MIA • 19 Apr 67, Major Tom Madison and Major Tom Sterling, 357 TFS, Ironhand, JCS 22.00, Xuan Mai Barracks, Route Pack VIA, both POW • 25 Apr 67, First I⸺ ⸺NANT Robert L. Weskamp, 354 TF⸺ ⸺ Pack VIA, KIA • 26 Apr 67, Major ⸺ N Al B. Meyer, 333 TFS, Ironhanl⸺ ⸺ack VIA, Pilot KIA, EWO POW • ⸺ ⸺YER, 469 TFS, JCS 13.00, Hanoi Rai⸺ ⸺Ɐi Bridge, Route Pack VIA, KIA • 28 Apr 67, Captain F.A. Caras, 44 TFS, JCS 20.00, Hanoi Railroad, Route Pack V, MIA • 30 Apr 67, Major Leo K. Thorsness and Captain Harry Johnson, 357 TFS, Ironhand en route to JCS 82.24, Route Pack V, both POW • 30 Apr 67, First Lieutenant Robert A. Abbott, 354 TFS, en route to JCS 82.24, Route Pack V, POW • 30 Apr 67, Captain Joe S. Abbott, 333 TFS, en route to JCS 82.24, Route Pack V, POW • 05 May 67, Lieutenant Colonel J.L. Hughes, 469 TFS, JCS 31.00, Ha Dong Army Barracks, Route Pack VIA, POW • 05 May 67, Lieutenant Colonel G.A. Larson, 469 TFS, JCS 31.00, Ha Dong Army Barracks, Route Pack VIA, POW • 05 May 67, First Lieutenant Jim R. Shively, 357 TFS, JCS 19.00, Hanoi, Route Pack VIA, POW • 08 May 67, Captain Mike McCuistion, 333 TFS, Route Pack I, POW • 12 May 67, Captain Earl Grenzebach, 357 TFS, Nguyen Khe, Route Pack VIA, MIA • 12 May 67, Captain P.P. Pitman and Captain R.A. Stewart, 34 TFS, *Ryan Raider* Strike on Ron Ferry, Pilot KIA, Gib MIA • 15 May 67, Major B.M. Pollard and Captain D.L. Heiliger, 13 TFS, Ironhand, JCS 39.43, Kep Army Barracks, Route Pack VIA, both POW • 27 May 67, Captain Gordon Blackwood, 333 TFS, JCS 18.23, Bac Giang Railroad Yard, Route Pack VIA, MIA • 02 Jun 67, Major D.L. Smith, 34 TFS, Kep Railroad Yard, Route Pack VIA, POW • 15 Jun 67, Captain J.W. Swanson, 34 TFS, Dong Khe Railroad, Route Pack III, MIA

100 MISSIONS NORTH

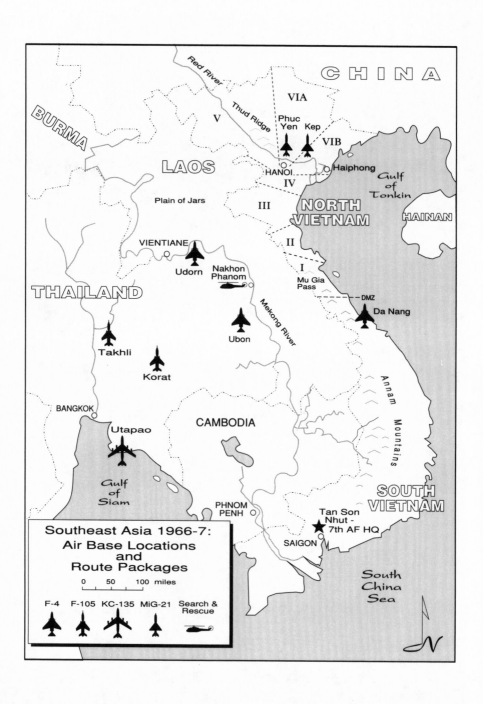

Southeast Asia 1966-7:
Air Base Locations
and
Route Packages

0   50   100 miles

F-4   F-105   KC-135   MiG-21   Search &
                                    Rescue

100 MISSIONS NORTH

Kenneth H. Bell

BRASSEY'S (US)
A Division of Maxwell Macmillan, Inc.
Washington • New York • London

Brassey's (US)

Editorial Offices
Brassey's (US)
8000 Westpark Drive
First Floor
McLean, Virginia 22102

Order Department
Brassey's Book Orders
c/o Macmillan Publishing Co.
100 Front Street, Box 500
Riverside, New Jersey 08075

Brassey's (US) is a Maxwell Macmillan Company. Brassey's books are available at special discounts for bulk purchases for sales promotions, premiums, fund-raising, or educational use through the Special Sales Director, Macmillan Publishing Company, 866 Third Avenue, New York, New York 10022.

Library of Congress Cataloging-in-Publication Data

Bell, Ken, 1931-
    100 missions north: a fighter pilot's story of the Vietnam War/Ken Bell.
        p.   cm.
        Includes index.
        ISBN 0-02-881012-0
    1. Vietnamese Conflict. 1961-1975—Aerial operations, American.
    2. Vietnamese Conflict. 1961-1975—Personal narratives. American.
    3. Bell, Ken, 1931- . I. Title.
    DS558.8B43   1993   92-31595   CIP
    959.704'348—dc20   Rev.

Designed by Lisa Chovnick

10 9 8 7 6 5 4 3 2 1

Printed in the United States of America

Dedicated to those who flew and fought so valiantly
over North Vietnam—especially those who did not return.

KHB 1993

"A man is not complete until he has fought a bull, raised a son, planted a tree, and written a book."

Spanish Matador

Contents

PREFACE

This book is an account of the missions I flew over North Vietnam in an F-105 fighter-bomber during the nine-month period of 23 October 1966 to 15 June 1967. It is based on a personal combat diary and notes that I kept during my tour of duty with the 355th Tactical Fighter Wing at Takhli Royal Thai Air Force Base, Thailand. I also researched training records, aircraft manuals, official orders, target photos, gun-camera film, checklists, maps, books, and newspaper articles in order to make this book as factual and realistic as possible.

My story is presented from the perspective of a line fighter pilot and builds gradually to develop the reader's understanding of the airplane and mission so that ultimately we go to Hanoi together in the cockpit of an F-105 to face the gunner's fire and experience the riveting danger of combat.

The period of 1966–67 was a time of fierce aerial struggle over North Vietnam. The strategy of the United States was to bring political pressure to bear on the outcome of the war in Southeast Asia by conducting air strikes against targets in North Vietnam. These strikes, known as Operation Rolling Thunder, were carried out by Air Force aircraft stationed in Thailand and South Vietnam and by Navy aircraft stationed aboard aircraft carriers in the Gulf of Tonkin. The F-4 Phantom, A-4 Skyhawk, F-8 Crusader, RF-101 Voodoo, and A-6 Intruder aircraft played major roles in the aerial campaign against North Vietnam, but it was the F-105 Thunderchief that bore the brunt of the burden of striking the heavily defended targets in the north.

Our fighter forces, supported by KC-135 tankers and other important supporting elements, faced unprecedented air defenses—both ground and air—and the consequent loss rate of U.S. fighters during this period was the highest experienced during the entire Southeast Asia conflict.

The story follows the order in which my missions were flown, and in some cases, quotes entries from diary notes usually made immediately after each mission. I kept these notes as a private record of the events and relationships that I experienced during combat, and they were never intended for publication. Therefore, you may sometimes find this book to be a straightforward, bare-knuckled, and intimate account of one pilot's experiences in combat.

Day after day, I left good friends and brave warriors behind in North Vietnam and Laos. I left them in exploding fireballs and hanging helplessly from parachutes. I listened to them on the radio as their damaged planes disintegrated around them. And I ached with frustration from the safety of my cockpit as they pleaded in vain for help and rescue from the certainty of a brutal captivity.

This is a book about people and feelings and not about national policy. Many have written about U.S. policies in Vietnam. This volume is about those who fought valiantly at the end of the policy whip. It is about the pilots and crewmen who found enough courage and patriotism each day to risk their lives flying in the hostile skies over North Vietnam. This book is written for those who shared that extraordinary experience with me and especially to honor my fellow pilots who never came home.

PROLOGUE

Time 1015
15 June 1967
Takhli Royal Thai Air Force Base
Thailand

"Takhli tower, Hotdog leader on initial for a one-hundred mission pass, over."

"Roger, Hotdog, this is Takhli, you're number one in the pattern, wind out of the south at five knots, altimeter setting two-nine-nine-five, cleared for a pass, the field is yours, over!"

"Takhli, Hot Dog one mile out on the trees, tuck it in Two!" With that cryptic exchange, I began my long awaited 100-mission fly-by, a series of high speed, formation passes signaling the end of a combat tour in Southeast Asia.

The 100-mission pass was a unique privilege that each of us completing a combat tour in the F-105 fighter aircraft looked forward to with growing anticipation. It marked the successful completion of 100 combat missions over North Vietnam and the end of a dangerous challenge that was appreciated by everyone, pilots and ground crews alike. It had become the traditional way to end an action-packed and emotionally charged combat assignment and, in a symbolic sense, was a fitting way for pilots to sound their final clap of thunder in the air war against North Vietnam.

The 100-mission pass was also a celebration that let time stand still for a breathtaking moment. The danger of the past and the hope that had sustained us from our first mission were riveted together with the joy and uncertainty of the future. In my case, that moment would also mark the final chapter in my flying career as a fighter pilot—something I sensed at the time, but did not fully appreciate for months to come.

My wingman was an outstanding young pilot. He had flown with me on several tough missions and I knew I could count on him to keep me out of trouble and hang in there during a final pass over the field. We discussed the maneuvers I planned for the fly-by but I cautioned him to be prepared for the unexpected. I was confident in his ability to stick with me through any maneuver, but I suspected that my instincts might respond to the enthusiasm of the occasion and I wanted him to be ready.

The 100-mission pass had become a very competitive game of flying one-up-manship. The commander's policy was very clear—your choice, but don't get hurt and don't go supersonic! Nonetheless, each succeeding finisher managed to push the limits a little farther, and those that turned out to watch soon came to expect it.

My adrenalin was pumping. At last, it was my turn to shine, to close my chapter of combat in the F-105. The day had come, I had faced the enemy, and the stage was set for an aerial celebration. I was on top of the world and anxious to do my best to provide a triumphant and memorable air show.

"Takhli, Hotdog approaching the field boundary!"

We were low and very fast. The runway markings disappeared quickly beneath the nose on the aircraft as I started a climbing turn to begin the fly-by. My wingman was glued in position and stayed there effortlessly through a series of tight, over-the-top maneuvers. We made three low passes crisscrossing the field from east to west followed by a formation roll down the runway as a final salute to the crowd.

For five glorious minutes, I basked in the spotlight of celebrated success. I had arrived. I had paid my dues and earned my wings as a combat veteran—a select fraternity of the world's greatest fighter pilots. I was king of the mountain and had made the most of it. It was time to land.

"Takhli tower, Hotdog one mile out reentering initial, request a pitch-up for landing, over!"

"Roger Hotdog, you're cleared to land, call base leg with gear check!"

I pulled too hard in the pitch-up and had to adjust my landing drastically. The airplane touched down long and hot, but the drag chute worked so I avoided the embarrassment of having to use the barrier to stop on my last mission. As I turned off the runway, I opened the canopy to cool my sweating face in the fresh morning air. The breeze felt good and it relaxed me.

Hotdog Two closed into close formation off my wing tip as we taxied back to the parking ramp. The customary parade of fire trucks met us and led the way with their water nozzles pointing skyward. A welcoming committee had formed on the ramp. The wing commander was standing beside his staff car proudly awaiting my arrival. He looked pleased, but a scolding twinkle in his eye told me I had pushed the fly-by limits too far.

As I braked to a stop in the blocks, the nose of the aircraft dipped sharply—almost ceremoniously. I stop-cocked the engine and began running through the checklist. A smiling and somewhat relieved crew chief climbed quickly up the ladder to the cockpit. He shook my hand and shouted, "Good show, Major, how's the airplane?" I gave him a thumbs up and he grinned broadly. The aircraft was scheduled for the afternoon "go" and another bout with destiny. I wasn't.

The crowd was beaming with excitement and I couldn't wait to join them. A bright red 100-mission welcome mat was rolled out at the foot of the aircraft ladder. I gathered up my gear and carefully backed down the side of the aircraft. My feet touched the ground and I turned to stand proudly in the place of honor on the welcome mat where only a privileged few had stood before. The commander greeted me, we exchanged salutes, and he shook my hand warmly. "You pushed a little hard, Ken," he said wryly knowing I understood his position.

Someone handed me my ceremonial 100-mission flying suit replete with several colorful patches. Instinctively, my eyes found the patch we coveted most. It was a large red, white, and blue shield sewn atop the left sleeve. The bold embroidered words read: "North Vietnam—100 Missions F-105." It was beautiful and signaled the finale I had dreamed about. Without hesitation, I stripped down to my skivvies and donned the colorful flying suit. I was bursting with pride. The crowd cheered as someone poured champagne over my head from behind. The sweet bubbles ran down my face, hiding the tears that were welling up in my eyes. I was overcome with joy and sorrow but felt very thankful.

After the celebration on the ramp, the next stop was a visit to the barber shop for a haircut, massage, and shave. I could hardly wait to get rid of my bulletproof mustache. It had served its purpose and was a terrible nuisance.

Later that afternoon, I hosted my 100-mission party. The stag bar at the Officers' Club was jammed by the time I arrived eager to outdo my predecessors—another combat tradition. The party was a roaring success but the bar outlasted me by several hours. My spirit was willing but my body was exhausted and I was emotionally drained. Reluctantly, I let my wingman help me to my trailer early in the evening as the party and the bar tab continued without me. By morning, I felt much better, but the cost of the party startled me. Even at twenty-five cents a shot, the final tally was staggering. I paid it gladly and counted my blessings.

As I walked back to my trailer, reality began to sink in. I realized more completely that I had flown my last combat mission and my part in the war was over. Without thinking, I passed by my trailer and continued across the airfield along a familiar path to the flight line. I wanted another look at the airplane I had flown on my last mission.

The ground crews were going about their normal duties and it was business as usual. No one noticed as I stood there quietly reflecting. I felt alone and terribly sentimental. In one short day, the celebrity was gone and I suddenly felt like a has been. It was a poignant moment indeed and it ended my combat story—a story I would remember proudly.

100 MISSIONS NORTH

1

GETTING THERE

In June of 1963, I received a Master of Science degree from the University of Colorado and reluctantly began my career in the technical Air Force. Before attending graduate school, I flew fighter aircraft for six years—F-86D and F-102A interceptors—and I hoped to continue my career in the cockpit after graduation. I planned to go on to test-pilot school as a prerequisite for training as an astronaut, but the Air Force assigned me instead to the Gemini Program Office in Los Angeles as a project manager.

Ironically, I found myself as a project engineer managing the rocket engines on the Titan II launch vehicle that I had hoped to ride into space as an astronaut. In a professional sense, the job in the project office was an excellent opportunity but it was also a frustrating disappointment, and the very thought of desk work ran counter to my instincts as a fighter pilot. I felt jilted, but pragmatically I didn't have a choice, so I decided to give it my best shot for the time being.

While the U.S. space programs were succeeding in the early 1960s the nation had also become deeply involved in the war in Southeast Asia. Pilot replacement in combat began to put some unexpected demands on the Air Force. The drain on pilot resources was felt across all major commands, but the squeeze was particularly noticeable in the Air Force Systems Command, where many experienced pilots were assigned off-line to management or technical positions.

Not surprisingly, the increasing need for combat pilots was a hot subject of discussion in our office. Accommodating as I was to my new technical career, I was anxious to return to the cockpit. My immediate boss was the original workaholic, and I was bored stiff with technical meetings and committee decisions. Each succeeding day dragged on a little longer and I was chafing for a taste of action.

As the air war in Southeast Asia gathered momentum, I tried several times to return to the cockpit, but my applications always stalled out in the front office. Our program director knew his turn to donate pilots would come soon enough without any volunteer statements to hasten the process. In desperation, I tried to short circuit the system by applying directly to the president for combat duty, but the White House never replied, and my zeal to fly continued to smolder unnoticed.

Late in 1965, the Gemini program office was tapped to return three pilots to the cockpit. Hallelujah! Out of twenty eligible pilots, only a handful met the criteria for selection to return to flying duty. The odds looked encouraging, but the program director was still a force to be reckoned with. It would take a bold stroke to convince him to release me.

The Gemini program director was Colonel Dick Dineen, a compact man with close-cropped gray hair and a craggy, weather-bitten face. He was tough as nails but fair and a very likeable guy, with a keen sense of humor. On the job, he was all business, but he loved a good laugh and liked to disarm difficult people with his piercing, blue eyes and just the hint of a sarcastic smirk. Colonel Dineen was a combat veteran and he was mission oriented, but I knew he wouldn't give up newly trained and productive project managers without a fight.

Hours after receiving the personnel order, all of the eligible pilots were called to a meeting in the front office. There were six of us and we met hastily amongst ourselves to discuss our tactics. We decided to present a solid front and agreed who would volunteer when the opportunity presented itself.

We met as a group with Colonel Dineen in his private office. The atmosphere was tense and he seemed grave as he greeted us and motioned to his secretary to close the door. We watched anxiously as he leaned back in his chair with his feet propped up on the conference table between us. "We have a message from headquarters requesting three pilots and I don't want any volunteers, is that perfectly clear," he said with conviction. "OK, ... there it is!" He looked stern as he slid the message down the long table toward us.... "Any volunteers?"

Without hesitation, three of us spoke in unison, "I do, sir." Someone stifled a giggle, but the room was dead silent as we stood at rigid attention waiting for his reaction.

Colonel Dineen knew us well enough to know what to expect, but I don't think he appreciated our audacity. He raised hell for a few minutes and made a tough speech about limited resources, but his emotions were clearly mixed. His mouth sounded angry but his eyes said, "I'd go too if I had the chance." He finally dismissed us with a disgruntled but fatherly gesture, and we returned to our expectant offices to share the news of our good fortune.

In less than a week, I received orders to report for F-105 training. The bad news was that I had to complete winter survival training first.

Survival Training

Stead Air Force Base, Nevada was forbidding in January of 1966. The thought of going through survival training in sub-zero temperatures was sobering, but I was thrilled to be aimed toward the operational Air Force once again. As far as I was concerned, three weeks of suffering was a price worth paying for a ticket back to a fighter cockpit.

At 120 strong, we were the largest class to enter Stead since the beginning of the war in Southeast Asia. Most of the officers in our class were second lieutenants just out of flying school and on their way to combat crew training for their first cockpit assignment in the Air Force. They were young, looked physically fit, and seemed well suited for the rigorous test ahead. In comparison, I felt somewhat inferior, but endurance would prove to be more a matter of mental discipline than physical stamina.

Survival training turned out to be more demanding than advertised. The winter of 1966 was one of the coldest on record in the Sierras, with temperatures dipping as low as 45 degrees below zero. As we struggled against the bitter cold, one couldn't help but wonder how those conditions would prepare us for survival in the hot, steamy jungles of Southeast Asia. The contrast seemed absurd at the time, but the value of the training would reveal itself soon enough.

After a week and a half in the classroom, we moved into the field for ten days of escape-and-evasion training. It began with a forced march at night to a remote location in the Nevada desert where we were told to proceed individually through enemy territory to a rendezvous point for a simulated predawn pickup and recovery.

We tried our best to evade capture but our fate was sealed. After several grueling hours of crawling through the desert on our bellies, we were captured and taken to a simulated enemy prison compound to spend two days and nights as prisoners of war.

The camp was supposed to be as authentic as possible. Short of serious physical abuse, our treatment was brutal and intimidating. Realism was paramount and emphasis was placed on psychological stress and brainwashing.

Conditions in the camp were realistic indeed, almost too convincing. Angry guards dressed in authentic enemy uniforms goaded us as we arrived tired and confused. They shouted threats with foreign accents as they herded us into a dimly lit, barren prison compound.

We were stripped to our underwear, searched, and processed for indoctrination and confinement. After a fiery political speech by the camp commander, we were separated, put into individual cells, and instructed to remain absolutely silent. Our tiny cells were cold, dark, and terribly uncomfortable. Patrolling guards harassed us constantly, making it impossible to sleep or rest.

After twenty-four hours in solitary confinement, I began to hallucinate. A small sliver of light under my cell door formed miniature cities in the gravel floor. They glowed brilliantly and changed with the angle of light. The illusion was fascinating, but I realized that I was losing my grip and wanted out of the cell, even if it meant a trip to interrogation.

At last, heavy footsteps stopped in front of my cell. The small door opened abruptly, and two guards led me blindfolded to another compound for questioning. As I stumbled along trying to regain my equilibrium, the thought crossed my mind that I had been tricked and actually captured as part of a bizarre conspiracy to overthrow our government.

The interrogation was more than convincing. The room was dark and austere. The setting was sinister, and the interrogator came across as a first-class bastard. He was so cunning I had to remind myself that he was acting. His questions were relentless, but I held my own at first with "name, rank, and serial number." The mood in the room shifted from tense to angry as the interrogator became impatient with my answers. Cleverly, he paused to offer me a cigarette. He was patronizing my weakness and I knew it. It was a textbook trap but I couldn't resist his offer. I was photographed "accepting favor from the enemy" and summarily dismissed.

Guards dragged me to the prison yard and crammed me into a small torture box. As I reflected on my lack of self-discipline, I wondered how I might react as a real prisoner of war. The odds were high that I would get a chance to find out, and the prospect troubled me. Thankfully, my body began to relax as I numbed to the tight enclosure of the torture box, and I was almost asleep when the guards opened the box and angrily returned me to my dank cell to await release.

The last phase of training was the trek, a week of survival in the mountains to help determine your strengths and weaknesses.

We started out in groups of ten, with an instructor as a guide. The mountains were covered with deep snow and more was forecast. We spent the first day on a tiring hike to reach the base camp. The weather was bitter cold and we had to get used to walking on clumsy snow shoes. The going was slow and exhausting.

We had barely enough food to sustain us. Each group was issued a few C-rations, some raw beef for making jerky, and a pitiful live rabbit. We had been instructed to fish and use snares to trap small game, but the streams were frozen, and the only animal within a hundred miles was the rabbit we had with us. The forlorn expression in his eyes indicated that he sensed he wasn't along just for the ride.

After two days in camp, the combination of cold and hunger had taken its toll. The jerky was good but it was consumed as fast as it was made. In short order, we were down to pemmican bars, coffee, cigarettes, and conversation by the campfire to sustain us.

The rabbit had become our mascot and a fellow survivor but we couldn't spare him any longer. Reluctantly, we gave him our regards and prepared a mountain stew. The warm broth was thin and tasteless—hardly a tribute to the rabbit's noble sacrifice—but it gave us the energy we needed to endure until morning.

Late on the fourth day, we broke camp quickly and formed into two-man teams for an overnight forced march. The objective was to evade an enemy force patrolling the mountains in order to reach a safe recovery point by morning to end the exercise.

We packed hurriedly and set out for the first checkpoint, carrying only the equipment we needed to survive until morning. The idea of facing a bitter cold night on foot in mountainous terrain was frightening. In less than an hour, it was pitch dark and we were in a blinding snow storm. We struggled desperately to make headway but by midnight the situation seemed hopeless. We were exhausted. The weather had turned a training exercise into a genuine fight for survival, and the only choice we had was to continue.

Without saying a word, my partner sat down in the snow and refused to move any further. His despair was genuine. He had reached his limit and was willing to give up. I tried preaching, ordering, and lifting, but nothing moved him. Finally I threatened him, "Buddy, if you sit down now, you're dead and I can't save you. You're gonna die right here because I can't carry you out!" It was a brutal message but I meant it. Slowly, he got to his feet and together we found the courage and strength to continue.

My partner was young and in excellent physical condition but he lacked mental discipline and toughness. Thankfully, he was able to reach a little deeper for hidden stamina. Others were not and came dangerously close to dying before they could be rescued. One had to be carried to safety by his trekmate, ironically the oldest man in our class.

We crossed the safe line just after dawn. The morning sun felt good. I relaxed as we walked silently to the collection point. As we rounded the last turn in the trail, an Air Force bus appeared in the distance, and our tired steps quickened. We looked at each other and smiled with a sense of pride and satisfaction. The ordeal was over.

Back at Stead, I turned in my equipment and hurried to enjoy the luxury of a hot shower and fresh sheets. I was too late for the hot water but the bed felt wonderful and sleep came very quickly.

That evening we attended an "I Survived" party at Harrah's Club in Reno. Traditionally, the club provided two drinks, a steak dinner, and two five-dollar chips to those who survived the training and showed up to brag about it. I had a couple of "deep dish olive pies" (double martini) and had trouble making it through dinner. The steak was delicious but too much for my undernourished system. Apologetically, I left early and drove back to the base fighting sleep all the way.

Early the next morning, I packed the car and headed for McConnell Air Force Base in Kansas to begin F-105 training. During the drive, I thought about Stead and what I had accomplished. The experience was invaluable. I had discovered my physical and mental limits and I was proud of that, but I wasn't sure I needed to do it again, ever. I was scheduled to attend jungle survival training in the Philippines en route to Southeast Asia, and just the thought of it nagged at me.

False Start with the Flying Tigers

After three weeks of exhaustive training in the mountains, a nonstop drive to Wichita, Kansas, was a piece of cake. I arrived at the base late in the evening and was greeted by a sign announcing, *"Welcome to McConnell Air Force Base, Home of the 23d Tactical Fighter Wing—Flying Tigers."*

The guard at the gate saluted and waved me through smartly. The base was very still except for the wind that always blows in that part of Kansas. I drove past the flight line, it was quiet. And rows of parked airplanes stood silhouetted in the last rays of sunset.

I found the wing command post and reported to the officer on duty. I was not expected, and the fact that I had orders assigning me to McConnell caused more than a ripple of confusion. I had a sinking feeling that my training in the F-105 was in jeopardy.

The senior officer on duty reinforced my doubts when he informed me, with some authority, that my orders were in error. "It will be several weeks before another class would begin," and as far as he knew, "all of the slots in that class are taken." It sounded like a classic example of hurry up and wait.

I got a room in the Bachelor Officers' Quarters (BOQ) and found the bar at the Officers' Club. The place was vacant except for the bartender. Instead of a martini, I got a fatherly lecture on the nuances of the liquor laws in Kansas. No drink without a locker, no locker without a bottle, and no bottles on Sunday.

Early the next morning, I returned to the command post. I was told that a call was expected soon from the personnel office at headquarters Tactical

Air Command (TAC). As I waited, I sifted through the possibilities. My experience with personnel offices in the past was not encouraging. I had a feeling that I may have traded a desk in the technical Air Force for a desk in the flying Air Force, with some grueling survival training sandwiched in between.

The call finally came and the duty officer relayed my choices. I could remain at McConnell to work in the command post or report to Nellis Air Force Base in Nevada for combat crew training in the F-105. If I chose Nellis, I had forty-eight hours to get there. Within minutes, I was back in my car and headed west. Goodbye to Kansas, goofy liquor laws, and windstorms.

F-105s in the Nevada Desert

The bright lights of Las Vegas appeared suddenly on the night horizon. They looked dazzling. The cool desert air smelled fresh, with just a hint of sage. My pulse quickened with anticipation.

The prospects of flying the F-105 at Nellis were exciting. It was the mecca of fighter flying in the Air Force, and I had finally made it. I was an experienced fighter pilot, on the promotion list to major, and still a single, class-A bachelor. Talk about "died and gone to heaven." I couldn't wait to establish myself as a member of the most elite flying fraternity in the business.

I was assigned to the 4526th Combat Crew Training Squadron (CCTS), the 26th Cobras. I had flown with the 26th Squadron several months earlier, on a dollar ride in a two-seat F-105F and was eager to join them for training. There were fifteen of us in the training class of 67-Alpha. We were all experienced pilots, and for the most part, everyone in the squadron welcomed us to the organization.

For reasons as old as pride itself, we were not immediately accepted by the student pilots in the class ahead of us. They were all second lieutenants who had joined the squadron six weeks earlier. Experience determines the pecking order in fighter units, and we posed a threat to the younger jocks. It was ironic because each group had something the other envied, experience versus a head start in the F-105. The barrier vanished in a matter of days, and once the new old-heads were accepted by the old new-heads we enjoyed a very competitive but harmonious relationship. Each group learned from the other. Our experience was refreshed and their vitality was challenged.

We spent the first day in the squadron doing routine paperwork and getting better acquainted. We were briefed on both the ground school and flying program and given schedules for the entire course curriculum. Late that afternoon, we were issued our flying gear and invited to the stag bar for beer call. The required uniform was a flying suit with a Cobra Squadron patch sewed proudly on one shoulder.

It was great to be back in patches, particularly after having come from the plain Jane flying suit world of support flying. Fighter jocks traditionally wore big watches and distinctive unit patches. Critics said that patches helped fighter pilots remember where to report each morning, but in fact, they signified a deep sense of unit pride. I was certainly proud to be a part of the 26th Squadron, and I was eager to begin flying the F-105 in order to earn the privilege of wearing the Thunderchief patch as well.

The 26th Squadron was a proud unit. Everything about it was top-notch. Lieutenant Colonel Fritz Treyz was the commander. He was a trim, lanky guy with a deep tan and ready smile, and results of his positive leadership were clearly evident. A can-do attitude permeated the outfit, and the instructor cadre represented the cream of the crop. They were experienced, credible, talented, and professional fighter pilots. Their esprit de corps was high and very contagious. It was a cohesive unit in a perfect setting with a dynamic and challenging mission.

The training program was concentrated, fast paced, and success oriented. In less than five months, we were scheduled to complete 190 hours of ground school and 70 hours of flight training, concentrating primarily on conventional weapons delivery. Toward the end of the course, two nights were set aside for night flying and night weapons delivery training.

There was always homework because each flight required an enormous amount of preparation. Balancing the school load against the lure of bright city lights was a constant struggle. Las Vegas after dark was life in the fast lane. "You pays your money and takes your chances," we used to say, "but school always keeps the next morning with a flight briefing at 0600."

Most of the F-105D aircraft in the Air Force inventory were assigned to the combat theater. Consequently, we flew the majority of our missions at Nellis in the two-place F-105F. The Fs were heavier and less agile than the single-seat D-model, but there was enough similarity to make the training realistic. We appreciated the few rides we got in the more nimble D-model and its increased performance stimulated our appetite for combat.

The F-105 was originally designed as a high-speed fighter bomber capable of delivering tactical nuclear weapons at low-level, day or night, in all weather conditions. It was complex and big by fighter standards at the time: 64 feet long, a 35-foot wingspan, and almost 20 feet tall at the top of the vertical stabilizer. It carried several external stores under the wing, and the landing gear was so tall that the wing was difficult to reach from the ground.

At a maximum gross weight for takeoff of almost 51,000 pounds, the F-105 was by far the heaviest fighter I ever climbed into. In fact, we used to say that "Republic Aircraft would have used concrete to build the airplane but someone in their design department discovered that steel was heavier." Perhaps overweight and certainly large, 833 of these sleek aircraft were built by Republic for the Air Force, never anticipating that they would be employed in Southeast Asia or that 383 would be lost in combat.

The F-105D was durable and straightforward to fly. "A simple combination perfectly suited to the mentality of a Thud pilot," the F-4 drivers used to say. In the air, you couldn't see enough of the airplane through the canopy to be conscious of its size, and it had the feel of a much smaller aircraft until you tried to turn. The airplane had a relatively small wing with high wing loading and was designed to fly fast and smooth at low altitude. By its design, the F-105 liked to go straight. Fast and low was the rule of thumb for getting the most out of the aircraft.

I had two dual rides with an instructor pilot in the F-105F before my first solo flight on 7 April 1966. I was tense at first but the flight went very well. Compared to other fighters I had flown, the F-105 was more complex and heavier, but it accelerated very quickly and was solid. Its powerful jet engine burned fuel quickly at low altitude. In less than thirty minutes, I was down to bingo fuel and headed back to the field for my first landing. The touchdown was a shade fast but the drag chute worked and no one booed from the tower, so I walked away delighted.

When I returned to the squadron, the older heads tried to look nonchalant while Colonel Treyz congratulated me and gave me an F-105 Arrowhead patch to mark the occasion. Silence is praise in the brotherhood of fighter pilots so I knew I had succeeded. It was a memorable day but just a beginning.

The training program was carefully planned and well executed. The art of tactical weapons delivery was new to me, but I caught on quickly with the help of some excellent instructors. Learning to dive-bomb, skip-bomb, and strafe ground targets was the easiest and most exciting because the targets were stationary, and we flew low and fast to hit them. Air-to-air gunnery against a moving target was a little more difficult and aerial refueling presented an entirely new challenge.

The aerial refueling phase of training was abbreviated for two reasons. Tanker resources for training were scarce and difficult to schedule. And it was assumed that pilots who were accustomed to formation flying would adapt quickly to flying on a refueling boom behind a KC-135 tanker.

I had plenty of experience flying formation in several fighters, and I didn't have any difficulty flying behind the KC-135 tanker until it was time to get stabbed with the refueling boom. Psychologically, I was intimidated.

I wasn't prepared for a mating dance at 30,000 feet over the desert. The harder I tried the worse I got. When I finally hung on the boom long enough to receive fuel, I didn't get enough to make the effort worthwhile.

At the mission debriefing, the instructor tried to encourage me. "Don't sweat the details, Ken," he said. "You'll get the knack of it next time. It's like learning to ride a bicycle, it just comes to you." Lacking "the knack of it" came back to haunt me sooner than I could have imagined, but for the moment I was satisfied.

Our class finished combat crew training in late June 1966, almost three months ahead of schedule. I received orders assigning me to the 355th Tactical Fighter Wing at Takhli, Thailand, but I was not scheduled to report until mid-October. I tried to reschedule an earlier port-call, but the personnel system refused to bend. They had their own schedule of schools, assignments, and reporting dates. Flights left Travis Air Force Base every-day with empty seats, but I was told to wait my assigned turn and find something productive to do at Nellis in the meantime.

Something productive meant a temporary job that would keep me out of trouble and allow me to fly enough to maintain proficiency until my sched-uled departure. Anything, even command post duty, would have been satis-factory, as long as it included flying the F-105.

"Top Gun" School

To my surprise, Colonel Treyz recommended me for a slot in the next class at the USAF Fighter Weapons School. It was a prestigious and unprece-dented opportunity and I was flattered, but I knew it was a long shot in view of my limited experience in the F-105. Colonel Treyz felt confident that I could handle it. "Ken," he urged me, "if you're ready for combat, you sure as hell can hack the fighter weapons school." Treyz was a practical, no-nonsense leader whose judgement was highly respected at Nellis, and I appreciated his confidence.

The fighter weapons course was seven weeks long. Eighteen of the top fighter pilots in the Air Force attended each class. The course was fiercely competitive, and only the most experienced pilots were considered in the selection process. By comparison, I was a pink-cheeked rookie, but I was available.

The commandant of the weapons school was a senior colonel who viewed his position as the "Archduke of the Fighter Weapons Fiefdom" very seriously. The idea of a freshman F-105 pilot attending the graduate school of fighter flying offended him. He felt it was unfair and improper to even consider letting me compete with some of the best sticks in the Air

Force. Given his predisposition, I was surprised he finally agreed to talk with me.

The day after the interview, I was told to report to the weapons school immediately. Audacity and determination had carried the day. I was elated but intimidated by the challenge. My future and Fritz Treyz's reputation were on the line. I knew I had to do more than my best, so I set my sights on being Top Gun in the class.

The other pilots in the class accepted me without question. They were all highly skilled, and several were more experienced combatwise than the instructors, but no one chided me about my lack of experience. They respected me as a rookie eager to make good, but it was obvious that they didn't consider me a serious threat to their prowess as veterans.

Everyone in the class was shooting for the Top Gun trophy. I was clearly the odds-on underdog, so I decided to turn that into an advantage. Experience can be a two-edged sword, and I sensed that if I hustled I might catch my classmates napping long enough to take an early lead in the scoring. The theory worked and I caught everyone by surprise. They were quick to attribute my success to luck rather than skill, but I smugly countered with the old adage that "the harder I worked, the luckier I got." In my heart, I knew I had picked a fight with a hornet's nest.

The course was everything it was cracked up to be: tough, challenging, competitive, exciting, and fun. The flying was the best that I had ever done. We flew early morning missions every day, followed by ground school and physical training of our choice. By 5:00 P.M. in the afternoon, we were ready for the camaraderie of the stag bar. It was a place to relax in a comfortable setting reserved for boisterous behavior and occasional punishment. Using our hands to illustrate maneuvers, we flew missions again and again to the accompanying din of humorous barbs and laughter. We rolled dice for double martinis and played a high-stakes game called Chilo (ace-two-three). Even if you lost, we reckoned "it was better than a sharp stick in the eye."

The individual competition between pilots was keen, but it was secondary to the tribal rivalry that stemmed from our unflinching loyalty to the airplanes we flew: the F-100, F-4, or F-105. Each tribe of pilots was certain that their airplane was best and was willing to do anything to prove it. In our case, the honor of the Thunderchief was at stake.

The F-100 pilots were competitive but the F-4 crews in the class were our arch rivals. The F-4 and F-105 were designed for different missions and flew roles supporting each other in combat, but by necessity, the airplanes were flown against each other in air combat training. The F-4 could outmaneuver the F-105 in a dogfight, but the F-105 was faster and could outrun the F-4 on the deck. Consequently, each enjoyed a tactical advantage that was difficult to exploit. The result was a built-in tension that served to fuel the fires of competition.

We were proud of the F-105 as a single-seat fighter, and we heckled the F-4 pilots because it took two pilots to fly their machine. The need for a pilot in the back seat (GIB) of the F-4 was a sore point that we often exploited. In turn, we took some heat about the weight and turning performance of the F-105, but we tried not to lose our sense of humor. The F-4 crews, on the other hand, took themselves very seriously, and at times the rivalry got pretty touchy.

On one occasion after a particularly hard-fought air combat mission, things got ugly. As our flight was approaching Nellis to land, the leader of the F-4 flight following us made a sarcastic remark on the radio that did not go unnoticed. "Nellis Tower, Shotgun turning initial ten miles out behind four Thuds strung out on final." Oh, oh! In jest, he had used the term "Thud" irreverently and implied that our traffic pattern was less than professional, a cardinal sin in a fighter.

After we landed, Shotgun leader swaggered through the door to the debriefing room only to be greeted by the exploding fist of my flight leader, an instructor and combat veteran. The room was stunned, but not a word was spoken. The message was clear. Thud was a term of endearment reserved for use by F-105 pilots. Besides, the quality of our traffic patterns was strictly the business of our instructor pilots and not subject to comment by F-4 student pilots.

The school missions were as demanding as the pilots who flew them. They ran the gamut of tactical specialties: strafe, dive- and toss-bombing, and air-to-air gunnery with the 20mm Gatling Gun and Sidewinder missiles. Air combat training (dogfight) was an integral part of each mission and was flown as close to a combat environment as safety would permit. It was training at its very best: unpredictable, realistic, and effective.

All of our missions were flown in clean aircraft, without external stores except the weapons to be expended. Consequently, we were limited to internal fuel duration. The sorties were short and compact. Because of the desert heat, we flew early in the morning when the air was cool, calm, and very sweet. Under those ideal conditions, students got a rare opportunity to experience the maximum design performance of their aircraft in a training environment. An F-105 accelerating in afterburner on the deck in smooth air was a breathtaking experience that ranked somewhere between sex and a good drag chute on a short runway.

The Fighter Weapons School was the focal point for developing tactical fighter doctrine in the Air Force and prided itself in offering training that was both realistic and relevant. Quite often, commanders were invited in to share their experience with the students and instructors. Because the situation over North Vietnam was so dynamic, we particularly welcomed visits by pilots from the combat theater.

On one occasion, two pilots who had been instructors of mine in the 26th Squadron, dropped in unexpectedly to share their combat experience. Both had been flying missions less than forty-eight hours earlier, and their stories were electrifying. One was a Wild Weasel pilot who had been shot down and recovered at sea on two consecutive missions. The other pilot had flown twenty-five missions and had returned to the United States to ferry a F-105 back to Thailand.

Both pilots described their encounters with the surface-to-air missiles (SAM) the North Vietnamese had begun to employ during the previous summer. The increased SAM threat coupled with a sharp rise in the F-105 loss rate had dictated some dramatic changes in our tactics. The importance of mutual support between aircraft and the need for electronic counter measures became very evident. There was no doubt that the addition of a SAM threat to the enemy's defenses had significantly changed the complexion of the air war over North Vietnam.

Nuke Training

Nuclear weapons delivery was an important part of the curriculum at the Fighter Weapons School. Although not a training requirement for the war in Southeast Asia, nuclear delivery techniques were vital to the performance of the Air Force mission worldwide. Ironically, nuclear tactics played an important role in shaping the conventional tactics that were used during our initial air strikes against North Vietnam.

There was nothing fancy about dropping nuclear weapons with the F-105. Timing was critical and safe escape was of utmost importance. But delivering nukes boiled down to getting into the target low and fast, making a precise release, and getting the hell out of the way. Something akin to a pony express drop in the middle of Indian territory, just faster.

We used practice bombs or nuclear shapes on the range at Nellis. Good weather and the absence of enemy defenses no doubt resulted in better than expected accuracies, but a long mission at low-level, particularly one flown under a hood simulating radar bombing conditions, was a demanding test of pilot proficiency.

My scores in the nuclear phase were excellent until my last mission. It was a low-level, simulated-instrument delivery of a Mk 47 nuclear practice shape against a target deep in enemy territory. We had just entered the range, and the instructor was flying the airplane from the front seat while I set up the switches on the nuclear armament panel in the rear cockpit.

Without warning, the left wing thumped as the fire-control system accidentally released the bomb, pylon and all, 50 miles short of the target. I rechecked the switches. They were all in checklist order, but the bomb was gone and my instructor was about to go unstable. "What the hell happened?" he asked frantically, as he rolled the airplane into a steep bank, trying desperately to spot the impact of the bomb in the desert. "That was a nuke shape, buddy. The whole world will be on the horn before beer call," he added in a disgusted tone. I was disgusted too and terribly disappointed. My last shot at Top Gun in the class had just fallen incredibly short of the target. In a competition decided by inches and feet, a 50-mile error would never wash.

On the flight back to Nellis, the instructor talked to the command post and warned me to leave all the switches just as they were. We had experienced a nuclear incident, which would require a full investigation. Before we landed, it seemed as though everyone in our chain of command short of the four-star himself called us on the radio.

Sure enough, a large welcoming committee met us as we parked on the ramp. They were concerned about a possible compromise in nuclear safety and security, but I was worried about my standing in the Top Gun competition. "Even if I got another chance, it would take a thousand shacks [bull's eyes] to average out a dumb error like that," I thought angrily. As it turned out, the bomb counted for score, and I moved from the top of the ladder to dead last in the run for class honors.

I spent the rest of the morning answering questions from Washington and the afternoon searching the desert for the missing bomb in a HH-43 Pedro helicopter ... whop, whop, whop, of the rotor blades beat relentlessly on my tired ears and body. We didn't find the bomb, and no one was able to figure out why it jettisoned in the first place. I was sure it wasn't pilot error.

That night, I went out to eat with the only F-4 pilot in our class with a sense of humor. Next to flying, his favorite pastimes were eating and drinking. In a highly competitive environment, where rivalry often turned petty, he never took himself too seriously. He sensed my bitter disappointment and tried to encourage me. "Babes," he said, "as long as you have your sense of humor and plenty to eat and drink, you haven't lost anything."

On 22 September 1966, we graduated from the Fighter Weapons School and earned the privilege to wear its distinctive school patch on our flying suits. At a formal graduation ceremony in one of the casinos in Las Vegas, we received our diplomas, applauded the Top Gun in each of the fighter sections of our class, and endured the remarks of a fast-burning two-star from Washington who waxed eloquently about his bomber experiences during World War II. He was long-winded, but the food was good, and the drinks were on the house.

As I checked out of the weapons school, it dawned on me that I was finally headed for combat where the gunnery range shot back with a vengeance. Everyone gave me the same grace advice, "Keep the airplane moving, check your six o'clock, and you might live to tell about it." Suddenly, I realized how much I admired and envied the guys who wore the 100-mission patch so proudly.

The next few days were devoted to the odds and ends of going overseas: shots, orders, travel schedule, a last minute physical, and an official-business, diplomatic passport. Our presence in Thailand was the worst kept secret of the war, but we were required nevertheless to carry a passport attesting to our civilian status. It didn't make sense at the time, but it seemed more logical than undergoing more survival training.

The orders assigning me to Thailand routed me through Clark Air Base in the Philippines for jungle survival training. Winter survival was still fresh on my mind, so I was delighted when I got a last minute opportunity to ferry an F-105 to Takhli without a stop at Clark for snake school. I was anxious about crossing the Pacific for the first time with tankers, but the thought of encountering serious refueling problems was overpowered by the joy of not having to face jungle survival training. As it turned out, my good fortune would come back to bite me.

One Didn't Want to Go

Several nights before I left Nellis, I was alone in my room preparing for the flight overseas when an unexpected knock came at the door. It was one of the lieutenants who had trained with us in the 26th Squadron. He was handsome, bright, and a little too cocky for his own good, but I had always admired his spunk and quickness. He was the model of a young fighter pilot and usually very confident, but he was uneasy and seemed shaken as he entered my room nervously.

He came right to the point. He was afraid to fly combat. His port-call was in two days and he didn't know what to do. He had just returned from several weeks leave with his family and girlfriend. They were all convinced that he would not return safely from Southeast Asia. Worse, he had dreamed that he would be killed and he couldn't shake the vision. He was gripped with fear. As he talked, I thought to myself, "What a pity, with all of his skill and talent, his confidence has turned to jelly."

He explained that he had come to me because I was the only one left at Nellis he knew well enough to share his heavy burden. "Damn," I thought, "I barely know the kid and he needs help now." He had the guts to share his problem but I couldn't seem to find the words to encourage him. I was as frustrated as he was scared. I felt terribly inadequate but I was on a spot to do something.

I began by assuring him that everyone going into combat had to overcome fear, myself included. Only fools or liars were excluded. He tried to crack a weak smile but his lips quivered, and I knew I was not convincing. I urged him to discuss his feelings with Colonel Treyz as soon as possible. It was a tough decision but Colonel Treyz might be able to help, and it was the only way to confront the problem honestly. He was hesitant so I offered to go with him, but he declined.

We shook hands and he left my room with a look of hollow resignation on his face. I poured a drink to soothe the knot in my stomach. The fear in his eyes was etched in my mind. I didn't know what he might do, but I doubted if he would make it back.

2

CROSSING THE PACIFIC

IT WAS TIME TO go to war. I was well trained, tuned as a fighter pilot, and eager to test myself in combat. A sense of urgency had pulled at me for months. I was ready to get on with it.

The airport outside my hometown was crowded with busy tourists. Warm sunlight reflected off the painted Spanish tiles lining the corridors of the terminal. Slowly, my parents and I made our way to the departure gate trying to make light conversation but feeling the ache and solitude of parting. Difficult as it was, I was anxious to say goodbye. I was prepared for sacrifice and it was time to overcome fear and sentimentality. The time had come to begin the final leg of my journey to combat.

The door of the airliner swung closed with a soft thump. As the stewardess turned the locking arm, I sensed a subtle note of finality. The cabin pressurization popped in my ears as the plane's jet engines whined to life. Moments later, a remote scream of power moved the airliner gently away from the terminal. I leaned forward and squinted through the small window for a last glance at my parents. They were standing bravely in the crowd at the gate and waving anxiously. I waved back, hoping to reassure them but the terminal swung out of view too quickly. I felt lonely but was relieved to be on my way.

Within minutes, we were airborne. As we climbed, I watched the streets of El Paso slip beneath the wing of the aircraft. Fondly, my eyes traced a familiar route through the city to my neighborhood and the small house I had been raised in. Pleasant memories filled my thoughts as I reminisced and pondered the future. Too quickly, the city faded into the barren desert of New Mexico. I sat back and flipped nervously through the pages of a magazine. Our flying time to Los Angeles was two hours and fifteen minutes. A connecting flight to Sacramento would complete my rendezvous with the F-105 fighter aircraft which stood ready for a flight across the Pacific and a date with destiny.

Off with the Patches, on with the War Paint

McClellan Air Force Base near Sacramento, California, was the F-105 maintenance depot. All major periodic maintenance on the aircraft, including the latest modifications necessary for combat, was performed at McClellan prior to flights overseas. The most obvious change was a camouflage paint job—war paint fitting for a Thunderchief.

At McClellan, I checked into the Visiting Officers' Quarters and found the other pilots scheduled for the flight. All three were 100-mission veterans in the F-105. As the "junior bird man" in the flight, I was assigned to bring up the rear as number four.

The flight leader noticed my weapons school patch and asked about it in a way that suggested he wanted to compare my training with his recent combat experience. He listened with a discerning look as I praised the realism of the course enthusiastically. When I finished, he smiled politely and cautioned me to be ready for a surprise or two in combat. "By the way," he concluded, "you won't need your patches over Hanoi. You might as well cut'em off here so you'll look ready to go when we get there."

We boarded a shuttle bus and went to base operations for our flight briefing. I expected a full-blown presentation, but we were greeted instead with a do-it-yourself, recorded briefing that covered the essential requirements and procedures for the flight, including routes and other pertinent flight data. Grease-pencil entries on a clipboard listed our call signs, takeoff time, cruising altitude, tanker rendezvous time, and location. It was the ultimate of brevity and standardization in one briefing. I was underwhelmed but the other pilots seemed satisfied so I kept my thoughts to myself.

A section covering the administrative procedures followed the flight plan instructions. As I listened, the first prerequisite requirement hit me right between the eyeballs. Ferry pilots were required to be current in the F-105, have landed the aircraft in the last sixty days, and *must have accomplished a wet aerial refueling [actually taken on fuel, no dry hook ups] within the past sixty days using both the boom/receptacle and the probe-and-drogue systems.* Oh, oh! I hadn't seen a refueling boom in over two months, and the probe-and-drogue phase of our refueling training had been quick and dirty at best.

I was between a rock and a hard place. By regulation, I was not qualified to make the trip, but it was too late and unthinkable to ask for a replacement because of a technicality. With any luck at all, I felt that I could hack the mission. Pilot proficiency depended on a number of factors, the least of which were technical. Confidence and pride had as much to do with a pilot's motivation as anything, and it was pride that told me to sign-off the compliance square in the briefing book that fateful afternoon. I knew I was setting myself up for the inevitable "I told you so" committee if anything went wrong, but I decided that the flight was important and worth the risk.

A weatherman gave us a quick-look forecast for the next day. Early morning fog at McClellan would burn off in time for takeoff, with clear skies and light westerly winds en route to the Hawaiian Islands. We were set for a morning departure.

After a restless night, I was up early to make final preparations for the trip. It was Columbus Day, 12 October 1966. My airplane was F-105D number 62-4274. It had just rolled off the overhaul line with all of the latest modifications. The airplane looked new and crisp. It was ready to go to war in its fresh coat of war paint.

I began a routine preflight inspection of the aircraft. The crew chief pointed out an electronic pod mounted on the fuselage centerline station instead of the 650-gallon fuel tank normally used for long range ferry flights. The pod looked unusual. It had several rows of antennae stubs protruding out of its long, cylindrical body. The crew chief explained that it was some sort of radio relay pod that had been developed quickly on a top-priority basis. The pod was highly classified, and a note in the aircraft forms warned that it could not be jettisoned even in an emergency. The message was abundantly clear. The pod was important and it wasn't going anywhere without the airplane.

I completed the preflight check and returned to base operations to compare notes with the other pilots. An identical pod was mounted on each aircraft in the flight. No one knew much about the pods, but the base operations officer assured us that they were extremely important and their deployment to the combat theater had been ordered by the White House. When questioned about the added fuel requirements imposed by the drag of the pods, he smiled and assured us that the matter had been fully coordinated and there would be ample fuel on board the tanker to meet our needs. We would simply need to take more fuel, more often. "Any other questions, gentlemen?"

Hickam Bound, First Try

The weather office was our last stop before heading for the airplanes. Morning fog had reduced the visibility to zero-zero but was forecast to improve in time for takeoff. With that assurance, we picked up our flight gear and loaded in a van for the short trip to the flight line. "Start engines at three-zero [0930] and come up on Channel Two, ready to taxi at four-five [0945]," the flight Leader reminded us as we arrived at the aircraft.

The airplanes were packed and ready to go. I took a quick look around the outside and climbed up the ladder into the cockpit. With the help of the crew chief, I got settled in the seat, adjusted my equipment, and completed the prestart checklist in time to relax and think about the mission.

As the second hand swept through three-zero on the instrument panel clock, I signaled the crew chief to begin the engine start. The powerful J75 engine came alive quickly. It's shrill whine pierced the morning calm. My ears resonated with the pulsing screech of the engine inlets as torrents of air raced through them to be devoured by the huge compressor. The noise and smell of jet engines settled my nerves and the cockpit routine began to feel natural again as I checked out each system in preparation for the command to taxi.

The fog was still patchy when we started down the taxiway but the visibility had improved enough for takeoff. After our final ground checks, we lined up on the runway for takeoff. On a signal from the Leader, I pushed the throttle up to full power and checked the engine carefully. One by one, we motioned that we were ready to go. Dark exhaust boiled out of the thundering jet engines as the shuddering aircraft strained to be released. Finally, the Leader snapped his helmet forward and began the takeoff roll, with Number Two in close formation. It was exactly 1000 hours. Number Three waited thirty seconds and then followed with us in formation behind the lead element.

The afterburner kicked in with a hard bang and the aircraft accelerated quickly down the runway. The morning air was smooth and the acceleration forces were exhilarating. In a matter of seconds, we reached rotation speed. Three's nose-wheel lifted up, barely skimming the runway. I eased back on the stick and moved the throttle back and forth gently to maintain position on his wing as we gracefully reached for the sky. In no time, we were safely airborne and climbing high above the fog bank below us. As we joined up in four-ship formation, the Leader turned to the west toward a bright blue horizon over the Pacific. I thought to myself, "This is it babes, no turning back now. Next stop Honolulu."

We had just settled down in spread formation when things began to unravel. The flight Leader was busy answering a barrage of radio calls, and we were just about to coast out when Number Three radioed that he smelled smoke and strong fumes in his cockpit. What a jolt! He started an immediate turn back toward McClellan and I moved in close to check his airplane for signs of trouble. Halfway through the turn, he gave me a hand signal indicating that he had also experienced total radio failure. The cheese got more binding.

The flight Leader decided to press on as planned with two aircraft but directed me to lead Number Three back to McClellan for an emergency landing. "Four, this is Lead, I'll press on with Two. Get Three back on the ground ASAP ... see you in Hawaii, over!"

"Roger, have a good trip," I said, as I motioned Number Three to join on my wing and headed straight for McClellan.

Oakland Center cleared us for an emergency descent and an immediate instrument approach to McClellan. Since our departure, the weather had deteriorated to less than one-quarter of a mile visibility due to ground fog. What a pickle. I looked at Number Three to see how he was doing and he gave me a hurried thumbs up. He was tucked in tight on my wing and anxious to get on the ground. Ready or not, the ball was in my court.

McClellan approach control cleared us for an instrument (ILS) approach. I acknowledged the clearance and started a turn onto final. "What a way to get recurrent on instrument approaches," I thought as the steering needles on the attitude gyro started to center. We had flown instrument training missions at Nellis on the gauges but never as a matter of necessity. It had been months since I had seen anything but clear weather out of the cockpit of an airplane. Fortunately, my experience as an all-weather interceptor pilot served me well.

We stabilized on final approach with the landing gear and flaps down and began a shallow descent, following the glide slope indicator. I could see glimpses of the ground straight below us, but the slant range visibility was zero. Regardless of the weather, I knew I had no choice but to fly Number Three all the way down to the runway. I kept telling myself, "Just stay cool and smooth, center the dials, hit the runway, and pray for good drag chutes."

Less than 100 feet from touchdown, the fog broke enough to see the runway. We were lined up on the centerline and aimed right at the runway numbers. I eased back the power and held on. Kaplunk! The tires squeaked and we rolled down the runway. By the grace of God, we had cheated death again and made it look like we knew what we were doing.

We turned off the runway and taxied back to the ramp. I was emotionally and physically exhausted, but Number Three was safe and in need of maintenance. We asked for a fast turn around in order to try again the next morning—the thirteenth of October but not Friday, thank heavens.

The maintenance report on the number three aircraft was sobering. Major Vic Cole was very lucky. The smoke in his cockpit was caused by a hairline crack in the oil cooler, which allowed oil to leak into the hot compressor section of the engine. If the problem had waited an hour, the aircraft, classified pod and all, would have gone into the drink, and Vic would have been a swimmer big time.

After a night's rest, we departed McClellan again the next morning. Vic was leading and our flight plan was essentially the same but the weather was considerably better. The Pacific looked calm as we made an uneventful rendezvous with our tanker, Levi 66, and headed for Hawaii.

My doppler navigation system was on the blink but Vic's was working and the tanker was navigating, so I sat back to enjoy the ride and smoke a cigarette. The ocean temperature was not cold enough to require the use of bulky poopie-suits so there was enough room in the cockpit to move around a little and keep my butt semicomfortable.

In spite of the clear weather, I was anxious about crossing the Pacific. From cruising altitude, the waves looked motionless and the ocean reached the horizon in all directions. It was vast and made me feel small and very insignificant. As the shoreline disappeared behind us, my aircraft began to make some peculiar noises and the engine felt like it was surging. I stared at the instruments anxiously but the needles were solid, not even a flicker. It was the ocean working on my imagination, and I knew I had to relax or it would get the best of me.

First Refueling

Before we reached the point of no return, we each made a test hookup to check our refueling systems. As I watched Three move into position behind the KC-135, it dawned on me that I was about to make my first operational refueling. Training was over, this one was business and my life depended on it.

Aerial refueling was not too difficult but the F-105 could be tricky at heavy weight with external stores loaded on the aircraft. In a nose-high attitude at relatively slow speed, the airplane had a tendency to yaw in a Dutch roll. The refueling receptacle was located in front of the cockpit and slightly left of the centerline of the aircraft. Just the force of the nozzle in the receptacle was enough to aggravate the yawing motion and cause the roll to go unstable quickly. To compensate, we learned to use a touch of left rudder and right aileron, a subtle cross-control combination that was effective but easy to overdo.

Number Three refueled and his system checked out okay. As soon as he was clear, I moved into position, stabilized, and before I knew it, I had my first drink of fuel over water. "A piece of cake," I said to myself with some relief.

Instead of disconnecting, I stayed on the boom and tried moving around slightly in the refueling envelope to get a feel for the control pressures required. The aircraft felt solid but the nose did have a tendency to roll to the right. Before I could fine tune my corrections, the boomer disconnected and stowed the boom. I was tempted to ask for more practice but decided to quit while I was ahead, even though I felt uneasy. The next refueling would be for the record with zero room for error.

We refueled five times during the four and a half hour flight to Hawaii. Although I had succeeded, my hookups were consistently erratic and got progressively rougher. The boomer was patient. He made an extra effort to encourage me, but I could sense anxiety building in his voice with each successive refueling. Something was wrong and we both sensed it.

I blamed the problem on my rusty technique even though I felt that something was wrong with the airplane. It was strange, but at times the controls seemed to react backwards. I couldn't figure it out. The flight controls checked out okay during preflight and the airplane was fresh out of overhaul at McClellan, so the likelihood of having a system problem was remote. All logical fingers pointed at the pilot.

During the next, longer leg to Guam, refueling would be even more critical because we would be out of range of the destination for most of the flight and dependent on auxiliary bases for emergency recovery. At times, continuous refueling contacts would be necessary. The consequences gnawed on me as I landed at Hickam.

As we taxied to the parking ramp, it was obvious that the first two aircraft in our flight had departed without us. A note in base operations said they hoped to see us in Thailand. "Have a good trip and hang in there on the tanker," it concluded ominously.

The maintenance crew checked my airplane carefully but found nothing wrong with the flight control system. Damn, it had to be me. That night, my sleep was restless and morning came early.

The flight to Guam was planned for seven hours with no room for error. The departure visibility at Hickam was marginal, and the winds en route were out of the west but slightly higher than normal. Consequently, every pound of fuel counted.

In order to save time and fuel, we made a formation takeoff with the tanker. Our unorthodox departure took us straight over downtown Honolulu at low altitude. The noise and smoke from the four engines of the KC-135 blanketed the city. The racket must have been loud enough to wake the drunks on Waikiki Beach, but we didn't lose sight of the tanker and saved a few hundred pounds of precious fuel in the process.

As soon as we reached cruising altitude we began topping off our fuel tanks. The idea was to keep them full in case we had to divert to an emergency recovery base short of our destination. The pressure didn't improve my refueling technique one iota. Again, the boomer did his best to encourage me but his calls only made things worse. Boomers were usually very quiet so I knew I was in trouble when ours started talking me onto the boom.

Halfway to Guam, the navigator on board the tanker radioed that his navigation equipment was unreliable. In order to maintain a straight course for Guam, he needed frequent position updates from our Doppler systems. I chuckled to myself, "My navigation system hasn't worked since we left California, and all of a sudden, the mother ship needs help." Vic's Doppler system was intermittent, so the tanker navigator was faced with getting us there the old fashioned way, with sun shots using a mechanical sextant.

The tanker commander told us to stay close and cycle on and off the boom until we were within range of Guam. I took a nervous drag on my cigarette, switched to 100 percent oxygen, and secured the cockpit for refueling.

I was very tense as I slid in behind the tanker. I tried to stabilize in position but I could feel myself starting to overcontrol the airplane. Before I could settle down, the boomer took a chance and stabbed my receptacle. Away she went! In seconds, my airplane rolled to the outer limits of the refueling envelope, triggering an automatic disconnect. I backed off and tried to settle down. "If only I could calm down enough to get a full load, just two measly minutes. Then I could relax and regroup," I chided myself. The boomer extended the nozzle and stabbed me again.

The harder I tried the worse it got. The oscillations were so large that the boom began to flex badly. The nozzle was jammed in the receptacle. I tried to disconnect, but the side loads on the boom were too high for the locking jaws in the receptacle to release. After several more futile attempts to stabilize, the situation came unglued. I heard a loud snap, the nozzle tore out of the receptacle, and the tanker and I parted company. The refueling operation was over. The boom was bent and my receptacle was broken. Thank God that Number Three had already taken a full load of fuel. We could make an emergency recovery at Wake Island if we acted quickly.

The tanker gave us an initial vector and our estimated range to Wake Island. We turned north as the tanker continued west on course for Guam. "Levi Six-Six, we are diverting to Wake, advise your control and alert the system. Thanks for the gas, sorry about the boom," Three radioed laconically. Quickly, the silhouette of the lone KC-135 shrank to a silver glint on the ocean horizon.

Wake Island Here We Come

If we could find it, the thought of landing on Wake Island was exciting. Until that moment, it was a place that only existed in old war movies. Just its name conjured up memories of John Wayne, a grizzled Marine with set jaw, dug in on a bloody beach with his machine gun blazing away at the enemy. To a young Saturday matinee worshipper, Wake Island was an imaginary symbol of action and glory. But it had suddenly become a reality as a desolate atoll in the Pacific, our key to recovery.

From 30,000 feet, Wake Island was a speck in the ocean. As we descended, the tiny island took shape as a small horseshoe reef that had been fashioned into an airfield. A narrow runway spanned the opening to the shallow lagoon inside the island. Rows of small waves broke against the coral jetty that extended both ends of the runway into the crystal clear, green ocean. From either direction, landing an F-105 was going to be a tough challenge.

As we lined up on initial approach, I reminded myself that Wake Island was a normal fuel stop for commercial jet airliners, but the thought of stopping a high-performance fighter in the same distance without getting wet bothered me. The runway looked like a beached popsicle stick as we pitched out to land.

I touched down seconds behind Three knowing that drag-chute failure could spell disaster. Both chutes deployed so we turned off the runway together and paraded past the terminal to the ramp in show formation. I wanted to make sure that it looked like we knew what we were doing.

In spite of the bravado, I felt conspicuously guilty. The Pan Am agent in charge of the airport met us as we parked. F-105s were a rare sight at Wake and he was curious about our unexpected visit. I could tell by the expression on Vic's face that he wasn't anxious to explain it.

Wake Island was not renowned for its maintenance or hotel accommodations. The closest F-105 unit was stationed on the island of Okinawa. It would take several days to deploy a maintenance team to fix my airplane. Meanwhile, we settled into some rather austere visitors' quarters and spent our time fishing and drinking at a makeshift bar known affectionately as the "Beach Club." The surf was inviting but we weren't allowed to swim because of sharks, and we couldn't eat the fish we caught because of possible coral poisoning. The only safe bet was the whiskey.

To help pass the time, we took frequent walks across the island to the Pan Am terminal to play the pinball machines and watch the charter flights as they stopped in for service. The stewardesses were off-limits to visitors but they were refreshing to watch and sexy to think about.

The eastbound planes were packed with battle-weary soldiers returning from Vietnam. They were young men with grave faces but their tired eyes conveyed a sense of genuine relief. Their macho attitude contrasted sharply with the uncertainty in the faces of the new troops going the other way. The neatly pressed replacements looked frightened. Their bright eyes were filled with anxiety, yet they seemed curious and ready for adventure. As I watched, I knew I was looking at some who would not return. I thought about their families and about my own.

When the C-130 carrying our maintenance crew finally arrived, we were grim and anxious to get going. After three days of tedious waiting, we had bruises on our hands from bumping the pinballs and had consumed all the liquor the Beach Club had to offer.

A flight control specialist found the problem in my airplane quickly. The stability augmentation system (STAB AUG) was hooked up backwards. The young mechanic collected his tools and looked at me curiously. "That must have been one hell'uva ride. Why didn't you disconnect the system and fly without it?" he asked sarcastically. I fought the temptation to give the cocky kid a lecture, thanked him for his help, and turned my attention to a group of mechanics examining the receptacle.

The STAB AUG system wiring was fixed in a matter of minutes but the receptacle was another story. It could not be repaired without an extended delay at Wake. We could wait another week or two or chance flying to Guam using the probe-and-drogue system for aerial refueling. The Pacific Air Force command post (PACAF) in Honolulu chose the latter. Ouch!

I was not proficient with the probe-and-drogue system even though I had signed the currency statement back at McClellan. The last time I had even extended the "pecker" was to salute a flight of F-4s on the ramp at Nellis. Irony or poetic justice? Either way, I was in a well-deserved jam.

The decision to go with the probe-and-drogue troubled Vic as well. He had also fudged a little on his currency requirements. We talked it over and decided we didn't have a choice. We had to press on regardless of the consequences. Our skill and cunning as fighter pilots were on the line.

Vic filled me in on the fine art of sticking a drogue. "Aim the probe high and to the right of the drogue. It won't look right but the basket will move up to meet the probe as you move in," he assured me. "Once you're in there, keep a bend in the hose and push hard to stay there."

We packed the airplanes and waited for the order to scramble from PACAF. When it came, we started up and blasted off leaving Wake Island behind us in our jet wash. It was a bold stroke and I was nervous but glad to be back in the air and on our way.

Levi 85, a drogue equipped tanker from Guam, met us as we leveled off after departing Wake. The time en route to Guam was relatively short, two and a half hours, so all we needed was one good drink of fuel and a release from the tanker to proceed on our own.

When we joined up on the tanker, the refueling boom was stowed with the hose and drogue attached and trailing in the slipstream. The basket was oscillating slowly. It looked ominous. I felt my hands begin to sweat when the boomer lowered the boom and drogue into the trail position for refueling. "Cleared in for contact, little buddy," the boomer called cryptically.

I would try first. If I didn't succeed, we could return to Wake and wait for maintenance. "What pressure," I thought as I moved in for a stab at the basket. My heart was pounding and I could feel the rush of adrenalin in my veins. I was determined to succeed and redeem my past performance.

To my surprise, I hit the target on the first try. I took a deep breath, added power, and concentrated on staying on the drogue. The flight controls were responding properly and I began to gain confidence. After a couple of minutes, my airplane began to drop off slowly. It was gaining weight, and even at full power I could not maintain a proper connection on the drogue.

I backed away a safe distance to stabilize, lit the afterburner, and used a combination of throttle and speed brakes to maintain a slow, positive closure on the basket. Again, the hookup was easy, and in less than three minutes, I had a full load of fuel. I pulled back the power, stowed the probe, and slid out on the tanker's wing to watch Number Three refuel. I was so relieved that I almost cried. The monkey was finally off my back.

Vic extended his probe and moved in on the basket. He was smooth and made several stabs but couldn't stay on the drogue. With each hookup, he took on some fuel but not enough to compensate for the amount he was burning. He was having a difficult time, and we were getting dangerously close to a bingo point for a recovery in either direction.

Vic was frustrated and the tanker commander was getting nervous. With luck, we could have made Guam without taking on more fuel, but Vic wanted another 2,000 pounds to make it safely. He backed away from the basket to stabilize the airplane and collect himself. As he started in, he called, "Three is moving to the precontact position. I'll get it this time, no sweat!" The determination in his voice was deliberate.

Without thinking, I gave Vic some advice he didn't need. "Lead, this is Four. Try a little burner," I said quickly.

My timing was terrible. Vic's afterburner lit just as the probe entered the basket. His aircraft accelerated, and zingo, the probe hit the basket and kept right on going. The basket tore loose from the hose and fell to a watery grave in the Pacific. Vic's probe was bent and the basket was gone. Another refueling ended abruptly. We were batting two-for-two and becoming notorious.

I had enough fuel to make Guam but Vic was hurting. Our best bet was to leave the tanker and accelerate to an optimum cruise speed to save fuel. We didn't have another choice. We had to press on with what we had and sweat out the fuel minute by minute. By comparing the fuel remaining with the amount the engine was burning, we could tell exactly how many minutes of fuel each of us had remaining. It was a computation fighter pilots made more often than they cleared their ears.

We let the "world" know that we were in trouble and what we intended to do. The system started to react to our distress but the tanker commander would not agree to release us. The rule book said that he was in charge of the formation until we reached our destination, and he was sticking by the rules. "If you proceed without us, be advised you're on your own," the radio crackled as we accelerated away from the tanker.

"Roger, Levi Eight-Five, thanks for the help. Andersen is seven hundred nautical miles at two-six-zero degrees, your position is one-five-one-five north, one-five-seven-zero-zero east. See you on the ground, Plink Seven-Three flight is going to three-zero-five-four for Duckbutt control," Vic replied calmly but with a touch of sarcasm.

We were an hour and a half from Guam, Vic had 8,000 pounds of fuel, and we were praying for light head winds. We checked in with the Duckbutt SA-16 rescue aircraft on station below and began the agonizing process of counting minutes and pounds of fuel remaining.

As soon as we were within radar range of Guam we established radio contact with approach control at Andersen Air Force Base and started a shallow descent to the runway. A string of B-52s were recovering from a bombing mission over South Vietnam, and we were advised that they would have first priority in the landing pattern. Priority be damned, we had to land without delay. Vic acknowledged the call knowing that we could fit in between bombers easily.

About 20 miles out, we spotted the steep cliffs of Guam and the runway at Andersen. We were lined up on final approach but the B-52s started complaining about pattern spacing and screaming "minimum fuel." The command post asked us to hold short of the island until the bombers landed but we didn't have the fuel to spare, so we switched to tower frequency and landed straight in without further ado.

The runway was long enough to stop without a drag chute but we deployed them instinctively. Consequently, it took an extra minute or two to clear the runway and one of the B-52s on final approach nearly had a baby. He was low on fuel and convinced that we were going to force him to make a go-around. "Tower, get those damned fighters off the runway," he screamed in a trembling falsetto. We made it off with time to spare, but for an instant, I hoped the jackass would have to go around.

They parked us on the back forty and as soon as we were in the chocks I knew we were in trouble. A colonel in a blue staff car with a flag on the front fender met us at the airplanes. It was the bomb wing commander and he was hopping mad. His jaw was set and his eyes were on fire. As I climbed down the ladder, I reminded myself to keep quiet and let Vic do the talking. He was the flight leader after all, and leadership had its moments.

It was clear from the outset that the colonel intended to do the talking. He had been following our progress across the Pacific, and in his view, we hadn't covered either the Tactical Air Command or the Air Force with glory. "How did you manage to bend a boom in the first place?" "Why did you leave Wake island without a backup system?" "How in the hell could a hotshot fighter pilot bust up a refueling basket and then leave the tanker without permission?"

I figured it was our duty to endure his questions and be ready for the punch line when he got to it. "Who in the hell do you think you are busting into the traffic pattern like you did? Don't you realize that B-52s returning from combat have top priority?"

The colonel paused briefly looking for an answer. I was willing to settle for "yes, Sir, ... no, Sir, ... no excuse, Sir" but Vic chose to set him straight. It was a mistake. Like most commanders, he didn't set straight easily, and we both got our butts chewed thoroughly before he dismissed us. It was a small price to pay for the luck we had enjoyed that day so we counted our blessings and headed for maintenance control.

We were pleasantly surprised to find a cadre of experienced F-105 maintenance troops waiting for us. They assured us that our aircraft would be fixed and ready to go by morning. Ironically, the biggest problem they had was repacking the drag chutes. One of the mechanics reminded us that we had used our chutes unnecessarily. He added that there was a published "Notice to Airmen" that "advised F-105 pilots not to use drag chutes at Andersen because spares are not available." After a deserved ribbing, we asked for a ride to the Officers' Club. The sun was setting and my "martini low light" was on steady.

We stashed our gear in the BOQ room and headed for the stag bar. The place was wall-to-wall bomber crews. They looked like peacocks in their pressed flying suits adorned with arrays of colorful velcro patches. Vic's single 100-mission patch stood out like a beacon. When they was saw us, an uneasiness came over the bar.

Vic walked over to a guy sporting a "100 Missions: South Vietnam: B-52" patch on his flying suit. "That patch offends me," Vic said in a loud voice. "How dare you compare a B-52 mission over South Vietnam with a mission north in the F-105!" In a flash, tempers flared and we were in a heck of a fracas. Drinks spilled and two guys wound up on the floor before a couple of the bomber crews broke it up with a stern lecture about growing up. The poor guy with the patch on his suit got the message and nearly crapped his pants in the process.

Dinner was tense but we made it to bed early with the help of the base provost marshal.

The Last Leg

The morning briefing was conducted at the tanker squadron in wing operations. Levi 81 was assigned to fly the final leg as our tanker. Maintenance reported that both aircraft were repaired and ready to go. As we left the operations building, the aircraft commander of Levi 81 cleverly reminded us that we had earned a terrible reputation with the Pacific tanker fleet. "Try to make it the rest of the way without busting up any equipment," he urged us smugly.

Our route of flight lay west across the Philippines and the South China Sea to Danang on the Vietnamese coast south of the Military Zone of Demarkation (DMZ) between North and South Vietnam. From there, it turned southwest across the southern tip of Laos to enter Thai airspace for a flight across Thailand to Takhli Royal Thai Air Base. The flight plan estimated five and a half hours en route, including the letdown and recovery.

The flight went according to plan. After two refuelings, I was still having trouble on the boom so I disengaged the STAB AUG and flew the remaining hookup without the help of electronics. It worked. We completed all three refuelings without a scratch and redeemed ourselves as professional receiver pilots, at least with Levi 81.

As we entered the Southeast Asia peninsula, I felt gripped with a combination of anxiety and curiosity. It was both exciting and disturbing to look down on a land where a war was being fought. There were no visible signs of violence, none of the details delivered by the media, and everything looked quite peaceful. Even so, the land had a sinister look, which was intriguing and a little fearful.

From altitude, I could see the Gulf of Tonkin and the southwest corner of Hainan Island. The Vietnamese shoreline looked serene. It stretched from north to south without any visible boundaries. Naively, I looked for the infamous DMZ but couldn't find it and laughed at myself for thinking I could see it from the air.

To cross into southern Laos, we switched to the tactical control of Red Crown, a U.S. command and control aircraft that monitored all airborne traffic over Laos and north of the DMZ. The radio chatter was interesting. I was fascinated by a constant stream of cryptic messages that overlapped each other. In the background, radio transmissions from ground units engaged in combat were audible. There was a sense of urgency in their clipped, often profane messages. "Damn, it sounded just like the evening news," I thought excitedly. It was ironic that the pods we were carrying might one day carry the same message traffic directly to high places in Washington, heaven forbid.

We crossed the Mekong River and entered Thailand heading directly for Takhli, 300 nautical miles away. As soon as we were in Thai airspace we were passed from one radar control to another in quick succession. From Crown to Cricket to Lion to Dressy Lady and finally to Takhli approach control for descent and landing. I was thankful that Vic was leading because we were busy and he was familiar with the system.

Ground control cleared us to descend. We took one last drink of fuel from Levi 81 and received clearance to proceed on our own. "Thanks for the lift Levi, see you on the ground. Four, Lead here, go Channel One-Five, over," Vic said calmly as we switched to approach control frequency.

Takhli approach control cleared us to proceed to Point Alpha, to descend to 5,000 feet and to depart Alpha heading 250 degrees for Point Bravo, the 9-mile gate for Channel 43 (Takhli Tacan station). We throttled back and started descending.

As we got closer to the ground, I could see details in the beautiful jungles of northern Thailand—"up country" as it was referred to colloquially. The jungle was lush and green. It was very dense with a few meadow clearings. The trees were enormous. Smoke from small camp fires dotted the countryside. Even at 5,000 feet, I could smell the aroma of their wood fires, an odor unique to the Thai jungle.

The dark jungle cover spread evenly over gently rising hills with a few sharp ridges jutting up a few hundred feet. Like all foreign lands, Thailand had a character all its own and one that would leave an indelible mark on all those who served there.

We hit Point Bravo and turned due south. As we did, I looked through the lead aircraft and saw Takhli Air Base for the first time. It was carved out of the jungle and looked much smaller than I had expected.

As we approached the field, Vic checked in with the tower. We had arrived during the recovery of the morning strike force. Traffic was heavy and there was lots of interesting radio chatter. The tower advised us to take spacing behind Tico flight, a flight of three F-105s approaching the field from the west for a landing on runway three-six. I relaxed my grip on the stick and adjusted my sweaty helmet. It was intimidating to be in the traffic pattern with F-105s returning from combat. My heart was pounding.

"Takhli, Tico Lead turning initial for runway three-six two miles out with three aircraft. Tico Four recovered at Udorn with battle damage." "Tico check in."

"Two!"

"Three!"

"Roger, Tico. You are number one in the pattern, cleared to land. Call turning base leg, winds calm." "Tico, this is Tower, use caution on the landing roll. We have a disabled B-66 halfway down the runway blocking the left hand side, over."

"Roger ,Tower. Tico has a tallyho."

"Tower, this is Dobe with four, on initial five miles behind two ferry birds. Have them in sight, over."

"Roger, Dobe, call on the break." "Flight of two on initial [that was us] cleared to land behind Tico, a flight of three turning base now."

"Tico on base with three green and pressure."

"Two, same."

"Three, Rog."

"Everyone clear right for the burning B-66."

Vic broke left over the end of the runway. I waited three seconds and followed. "Tower, Plink Seven-Three turning base with three green," Vic called.

"Roger, Plink Seven-Three and Seven-Four are cleared to land."

I touched down smoothly, lowered the nose wheel, and deployed the drag chute. The deceleration felt good. I steered to the right to avoid the B-66 that was resting in the grass halfway off the runway. It was still smoking as the firemen watched with hoses poised. "Must've collapsed the left main landing gear on landing roll out," I mused out loud.

As we turned off the runway, ground crews signaled us to enter the de-arming area. They had mistaken us for two mission aircraft and seemed confused by the strange pods we were carrying. After some discussion, they safetied our tank pylons and waved us on.

Halfway down the taxiway to the parking ramp, I saw a large wooden sign, "WELCOME TO THE 355TH TAC FIGHTER WING, COL BOB SCOTT, COMMANDER." "No question about who's in charge here," I thought. It was my first encounter with the command authority that prevailed at Takhli. I sensed that there was nothing ambiguous or shy about the way the wing was run and my perception proved to be right on the money.

Takhli Air Base

The Japanese built the airfield at Takhli and used it as a fighter strip during World War II. It was a small, compact base. The parking area paralleled the runway to the west and was literally jammed with F-105s. Almost 100 aircraft were parked diagonally in two rows facing each other like feathers on an arrow—big camouflaged feathers.

It was difficult to taxi in such close quarters. I inched my way through the parking area twice before I found the right parking place. Everyone looked at me like there was a sign on the side of the airplane announcing the arrival of the new kid on the block. What an entrance for a hotshot graduate of the weapons school.

The ramp was busy. Ordnance crews were loading bombs and missiles while mechanics worked on the airplanes. The ground crews were dressed to suit the hot weather. Many went without shirts and some worked in shorts but they all had on their squadron caps. It was apparent that stateside spit and polish had given way to hard work, unit pride, and the war.

A beaming crew chief directed me into the blocks with precise hand signals. It didn't look to me like the airplane would fit so I followed his directions cautiously. A large group had gathered to meet the aircraft and examine the unusual pods we were carrying.

I stop-cocked the engine. The crew chief came up the ladder, smiled, and welcomed me to Takhli. He thanked me for bringing him an airplane. His last one had been shot down only weeks earlier on a costly strike against a fuel storage area just southeast of Hanoi.

As I came down the ladder, I was surprised to see an old friend waiting to greet me. Major Bill Egan, a West Point classmate and close associate during our years in the Air Force, smiled and shook my hand warmly. Bill was a B-66 pilot and had only been at Takhli for a couple of months. The strain of combat had already left its mark on his broad smile. There were lines in his ruddy complexion, and the graying, red stubble on his face was evidence that he had spent the night before patrolling the skies over North Vietnam.

I gathered up my gear and jumped in Bill's truck for a ride to the command post. He had a small Datsun pickup with right-hand drive, which I found peculiar. "You'll get used to it," he chuckled as he maneuvered through the congested flight line.

As we left, maintenance crews were already preparing number 274 for combat. I looked back and wondered if we would both make it. Our relationship had been short but intimate. Eighteen hours and forty-five minutes in the air, a dozen or so exciting refuelings, and we had finally reached our destination. "Here's to you 274," I saluted, "hope we both make it." Time would tell, but despite some very close calls, I would do better than 274. Less than five months later, the aircraft was shot down and crashed in Laos, the pilot killed.

I said goodbye to Vic Cole in the maintenance shack. He wished me luck and we shook hands, promising to keep in touch. We had shared some exciting experiences but we didn't really have much in common. Vic had "done his tour" and was anxious to catch an early hop to Bangkok. It wasn't until we had parted that I realized that I had never asked him where he was stationed.

Bulletproof Mustaches

After a brief stop at the wing command post, we were off to the club for a relaxing breakfast. I walked into the Officers' Club trying to look seasoned and sure of myself.

"Ken Bell, you old son of a gun," someone shouted from across the dining room. It was Max Brestel, an old friend from a fighter squadron in Spain. Max was an interesting guy but I figured his wife had long since shot him. He was a very junior pilot when I had known him in Spain, and I envied the fact that someone once so junior had gotten a head start on me in combat.

Bill and I joined Max at his table. Max had logged over twenty missions and was thankful that he wasn't starting over. As a matter of fact, he doubted if a guy "just starting now could make it." That got my attention and Max enjoyed it. He twisted his fledgling mustache. "Better start one right away, Ken," Max said as he rolled the dark, waxy tips of his mustache between his fingers. "It's bulletproof. You'll need one to stand half a chance of finishing."

With or without a mustache, the odds were sobering. That fall, the F-105 losses had gone up dramatically. In October, we lost five airplanes and only one pilot was recovered. By the end of 1966, 111 F-105s had been shot down in the worst year of the war. Statistically, in a 100-mission tour, pilots faced a fifty-fifty chance of getting shot down and only half of those shot down were recovered.

The likelihood of going down over Hanoi presented a grim scene, but Max had a lighthearted way of expressing it. "Ken, you know I'm fearless," he jokingly boasted. "But I come back from every mission scared speechless." I smiled. Max Brestel was a lot of things but he was never speechless.

A young Thai waitress handed me a menu. She had a willing smile but spoke no English. Bill Egan told me to order by the numbers and to add sahwahdee as a polite Thai gesture. "If you want eggs," he said, "pick any number. They all come the same way, hard over with toast, bacon, and salt tablets."

A prominent dish of pills on the table prompted more sage advice from Max, who was enjoying his role as my combat mentor. "You know the only way to tell that it's Sunday around here?" Max asked rhetorically. "They serve malaria pills with breakfast and the date on your Seiko watch turns red." We laughed nervously.

3

CHECKING IN

THERE WERE THREE SQUADRONS in the 355th Tactical Fighter Wing, the 333d Lancers, the 354th Bulldogs, and the 357th Dragons. Each squadron had its own traditional color (red, blue, and yellow) and insignia dating back to World War II. Signs bearing these insignia and the name of each squadron commander marked the location of their operations buildings along the flight line.

The command post was the nerve center of combat operations. It was centrally located on the flight line in a complex of small frame buildings set up on short wooden posts to protect them from the jungle. Just the setting made the war seem real and imminent.

Three hours after arriving on station, I had completed my in-briefing at the command post and was headed for the 354th Squadron. The Bulldogs were hurting. They had suffered some punishing losses during the previous weeks and were down to only eleven pilots out of the twenty-four usually assigned to a squadron. Most of them were relatively inexperienced lieutenants I had known at Nellis. The commander, Lieutenant Colonel Don Asire, also a friend from Nellis, and three other experienced pilots were struggling to hold the squadron together. My weapons school experience would be a welcome addition to the beleaguered squadron.

The 354th was located south of the command post in a low, tin-roofed building marked by a blue and white flag and a distinctive bulldog emblem. A small, well-kept garden welcomed me as I walked onto the low wooden porch surrounding the frame building. The air was heavy with the scent of musty teak wood.

As I entered the building, I saw two familiar faces from Nellis, Lieutenant Stein and Lieutenant Glenn Gidel. They had just returned from a mission and explained that Colonel Asire and the other pilots were still in debriefing. It was a tough mission, but they had hit the target and come home without any losses. It was only their second mission counter up north and they were concerned about the losses the squadron was suffering, but they were proud to be part of the air war over North Vietnam.

As we talked, my thoughts slipped back to our days in training. Stein and Gidel were quite different. Steiny was a big, freckle-faced kid with discouraged, faint eyes. He meant well but was clumsy and slow. Glenn Gidel was just the opposite—lean and alert with a genuine spark of brightness in his eyes. Glenn was a quick pilot and natural wingman. But, despite their differences, they both faced the same threats in combat and they agreed that their prospects were not favorable.

I heard several pilots enter the hall from a room in the back of the building. I recognized Don Asire's deep voice and turned to greet him. His confident tone seemed out of place with his small frame and somewhat scholarly manner. He was gaunt and his deep-set blue eyes looked especially hollow. "Ken, welcome aboard. It's a relief to see you," he said as he introduced me to the others. "This is Vern Frye our D flight commander. I'm going to put you in Vern's flight until you have enough experience to take a flight of your own," Colonel Asire concluded.

Vern Frye was also a major. He welcomed me but registered some surprise to find that I had been promoted. Vern was athletically trim with a square jaw and short, dark hair. He was clean-cut, seemed energetic, was pleasantly outgoing, and apparently in a hurry. Vern gave me directions to the trailer we would be sharing and explained that he was on his way to mission planning. "You'll need the wing orientation briefings before we can put you on the schedule, so relax and have a look around," he said. "I'll see you at the trailer in a couple of hours."

As I turned to leave, I noticed a letter predominantly displayed on the squadron bulletin board. It was marked

> "All Read and Heed!"
> After repeated warnings, rowdiness in the stag bar has gotten out of hand. The recent destruction of several slot machines is evidence that some have lost their appreciation for the few creature comforts being provided them. I view this act as a direct challenge of my authority and I am prepared to meet that challenge. Signed, Robert R. Scott, Colonel, USAF, Commander.

I was scheduled to report to Colonel Scott early the next morning. His stern, rather direct letter gave me the impression that I would meet a man who knew he was in charge. I tried to visualize him as I followed Vern's directions to the trailer.

Trailer 30A

Flight crews lived in a complex adjacent to the Officers' Club. Junior officers were assigned by squadron to small, dormitory style buildings called hooches. As a new major, I was entitled to the privacy and comfort of one of the air-conditioned, two-man trailers. They were convenient to the stag bar and only a five-minute walk from the flight line. It wasn't the Ritz, but it was far better than I had anticipated.

I found the trailers easily. They were set in rows behind the Officers' Club and their symmetry contrasted sharply with the jungle landscape surrounding them. Nothing was moving. Freshly laundered socks, skivvies, and flying suits hung motionless from clotheslines between the trailers. The afternoon sun was hot, and the only sound was the drone of two auxiliary electrical power units.

The trailers were set on skid-rails over a bed of heavy gravel to provide drainage for the monsoon rains. The loose rock made walking difficult and amplified the sound of my clumsy footsteps as I searched for a trailer with my name on it. Even though it was broad daylight, I somehow felt like an intruder.

The doors on the trailers were numbered and marked with names stenciled on wooden replicas of the squadron patches. I zeroed in on the 354th area and finally stumbled upon my trailer. Voila! Number 30A had a freshly painted bulldog plaque bearing the name of "Major Bell."

I opened the door to the trailer cautiously. To my surprise, the few items I had shipped from Nellis were stacked neatly in the corner between the desk and wall locker. I was impressed. "Nothing's too good for a one-o-five jock," I boasted quietly as I stepped into my new combat quarters.

There was a bedroom at each end of the trailer with a toilet, shower, and a small sink in between. My room was furnished with a dresser, straight-back chair, small refrigerator, and a G.I. issue double-decked bed. I was surprised to find two flight bags, a flight jacket, and a khaki side-brim campaign hat resting on the top bunk. The name tag on a flight suit in the wall locker matched the one on the jacket: *Major Charles "Vas" Vasiliadis, Pilot, USAF.* "Who in the hell is Vasiliadis and what were his things doing in my room?" I asked myself out loud.

Suddenly, the door burst open behind me. "Hi, I'm Vas," the surprised visitor said with a confident look on his face. "You must be Ken, Vern's new trailermate. Welcome to the three-five-five." He gripped my elbow as we shook hands. His square jaw ground to one side as he spoke, and his piercing, black eyes riveted each word. "I'm Greek, but I'm not bearing gifts and I'll be out of here by morning," he assured me with a broad smile.

I liked Vas immediately. He was forceful, confident, and cocky enough to be interesting. I sensed that he was genuine. "What are you doing here?" I asked him. "Vern didn't mention you."

Vas had been temporarily assigned to Takhli from Kadena Air Base on the island of Okinawa. He had a long history in the F-105 and Colonel Scott had invited him to help the wing through its critical pilot shortage. Vas didn't need much of an invitation. He loved to fly, he was good at it, and he was a skilled leader. Vas seized the occasion to give me the benefit of his insight and experience. Our conversation was an intense, mostly one-sided lecture. During a lull, I suggested we adjourn to the bar. It had been a long day, and a my jet lag told me it was way past martini time. Vas agreed with his characteristic closing shot, "Rog, you got it, buddy."

On the way to the club, an afternoon squall hit with full force. Heavy rain quickly covered the gravel around the trailers. A wooden walkway that normally marked the path to the stag bar was floating uselessly behind the club on a lake of rain water. As we splashed through the puddles, I noticed several enormous beetles collecting on high ground. They dwarfed the largest cockroaches I had seen as a boy growing up in west Texas. As they crawled, their grotesque bodies were thrust forward in a menacing stance by their long rear legs.

We were soaked when we reached the short wooden steps at the back door of the stag bar. "What kind of bugs were those?" I asked Vas as we jammed through the door.

"They're rice bugs and they're a delicacy," Vas replied. "The Thais like to suck the eggs out of the female and eat them. The only trick is sorting out the females," he went on. "They do it by smell," he grimaced. "In just the right place."

The stag bar was crowded, the smoke was thick, and the humidity was heavy. The only fresh air in the room came as a weak stream of vapor from a small, overworked cooler sitting in the corner. A row of slot machines stood in front of a long, battered wall opposite the bar stools. Each machine had drawn a crowd of boisterous and relentless players. As I watched, I was reminded of the commander's strong letter. It was my first exposure to combat pilots at their leisure.

No one seemed to notice us. Vas was relaxed and buoyant but I felt self-conscious. I was the only guy there in a new flying suit with zero combat missions. We ordered a round of drinks and Vas continued his lecture.

I looked down the bar and saw Lieutenants McCaffrey and Haggarty—Mac and Hags—the gold dust twins from Nellis. Mac resembled a big Irish cop and Hags complimented him nicely as his short, cocky sidekick—always smiling but unpredictable. They had been at Takhli several months and I knew I was in for a ribbing.

They let me have it. "Well, well, if it isn't Major Bell!" Both had forty missions and would soon be checked out as flight leaders. According to them, they would be through by Christmas, and I was lucky I had made it over before they finished the war single-handed. "As usual, the lieutenants are doing all the work and the brass is taking the credit," they asserted humorously. And as a new major, they let me know I had "passed from buddy to brass."

After a good laugh, Hags asked how I had gotten into the stag bar. "Not through that door I hope," he said pointing to the back of the stag bar. "It is reserved for people who have flown up north, no exceptions." Reluctantly, they let me off the hook for a round of drinks, but I sensed that the back door tradition was not to be taken lightly.

I commented on their mustaches. Hags's was very dark and doing much better than Mac's and I needled him. "Frankly Sir, it's a pain in the ass. More trouble than it's worth," Mac said as he stroked his fuzzy upper lip. "Don't even start one," he went on, "and chances are even you'll make one hundred missions without it."

"What do you mean, even," I snapped back. "What does a mustache have to do with getting shot down?"

"It's superstition Sir, and we don't miss a trick when it comes to dodging the golden BB," Hags said wryly. "Mustaches worked good at first, but lately a couple of guys have gotten hammered who had'em," Hags added. "The real kick in the ass is that each one of the guys who cut them off early got hit in a matter of days." I laughed but they were dead serious.

Grimly, Mac told me that one of his classmates had been killed at Korat during a crash on takeoff. Instinctively, I knew it was the lieutenant who had come to see me at Nellis. When Mac told me his name, the full weight of my intuition hit home and I felt numb all over. Thoughtfully, Vas interrupted with an offer for dinner but Mac and I stayed at the bar to talk things over.

Takhli Village

After a few more drinks, my body said it was time to eat and go to bed, but Mac talked me into going to town for a Thai meal and some late entertainment. He had a day off the schedule and felt like celebrating.

On my way to the trailer, I was overtaken by Vern Frye. He was scheduled for the early go and had already had supper. Vern urged me to get some rest and counseled me on the hazards of drinking. "I'd stick to U.S. Pepsi, if I were you," he said. "Whiskey dulls the senses, and you'll need all the sense you can muster to survive this test." He went to bed trusting I would appreciate his advice so I changed clothes quietly.

Mac and I hired a cab in front of the club. It was an old Mercedes driven by a moonlighting Thai officer with all of the necessary base credentials. I settled back for an evening tour of the countryside.

It was less than 10 miles to Takhli village. The excitement of seeing a new and strange country at dusk revived me. We were on a narrow road between two small dikes with a flooded klong (swamp) on both sides. The small houses dotting the landscape were set on pilings, and smoke from their cooking fires filled the air with the pungent aroma of charcoal.

In a matter of minutes, we reached the village. It wasn't much by Las Vegas standards but it did have some encouraging signals. A faded neon sign marking the Takhli Villa bore a universal message. The driver pulled up in front and agreed to wait for us.

The bar was dimly lit and deserted except for a couple of girls perched on stools and an older Chinese man seated at the cash register. Mac encouraged me, "Don't let the atmosphere bother you, it's a great place to eat." I was hesitant but Mac assured me that hot beef and peppers were the house specialty, and they turned out to be wonderful. They were eye-watering hot, but with the help of several bottles of Singhah beer, the meal filled a void my stomach had been crying for since breakfast.

The choices after dinner were standard—dancing, drinking, and a massage in a lukewarm hotsy bath. My day had begun several time zones earlier and I had an early appointment with the commander but I couldn't resist the temptation to sample the local agenda.

I fell asleep in the cab going home and tiptoed into the trailer, hoping not to disturb Vern. To my surprise, he had already gone to the morning briefing but had left a six-pack of Pepsi and a note on the desk reminding me of my early schedule. It hurt, but I made it to breakfast on time. I chose the number on the menu for scrambled eggs, hoping they would be soft enough to swallow with dry toast and butter.

As I sipped my coffee, I watched the Thai waitresses. They were unusually young and graceful. They giggled bashfully as they skipped between tables, and their broad smiles embarrassed quickly if you tried to catch their eye. Their names were difficult to pronounce and impossible to read so they were identified by number. It was a rude system, but they were proud of their numbers and seemed to enjoy their anonymity.

My eggs came hard and looking straight back at me. As I ate, Colonel Scott entered the mess and made his way to a table set especially for him. He was well groomed, trim, and small compared to what I had expected. His crisp summer uniform and stride reflected his confidence and poise.

Several waitresses gathered attentively around a table at the end of the dining room. It was on an elevated platform with a place set elegantly for one. I watched Colonel Scott as he was seated, but he didn't acknowledge me and I didn't expect to join him.

I finished breakfast quickly and headed for wing headquarters. It was a short walk, and the early morning air was surprisingly cool and refreshing. The hot sun was just beginning to break through some low-hanging clouds to the east. As tired as I was, I felt alert and excited with a genuine sense of purpose and destiny.

The jungle canopy surrounding the base was beautiful. The trees were extremely tall and their heavy foliage was dark green with just a touch of vermillion. A thin layer of smoke hung over the tree line like a mysterious morning shroud. The air was still and laden with the smell of teak fires.

The quixotic feeling that gripped me was broken by the realization that three tiny snakes were crawling on the road beside me. I stopped abruptly and their hooded heads arched up in unison. They were cobras. Where was mama? Bill Egan had warned me that King cobras were known to stalk humans but I thought he was joking. I moved to the crown of the road and picked up the pace hoping to out-distance the mischievous baby snakes and their mother, wherever she was.

As I turned down the ramp toward the headquarters, a blue sedan pulled to a stop in front of the building. It was Colonel Scott. I checked my watch. I had plenty of time but I lengthened my stride instinctively. I didn't want to risk keeping the commander waiting.

The commander's office was easy to find. A sergeant at an outer desk greeted me and ushered me in quickly. Colonel Scott was seated alone, facing a large window overlooking the flight line. His gaze seemed fixed on the men and aircraft he commanded. Cautiously, I interrupted him, "Major Bell reporting for duty as ordered, Sir!" I saluted smartly as Colonel Scott turned and motioned for me to be seated.

"Ken, welcome aboard the 355th, the best fighting team in Southeast Asia. We have an extraordinary mission and we are doing a outstanding job in spite of some very difficult odds," he said proudly. His steel blue eyes were intense, almost harsh in their focus and determination. "There are those in this wing who may tell you that I am too tough and demanding, but we are here to do a job, and my job is to command and lead," he said resolutely. "Whatever goes on at Takhli, on base or in the air, I can assure you that I am in command."

Colonel Scott rose to shake my hand. His message was clear. He was in charge and made no bones about it. As we walked toward the door, he grinned shrewdly. "We'll get along fine, just do your job and mind your manners," he quipped as he measured my reaction. His head was cocked up slightly and his piercing eyes danced sideways. He was satisfied that I had understood his message. As quickly as it had begun, my welcoming interview with the commander was over.

As I left the building, another blue sedan arrived abruptly. It was the vice wing commander, Colonel Jack Broughton. He was in his flight suit and obviously in a hurry. I stepped aside and saluted. He smiled and returned my salute briskly without speaking. He was a big, forceful-looking man, and the stern expression on his face told me that he had something urgent on his mind.

I walked to the Tactical Operations Center (TOC) anticipating an early start on my orientation briefings only to find that they had been delayed because I had arrived without confirmation of a Top Secret clearance. Apparently, my unexpected flight across the Pacific had short circuited my orders, and I had outdistanced my clearance in the process. It was a trivial administrative detail, but the intelligence types wouldn't budge until I could produce evidence of a clearance. Disgruntled, I filled out an application for an interim clearance and walked back to the club for coffee.

On the way to the club, I stopped by the trailer and found Vern cleaning up after the morning mission. He had just finished shaving in the bathroom. "Another crummy Sky Spot," Vern said as he splashed his face with water. "I'll be done in a jiffy but come on in if you need something. We don't stand on ceremony around here, partner."

As Vern spoke, I saw the maid standing beside him washing some clothes in a small basin. Vern sensed my surprise. "This is Suwahne, our maid. She doesn't understand a word of English. I call her Water Buffalo because she moves so slowly." Suwahne smiled as if she understood and kept on washing. "You have to watch her, Ken. She'll use half a box of Tide on one flying suit if you let her. She thinks laundry soap is magic and the more the better." In sympathy, I thought that Suwahne was a prettier name, but Water Buffalo somehow suited her.

Vern commented on my late hours. "If you don't shape up, you'll probably be late for your one-hundredth mission," he noted sarcastically as he smiled and invited me to join him in the club for brunch and coffee.

Meeting at the club after the morning mission was a daily ritual. The returning crews were relieved and in a mood to relax, eat a meal they could digest, and discuss the mission.

The morning edition of *Stars and Stripes* was an important part of the brunch ritual. The front-page coverage of the air war was usually current and of primary interest to everyone. Stateside news was several days out of date, but it was more current than the mail so it didn't matter. Once you adjusted to the delay, you felt in sync with the world back home. Sports news was terribly outdated for some reason and ran a poor third with the jocks at brunch. The center page of the paper was a must—comics, the crossword puzzle, and a sexy picture of a lovely American girl looking seductively come hither. Talked out and full, the pilots usually left the club and retired to their hooches, *Stars and Stripes* in hand, for a well-deserved morning nap. Compared to the night before a rough mission, sleep came easy, believe me.

Instead of a nap, I went to base headquarters to follow-up on my security clearance and complete in-processing. The headquarters building had been built by the Japanese and was the only large building on base. It contained staff offices, a small base exchange (BX), the post office, the flight surgeon's clinic, and a staff judge advocate's office. I didn't want any legal advice, but I did need a security clearance so I could get on with the war.

The intelligence clerk was understandably confused. I had arrived without a clearance and he didn't have the foggiest idea what to do. I explained to him that I had already applied for an interim clearance but he continued to draw a blank. When he mentioned a six-month delay, my fuse got shorter, and the problem escalated quickly. The base commander turned out to be a practical man. He was a lieutenant colonel who had suffered the "who's in charge" lecture more than once and appreciated the commander's views on innovative rather than bureaucratic thinking.

Armed with assurances for action on a security clearance, I braced myself for an encounter with the finance office. Bean counters were known the world over for their deliberate adherence to procedure and Takhli was no exception. Mission be damned, finance marched to a different drummer. All I needed was a new allotment form, but I was obliged to wait while a fastidious clerk reviewed my entire record. I had no choice, it was a matter of patience or no money.

On my way out of the building, I stopped at the post office. The clerk assigned a mailbox to me with one of those combinations that never work the first try. The box was empty but the nuisance was worth a chuckle.

The small exchange was located next door. It was stocked with the essentials but I was looking for something special. I needed a Seiko watch and a campaign hat like the one Vas and the others had. With a polite smile, the young lady at the cash register gave me directions to the Thai exchange. It wasn't far and she was certain that they had what I was looking for.

As I crossed the base, I discovered that Takhli was larger and more diverse that I had imagined. It was the basic training center for the Royal Thai Air Force and home for one of their F-86 Fighter Wings. Although separate from our operations, the Thai Air Force provided all of the support functions normally associated with running an air base.

The Thai BX was not what I expected. It was an open market consisting of small shops specializing in certain products. There were brass candlesticks, fine and not so fine jewelry, ceramic elephants, knives, clothing, watches, bikes, and hats. It was a street bazaar in a jungle setting.

I was surprised by the din of shrill music and jabber that emanated from small television sets playing in shops throughout the marketplace. Finding television in the up country of Thailand was a pleasant surprise, but it was clear that there was no need to buy a set. Programming was strictly Thai and it was difficult to listen to the unusual songs, which sounded like high-pitched, chanting noise to my unaccustomed western ears.

The Seiko was easy but finding a Thai campaign hat large enough to fit my head was a problem. I finally settled for a size 58, the largest one they had, hoping it would stretch, but it didn't. It was too tight but I figured a snug fit was better than no fit at all and it served my immediate purpose. I was dressed for combat. As I swaggered out of the shop, I had no idea that I had my new hat on backwards.

The bicycle shops stocked one model in a choice of two colors. Thirty bucks bought the best bike in the store, and the Thais knew we would buy more than one bike over the course of a tour. It was open season for bike theft and, without extraordinary precautions, bikes disappeared as fast as we could buy them. The Thais reasoned that a parked bike was a useless bike just begging to be put into action.

As I walked back toward the club, I passed a large drill field where new Thai recruits were undergoing rigorous training. It was hot and their drill sergeants were disciplining them ruthlessly. They used long billy clubs to correct mistakes and their brutality shocked me. I thought about getting shot down and I wondered how their actions might reflect the treatment I could expect in the hands of the North Vietnamese. The thought frightened me.

By the time I returned to my trailer, I was ready for some rest and quiet reflection. Vern was writing letters at his desk. He told me that Vas had caught a hop back to Kadena. I noticed that the extra bunk was gone and I felt relieved. As much as I enjoyed company, I realized how much I also appreciated privacy. While camaraderie was an essential part of flying fighters, there was always an occasional need for peace and quiet.

As I reflected, my thoughts centered on the people I had seen and their attitudes. After just two days at Takhli, it was obvious that everyone in the wing was highly motivated—pilots, ground crews, and support personnel as well. Their attitudes illustrated the vital importance of having a challenging mission. I was particularly impressed with the airmen. Their morale was high, they wanted to work, they took pride in what they were doing, and the results were outstanding. All of them were dedicated. The crew chiefs, mechanics, armorers, electricians, specialists, and their supervisors worked tirelessly. It was clear that the success of the mission hinged largely on their efforts.

It was too soon to draw any conclusions about the Thai people. Their language and culture were certainly unique but my initial impression of them was ambiguous. An entry in my diary noted my dilemma. "Takhli has been a very pleasant surprise. The Thais are like happy children, always smiling and laughing. But I can't figure out whether they are laughing with us—20 Oct 1966."

The next morning marked my birthday. I was thirty-five but the occasion had slipped my mind as I stood half-asleep in the shower. Through the steam, I saw a figure slip quietly into the bathroom. It was Water Buffalo, she had come in to do our laundry. What an embarrassing predicament. I tried asking her to leave but she didn't understand and I ruled out trying to outlast her. Timidly, I drew back the curtain and grabbed a towel for cover. She smiled unashamed and continued with the laundry. "What a way to start a birthday," I thought as I chuckled about my American modesty.

In-Briefings

The orientation briefings took most of the day. They covered policies, organization, ground and flight operations, intelligence estimates, the enemy air order of battle, search and rescue procedures, and a recap of the Rolling Thunder operations.

It had been a tough year for the 355th. In the first nine months of 1966, the wing had lost fifty-six aircraft, bringing the total to seventy-one aircraft downed since deploying to Thailand. The 354th Squadron was the hardest hit, having suffered almost half the losses. The Wild Weasels, who attacked the enemy radar defenses, had lost all of their aircraft to surface-to-air missiles (SAM) and were sitting around anxiously waiting for replacements.

The most serious threat we faced was enemy ground fire—antiaircraft artillery (AAA) and SAMs. MiGs were a threat as well, but they were relatively ineffective compared to ground fire. In addition, the location of the North Vietnamese defenses was very difficult to predict accurately, particularly the activity of SAM sites. All of the targets were heavily defended but the location and concentration of their defensive fire varied considerably. Intelligence was vague and most of the target photos we had were as much as a year out of date. Consequently, we had to rely on our wits and day-to-day target experience to pick our way through the defenses.

The rugged mountainous terrain in North Vietnam looked almost uniform. Approaching from northeastern Laos, the most prominent landmarks were the Black and Red rivers, which joined northwest of Hanoi to flow southeasterly across the Red River delta. In the surrounding agricultural countryside, there weren't many ways to take advantage of surprise or use the terrain for radar masking.

Just to the northeast of the Red River, a short chain of small mountains less than 40 miles long and barely 5,000 feet high was the most prominent terrain feature in the Red River valley. Dubbed "Thud Ridge," these low mountains offered the only hope to mask ourselves from the controlled ground fire concentrated in the defense of the Hanoi region.

The likelihood of being shot down was high so a lot of time was spent reviewing search and rescue (SAR) procedures during the briefings. We were assured that a coordinated effort would be made to recover us from enemy territory but, if captured, we could expect brutal treatment. We reviewed our rights as prisoners of war and received a Geneva Convention card, printed in English, which identified us as members of the U.S. Armed Forces. If taken prisoner, we were expected to abide by the Code of Conduct and resist giving more than our name, rank, and serial number. In any event, we were told not to admit that we were based in Thailand. The fact that we struck targets in North Vietnam daily from bases in Thailand was the worst kept secret of the war, but for political reasons, neither government was ready to own up to it. No wonder I needed a Top Secret clearance.

We joked about telling the North Vietnamese that we were desperate men on a one-way mission from another planet, but we all knew that a cover story would be futile. The whole world knew we were flying out of Thailand. Our strikes were front-page news in most foreign papers and reporters frequented the bars in Bangkok ferreting out stories. To the press, we were "tourists visiting from up country." It was absurd but most reporters reluctantly went along with the story.

Route Packages

For the purpose of managing and designating targets, North Vietnam was divided into six geographical areas called Route Packages. These were numbered in sequence starting from the DMZ north to Route Package Six, which included Hanoi, Haiphong, and most of the industrial targets in the country. Route Package Six was further subdivided into two sectors. The Air Force was given primary responsibility for targets in Package Six-A, the northwestern sector that included the MiG base at Phuc Yen, and the highway and railroad connecting Hanoi with the industrial area around Thai Nguyen, 40 miles to the north. Package Six-B, which bordered on the northeast railroad to China and included the important port at Haiphong, was assigned to the U.S. Navy. Because Package Six contained most, if not all, of the significant targets in North Vietnam, the defenses there were formidable.

Route Packages were conceived by Washington as a set of clearly defined targeting steps that could be taken to demonstrate U.S. determination through a strategy of graduated response. The theory was that the United States could gauge its air strikes in the north to respond gradually to North Vietnamese support of the war in South Vietnam. High-ranking civilian analysts in the White House and Pentagon argued that we could graduate political pressure on North Vietnam by striking targets of increasing importance to Hanoi thereby demonstrating our resolve without risking war with China or the U.S.S.R. It was a naive strategy steeped in an abiding fear of the consequences of decisive action. Glibly, the analysts treated war as an intellectual exercise rather than as a real and deadly confrontation of national wills.

Further, the strategy of graduated response was politically ignorant of a people and a determined leader the analysts didn't understand or appreciate. Rather than bring internal political pressure to bear on Ho Chi Minh, it served to galvanize the North Vietnamese people in support of their government and in their hatred for Washington and the American pilots overhead.

Tactically, the Air Force and Navy were obliged to patronize the concept of compartmentalized targets. Efforts to combine fighters operating out of Thailand with those operating off the carriers in the Gulf of Tonkin in a coordinated attack were rare. We were denied the opportunity to combine our capabilities where we needed them most. Together, we could have formed a mutually supporting force of fighters to outsmart the enemy defenses effectively rather than squander our forces separately.

After the last briefing, a photographer took two pictures of me for my rescue identification folder. I looked terribly grim and rather pathetic, with only meager signs of a budding mustache. The folder also required a set of confidential questions and answers that could be used to validate my identity during recovery. I chose Fast, Blue, and Buick because they described the car I had left behind and would be easy to remember.

Number "8"

It was late afternoon when I reached the 354th Squadron. Sergeant Perry, the NCO (noncommissioned officer) in charge of the personal equipment section, was waiting to begin fitting my equipment. He greeted me cheerfully and escorted me into the building. His professional attitude and repu-

tation for meticulous attention to detail were hard to resist. He was a stickler but he had a way with pilots.

The personal equipment room made me think of a gladiator's locker
room. Everything was neat and very compact. Each pilot's equipment hung
on a rack below a numbered peg holding his helmet—G-suit, survival vest,
shoulder holster, life preserver, parachute, and a "brain bag" stuffed with
checklists. Leaving out #13, there was just enough room for about twenty-
five pilots.

"Sir, you are number eight," Sergeant Perry said as he led me to my
equipment. I was tempted to ask about my predecessor but decided not to.

Each piece of my equipment was new and marked with #8. The helmet
was camouflaged and had a blue visor cover signifying the 354th squadron
color. Everything else was government-issue green. No reflective surfaces
and nothing to indicate the organizational origin of a downed pilot. It was
simple. If I got shot down, I had my nameplate, a Geneva Convention card,
and that was it. The equipment belonged to #8 from someplace but not
Thailand.

We started by fitting the helmet. The trick was to get a snug fit without
creating hot spots that could drive you crazy on long missions. By varying
the thickness and shape of the liner pads, Sergeant Perry was finally able to
fit the inside shell of the helmet to my peculiarly shaped head. The helmet
later needed further adjustment but it fit well enough for the time being.

The oxygen mask was next and, as usual, a challenge. The mask clipped
to the front of the helmet and was held tight against your face with four
adjustable straps. A small microphone was built into the mask and interconnected with a headset in the helmet to provide radio communications.
Consequently, the mask had to fit tight enough to hold under pressure
without inhibiting your speech, blurring your vision, crushing the bridge of
your nose, or causing enough discomfort to distract you from your mission.
It was a tough combination to achieve and one that took several flights to
balance properly.

I fastened the mask over my face and Sergeant Perry plugged me into a
portable oxygen regulator and radio test set. I could hear myself breathing
through the headset and the pure oxygen was cool and refreshing. As the
pressure increased, it became more difficult to exhale, but the mask didn't
leak until Perry hit the highest altitude setting. Suddenly air started
leaking around my nose, and the mask felt like a facial whoopie cushion.
It wasn't a perfect fit but at the altitudes we flew it wasn't likely to be a
problem.

I pulled off the helmet and mask. It was time to try on the heavy stuff,
one layer at a time. As I struggled with the tangle of straps and zippers, I
was reminded that flying fighters was not all high tech and glamour.

Although it became routine, just getting ready was hard work and often stressful as you anxiously prepared for a tough mission.

I fastened the G-suit around my waist and zipped the chaps down around both legs to the ankles. The new G-suit felt stiff and pinched as Sergeant Perry adjusted the laces to work out the wrinkles. He snapped the connecter hose into a suit tester and gave it a shot of pressure. The G-suit inflated quickly and caught me by surprise. The stomach bladder swelled up the size of a football and squeezed me like an angry gorilla. My legs were rigid. I grunted in pain and passed gas loudly. Like a good soldier, Sergeant Perry smiled and went on pretending not to notice.

Donning the survival vest was a new experience. It was bulky and zipped up the front between a row of chest pockets that bulged with items essential for survival: a signal mirror, day and night flares, water, and ammunition for a .38 caliber service revolver. The items in the vest varied, but most pilots opted for extra water and ammunition. I was determined not to become a prisoner of war so I packed several rounds of extra ammunition.

The underarm life preserver harness fit over the survival vest. A madman must have designed it. A pair of inflatable water wings were held in your armpits by a nylon strap, which made a figure eight around your chest and shoulders. The strap was too long, always loose, needing constant adjustment. Fit under a tight parachute harness, the preserver packets felt like huge deodorant pads that forced your elbows out in an awkward position.

The parachute went on over the water wings and survival vest. I was used to a backpack but had never squeezed into one wearing a bulky survival vest and a loaded revolver. After a struggle, I got the chest strap fastened while Sergeant Perry worked on adjusting the seat harness and leg straps. The seat straps had to fit very snug. The slightest bit of slack could play havoc with your essential parts during the opening shock of the parachute. When the straps were adjusted properly for bailout, they were comfortable for sitting but very uncomfortable for standing and made walking cumbersome. All trussed up, even the most agile fighter pilots resembled top-heavy crabs walking very tenderly.

The rest of the fitting session went quickly. Gloves, minor adjustments to the helmet and visor, and an introduction to a gadget called a tree penetrator and descent device (TPDD).

The TPDD was little more than a roll of 1-inch nylon tape that fit neatly in the lower pocket of the G-suit. It had been improvised by pilots who had survived parachute landings in large jungle trees and found themselves caught dangling in the canopy and unable to descend or judge height accurately. A stranded pilot could loop the tape through his parachute harness and rig a pulley to lower himself to the ground gently. The trick was getting the device out of your G-suit pocket and attached properly.

Sergeant Perry took me outside and hooked me up in a simulator he had built to demonstrate the use of the descent device. As I struggled to rig the strap, the parachute harness dug into my groin unmercifully. Almost numb with pain, I finally reached the strap and desperately rigged a pulley. I was exhausted and shocked about my reaction to pain but I had learned a valuable lesson.

We went back inside and Sergeant Perry showed me how to stow my equipment properly. He cautioned me several times about using the parachute D-ring as a handle. Deploying the parachute in the locker room was embarrassing enough but to trigger the wailing scream of the emergency locator beeper by accident gave widespread evidence of a mindless act by a clumsy fighter pilot.

The last thing in my equipment bin was a shop-made ditty bag we called our "brain bag." It carried everything we needed to know to fly combat: checklists, emergency procedures, weapons settings, radio frequencies, tanker refueling tracks, a clipboard, pencils, and even a small, circular slide rule. There was always just enough room in the bag for the ream of charts and target photos we needed for each mission.

The brain bag was a necessary item and hard to forget, even for an F-105 pilot. As a counterbalance to the helmet bag, the brain bag gave us something to carry in both hands on the way out to the aircraft. Without one, an "uneven light" came on in your brain that said you weren't prepared for combat.

After a short breather, I put on my flight gear and headed for an airplane. With all of the equipment, I weighed more than double my normal weight and needed to practice going up the ladder and getting in the cockpit. As I plodded down the ramp looking for an empty airplane, my footsteps were so heavy that I was tempted to look back to see if I was leaving footprints in the tarmac.

I finally spotted an airplane and made a beeline for the cockpit ladder. The crew chief smiled, took my helmet and brain bag, and helped me toward the ladder. Halfway up, I almost fell over backward but caught myself just as the crew chief reached to steady me. Awkwardly, I eased down into place in the cockpit. It had been meticulously prepared. All of the straps and connectors were carefully arranged and ready to receive a pilot.

The crew chief helped me attach my parachute harness to the survival kit in the seat beneath me and cinched the straps up snugly. As I attached the lap belt across my waist, he carefully guided the shoulder harness over my shoulders and down to lock into place in the buckle. Snap! I was all thumbs and sweating profusely, but I had become a part of the airplane. I took the helmet off its perch on the windscreen and donned it carefully. As I fumbled with the chin strap, the crew chief plugged in the oxygen and radio connections and I heard the intercom system crackle in my headset. Just for the heck of it, I fastened my oxygen mask across my face and pulled down the helmet visor. I was breathing heavily.

I felt like 10 pounds in a 5-pound container. The survival vest bulged up under my chin awkwardly and I could barely see my legs or the control stick, which was somewhere between them. I must have looked very uncomfortable and frustrated. The crew chief offered me a drink from the built-in water bottle and tried to reassure me, "Don't sweat it sir, you'll get used to it."

After several minutes in the cockpit, I had had enough and started unstrapping. As I tried to stand up, something was holding me in the ejection seat. I had forgotten to unfasten the straps to the survival kit. The crew chief laughed politely. It was a common mistake and one I would make again and again in my haste to leave the cockpit.

I thanked the crew chief and started back to the squadron. The sun was setting and I was weary. My steps seemed even heavier so I did look back over my shoulder but there weren't any footprints in the tarmac.

After my dry run in the cockpit, I was looking forward to a drink at the stag bar. As I entered, I checked the "Top Secret" bulletin board, hoping I might be scheduled on the morning mission, but my name was still missing.

"Saw you out there practicing this afternoon, Major," rasped the unmistakable voice of Lieutenant Stein. "Cockpit fit will be the least of your problems when you start flying missions," he said sarcastically. "How do you like being assigned to D flight?" Steiny asked, expecting I might be surprised or react bitterly. It was a rude question and a clumsy way to fish for information so I brushed it off pretending not to notice.

As I moved past Stein, I saw Gene Conley, another friend from Nellis, and Don Asire, huddled over drinks at the bar and engrossed in conversation. Gene was the operations officer of the rival 357th Squadron and had been promoted to lieutenant colonel. He tried to have me assigned to the 357th but had been outmaneuvered.

"So you finally made it through training," Gene greeted me with a characteristic needle. "I thought we had you in the top squadron but Asire snatched you out of our clutches." Gene kidded me about dragging my feet at Nellis and about being prepared for combat. "The 354th is the number two squadron here and they're sucking gas, so I hope you're ready," he warned me. "Combat is a far cry from the weapons school." Colonel Asire grinned wryly, needling Gene about my assignment to the 354th Squadron.

It felt good to be among familiar faces. We dusted off a few training memories but the conversation quickly turned to combat and "things to look for." Gene Conley had already completed two tours in South Vietnam in A-1Es and had volunteered to fly another in the F-105. He sounded cynical but he was very straightforward and conscientiously wanted to share his experience with others to help them avoid making costly, if not deadly, errors. Don and Gene were quite different but they were both experienced, and it was a privilege to be on their team, whichever squadron.

Don Asire kept long hours as a squadron commander. He always looked very serious but he had a quick, sophisticated, and sometimes prophetic sense of humor. "I've got the toughest, most gratifying job at Takhli," Don said. "And Gene Conley is the only guy I know who deserves it more than I do." Gene smiled, lifted his drink, and toasted Don graciously. They were close friends who appreciated their squadron rivalry.

Colonel Asire told me again that he was expecting a lot out of me. I started to question my assignment to D flight but decided to wait, suspecting that combat would discern leadership quickly.

Bad news from the afternoon mission made the rounds at the stag bar. The 388th Wing at Korat had lost an F-105 and the pilot was not recovered. For some reason it hit me kind of hard, much harder than those around me. Maybe it was because I was new? I remembered my birthday and wondered where I would be on the next one.

After a few more drinks, we decided to have dinner. At first, I thought it might be the right occasion to celebrate my birthday but decided against it. On the notable list at Takhli, birthdays ranked somewhere between a weather abort and an aircraft no show. Everyone shared the same future, now and tomorrow morning. Growth was only measured in missions. We talked about counters, MiG kills, flak, battle damage, and R&Rs, but not about birthdays. Only one day really mattered—the day of your 100th mission.

While I was reflecting on my birthday, someone at the table brought up the subject of cobras. One of the pilots smiled and said that jungle snakes were graded by the number of steps a victim was likely to take after being bitten. Cobras were five steppers, the King cobra was a one stepper, and the dreaded Russell's viper was only a half stepper. They all laughed sardonically and I came to learn that they weren't kidding.

After dinner, I went back to the trailer and poured a drink to help sort out my thoughts. I was one day closer to my first mission and anxious to get started, but I couldn't get the guy who went down from Korat off my mind, even though I didn't know him.

The next morning broke early in our trailer. I had decided to tag along with Vern as an observer in the planning and briefing process for the early go. It was a convenient way to learn something and ease into the schedule at the same time. Vern was a teacher at heart so he enjoyed it as well.

The mission planning room was well stocked with maps, markers, photos, and glue. There were several large tables where flights were plotted carefully on run-in maps. Missions were planned in exacting detail each day as new targets were assigned. When the planning was complete, each member of each flight had an identical set of maps, charts, target photos, and flight data for the primary and secondary targets. Pilots left the mission briefing with enough paperwork to smother the enemy but it was all essential and as accurate as possible. The target photos were usually outdated and the intelligence estimate was a "WAG" (wild ass guess) at best, but it was all we had under the circumstances. Over time, we started using prints from our own bomb damage assessment film to evaluate and better identify targets, and the planning improved remarkably.

Mission planning started each day with the receipt of the frag order from Seventh Air Force in Saigon, usually late in the afternoon. A force or mission commander was designated by the wing commander, and sortie requirements were assigned to the squadrons, usually five or six flights of four aircraft per mission. The squadrons in turn assigned flight commanders, element leaders, and wingmen to each flight and provided aircraft, by tail number, to support them.

Next, the force commander met with the flight leaders and key members of the wing staff to discuss routes to the target, tanker assignments, defenses and defense suppression, tactics, weapons loading and fuzing, individual flight assignments at the target, and coordination with other forces. With the groundwork laid, the flight leaders could begin the detailed planning necessary to prepare the charts and flight data required for the morning mission briefing.

The real dog work of plotting run-in maps and calculating flight data began after supper. Usually, it was done by the junior man in each flight—affectionately called "yellow nineteen"—as part of an accepted pecking order that worked very well. No matter who they were, the number four men in the flights gathered in the flight planning room to grind out the details for each of their flight members. It was a process that started fresh each day with every mission because none of the maps or other mission data could be used more than once. Even if a mission was scrubbed or delayed, the planning always started with a "blank piece of paper."

Although the process was a drudgery, there was an obvious incentive to do it right the first time. The confidence and trust placed in those doing the detailed planning was remarkable and always a source of great pride—notwithstanding the drudgery. A careless error could screw up the entire mission or, worse, cost a buddy his life or a long stay as a prisoner of war in the Hanoi Hilton.

Mission Briefing

It was exciting to sit in on the mission briefing even though I wasn't on the schedule. I didn't have a proper clearance but no one knew or really cared. The briefing started with a precise time hack to accurately synchronize our watches. The briefing officer covered the mission in general terms and highlighted any changes that may have occurred during the short night. An intelligence update was included as part of the standard fare, and the briefing concluded with a guess at the weather and questions.

Characteristically, mission briefings were short and to the point. They provided an opportunity for the crews to assemble as a team, see the mission commander, account for last minute changes, share their anxiety, and prepare for the detailed flight briefings at the squadrons.

If Seventh Air Force executed the mission during the briefing, the intelligence officer announced the executing code word used each day to designated the target. "Have words" always brought an anxious hush to the briefing room. "Go primary" meant we were going "downtown" to a target near Hanoi in Route Pack Six. "Go secondary" meant that the weather around Hanoi was probably bad and we were being executed to strike a secondary target in an outlying region of North Vietnam or Laos. The order to go to a secondary target was most often met with a sigh of relief but it was a mixed blessing. It only delayed the inevitable. We knew we would be fragged to hit the primary target again the next morning and the day after, until we finally got there.

After the mission briefing, the pilots went to their squadrons for the individual flight briefings. Transportation was often a problem. Squadron commanders drove jeeps or small Datsun trucks, the four colonels in the wing had staff cars, but the rest of us relied on our feet or a bicycle, if we chose to make the investment. Each squadron also had a crew bus we called the "bread truck" but it was seldom available at 3:00 in the morning. If you didn't catch a ride or have a bike, the walk from the wing operations center to the squadron buildings after the morning briefing was a time for quiet reflection.

We caught a ride to the 354th Squadron with the other pilots on the morning mission and arrived just ahead of Colonel Jack Broughton, the force commander for the mission. He screeched to a dusty stop in his parking spot outside the squadron building and hurried up the walk, adjusting the bill of his blue 354th Squadron cap. The duty officer at the front desk was poised and called our group to attention as Broughton entered.

Colonel Broughton was a large man with a square-set jaw, stern eyebrows, and close-cropped hair, which he brushed straight up from his forehead. He exuded confidence, with just a trace of danger. His presence commanded your respect and you could sense that he expected it. He reminded me of a rugged football captain eager to call the toss and lead his team into action. Broughton told us to relax as he joined his flight in their briefing room.

At that point, I felt like an unnecessary bystander so I decided to visit with Sergeant Perry in the personal equipment room. As I expected, he had everything under control. All of the equipment was laid out and ready for the mission. When the crews starting filtering into the room to suit up I knew it was time to get out of their way. Like matadors preparing to dress, each pilot had his own routine, with two things in common: They all took a nervous pee at the last minute, and their laughter gradually turned to serious reflection as they headed out to the bread truck for a ride to the flight line.

I had mixed emotions. On one hand, I wanted to go with them, but, at the same time, I didn't feel quite ready. I spent the morning chatting with members of the squadron as they came in to drink coffee and wait for news about the morning mission.

Colonel Asire was understandably anxious but we talked some before he left to prepare for the afternoon mission. Almost in passing, he told me that I would be on the morning schedule. "Probably a lower route package just to get your feet wet and get the feel of a heavy F-105," he said nonchalantly as he turned to leave for the operations center.

"Typical understatement by Don Asire," I thought. "But that's it, I'm on the team and finally going to go." I was happy but I felt myself getting apprehensive and a little nervous.

I left the 354th Squadron and went back to wing headquarters for some last minute orientation briefings and the final paperwork on my Top Secret security clearance. By midafternoon, I found time to rest for a while in the trailer.

Water Buffalo had finished her chores and was sitting beside the trailer enjoying her afternoon meal. Shaded from the hot sun, she had spread a tattered cloth on the gravel and was squatted down eating small servings of food from a stack of chipped ceramic canisters held between her legs. She carefully mixed each portion on a large green leaf and whisked the food into her mouth with her fingers with great dexterity. After each serving, she folded the leaf and placed it on top of the serving stack while she patiently chewed her mouthful. When she was through, she folded the cloth and wrapped it neatly around the stack of canisters, which she clipped together and tucked away in her small wooden cart. This simple but resourceful village girl had fashioned a useful mess kit out of a few discarded dishes and a large jungle leaf.

The trailer was cool so I decided to sneak in an afternoon nap. In seconds, I was asleep. I couldn't have resisted sleep for a million dollars.

I was awakened by the thunder and lightning of an afternoon monsoon storm. Rain was coming down in sheets, and by the time I looked out the door there was an inch or two of water standing in the trailer area. Our laundry was hanging dutifully on the line, getting a rinse in fresh rainwater.

It struck me that I was looking at almost everything Vern and I possessed in our tiny, obscure corner of the up-country jungle. We had two of everything. Two flying suits, skivvies, undershirts, heavy flying socks, and two pairs of boots. With the exception of the boots, most of it was hanging out to dry in the rain. As far as Water Buffalo was concerned, whatever we weren't wearing went into the wash or got polished daily. Without a doubt, we were the best-washed pilots to ever fly combat.

Morning "Go," Devil #2

By the time I got to the back door of the club, the stag bar was jammed. Both missions had gotten to Hanoi and returned without a loss so the guys were really into the gin. I checked the schedule just inside the door, and, sure enough, I was on it. I was listed as Devil Two flying Vern Frye's wing on the early mission. Even though I was relieved and proud, I felt a warm shot of adrenalin spread through my body. The best training in the world cannot adequately prepare you for that moment. I was finally committed.

Vern spotted me on his way through the bar and invited me to join him for an early supper. "Tommorow's the big day, Ken," he said enthusiastically. "You'll need your best head in the morning, babes, so let's get some food and a big U.S. Pepsi." It was an offer I couldn't afford to turn down.

After supper Vern and I went to mission planning to look at the fragged target. Buck Buchanan and Bob Keller were already there making up charts and the flight lineup cards. The primary target was a small river ford west of Dong Hoi in Route Package One but the weather forecast was not promising. The secondary mission was a Sky Spot radar-controlled bomb drop on a target in the same area.

Vern highlighted some of the mission details and explained what to expect on a Sky Spot mission. In the event of bad weather in the target area, we would join up with another aircraft, either a B-66 or an F-100, equipped with a radar beacon, and receive directions to a bomb-release point from a ground controller. It would be a piece of cake and go in the record as my first counter. "Think about it, and we'll answer questions in the morning when we get a better look at the weather," Vern said. It was clear that Buck and Bob were banking on bad weather.

Vern and I made small talk on the way back to the trailer. He had just turned thirty missions and I was envious. For him, a combat mission in the lower panhandle of North Vietnam was a breather. For me, it was number ONE!

I went to bed thinking about the odds of being shot down on the first mission. What a humiliating way to start and possibly end a combat tour. I fell asleep praying for God's blessing and asking for the strength and courage to see me through the first one.

4

NUMBER ONE

I STARED AT MY Seiko. It was 0330 in the morning and a red-letter day, Sunday, 23 October 1966. My end of the trailer was pitch dark, but Vern was already up and almost finished in the bathroom. Steam from the hot shower curled around the partially closed door into my bedroom.

I had spent a restless night thinking about the mission and worrying about hearing the alarm clock. I still had a couple of minutes to sleep but I was too anxious to wait in bed any longer. I decided to skip a shower and got dressed quickly. My boots were beside the bed and my flying suit was laid out carefully over the desk chair. Everything I needed was already in the pockets.

I was nervous and felt impatient and uneasy. I gulped down a glass of ice water and flicked out the goose-neck lamp on the desk. "Vern, it's getting late. I'll meet you in the club for breakfast," I shouted as I stepped out of the trailer into the damp night air and headed for the club. The crunch of my steps on the gravel broke the silence of the early morning.

The dining room was nearly empty except for a few busy waitresses, a handful of pilots scheduled for the early mission, and two B-66 crews who had flown all night and were celebrating with champagne, boisterous toasts, and shots of whiskey. I joined Buck Buchanan and Bob Keller at their table. They nodded but continued sipping their coffee silently.

Vern joined us and we began to talk about the mission. Buck and Bob seemed relaxed, but I was tense and had a hard time facing breakfast. My appetite was a victim of the jitters. The fried eggs were runny but too crisp around the edges; my throat was so dry that the toast wouldn't go down without gulps of coffee. I drank several glasses of ice water and chewed the ice nervously, trying to look calm and ready for action.

With Vern's urging, we left the club for the ride to the flight line in the squadron truck. It was a right-hand drive Datsun with 354th stenciled on the side. I sat alone in the truck bed. The wind over the cab buffeted my ears, and the jungle air felt unusually cool. I pulled my flight jacket up over the back of my neck and crouched forward. The scent of teak wood permeated the moist air. Dark silhouettes of huge trees sped by in the distance, and a plume of fine red dust billowed up behind the tailgate as we sped through the morning darkness.

As we swayed along the narrow, clay road to the flight line, I thought about the weather in the target area and wondered what the people there were doing. The thought vanished with the sound of the brakes as we parked and piled out of the truck quietly. My legs felt tense and my knees almost buckled as I jumped to the pavement, hurrying to keep up with the others. One by one, we filed by the guard at the door and went into the flight-planning room to pick up the charts that had been prepared for the mission. The briefing was set to begin in five minutes.

As we entered the briefing room and sat down with the other the pilots, I felt conspicuous. The fact that I was going on my first mission had really hit home. I felt my breath quicken. My throat was tight and my hands felt wet and clammy. As I reached for a cigarette in my sleeve pocket, I noticed a large sweat ring in the armpit of my freshly laundered flying suit. I lit up and took a deep, relaxing draw of smoke as the door to the briefing room was closed behind us.

Time Hack, Gentlemen!

The briefing officer was at the podium and waiting for us to take our seats. He was the only one in the room in a khaki uniform, and he seemed very comfortable and poised. Vern whispered that he was one of the staff duty officers and a regular mission briefer but was not a mission pilot.

He was soft-spoken, very articulate, and chose his words carefully. "Gentleman, in ten seconds it will be thirty minutes after the hour. On my count—five, four, three, two, one, ready, Hack. The time is now zero-four-thirty. Did everyone get it?" he asked as he began the briefing.

Seventh Air Force had already passed code words to execute the mission on the secondary targets. Bad weather was covering most of North Vietnam. As planned, our flight was assigned to a Sky Spot bomb drop over Mu Gia Pass along the Ho Chi Minh Trail, just inside the North Vietnamese border. The other flights were assigned to bomb other targets in the same area or to work with forward air controllers (FAC) against specified targets in northern Laos. For the veterans, the order to go secondary signaled a brief respite from the relentless pressure of going to targets in Route Package Six.

Tension in the briefing room eased, but I still felt very apprehensive. The unknowns of a heavyweight refueling coupled with my unpleasant experiences over the Pacific bothered me almost as much as the prospects of combat. The thought of having to abort my first mission because of a refueling problem nagged me. Over and over again, Vern had stressed the importance of timing on the prestrike tanker. "Get on and get off the boom quickly, there is zero time built-in for training." Oh boy. I could visualize the whole flight thrashing around hostile skies in formation, with a tanker trying to get a new klutz on the refueling boom in order to complete the mission. The pressure was building.

The briefer read a message from Seventh Air Force regarding Sky Spot missions. Bomb damage assessment showed that Sky Spot bombs had been hitting consistently long, and Seventh recommended that flight leaders compensate slightly by anticipating the command for bomb release from the radar controller. The pilots chuckled. "That might help for long bombs, but what kind of bugger factor can we crank in for lateral errors in radar? And who in the hell is making damage assessment down there in the first place, the North Vietnamese?" someone quipped sarcastically.

The purpose of Sky Spot bombing was to surprise and disrupt supply traffic along the Ho Chi Minh Trail under weather conditions that otherwise precluded direct air interdiction. The concept was sound but it was difficult to find out how we were doing. If the intelligence guys knew, they apparently weren't telling the units doing the bombing. Under the circumstances, we had to trust that someone knew what they were doing and hope that we were accomplishing more than just making potholes that could be repaired in a matter of hours.

The intelligence briefer stressed the possibility that some surface-to-air missile (SAM) sites may have been placed in the southern region of North Vietnam near Vinh and Dong Hoi. There had been a steady increase in radar and electronic signals from those areas in recent weeks, and the briefer cautioned us to be alert for a possible new SAM threat. Our bomb release point was within SAM range from Dong Hoi, so we were advised to keep an eye on our Radar Homing and Warning (RHAW) equipment—a warning I intended to heed.

After a few routine questions, we were dismissed and went to the squadron for our flight briefings. The squadron duty officer gave us our assigned aircraft tail numbers as we grabbed fresh cups of coffee and gathered in the flight briefing room to discuss the mission.

Devil Flight Briefing

"Guys, this is Ken's first mission so I'll cover everything in detail," Vern said as we drew our chairs closer to the table. The most important briefing reference charts were under the Plexiglas cover. "I'm Devil Leader. Ken, you're Number Two on my left wing. Buck is Number Three, and Bob, you're Devil Four. Standard formation practice, okay?"

We double-checked our watches, copied the tail numbers and ramp positions of each other's aircraft, filled out all of the takeoff data on the flight lineup cards, and went through the Combat Mission Briefing Guide in detail—too much detail as far as Buck and Bob were concerned, but I needed the schooling.

Talk about drinking from a fire hose; we covered everything in the twenty-page briefing guide in twenty minutes. Vern was breathless when he finished and I had a brain cramp. Start engine time was less than an hour away, and I began to feel panicky about getting everything done on time.

The mission briefing was finally over. As we started to get all the charts in our brain bags organized, Vern took me aside to emphasize some of the peculiarities I could anticipate with a heavyweight airplane.

Fully loaded with fuel and bombs, the F-105 weighed in just over 50,000 pounds (including 16,000 pounds of fuel and some 5,000 pounds of armament). The J75 engine developed 26,500 pounds of thrust at full power with afterburner, water injection, and the pilot leaning full forward gripping on the seat cushion. Depending on the temperature, the aircraft required a ground roll of 6,500 feet to reach a liftoff speed of 190 knots for takeoff at 220 miles per hour (mph). That amounts to accelerating 25 tons to 130 mph in just under a half-mile and plummeting another three-quarters of a mile to liftoff at 220 mph with 1,500 feet of runway to spare on an 8,000-foot runway.

Vern warned me that a heavyweight airplane had some peculiar characteristics that I ought to anticipate. It brakes and turns much slower on the ground, but once it gets rolling, it has a mind of its own. At maximum gross weight, the airplane likes to fly off the runway gradually, with smooth back stick. It climbs slower and it can be a bear to refuel when it starts to Dutch roll on the boom. Oh, oh, just the mention of a Dutch roll got my attention. "Remember," Vern reassured me, "anticipate the roll with a little cross control as you come up into refueling position and stabilize that way!"

"Let's suit up in five minutes," was the last thing I heard as I entered the latrine for one last, nervous pee. All the coffee had finally found its way through my overzealous bladder. Anxiety hits hard and takes no prisoners.

Four of us all but filled the narrow aisles of the personal equipment room. Sergeant Perry and his assistant had everything carefully prepared and were there to help if needed. As we dressed, I noticed that I was slower than the rest, and I was thankful that I had practiced at least once. How could something so easy for the other guys be so difficult for me? Sergeant Perry read my mind and came to my assistance.

Bob Keller was the first one suited up and ready to go. With his own extra recording gear, Bob looked like a cross between a camouflaged warrior from outer space and a war correspondent. He had a movie camera attached to the side of his helmet and a small, portable tape deck, which he plugged into the intercom to record the radio calls. "How about that," I said with surprise. "Movies of the war, live from the cockpit for a souvenir." It seemed like a lot of unnecessary trouble to me, but Bob said it was worth it and I envied his confidence.

After a struggle with my equipment, I was finally ready to go. I was uncomfortable and felt disorganized as hell but I was ready. We double-checked the emergency locator beacons in our parachute backpacks and headed for the door to catch the squadron crew bus. My nerves were under control but I could feel some tightness in my chest that I had never felt before.

The bus had not arrived yet so we waited for a moment on the sloping, wooden porch overlooking the flight line. The boards were weather-beaten and slightly warped and uneven. The sun was just breaking the horizon, and the rows of aircraft tails made a beautiful, sawtooth pattern silhouetted against the pale sky. It was a Takhli morning that I would experience often.

The moisture in the jungle air gave the sky an eerie steel gray luminescence that streaked up from the horizon like wispy brush strokes toward the morning clouds. As the sun burned through the overcast, the retreating clouds drifted toward a low mountain ridge to the east of the base, where they stayed to build and gain strength for the afternoon rains. Gradually, the gray sky turned pale blue with just a touch of rose as the clouds gave way to sunlight.

The aircraft silhouettes were beginning to fade into the light of day as the bus rolled into view. The sound of its brakes caught my attention. It was time to go. I finished a prayer and stepped out smartly toward the truck as it squeaked to a stop.

The crew bus was a large blue van that had been converted to carry pilots back and forth to their airplanes. Inside the sliding door, there were two long benches on opposite sides of the van that would accommodate up to six pilots and all of their flight gear.

The driver was a wiry little guy named Tui. He was a Thai civilian, and he welcomed each of us aboard with a broad grin and just the hint of a bowing gesture. He had a narrow face and bright, cheerful dark eyes. His black, unkempt hair stuck out under the 354th Squadron hat that he wore proudly on the back of his head. The bill of the hat was cocked back and tilted slightly to the side, giving him a jaunty, boyish look, which was probably unintended. A large white dress shirt fit loosely on his slight frame, and his pants were gathered by a long belt at the waist and rolled up at the cuff, revealing his American sneakers. The end of his belt hung down from a loop over his hip pocket. His pants were too large and probably borrowed, but it was obvious that Tui was proud of his job and the work he was doing. Tui and the 354th bread truck were an institution in the squadron and a familiar sight along the flight line.

As we entered the van, we gave Tui our aircraft numbers and parking locations, which he checked against numbers he had scribbled in grease pencil on a plastic board on the instrument panel. The aircraft order on the ramp was very important and Tui took pride in knowing it.

Tui threaded the wide van carefully down the center of the taxiway between the noses of the parked aircraft. As he stopped the first time, Buck moved confidently out through the sliding door and walked toward his aircraft. Vern sensed that I was not comfortable and tried to reassure me. "Pay attention to the order of parking spots as we get off and make sure you pick up the right flight sequence to taxi to the arming area. I'm parked a few spots to your right, so don't come off the chocks until I pass you. Then tuck it in trail about two ship lengths back. Buck and Bob will follow you out," he finished.

The van slowed again in front of Vern's aircraft. "This is my stop, old buddy," he said. "See you on Channel One. Have a good one!"

The last stop was mine. I spotted the airplane in the next revetment. The crew chief was waiting expectantly by the nose gear. Tui stopped the van. As I stepped out, the crew chief greeted me with a salute and offered to help me with my equipment. I returned his salute and shook his hand warmly. He had a firm grip and a confident grin, which I appreciated. When I gave him my parachute and helmet bag, the weight off my shoulders felt good, but the sudden change made my legs feel almost flimsy. I was trying to look calm and hoped that my anxiety wasn't too obvious.

"Your first one, hey Major," the crew chief said as he turned to take my parachute up the ladder. "Don't worry, she's a good bird and she always comes back. So relax and check out the bombs while I get your gear set up in the cockpit. Take your time and have a smoke. I'll meet you at the blast fence behind the aircraft."

We let the crew chiefs perform the aircraft preflight inspection so we could concentrate on checking the armament load. It bent the regulations a little but it gave the crew chiefs the respect and trust they needed. They were vital members of the team that got the aircraft to the target and their high esprit de corps reflected the responsible job they were doing.

I walked under the airplane to inspect the bomb pylons. I had checked practice bombs in training and had watched from a distance as other pilots inspected their weapons, but this was my first encounter with live bombs.

At the left inboard wing station, I found myself nose-to-nose with a 2,000-pounder. It looked lethal, and its olive drab paint and stenciled markings added to its authenticity. It was ready to go except for safety pins in the fuse and the pylon release mechanism. Red streamers hung down from the arming pins and fluttered gently in the breeze. The bomb shackles were secure in the pylons, and the sides of the bomb were snug against the sway-braces. An arming wire was threaded through the fuse. Less than an inch of ordinary piano wire kept the arming vanes from turning until after bomb release. Instinctively, I held my breath as I rechecked the connection carefully.

I ducked under the fuselage to check the bomb on the other side. Everything looked all right so I decided to take the crew chief's advice and have a last minute cigarette. I relaxed and watched as the flight line came alive in the morning light. When the crew chief finished in the cockpit, he joined me at the blast fence. "Everything is set when you are, Sir," he said reassuringly.

The crew chief and I talked about the weather and the mission. Just as we started back toward the airplane, a tug pulling a low trailer loaded with six bombs clattered by slowly. The weapons crews were already setting up for the second mission. Nervously, I glanced at my watch. I had barely fifteen minutes until flight check in and engine start time.

I was frightened and panicky as I hurried up the ladder. I ducked under the canopy rail and stepped down into the cockpit carefully. As I sat down, the crew chief helped me squeeze into the parachute harness and attached the shoulder harness and seat belt. The practice session of getting into the cockpit had been helpful, but I still felt uncomfortable and out of sorts. The crew chief tightened up all the straps, attached the oxygen hose to my mask, and handed me my helmet. I was finally in the cockpit but could I fly the airplane?

I squirmed around trying to arrange everything. My butt wasn't back far enough in the seat for a comfortable fit in the parachute. The harness felt like it was pulling me back, making it difficult to see over the instrument panel. My survival vest was pushed up under my chin by the parachute chest strap and it felt terribly bulky and uncomfortable. The struggle of getting settled was about to get the best of me, when I heard the crew chief come up on the ground intercom system. "Sir, how do you read on ground intercom, over?" crackled in my headset over the din of the flight line.

"You're five-by, Chief, standby one for the prestart checklist." I was slightly behind, but his voice was comforting, and the coordinated routine of going through the checklist would help calm my nerves and put my mind on business.

Before I did anything else, I took time to write my call sign on the inside of the canopy with a grease pencil. I had been warned that I would forget it in the heat of battle so I wrote "Devil #2" legibly in the lower front corner on both sides of the canopy.

"I'm back with you, Chief. How do you read me, over?"

"You are five-by, Sir. Ready to run the checklist when you are!"

"Rog, go ahead," I said and began the system checks required prior to starting the engine.

When the checks were complete, I looked at my watch. I had a minute to spare before flight check in on the radio. I noticed the background radio chatter on the command post common frequency, Channel 1. As I listened and collected my thoughts, the crew chief broke in unexpectedly, "Don't forget Sir, this will be a cartridge start. No sweat, just a reminder, over."

It dawned on me that I had never made a cartridge start. During training, I had always started the engine using the normal pneumatic starter with an external electrical power supply, but I had never used the self-contained pyrotechnic cartridge system. What a time to learn.

I flipped through the checklist to the page describing the cartridge start procedure. It was simple. Depress the CART START button and advance the throttle to idle at 8 percent engine rpm. The system did the rest; all I had to do during the start was monitor the engine instruments.

The start cartridge was a replaceable canister of black powder that fit into a compartment on the bottom of the aircraft fuselage next to the engine starter. The rapid combustion of the powder in the cartridge produced enough hot gas under pressure to power the starter turbine and start the engine using the normal ignition sequence. The rest of the process was automatic and happened very quickly. The cartridges were messy and expensive, but they provided the only way to start several airplanes at the same time without having to move a number of cumbersome ground power units.

My thoughts were interrupted by the radio call I had been waiting for, "Devil flight, check in!"

That's me. "Devil Two!"

"Three, Four," followed in a quick, neat cadence.

As the second hand hit "twelve" on start time, the radio cracked, "Roger, Devil, let's turn'em. Start carts, ready now!" I pushed the start button without hesitation.

The whine of four engines coming alive together permeated the flight line. Black smoke from the start cartridges blanketed the ramp. The smoke from my own starter exhaust blew back over my cockpit, shrouding me in darkness. For a split second, the cockpit was filled with the smell of burning cordite. I was startled by the smoke and thought for a moment that the airplane had exploded. The high pitched scream of the engine inlets pierced through my helmet into my ears and resonated down to the pit of my stomach.

The hot exhaust of the engines began to clear the air, and I noticed through all the noise and smoke that the crew chief was signaling me with a thumbs up that everything looked normal.

In the cockpit, the engine instruments were winding up quickly, and the lights on the master warning panel were blinking like a pinball machine. In less than a minute, the engine was started, and all of the instruments and warning lights were stabilized and reading normal. I completed the pretaxi checklist and waited for the radio call to taxi.

What an experience. My pulse was racing and I was poised for action. The noise of the engines, the smell of cordite mixed with warm gusts of jet exhaust fumes, and the familiar smell of burning jet fuel was intoxicating. My fear had turned to anticipation. I was more confident and ready for the mission.

"Devil, let's taxi," Vern called with authority.

The aircraft checks were complete. The crew chief had buttoned up the underside of the airplane and was ready to disconnect from the intercom. "Major, give'em hell and bring her back in one piece," he said as he cleared off the radio.

I pushed the brake pedals to hold position and gave the crew chief the signal to remove the chocks. As he reappeared in front of the aircraft, I saw Vern's aircraft approaching from the right. When he passed, I applied enough power to move forward slightly and check the brakes. When I tapped the brake pedals, I felt the full momentum of 50,000 pounds as the airplane lunged to a stop putting an enormous load on the landing gear. "Take it easy, buddy," I told myself. "Don't bust the bird getting out of the parking spot."

The crew chief smiled and gave me an encouraging thumbs up. As the aircraft turned, he saluted and motioned me on my way. I was shocked at how close the wing tips came to the aircraft parked on either side of the taxiway. I inched along slowly, concentrating on keeping the nose wheel on the centerline. There was barely enough clearance, with only inches to spare.

Because of the enormous momentum of the aircraft, I had to tap the brakes constantly. Straining forward in the seat, I held the throttle firmly against the idle stop, instinctively trying to hold the aircraft back. Just as Vern had warned, the airplane seemed to have a mind of its own.

In trail, we snaked our way north along the taxiway toward the arming area at the end of the runway. It was the area designated for arming the weapons on board and making a final check of the aircraft prior to takeoff. The armament crews were a special breed. Because of the risks involved, they were highly motivated and worked together as a disciplined team. A single mistake could be devastating. Consequently, the procedures they used were precise and strictly adhered to.

Devil Leader turned and came to a stop in the first parking spot farthest from the runway, with the nose of his aircraft pointed away from the airfield. I parked on his right, and Three and Four followed in turn to complete the echelon. When the wheels were chocked, I put both arms outside the cockpit to signal that it was safe for the armament crew to work on the aircraft. This procedure assured that our hands were clear of the armament switches while the bombs were being armed and the armament system was being checked and readied for use. It was a safeguard intended to avoid a lesson we couldn't afford to learn the hard way.

To my surprise, the chaplain was in the arming area. He made his way patiently from airplane to airplane, pausing briefly to give prayers and exchange gestures with each pilot. It was not possible to hear what he was saying, but his thoughtfulness and presence were reassuring. When he stood below my cockpit looking up, our eyes met easily and we paused for a prayer.

When I looked up, the arming crews were standing in a line in front of us. Each team chief held a set of pins and streamers over his head to signal that the aircraft was armed and ready to go. With his thumbs turned outward, Devil Leader signaled to remove the chocks and we each followed suit. The ground crews saluted and gave us an enthusiastic thumbs up. Vern's aircraft moved forward and turned right in front of the flight toward the runway. I saluted my arming team and followed Vern to a position just off his left wing, as we stopped short of the runway.

We were number one for takeoff. Broad, white hatch marks and the number eighteen were painted on the end of the runway. It was smeared with black tire marks left from repeated landings. The crown in the runway exaggerated its narrow width, but I knew that a flight of four, with wings overlapped, would barely fit across it. I was only seconds away from my first combat takeoff and my knees began to tremble slightly.

The radio cracked, "Devils, let's get the canopies [down and locked], go to Channel Two and check in."

"Takhli Tower, Devil is number one for runway one-eight with four. Devil check in!"

"Devil Two!"

"Three!"

"Four!"

"Roger, Devil. Cleared into position and hold. Winds are light out of the south, altimeter two-nine-nine-zero, the temperature is seven-nine degrees with an EPR [Engine Pressure Ratio] setting of two-four-three, copy?"

"Roger, Tower. Devil copies. Leader has pins, canopy, lanyard."

"Devil Two has pins, canopy, lanyard."

"Devil Three samo."

"Devil Four same, same!"

With the acknowledgment that each one of us had removed the ejection seat safety pin, locked the canopy, and connected the emergency parachute lanyard, the flight lined up on the runway and came to a stop in close fingertip formation.

"Devils, let's run'em up," Vern commanded over the radio, as he circled his hand several times over his helmet.

As I came to a stop on the runway, I turned on the brake antiskid system, clamped down on the brake pedals, pushed the throttle up to full power, and waited for the engine to stabilize. Within seconds, I felt the power of the engine straining for release. I pushed the brakes harder, knowing my legs would tire quickly.

Things were happening fast and my mind was racing. After a quick scan of the engine instruments, I signaled to Vern that I was ready. My knees began to shake so bad that my feet were trembling on the rudder pedals. It was a sure sign of stress, and I wondered if anyone in the flight noticed my rudder flapping in the breeze. Time stood still. Seconds ticked by like minutes. It seemed like we would never roll.

"Devil flight, this is the Tower. You are cleared for takeoff. After airborne, contact Dressy Lady on button three. Have a good one, over."

"Roger, Tower. Devil is rolling. Two, don't forget your water," Vern called, reminding me to turn on the water injection system that was needed to achieve maximum thrust for takeoff.

Vern started the takeoff roll and lit his afterburner. A torch of flame the length of his airplane shot out of the tailpipe and ignited like a giant Bunsen burner. The white-hot cone of flame illuminated the runway, and the noise from its shock wave cracked violently. Turbulence from Vern's afterburner rocked the wings of my aircraft, and his exhaust fumes filled my cockpit. I punched the clock on my instrument panel and began a five-second countdown for aircraft separation. The mission had begun.

Five seconds after Vern rolled, I released my brakes and pushed the throttle outboard to light the afterburner. The burner lit with a solid bang, and the acceleration pressed me back in the seat with authority. The brute force of the afterburner as it lit gave me a thrill that always felt great.

When the burner stabilized, I switched on the water injection, checked the water light, and looked ahead for the 2,000-foot marker where I would make an acceleration check for a takeoff decision. By the book, I needed a minimum of 110 knots at the 2,000-foot checkpoint to continue takeoff, but I was determined to continue. The airspeed checked right on the money, so the decision to press on was easy.

As the airplane approached liftoff speed, the aircraft felt heavy, but the controls were responsive. With gentle back pressure on the stick, the nose came up gradually. The runway raced by and I could feel momentum building quickly. At the 6,000-foot runway marker, the airspeed indicator passed through 190 knots as the airplane continued to accelerate under the powerful thrust of the roaring engine. After a light skip or two on the runway, I was airborne and flying beautifully.

I began cleaning up the aircraft—landing gear and trailing edge flaps up. At 200 feet in the air, I eased off on the back pressure and let the nose down just enough to let the airplane accelerate more quickly. The morning air was smooth as glass, and the aircraft responded like a thoroughbred answering the whip in the stretch.

The flight controls were solid and responsive. A whisper of wind noise across the canopy was the only audible evidence of speed in the cockpit. I could barely hear the roar of the afterburner, but the acceleration was still building as the airplane passed through 350 knots airspeed. I had my eyes glued on the lead aircraft and my jitters were gone. The airplane and I were in tune, and although I was excited, I felt at home in the airplane.

When Devil Four called airborne, Vern started a left turn to the northeast so that we could join up in close formation. In the dawn sky, our afterburners looked like four Roman candles rising in trail toward heaven. It was a beautiful sight and a thrilling way to start the morning.

Number Four joined quickly in a tight fingertip formation. We checked in with Dressy Lady, a nearby ground control radar station assigned to monitor our climb and facilitate our rendezvous with the tanker, some thirty-five minutes away. Once we settled down, Vern told us to loosen up the formation and check out our aircraft systems. For the first time since leaving the parking blocks, I had time to look at my checklist. I went through each procedure step-by-step and double-checked each item. I didn't want to drop my bombs inadvertently over Thailand. My accidental short bomb at Nellis was still haunting me.

Green Anchor Two-Two

As we approached cruise altitude and the eastern edge of the Thai-Laotian border, we entered a layer of high clouds surrounding the weather system that was dominating North Vietnam and its entire coastal region. "Tuck it in close, Devil flight, until we top this," Vern ordered quickly. "The tanker is on radar at twelve o'clock, twenty miles."

"Green Anchor Two-Two, this is Devil flight. How do you read, over?"

"Devil flight, Green Anchor Two-Two here. Read you five-by and have a tallyho at our eight o'clock, low, just above the cloud deck. Four F-105s. Is that affirmative?"

"Roger, Green Anchor. That is affirm, and I have a tallyho. Confirm your altitude and heading, please."

"Green Anchor Two-Two heading zero-four-zero at flight level two-four-zero. Devil flight, check your noses cold. Cleared to join up and move into the contact position, this is Green Anchor Two-Two, over."

Vern reminded the flight to recheck the gun safe and switch the radar to standby. Looking down the business end of an armed Gatling gun made the tanker crews nervous. Energy from the radar antenna was also dangerous at close range and interfered with the operation of the tanker's electronic equipment. "Green Anchor, Devil flight is one mile out, noses cold."

"Roger, Devil Two."

"Devil Three."

"And Four!"

When I saw the tanker, I started to get nervous. My problems on the refueling boom during the ferry flight and Vern's repeated warning about the initial difficulty of heavyweight refueling had me spooked.

Vern and I moved to the right wing of the tanker and Devil Three and Four took the left. As we joined, an F-4 flight checked in with the tanker. The F-4s were scheduled to refuel when we were finished. That's all I needed, pressure from a flight of F-4 veterans kibitzing my first combat refueling with eight sets of critical eyeballs. I was in a first-class mental sweat and tight as a groom's hat band at a shotgun wedding.

Devil Lead had finished refueling and was disconnecting when the radio cracked with the call I had been dreading. "Okay, Devil Two, this is the Boomer. You're cleared into the contact position. If you read me, acknowledge, over."

"Boomer, Devil Two, copy," I answered as I moved down into position behind the refueling boom.

When I pulled the handle to open the refueling slipway door, the airflow over the receptacle made a loud, rushing noise that startled me. Gingerly, I moved up just under the boom nozzle and stabilized. I added a hint of cross-control pressure to the stick and rudder to counteract the tendency of the nose to roll and held my breath. The boom extended smoothly, and the nozzle slid into the receptacle, locking with a sharp clank. Great day! I was taking fuel without a problem. I didn't dare take my eyes off the tanker, even to look at the fuel lights in the cockpit. I just concentrated on holding a steady position. For the moment, I was so concerned about refueling that I forgot all about combat.

I had been on the boom for about thirty seconds when the nose started a slow arcing movement to the right. Oh boy, here it comes! I tried to make a correction, but the roll got progressively worse, so I triggered the refueling disconnect button and backed off to restabilize. The boomer broke the tense silence, "Devil Two, this is the Boomer. I'm reset. Relax and slide in again. We hit a little chop, no problem Sir, over."

Just as I started to move in, we hit more turbulence and I bounced up high enough in the tanker jet wash to feel a strong buzz on my rudder pedals. It gave me a jolt and an enormous shot of adrenaline. After several more ragged hookups, I had almost a full load of fuel, so I moved out to let Three and Four take some fuel. I had another try coming when we topped off just prior to leaving the tanker.

I tried to relax and figure out what the hell I was doing. There *was* some light turbulence but it wasn't really a factor, in spite of the encouraging remarks by the boomer. The stability augmentation system (STAB AUG) in the aircraft was working, so the problem was clearly the pilot. I was not controlling the airplane.

During refueling, a heavy F-105 was close to its stall speed and in a control region where pilot control technique was critical. Aerodynamically, bombs and other external stores added to the drag of the airplane, causing it to mush through the air in a nose-high attitude and respond sluggishly. I decided that I was being too gentle with the airplane. The F-105 was an honest aircraft, but like any thoroughbred, it required control and discipline.

When my turn came to top off the fuel tanks, I tried an exaggerated cross-control correction initially and gradually reduced the stick and rudder pressure to steady the airplane as I stabilized on the boom. It worked long enough to fill up the tanks, but I knew it would take a few more missions and more refueling experience to overcome the problem completely.

I was relieved but still skeptical. The knack of heavyweight refueling turned out to be much like riding a bicycle with someone on the handle bars. It seemed difficult at first but once you had it, you had it.

We arrived at our tanker drop-off point right on time. Number Four was completing his last refueling when the tanker commander called to release us. "Devil, this is Green Anchor Two-Two. We have you at the drop point, cleared to Cricket control on two-four-two-five. We'll be on station for the next thirty minutes if you need us. Have a good mission. Devil, confirm your strike frequency, over." Cricket coordinated most of the missions in the lower route packages and provided vectors to the Sky Spot drop zone.

The boomer held up a card in his window with our strike frequency written on it. Vern acknowledged it with a thumbs up so the tanker could listen in.

"Roger, Two-Two. Thanks for the gas, we'll see you later. Devil, let's go button eight for Cricket and check in."

"Cricket, this is Devil flight. How do you read, over?"

"Devil Two."

"Devil Three."

"Four is on."

We began a descending turn away from the tanker. Our course to the target would take us across the Mekong River into Laos and toward the southern, mountainous region of North Vietnam. I looked at the tanker as it slipped away over my left shoulder. The thought that I might not return to see it again crossed my mind and brought a lump to my throat. As the red, white, and blue star on the tanker disappeared, I felt like I was letting go of America. For a moment, I wished that I was in the tanker and able to eavesdrop on the action rather than face it first hand.

"Devil flight, this is Cricket. Take up a heading of zero-eight-zero. Your Sky Spot aircraft will be at your twelve o'clock position, level at two-one-zero. A two-place F-100F, call sign is Miscue One-One, over."

"Roger, Cricket. Devil copies. Devil, let's green'em up!" We were approaching enemy territory and cleared to arm the aircraft. I went through the checklist:—armament panel set and armed—trigger pin out—gun sight on and set—radar warning RHAW gear on—loose equipment stowed—100 percent oxygen—cabin pressurization to RAM air—helmet visor down—and get ready to pay attention.

"Devil Leader's green."

"Two, Rog."

"Three, Rog."

"Four green." Devil flight was set.

After a few minutes, my visor started driving me crazy. I felt like I was trapped and looking out of a tunnel. Worse, the visor lens was pressing against my oxygen mask and causing an annoying hot spot on the bridge of my nose. I decided to take my chances on being hit in the cockpit and pushed the visor up. I would learn to fly with a closed visor but, for the moment, the relief was very settling.

Vern spread the flight out into tactical formation and told us to "uncage our eyeballs." Translated, he meant look around, your life depends on it! "Cricket, this is Devil. I have a tallyho on an aircraft, twelve o'clock about five miles. Moving northeast, over."

"Roger, Devil, affirmative. That is Miscue One-One, cleared to contact Sky Spot on strike frequency, Cricket out."

We checked in on the radio frequency with the F-100 and joined up in close formation on his wing, two F-105s on each side. He was flying toward the bomb release point at 21,000 feet and about 2,000 feet above a solid layer of clouds that covered the entire area.

Our proximity to the clouds put us in a vulnerable position to SAM attack, but everything was quiet except for an occasional strobe on the RHAW gear and some interesting radio chatter. The strobe lines pointed in the direction of Dong Hoi, but it was difficult to tell if the warning signal was from a AAA gun radar or a missile site. We were out of range of any AAA guns we knew about, but a SAM would have posed a threat. My eyes and heart started to work overtime.

"Miscue One-One, this is Sky Spot. Your target is a bridge crossing on the Ho Chi Minh Trail. I have you one minute from bomb release. Bombers, recheck your switches!"

"Roger, Devil recheck."

I realized I had not double-checked the switch settings on the armament control panel. I couldn't risk an aborted drop due to an improper switch setting, but time was getting short and I had just gotten comfortable flying close formation on the F-100. I forced my eyes off the lead aircraft long enough to make a quick scan of the cockpit. A reflection of sunlight on the instrument panel made it difficult to see all of the lights without a closer look. The bomb release countdown was about to start so I moved out of formation slightly in order to look inside my cockpit.

"Better tuck it in, Two," Vern noticed. "We're getting close to the drop." His reminder was embarrassing, but I was satisfied that I was ready to drop.

I was concentrating so hard on flying formation that I was oblivious to the fact that we were over enemy territory and I was about to drop bombs on a target in North Vietnam for the first time. I was intent on releasing the bombs right on the mark and curious to see how the airplane would react to losing 2 tons of weight instantaneously. The thought of hurting someone on the ground didn't cross my mind but the mischief in me hoped that we would surprise the hell out of someone.

"Miscue One-One, this is Spot. Come starboard five degrees and stand-by for the ten-second count, over."

"Roger, Spot. Miscue is steady zero-three-five degrees ready for the count. Bombers, listen up!"

The ground controller started the final count at five seconds to go. A fraction of a second before the command "One, zero, mark." Vern pickled his bombs in order to provide the Kentucky windage that Seventh Air Force had suggested. What a sight. Our formation jumped up 20 feet as eight 2,000-pounders disappeared in deadly formation into the cloud deck below us.

As soon as the formation stabilized, we made a hard turn to the left to avoid getting any closer to the SAM threat at Dong Hoi. Strobes on the RHAW scope indicated that we were being watched more closely on enemy radar than we had expected. We were vulnerable and needed some maneuver room. Without visual warning, we were sitting ducks for missiles coming up through the overcast.

Armed Reconnaissance

Sky Spot released us to return to Cricket control. I had already worked up a
sweat and we hadn't done anything spectacular or dangerous. When Vern
asked Cricket for permission to enter Route Pack One to look for targets of
opportunity, I sensed that things might get more interesting. My subsiding
mission jitters began to quicken again.

We circled back through the eastern border of Laos northwest of the
DMZ in an area code named Doghouse, the only free-fire zone we had in
Laos. Vern started a steep, descending turn toward a range of karst mountains separating Laos and North Vietnam. "Tuck it in tight, Devils," Vern
said crisply. "Looking for a break in the clouds to get through the mountains for some recce, we might find some trucks today." I was on top of the
turn looking down through the formation at the terrain below. The rugged
karst ridges were shrouded by fog and low-hanging clouds forming an ominous barrier to what lay beyond in the valleys of North Vietnam.

After several tight turns, we had descended to less than 1,000 feet above
the karst. We had to maneuver with high Gs in order to thread our way
down through the ragged, dangerous cloud cover. Maintaining formation
was hard work, and my flight suit was drenched. Condensation steamers
curled off our wing tips as we turned through the moist air. The spiraling
streamers marked our flight path as we carved our way down toward the
valley floor.

At less than 500 feet above the ridge line, Vern reversed his turn quickly
and headed for a small valley that ran east and west. We were doing better
than 500 knots, really smoking. I watched Devil Three and Four maneuver
back and forth to hold position and admired the job Buck Buchanan was
doing as the element leader. The number three position in tactical, spread
formation was the toughest job in the flying book, bar none. Buck made it
look easy and I envied his skill. Watching our flight work together as a
team made me realize how much I had to learn. I thought that I had come
to combat well prepared until I saw the pros in action, doing an extraordinary job as a matter of routine.

Vern leveled off a couple of hundred feet above the high, jungle tree
cover and headed northwest. He was looking for an opening into the valley
to the east. I was on his left wing and scanning our right front quadrant for
a break in the clouds or a moving ground target. Through a clearing in the
trees, I saw an opening to a narrow mountain valley. Vern spotted it and
started a tight, diving turn to the right. "Devils, we have a road complex at
two o'clock."

My first glimpse of North Vietnam was breathtaking. The jungle mountains looked mysteriously beautiful but menacing. Beneath the tree cover,

bomb-scarred ridges were a patchwork of devastation. A network of narrow, dirt roads wound aimlessly through enormous pockets of concentrated bomb craters, some still half full of morning rainwater. The barren roads had been carved in the red jungle soil during months of use by vehicles carrying supplies to the south.

Absolutely nothing was moving. The area looked as desolate as the moon. Every road was cut with at least a dozen bomb craters. But, despite the damage, traffic had only been delayed or rerouted. Fresh vehicle tracks went around or down through the craters. The Ho Chi Minh Trail was severely damaged, but it was clearly in use under the cover of darkness or bad weather. The North Vietnamese were noted for their patience and an abundance of manpower, which they used to repair even the largest bomb craters in a matter of hours.

We made two runs down the valley at treetop level looking for a target. We were low enough to draw ground fire but nothing was moving. When Four called bingo fuel, Lead turned west and started a climb. "Devils, let's get out of here," Vern said resolutely.

The mission was almost over and the results seemed almost anticlimatic. In forty minutes I would be back at Takhli with my first counter, number one over North Vietnam. "A piece of cake," I thought as I de-armed the gun and moved the cockpit temperature control lever to the max cold position. The pressure popped my ears but the cool air pouring into the cockpit felt refreshing.

"Cricket, this is Devil. We are outbound from Doghouse with bingo-plus fuel, RTB [return to base] Channel Forty-Three [Takhli], over."

"Roger, Devil. Cricket here, do you have words?"

"Cricket, Devil was successful with Miscue One-One. No BDA [bomb damage assessment], negative on the recce east of Doghouse. Be advised the weather was beginning to break. There were numerous vehicle tracks and rolling targets may be in there later, over."

"Roger, Cricket copies Devil. Green Anchor Two-Two is still on station. Do you require post-strike refueling, over?"

"Negative Cricket. We are bingo-plus and ready for RTB."

"Roger, understand Devil. Cleared on course to Channel Forty-Three. Contact Brigham control one hundred miles out, Cricket out."

"Roger. Devil go button eight and check in!"

Brigham was a radar site northeast of Takhli that normally provided radar control for our recoveries.

The trip home was routine and gave me a chance to relax and enjoy a sense of relief and accomplishment. Brigham picked us up on radar 150 miles from Takhli and gave us vectors and instructions for the recovery. Their control was similar to routine traffic control back home, and it surprised me. I was expecting something different in a combat theater, something more makeshift, perhaps.

Brigham reported that a line of thundershowers was approaching Takhli and that the weather was deteriorating rapidly. The weather at Korat, our alternate, was still good. Vern elected to press on toward Takhli and delay a decision to divert until we passed abeam of Korat, roughly 100 nautical miles east of Takhli.

"Devil flight, this is Brigham. The supervisor of flying [SOF] at Channel Forty-Three advises that the main squall line has passed the base and the weather is improving. They are measuring a five hundred-foot broken overcast, two miles visibility with light rain, with winds out of the south at ten knots, gusts fifteen to twenty. Water is standing on the runway, braking action fair. Do you wish to recover at forty-three or divert to Channel One-Twenty-Five, over?"

There was a measured pause before Vern calmly reported his decision. "Roger, Brigham. Devil will recover at forty-three, break, break. Devil Three take Number Four and set up for a tactical approach ten miles in trail, over."

"Roger Devil, understand tactical recovery at forty-three. Brigham will monitor your descent. Contact Takhli RAPCON [radar approach control] approaching Point Alpha, over."

"Roger, Brigham. Devil copies. Devil Three take your spacing now, over."

"Rog, Three!"

I was amazed how matter of fact everyone seemed about the weather. In my experience, it loomed as a dicey recovery situation at best. After some thought, I realized that even the worst weather on recovery at Takhli was ho-hum compared to a mission up north. I was nervous as hell but willing to put my trust in the leader and count on the collective skills of a team that was more seasoned and certainly more accustomed to these conditions than I was. My job was very straightforward—hang on tight, fly the wing position, and try to learn from the experience.

"Devil Two, this is Lead. Check my hand signals and fly the wing position right down to touchdown. Get your drag chute as soon as we touch and call it so I can pull mine, got it?" he said as he looked back through his canopy at me. There was a lot of radio chatter so I gave him a thumbs up to signify that I understood his instructions.

The recovery was smooth until we hit a solid cloud deck at about 10,000 feet. There was moderate turbulence in the clouds due to wind shear but nothing that a good stick and rudder man couldn't handle under the circumstances.

At Point Alpha, some 40 miles from the base, we contacted Rapcon and they cleared us to proceed to Point Bravo, a position 2,700 feet above the ground and 15 miles north of the runway. At Bravo, we were directed to turn south to a heading of 185 degrees for the final approach to the runway. We were still in solid clouds but the air was quite a bit smoother. I was fighting a classic case of vertigo but my confidence was building. "Just fly on Lead, and forget how it feels," I kept telling myself.

At the 9-mile gate, we had descended to 2,000 feet and lowered the landing gear and wing flaps. I glanced down in the cockpit to check the landing gear indicators and noticed that the airspeed was steady at 250 knots. I had three green gear lights and was set for landing.

We began a gradual descent to start our final approach. As we descended, the smell of smoke from wood fires on the ground became faintly distinguishable in the cockpit. I sensed that we were within seconds of breaking out of the cloud deck and getting very close to the ground. I was tempted to look into the cockpit to check the altimeter but discipline kept my eyes fixed on the lead aircraft. Glimpses of the ground appeared through ragged breaks in the clouds and the jungle trees looked enormous under us. Vern's landing gear looked like it was almost touching them.

Vern signaled that he was reducing his power slightly. We broke out of the overcast at about 200 feet above the ground with good forward visibility, a quarter of a mile from touchdown and right on a shallow glide slope. The surface winds were holding steady out of the south. Condensation streamers spiraled off of our wing tips tracing our glide path against the horizon and accentuating the nose-high attitude that was so characteristic of the F-105 at low speed.

As we approached the runway threshold, I took a deep breath and concentrated on holding a steady position on the lead aircraft. Just feet above the overrun, I felt the ground effect start to cushion our rate of descent. I touched down with a solid screech a few feet short of the runway numbers. Vern landed a split second later. Puffs of white smoke rolled off his tires as his landing gear struts chattered under the shock of impact. We were rolling side by side in close formation on a narrow runway.

Almost simultaneously, I pulled the throttle to idle, lowered the nose gear to the runway, and pulled the drag chute handle. The chute deployed abruptly and opened with a sharp tug as the airplane started decelerating quickly. "Two has a good chute," I called as I saw Vern's chute start to deploy out of the tail of his aircraft barely a ship-length ahead of me. Our wheels sprayed up sheets of water as they splashed through pools standing on the runway. Our tires were hydroplaning, but because of the drag chutes, we were able to maintain directional control and stop safely.

As we rolled out toward the end of the runway, I cleared Vern for a right turn off the runway in front of me. "Roger, Two. Go to tower frequency and follow me into the de-arming area," he replied. "Tower, Devil Lead, clear of the runway."

After the ground crews de-armed the aircraft, we started north, up the long parallel taxiway to the parking ramp. I was relaxed and feeling a bit more like a veteran. I stowed the loose equipment in the cockpit and raised the canopy. The fresh air felt good on my face. As I looked out over the airfield, I saw Devil Three and Four touching down at the far end of the rain swept runway. Fortunately, they both had good drag chutes.

When I looked back up the taxiway, I saw Vern turning into the parking ramp, and it dawned on me that I didn't know where to park my airplane. My mind was blank. I had managed to remember my call sign during the course of the mission only to return safely and forget the parking block number. Crap, what a dumb trick!

I stopped on the taxiway to collect my wits and spotted my crew chief standing in front of the left parking line waving his arms frantically. I acknowledged his signal timidly, trying not to look too obvious. Relieved, he jogged back down the line to mark my parking spot.

My embarrassment turned to caution as I taxied slowly down the cramped space between the blast fence and the tails of the parked aircraft. Halfway down the line, I turned into an open, diagonal parking slot and brought the aircraft to a gentle stop.

The crew chief smiled as he gave me the signal to stopcock the engine. He chocked the wheels and crawled up the ladder to welcome me back. "How's the airplane, Major?" he asked, as the whining engine began to spool down rapidly. I gave him a thumbs up and he helped me unstrap in the cockpit. I took off my helmet and rested it on the windscreen in front of me. After a two and a half hour mission, removing a tight, sweaty helmet felt wonderful. I felt like scratching every hair on my head separately.

As I gathered up my gear, I noticed the number of the parking spot written in bold letters on the flight lineup card clipped to my knee board. If it had been a snake, it would have bitten me. I felt like a jerk, but I was in for even more embarrassment when I tried to get out of the cockpit. As predicted, I had forgotten to release the seat buckles attaching my parachute harness to the survival kit beneath me, and when I tried to stand up, I was jerked back into the cockpit. It was a another reminder that my act needed getting together.

I eased out of the cockpit and carefully worked my way down the ladder.

The Bread Truck

It felt wonderful to stand on the ramp and stretch. Tui was waiting in front of my airplane with the bread truck. After a few encouraging words with the crew chief, I picked up my gear and boarded the crew bus. Vern was sitting inside and smiled broadly. "Welcome to combat, big fellah. What did you think of that, a piece of cake, hey?" he asked with a grin. I shook his hand and went for my cigarettes. The first draw of smoke was absolutely delicious.

Tui ground the transmission into gear and began to thread his way down the crowded flight line toward the other aircraft. The ramp was crawling with maintenance crews preparing the aircraft for the afternoon mission. A steady stream of tugs pulling flat carts loaded with bombs and missiles had invaded the ramp, and crews were loading pylons on almost every aircraft.

We picked up Buck and Bob and headed for debriefing. The maintenance control shack was the first stop. Each of us reviewed the status of our aircraft with a team of technicians: mechanical, avionics, engine, airframe, flight controls, armament, and refueling. Every aircraft system problem was documented in the aircraft forms and discussed in detail.

From maintenance, we went to the intelligence section for a mission debriefing. The intelligence shop reviewed each mission carefully and summarized the results in a Wing OPREP report to Seventh Air Force immediately following each mission. Our mission was easy to debrief. It was accomplished as planned. Bomb damage was unknown, and the road reconnaissance was "negative" with no unusual enemy activity and no losses.

By the time we finished in intelligence, I had smoked five cigarettes and lit another in the truck on the way to the squadron. I could almost taste the cold beer which was a traditional part of the more informal flight discussions.

Our mission was "normal-normal" but Vern was a stickler for detail, so we knew we were in for some candid remarks in the privacy of the D flight briefing room. My difficulty during refueling drew the most attention. It was no surprise, but I was ashamed and hoped to be spared the bloody details. As we talked, Buck and Bob grew visibly restless, so Vern dismissed them, knowing the two of us could discuss the problem later in our trailer. It was humiliating but I realized that it was important.

When I returned to the trailer, I was surprised to find a note on my desk from Gene Beresik, another old friend from Nellis. Gene had ferried a replacement F-105F to Takhli from Kadena Air Base on Okinawa and was waiting for me in the stag bar. What a stroke of luck. He could help me celebrate my first mission with the gusto that Gene always brought to a party.

At Nellis, Gene had two indulgences: gin and high-stakes dice games. He was a marvelous, outgoing guy with a contagious sense of humor. I hadn't seen him in several months, but I was sure I would find him with a martini in one hand and a dice cup in the other shouting, "Shoot the bundle."

I changed into a fresh flying suit and hurried to the club expectantly. Sure enough, I found Gene with Don Asire and Gene Conley tipping gin and throwing dice at the stag bar. "By God, if it ain't Ken Bell, you old son-of-a-bitch, how in the hell are you?" he shouted as we greeted each other with a warm handshake.

"Look what the cat drug in from Kadena for your first mission party, old Twinkle Toes," Gene Conley said sarcastically, referring to a nickname we pinned on Gene at Nellis because of the way he walked on the balls of his feet after a few martinis.

We started to roll for a round of drinks. "Can't lose in a big game like this," Beresik said as he picked up the cup. "Boys, what's your pleasure?"

Don Asire stopped Gene and reminded me that I was obliged to buy a round to commemorate my first mission. I rang the bar bell proudly, and Don proposed a toast to the newest veteran in the 355th Wing. "Here's to the F——— NEW GUY," the bar cheered as they raised their glasses.

One of the more colorful pilots in the wing shouted his own brand of encouragement, "If I had ninety-nine to go, I'd cut my wrists and sit in a tub of warm water!" I joined the laughter. It wasn't exactly champagne across my bow, but the toast and the sound of the bell were the initiation I had been waiting for.

A stag bar was not complete without a brass bell. A bar bell had its origin in the Navy and spread quickly to become a permanent and sacred part of fighter pilot tradition the world over. At Takhli the bell hung conspicuously over the bar and close to the cash register. In addition to serving the spontaneous needs of generous patrons, it was also used to signal the entrance of any patron failing to remove his cap at the door or as a convenient trap for strangers naive enough to ring the bell out of idle curiosity. As fun-loving hosts, we welcomed any excuse to ring our bell. After all, money wasn't terribly important, and the best drink in the house cost all of a quarter.

After a few more drinks, we decided to treat our stomachs to dinner. We reminisced about our days at Nellis and speculated about the future. Gene Beresik was particularly disappointed because he had not drawn a combat assignment, and we discussed ways he might bend the personnel system to arrange an assignment to Takhli. He was chafing to fly combat and his F-105 experience would have been welcomed.

Ironically, our dinner turned out to be the last meal the four of us would share together. When we first met at Nellis, just eight months earlier, we all knew that we were in for a tough mission and stiff odds in combat, but we didn't dare dwell on that. Our future was the next mission and its outcome. Everything else was secondary and hardly worth worrying about. For the moment, fortune had united us for an evening of camaraderie and we made the most of it.

After dinner, we were tempted to continue our party in town, but we decided, instead, to have a couple of "shooters" at the bar and then parted company. As always, Beresik was smiling broadly and ready to roll the dice for another round of anything.

On the way out of the bar, I checked the morning schedule on the "Top Secret" bulletin board. I really didn't expect to find my name, but, as a bona fide member of the team, I felt obliged and proud to be able to check the flying schedule with more than just idle curiosity.

To my surprise, I was scheduled on the early go as Diamond Two. I shuddered to think that I had toyed with the idea of taking my celebration to town for a hot bath and whatever. Vern was the mission leader so I hurried out of the bar to find him. I was curious; why hadn't he let me know about the schedule earlier?

Vern was either at wing operations helping with the flight planning or in the trailer. I made a beeline for the flight line but decided to check by the trailer on the way. It was getting late and I felt out of sorts and a little panicky.

As I walked, I realized that I was scared. Down deep I felt somewhat cheated because I had expected more time to savor the celebration of my first mission. I had only gotten to enjoy the relief and satisfaction for a few precious hours and it was too soon to face danger again. Ridiculous, I scolded myself, how much time is needed?

The thing that really bothered me was the fact that for the first time in my life I recognized that I was staring at genuine fear, fear that had hit me as I read my name on the schedule unexpectedly and had turned my jubilation to anxiety. The idea that I was frightened made me uncomfortable because I wasn't prepared to accept that kind of a flaw in my character.

Vern was in the trailer. He apologized for surprising me with the schedule. He had added my name as a last minute change, and he encouraged me to get to bed early. "We might see some action tomorrow," he said. "There's a chance the weather will break. If it doesn't, the secondary mission is another Sky Spot." He didn't mention my absence at flight planning and I didn't press him.

As I prepared for bed, I sat down and reflected on what had been a red-letter day by any measure. I had finally tasted combat and had stood up to the test.

Through my own selfishness, I came to realize that the wing had an important mission to fulfill, one that transcended the needs or wishes of the individuals involved. Celebration was great and it certainly was part of the package, but success didn't turn on one mission or the feelings of one pilot. It was a team effort with no time outs until the mission was fully accomplished. I was an important member of the team, to be sure, but just one among many.

The physical and mental strain of the day began to weigh on me. The enormity of the challenge I faced as a professional pilot began to take shape and come into focus. Combat was full-time work and it required the talents of grown, disciplined men. The gunnery range and training were behind me. Everything I had ever learned about flying fighter aircraft had come together for one purpose, and my skills were going to be tested under fire again and again. It was sobering to realize that every day real lives were at stake and that the odds were serious and deadly. I thought about the "ninety-nine to go" toast in the bar and wondered if I would make it.

Combat Diary

I poured myself a stiff drink of Scotch and sat down at the desk to summarize the day in my diary.

> *23 October , Sunday—2+35 hours—Mission #1* First mission—a bit apprehensive. Half the battle was getting me and all the gear in the cockpit. Was a Sky-Spot mission just inside NVN near Mu Gia pass. Devil #2. Led by Vern Frye (good lead), 2 x 2,000# bombs. Rough at refueling again.
>
> Was impressed with the beauty of the rugged jungle. Worked up a hell of an unnecessary sweat.
>
> Beresik came to town. I rang the bell for #1, only 99 to go. Actually, I flew my 100th first.

It was getting late but I had one more thing to do. Using a red marker pen, I inked in the first mission stripe on the band of my campaign hat. It was a wing tradition and I decided to use red stripes for the most significant or dangerous missions. Before it was over, there were would be plenty of red ones.

I switched off the light and went to bed. I tried to relax but my mind was racing. There were less than four hours until wake-up for the morning mission. I thought about home and the task before me. I thanked God for my loving parents and asked Him to comfort them. I asked for strength and enough courage to master my fear with confidence. I prayed for the wing, our commander, and the guys who flew so valiantly. And finally, I asked God to bless America.

I was tired and finally relaxed. Everything I had prayed for was important to me, and I had faith that I was in good hands. I drifted into sleep knowing that I had done the best I could and that my strength would be renewed by morning.

5

WARMING UP

MY NEXT FEW MISSIONS were flown in the lower route packs to prepare for the big ones in Package Six. Everyone was anxious to taste Hanoi for the first time but conditioning was absolutely essential. Your reflexes, flying skills, hearing, eyesight, confidence, and mental discipline had to be tuned and ready.

Even though I was very well trained, it was necessary to go through a progression of missions that would prepare me for the high-threat environment. The wing commander insisted that each pilot go through this seasoning process, and his objective was clear. He wanted pilots to be effective, and he wanted them to have the skills and confidence necessary to survive. Putting bombs on target was important, but bringing the airplane home to return again was paramount.

Only combat can thoroughly prepare even the best-trained pilots for the hostile environment of armed conflict. Nothing is hypothetical and combat has two ingredients that are impossible to simulate in training: a real threat and fatal consequences. This combination was both intimidating and unforgiving. Even the most stubborn pilots soon recognized the consequence of failure and were easy to motivate as team players. One mission over enemy territory was usually enough to convince anyone that the game was real and the results were deadly.

To be effective and survive in combat, a pilot had to fully appreciate the importance of teamwork. The need to rely on the mutual support of all flight members was the most essential element of success. Interestingly, teamwork was often the most difficult principal to instill in training and usually the first lesson learned in combat. There is nothing more vulnerable, useless, or lonesome than a single aircraft over enemy territory.

The difference between a well-trained pilot and an effective combat leader was the ability to think instinctively as a team member under immense pressure. Missions in the lower route packs gave us an opportunity to learn to think and to fine tune our pilot skills so that we could work effectively as a team up north. Ironically, the threat in the lower route packs turned out to be almost as menacing in terms of losses, but it was not so obvious in terms of visible flak and SAMs.

In the seasoning process, each pilot learned to adjust to the environment differently. Flying and procedural skills usually came quickly, but the ability to think clearly under pressure was a more difficult skill to develop. The ability to fly wing and deliver weapons was essential, but the ability to think and anticipate was an absolute prerequisite for leading others.

During my first two weeks in combat, I flew progressively more demanding missions in terms of target location, defensive threat, and flight responsibility. I started out flying as Number Four in the flight in the lower route packs and finished as an element leader on a strike against an important bridge near the Chinese border. In that same period, five F-105s were lost and only two pilots were recovered. Statistically, it was a normal two-week period but, personally, it was a time of enormous growth and introspection. For the first time in years, I was doing what I felt I was best suited for and enjoying it immensely. Even though I was anxious about each mission, I could see my skills improving and feel my confidence growing daily.

I enjoyed being part of a squadron again. The sense of teamwork and camaraderie was especially gratifying, and I was determined to make the most of it. It was rewarding to take part in a vital mission, and I savored each moment. Paradoxically, I respected the threat, but I enjoyed the sense of danger, however horrible its cause or consequences. I wanted to make a significant contribution to the outcome of each mission and make my mark on the history of the war.

Missions two and three were replays of number one, Sky Spot drops near Mu Gia Pass. I hadn't seen the face of the enemy yet, but my refueling technique was improving steadily and that was very encouraging.

Several days of bad weather curtailed all operations, so I took the opportunity to relax and catch up on some loose ends. I needed an alarm clock and found an old-fashioned model on sale at the Thai exchange for ten Baht, less than a half-dollar. It had a big round dial that glowed in the dark and two alarm bells that rang like crazy for five seconds. It looked goofy, but it was loud and just what I needed when Vern wasn't around to rouse me.

On the way back to my trailer, I passed the Thai training area where the new recruits were eating their noon meal. The scene was right out of the movie *Bridge on the River Kwai*. Two lines of frightened recruits filed past large pots of steaming rice and gruel. They were served in wooden bowls and moved in a quick shuffle down long rows of wooden benches to sit and huddle over their food. They ate ravenously and only looked up long enough to make sure they had not fallen prey to one of the barking drill instructors. It was a grim scene and a reminder of the treatment I might receive in the hands of a brutal enemy.

I found my first letter from home in my mailbox. My 1963 Buick Riviera had sold for a handsome price and the money was in savings. My heart sagged. I had lost a one of a kind, and all I had left were the memories and the rescue passwords that I hoped I would never need.

Marlin Four Is Down!

After two days of monsoon rain, the weather finally broke enough for us to get into Route Pack One for another Sky Spot drop in the southernmost target package in North Vietnam.

Our flight had just completed the recce phase of the mission when the chilling sound of an emergency beeper began to wail on the radio, accompanied by an urgent call, "Marlin Four is down!" It was my first encounter with a shoot-down and I sensed something futile and ominous. We diverted to a post-strike tanker and returned to provide top cover for the rescue operation, referred to as Rescap.

Marlin Four had taken a direct hit from ground fire during a strafing pass in a deep mountain valley. When we arrived, Marlin Lead was trying desperately to direct the rescue force, a Jolly Green H-53 helicopter and two A-1E Sandys, to an area where he thought he had seen a parachute canopy hanging in the trees. The situation sounded hopeless, but the activated beeper was evidence that a chute had at least opened. After two hours of exhaustive searching, we were not able to establish contact with Marlin Four and the rescue effort was terminated. It had been my first taste of tragedy and I was disheartened and felt empty.

Marlin Four was Major Dale Johnson, our wing standardization and evaluation officer. I had just met Dale the day before and enjoyed a long talk with him about his job. He was frustrated because he was having a hard time convincing pilots that the threat in the lower route packs was serious. Tragically, Dale's loss was bitter evidence of the validity of his concern.

On the flight home, I had an uneasy feeling that I would be asked to take Dale's place on the wing staff. It made sense in view of my qualifications as a weapons school graduate, but I didn't like the idea of leaving the squadron. "Damn it to hell and back," I thought in disgust. "This will mean the end of my association with the 354th for sure." I sensed that my squadron days were numbered.

That afternoon I was told that I had been assigned my own squadron aircraft, number 723. I was thrilled and looked forward to giving the airplane a nickname but I feared it could be a short-lived privilege.

My next mission was a noncounter in Laos, part of Operation Steel Tiger. To strike targets in Laos, we were required to have a forward air controller (FAC). It was one of the rules of engagement that was strictly enforced. The FACs had unusual call signs and flew some strange-looking airplanes but they were real pros, mostly CIA Air America pilots flying clandestine operations.

Our FAC marked a target in a wooded area he said was a large truck park. Each of us was carrying six 500-pound bombs with instantaneous fuses. The FAC asked us to make a shallow delivery one at a time from the valley side coming slightly uphill toward the target. It was a risky way to bomb but he assured us that it was important.

The flight leader asked for another smoke rocket to mark the target and maneuvered the flight to a high perch for a dive-bomb pass. "Locust flight take five seconds spacing. Locust Lead is in now." I waited and rolled in just as Lead was pulling off the target. When I stabilized, I was in a shallow dive and a little hot on airspeed, a combination dive/skip bomb pass they hadn't taught us at Nellis. The ground was coming up fast. I was a split second away from release, when the bombs from the lead aircraft hit and exploded in the target area. I pickled and pulled up hard to avoid getting hit by debris and bomb fragments. Locust Three and Four followed in close order, putting their bombs right on target.

The FAC was ecstatic as he reported the extent of our bomb damage. "No wonder we were accurate," I thought. "We damn near put four F-105s into the truck park right behind the bombs." It was a good lesson on how to improvise and get away with it. I was excited.

After his pass, Locust Four lost sight of the flight. It took us fifteen minutes to find him and the delay put us low on fuel. We made it home on fumes, and at the debriefing the flight leader was furious. Locust Four was known for getting lost. He disliked flying formation and didn't understand or couldn't grasp the importance of mutual support and flight integrity.

That evening, I had a heart-to-heart with the wayward wingman at the stag bar. He was convinced that "we each have our own style" and that we would eventually adapt to his way of doing things. It was pitiful. He was a loner and couldn't last much longer. I urged him to change before he lost an airplane or took someone down with him. In a few weeks, he finally recognized his shortcomings and decided to ask for an early return. The wing commander agreed, and the guy was on the next C-130 bound for Bangkok.

I ate dinner alone that night and had a moment to gather my thoughts about moving to the wing staff. It was weighing on me and I felt trapped. I was about to fall into a bad case of "feeling sorry for myself" when I noticed three Thai waitresses watching my table. Sitsue, Nip, and Susie were young and uniquely beautiful. They seemed childlike yet innocently sensuous. They were cheerful and resilient, and they epitomized the character of the Thai people with their supple ambiguity. I smiled and vowed to stop taking myself so seriously.

The next morning, our flight was diverted to an obscure river ford in the Doghouse area of Laos. The area looked worse than the Ho Chi Minh Trail. It was barren except for a network of dirt roads that wound in and out of the woods through hundreds of bomb craters, many under water. It was obvious that enemy supply trucks were still able to get through, in spite of our efforts to halt the flow of traffic. The North Vietnamese were tenacious bastards.

When we landed I had a message to report to Colonel Bowman, the deputy for operations. I suspected that he would ask me to take the job of wing stan/eval officer and my intuition was right on. My heart sank even though I knew what was coming.

Colonel Bowman was a straightforward, thoughtful man whom we all respected. He had a reputation for being fair, but he didn't mince words and was used to getting his way. I knew he wouldn't ask me to join the staff unless he needed the help and was sure I was the right guy for the job.

He listened patiently to my reasons for wanting to stay in the squadron. His eyes were sympathetic, but I sensed that the needs of the wing were uppermost on his mind. Graciously, he asked me to think about it for a day, but the tone in his voice said his mind was made up.

I was in knots. I knew the wing came first, but I had worked so hard to get back in the cockpit and into a squadron again that I felt somehow betrayed. I wanted to be part of an organization and grow to a position of leadership. I kept asking myself, "Why couldn't someone else do the job, like Vern or a couple others who were well qualified? Why me?" I knew the minute I left the squadron that I would suck hind tit with the flight schedulers. As a staff wienie, I would eventually get my share of missions, but it would be on a fill-in basis. I didn't want to grovel for good missions or claw my way to Hanoi flying wing. I wanted to lead the way.

I decided to be truthful with Colonel Bowman and told him exactly how I felt. He looked disappointed and sympathetic but he was firm. I would report to the staff as soon as the move could be coordinated with the squadron commander. He agreed with me about squadron duty but added that I had a few things to learn about the operation of a wing staff. He suggested that I might welcome an opportunity to work and grow with the example set by three experienced colonels.

As it turned out, Colonel Bowman was right about my need for growth, but I had the squadron schedulers pegged to a tee. Once I moved to the wing, they couldn't remember how to spell my name. It was a challenge I soon mastered.

By my sixth mission I was progressing nicely and my confidence was building. I flew with Major Phil Gast on an early morning workout with five 1,000-pound bombs against a road intersection in Doghouse. Phil found the target but somehow misread the ground elevation, and our bombs hit 300 feet long in the woods south of the road. To our surprise, several large secondary explosions sent shock waves and flames belching out of the forest. By a stroke of sheer luck, we had caught several ammunition trucks parked in the trees waiting for us to leave the area. The poor bastards never figured we would miss long in their direction. What justice!

We popped over the mountains into Route Pack One and looked for targets to strafe but nothing was moving. At bingo fuel, Phil let me take over and lead the flight back for the recovery at Takhli. It was another step in the checkout process.

After the mission, I discussed my move to the wing staff with Major Gast. Phil was on the promotion list to lieutenant colonel and waiting on the staff for a job as squadron commander. I valued his opinion. He was bright, he knew the ropes, and was on his way up. Not surprisingly, his views mirrored those of Colonel Bowman and he encouraged me to approach the job positively.

The next mission I flew was very significant. For the first time, the weather was clear enough for me to get a good look at the geography of the southern regions of North Vietnam. It put things in perspective and gave me an opportunity to fly and reason at the same time.

I was Number Two in a flight of four sent out to destroy a suspected SAM site near the coastal town of Dong Hoi. From the outset, our flight leader was a bundle of nerves, and his anxiety showed during the mission. He was indecisive, he orbited the target too low and too slow, and, when we finally rolled in, we were strung out and too shallow to deliver bombs accurately.

We pickled and made a gentle pull-up toward the mountains. We were sitting ducks for a SAM attack. "Jesus," I thought, "this guy's days are numbered!" As we turned around for a strafing pass, I got a series of active SAM warnings on the radar detection system. The missile site was still intact but I couldn't see any missiles. We made a pass and pulled up toward the ocean. I looked back expecting to see a SAM come off the pad, but nothing happened. Fortunately, a supporting flight of F-4s had demolished a missile transporter near the site, so the launch crew apparently decided to stay low.

Leaving the target area, I heard Red Crown initiate search and rescue (SAR) for Cobalt Two, an F-105 from the 388th Wing at Korat. It was eerie knowing that someone was down and wondering what had happened. We had just cheated the enemy defenses successfully, but the search for the downed pilot made me realize that you never knew when fate might have it the other way. Just four days later, our flight leader would face his date with destiny in the jungle.

On 3 November, the morning mission was directed to strike the railway yards at Yen Bai on the Red River, just 50 miles northwest of Hanoi. In an attempt to confuse the defenses, our flight was diverted to strike a river bridge closer to Hanoi and hit targets of opportunity on the way out, armed reconnaissance at its best and riskiest. It was my eighth mission.

Diary entry: First Bridge

Finally flew my first one up north this morning. We were a single diversion flight to the Lang Trang bridge covering for twelve aircraft sent to the Yen Bai railroad yards. I was Mambo Four in the last flight in. Crossing the Red, I felt like I was going to piss my pants.

Went halfway between Yen Bay and Phu Tho for the target—200 x 20 concrete bridge. I was shallow, low, and fast with five 1,000-pounders and got it! Good breaks in the concrete bridge, particularly the south end. Got shot at during recce but I missed seeing the flak because I had my head in the cockpit looking for the fuel system circuit breaker. The bomb bay tank wouldn't feed.

Had a three ringer coming out, it was a SAM. Post strike refueling and low level back home. What a dense jungle.

I had flown my first mission into the high-threat area, hit the target using an unorthodox bomb pass, luckily missed getting hit and come home unceremoniously. Perhaps it was beginner's luck, but I was excited and ready to go back.

The next day I flew two missions back-to-back and crossed the ten-mission threshold. With each mission, I was growing more accustomed to the threat and getting closer to a position on the starting team. My goal was to become a qualified flight leader as early as possible in order to establish my flying credibility with the wing commander and each of the squadrons.

On the morning mission, Max Brestel made his debut as a flight leader. Major Gordon Mickelson, the senior flight commander in the 354th Squadron, "mother henned" the flight from the number four position.

Max had good eyes and a cool head, so I relaxed to enjoy my job as his wingman. I knew Mick would give him more help than he needed if he faltered.

After several last minute changes, we wound up in the Doghouse area with a FAC who sounded like he had the entire North Vietnamese army cornered in a suspected truck park just waiting to be annihilated. The FAC marked the target with a smoke rocket, and we put our bombs right on his mark. There was lots of smoke but no secondaries. The FAC had let his enthusiasm sway his judgment. The best we could claim was more splintered trees and a fresh crater or two to complicate life for the North Vietnamese truck drivers. Considering the circumstances, Max did a good job and got his ticket punched as a bona fide flight leader.

On the afternoon mission, I was number three in a flight of three looking for a remote bridge near the nasty little beach city of Vinh in the lower route packs. It was a chance for me to flex my new muscles as an element leader without having to worry about flinging some poor wingman all over the sky. Without a wingman, my six o'clock position would be wide open unless I stayed close to the leader. It was the incentive I needed to hold a good position.

The weather was very hazy and there were distracting radar signals coming from the defenses surrounding Vinh but we finally found Bridge 520, a small wooden structure that turned out to be a flak trap. The road had been cut on both sides of the bridge, and the only gun emplacements shown on the target photo were marked as unoccupied, but as soon as we rolled in for a dive-bomb pass, the little buggers started shooting. Orange goofballs of flak and tracers from automatic weapons crisscrossed beneath my nose as the bomb release pipper approached the target. I pickled and pulled up hard to join the lead element.

Our bombs hit all around the target but didn't get it. As we jinked out toward the mountains, I suspected that we would get another shot at that target. Even though the bridge was small and looked insignificant, it would not be left standing. The fact that the North Vietnamese thought it was useful enough to defend would whet the appetites of our intelligence people. It had all the earmarks of a return engagement.

On the way back to the tanker, we were instructed to take on a full load of fuel and divert to an area southwest of Hanoi to provide Rescap for the main strike force. They had gone after a JCS target that had never been hit before. As soon as we got on the strike radio frequency it was obvious that the guys were having an extraordinary day with flak and SAMs. The radio chatter was enough to make your hair turn gray.

Flapper One was down and holed up in the foothills close to the Black River. A chopper and A-1 Sandys were on the way in, and our flight was directed to maintain top cover until the rescue was complete. "Holy mackerel," I thought. "It's our flight of three against the whole damn North Vietnamese Air Force for at least an hour, maybe two."

We established a weaving pattern above the rescue area and tried to establish radio contact with Flapper One. The radar warning display looked like it was "growing hair" with dozens of warning strobes that were impossible to interpret. The SAM launch warning light flashed on constantly. I was tense and scared, my mouth as dry as cotton. We maneuvered constantly. I had to divide my attention between covering the lead element and watching for SAMs coming out of the threat area. My head was on a 360-degree swivel and I was in a drenching sweat.

The Wild Weasel flight covering the strike force was the last flight out of the target area. On his way out, Machete leader spotted a SAM with his number on it. He sounded hysterical and absolutely helpless on the radio. "PULL, PULL … it's gonna get me, damn it." There was a scream and then silence.

Seconds later, a call came from one of the other flight members. "Machete Lead is hit. SAM head on, no chute, no beeper."

I felt sick enough to cry. The last desperate words of Machete Lead were ringing in my ears.

We recycled to the tanker four times covering the rescue of Flapper One, evidence of the determination and guts of the rescue team in the face of stiff odds. There were no more SAMs launched and no MiGs showed up to hamper the rescue operation. It was the longest mission I had flown, six hours and forty-five minutes. I was so exhausted during the last refueling that I fell asleep on the boom for a second or two.

Friday, 4 November 1966 had been a sobering day. Two missions, two tragic losses, only one pilot recovered, and almost four hours on Rescap in the high-threat area. Sleep came easy that night.

First Flight Lead

The next day I was turned loose with a flight of two as a flight leader. Buck Buchanan was on my wing as my supervisor and flying nanny. Buck was a lanky, low key country boy and a real pro. He only spoke when something needed to be said and usually chose his words carefully. He was an ideal wingman for my first shot at flight lead.

Our target was the Bau Khe Highway river ford 15 miles north of Dong Hoi in Route Pack One. The ford provided a river crossing for Highway 1A, which paralleled the coastline and was a main supply route linking Hanoi with the south. The ford at Bau Khe was nicknamed the "Sandpile." It had been hit so many times that the bomb craters had actually changed the course of the Nguon Nay River.

I had trouble finding the narrow ford amongst the network of craters and vehicle tracks that marked the area. Compared to its marking on the map, Highway 1A wasn't much of a road, but we finally interdicted a point that looked important. Our bombs cut the ford, and within minutes, the craters filled up with water.

On the way back I tried out a tactic that I felt would improve our effectiveness and, at the same time, reduce our vulnerability to ground fire: high-speed road recce above 400 knots minimum. It worked well in terms of maneuver and security, but there was nothing moving on the roads and no one to surprise. We might as well have been working the back side of the moon. In my vain effort to find something worth strafing, I let our fuel get a shade too low, but we made it home with a couple of hundred pounds to spare.

Buck gave me mostly high marks during the debriefing. He liked high-speed recce, but he wasn't as impressed with my fuel management and let me know it very subtly. "One of the things you'll learn as a leader is to anticipate the fuel needs of your wingman, particularly if he's your buddy," Buck said wryly.

On my next three missions, I was given the opportunity to demonstrate my ability to lead an element. Each time I learned a valuable lesson. Leading the element required the formation skills of a wingman and the thinking skills of a leader. It required the ability to lead and follow at the same time.

Early Sunday morning, the sixth of November, I found myself on my way back to Bridge 520. I was leading the element in a flight of four. My wingman had much more experience than I, so I assumed that he would be able to compensate for the errors I was bound to make my first time out in that position.

We were superstitious about suffering high losses on Sunday so something in my gut felt very apprehensive as we started our run-in to the target. It was a beautiful morning and everything was going well, but I sensed that we were flirting with disaster. We had given the gunners two days to reload and tune up their defenses, and the mission was a duplicate of the one that had failed earlier. "Hang in there, Ken," I scolded myself. "Concentrate on flying the element and stop worrying about winning the war, or you will get your ass shot off."

All hell broke loose when we pulled up to look for the target. The bastards were waiting for us again and started shooting early. As we searched for the bridge, we got higher and slower and easier to hit. My radar warning equipment was going crazy. It cycled from low threat, to high threat, to a SAM launch light in less than a second.

I was still looking for the target when the lead element rolled in. Instinctively, I followed, but our hesitation on the perch resulted in a long, shallow pass, the most vulnerable way to attack a defended target. I was halfway down the chute before I spotted the bridge. Four was a little wide but right with me. I made a slight correction and pickled just as the bombs from the lead element hit the target. We got the bridge but we didn't silence the gunners. From the looks of the ground fire, they were tracking us.

When I pulled off the target, I looked over my shoulder to check Number Four. He was nowhere in sight and didn't answer the radio. I was frantic. I had the lead element in sight, but I feared that we had lost Number Four over the target.

We joined up and made another pass through the target area. I expected the worst, but there was no sign of a downed aircraft, and the North Vietnamese didn't fire a shot in anger. They were either out of ammunition or caught totally by surprise. In either case, they probably thought that we had lost our minds.

Our recovery was complicated by poor coordination between our flight, ground radar, and the post-strike tankers. When we did find our tanker, he informed us that Four had come out by himself with radio failure and was on another tanker. I was relieved but upset as hell because we had lost flight integrity. It was comforting to know that Four was not down, but the results of not knowing his whereabouts could have been disastrous.

The mood in the debriefing was strained. We had downed the bridge but had not performed well as a team. The flight leader was upset but didn't know exactly how to express it. He felt bad about stringing us out looking for the target, and I was inexperienced, but my wingman should have been able to stay with me. The thought that we could have busted our ass because of a simple radio failure was troubling. Ironically, it pointed toward the tragedy that awaited the Number Four man only days later.

We were on our way out of debriefing when we heard that the wing had lost two airplanes on the afternoon go. A 354th pilot, Captain Vic Viscarra, was flying with a Wild Weasel flight, and was down in Route Pack One. A 357th Squadron pilot had crashed at Danang trying to land with heavy battle damage. Vic was later recovered by the Navy, and the other pilot walked away from a flaming wreck, but the "low threat" in Route Pack One had claimed two more graduates. It was another typical Sunday at Takhli.

After thirteen missions, I was ready to go against primary targets in the Hanoi area. I felt prepared but uneasy. The warmup was over. To fly Rescap on the fringe of the action or to hit a bridge several miles from Hanoi was one thing, but to go downtown in a twenty-four-ship gaggle of thundering airplanes was quite another. The prospects were sobering.

6

STAN/EVAL

IT WAS OFFICIAL. THE special orders assigning me to the staff were published, and I moved to a solitary desk in a corner of wing headquarters to begin my duties as the standardization/evaluation flight examiner and flight manuals control officer. What a title and what a day to remember!

Once I accepted the fact that I had been selected for the job, I decided to give it my best shot. I had the right training, there was a lot of work to do, and the job offered a real opportunity to make a meaningful contribution to the wing mission. I didn't like losing my close ties with the 354th Squadron, but I figured I might find a way to build a unique and rewarding relationship with all three of the squadrons in the wing. To be effective, I had to build my credibility with the squadrons quickly. My first challenge was to gain their confidence.

I knew the job would be lonesome. Right or wrong, standards and their evaluators were viewed much like the IRS or the Inspector General, as persona non grata. Even though procedures and checklists are fundamental to disciplined flying, anyone who professed or evaluated them was automatically suspect by pilots.

Most pilots asked why the Air Force applied standardization rules that were necessary in training to combat. They reasoned that the North Vietnamese gunners were the best evaluators of our ability to get to the target, hit it, and return safely. If we passed their test, why bother with formalities? Surely, mission results were the measure of success in combat. Who needed stan/eval under those circumstances? It was a question I had asked myself and one I had to answer each time I briefed new pilots reporting to the wing.

There were regulations and standards that applied to all aspects of flying: flying hours, training requirements, standard procedures, currency requirements, and proficiency standards for evaluation. The provisions of these regulations were broad and changed frequently. Consequently, a standardization and evaluation officer was needed to administer the process for the commander. The stan/eval officer was expected to know the "book" verbatim, interpret the standards realistically, recognize necessary changes, and be able to demonstrate the standards in flight. In our wing, I was also expected to be the expert on weapons: their use, loading, fuse selection and settings, delivery techniques, and effectiveness in general.

To help me do the job, I had an administrative sergeant and an assistant who was the wing weapons officer. Together, we worked as a team to insure that the pilots were well informed, trained, and capable of carrying out a dynamic and difficult mission. Probably the toughest part of our job was convincing the pilots that standardization and flight evaluation were necessary in combat. We had to convince them that we were there to teach and help rather than to inspect.

Because of the demands of combat, most of the provisions of the regulations requiring rigorous standardization and evaluation were waived. In fact, the waiver stated: "All annual aircrew academic refresher courses, physiological refresher training, instrument flight checks, proficiency checks, and written examinations were waived until the aircrew returned to the CONUS [Continental United States]." Most pilots interpreted that statement as a hiatus from anything smacking of stan/eval, but that was not how it was intended. Rather, the waiver was intended to let us place emphasis on the use of realistic evaluation methods, encourage innovation in tactics, and enhance training so that we could adapt to a rapidly changing and sophisticated threat.

In short, the stan/eval officer was supposed to study the lessons learned and act as a focal point for the evolution and implementation of tactics and weapons techniques that would help pilots survive and be more effective. Our tactics had to change with the threat, but there was also an equally important need for consistency. Consequently, there was tension between stan/eval the "inspector" and stan/eval the "helper and trainer." The trick was to make the tension work for the benefit of the wing and the survival of the aircrews.

After the first week in the job, it was clear that I was overloaded. I needed help and decided the best way to improve my span of control and influence would be to designate one of the most experienced pilots in each squadron as the stan/eval representative, with the authority to train and evaluate pilots in that unit. I suspected that the squadron commanders might view this as an invasion of their authority and resist the idea unless it was presented and sold with tact and savvy.

The wing commander endorsed the plan, and I was able to gradually gain the confidence I needed in the squadrons, but the idea did not meet with the universal acceptance of the squadron commanders or their operations officers. In their view, stan/eval was *waived*, and they didn't have time to worry about procedures and evaluations, with all the other demands of combat.

Every day I learned a new lesson in tact and diplomacy and gradually evolved a system that not only worked, but was ultimately welcomed. The secret was my willingness to fly a stan/evaluation check on any mission, go anywhere the pilots were asked to go on short notice, and make a fair evaluation with positive recommendations. It was a formula that was hard to resist, and it enabled me to spot weaknesses and correct them quickly.

For new pilots and electronic warfare officers (EWO), I developed a combat orientation and training program to provide the squadrons with more confident and effective aircrews. I briefed every new crew member before he reached his squadron and expanded the program to include coordination conferences with the tanker crews at Takhli, the 388th F-105 Wing at Korat, and the supporting F-4 wings at Ubon and Danang.

During a seven-month period, I briefed each new aircrew member assigned to the wing and made a combat flight evaluation on every pilot in the wing, including the commander. I was busy, sometimes frustrated, always tired, but the effort paid dividends.

On 12 November 1966, I was put on orders as a flight leader. Coupled with my position as a flight examiner, it gave me the requisite tools I needed to do my job with confidence. I was still a relative newcomer, so it would take time to build experience and credibility.

Conducting a flight evaluation in combat was more straightforward than doing it in a peacetime, training environment. If the Weasel crew or pilot being evaluated were new, their first flight was always preceded by an extensive briefing covering the air operations and the procedures they would be required to follow. Time permitting, I scheduled a training sortie to introduce them to the peculiarities of our operation gradually and, at the same time, allow me to spot weaknesses that might require a tune-up before introducing them to combat. Heavyweight takeoffs, air refueling, combat tactical formation, and dive-bombing with real bombs were some of the challenges facing new pilots fresh from leave at home and slightly out of touch with the airplane.

Training flights were very useful but always difficult to schedule on top of an already taxing combat load of some ninety sorties per day. The chief of maintenance was a dedicated man, but he didn't think much of the idea of using his precious resources for training. He felt I was trying to do a job that should have been done by the training wings supplying the pilots. I appreciated his position, but when push came to shove, I usually got the training sorties.

When a replacement pilot was ready for combat, I often flew in his flight on one of his first missions. Usually flying in the number four position, I could evaluate the new pilot and two other seasoned pilots in the squadron at the same time. It was a full-time job evaluating the flight leader, the element leader, the new pilot, and do my job as a wingman in combat simultaneously. The challenge was enormous, but I learned a lot about tactics and more about myself in the process.

The key to making these difficult flight evaluations useful was the ability to anticipate and learn from any new situation and then demonstrate the value of the lesson learned to the flight during the debriefing. Later, after more study and thought, changes could be applied through the stan/eval representatives in the squadrons and implemented in wing tactics through evolutionary, sometimes revolutionary, doctrine changes. The object was simple. We had to be able to anticipate and react to changes in the defense quickly, and we couldn't afford to do anything stupid in the process.

The "Average" Pilot

There is no such thing as an average fighter pilot; even new ones have more than enough drive and self-confidence. While confidence was absolutely essential in combat, it could be deadly if it came wrapped in complacency or individuality.

None of our new pilots arrived with a complacent attitude but some did get through training still thinking like individuals. They were easy to spot and usually came from a flying experience that did not stress the need for mutual support in formation flying. Consequently, they were required to learn new tricks in training that were sometimes very difficult to master mentally. But even the toughest nuts soon appreciated the essential need for mutual support in combat. It was something I stressed again and again in the orientation briefings and during flight evaluations.

With very few exceptions, all of the F-105 pilots I flew with at Takhli had better than average pilot skills when they arrived, and each one of them tuned their skills quickly in combat. Learning to think under pressure was more difficult to develop and next to impossible to predict from pilot to pilot. Some were quick and some were early leaders, but each one of them eventually learned how to make a team contribution. Flak and enemy missiles were great prompters.

Given the flying skills and the confidence to think, pilots had to learn to see the target and concentrate on delivering weapons in the face of some very determined and distracting defenses. Dive-bombing accurately in heavy flak and in the intimidating environment of SAM missiles was difficult for everyone, and it never got easy. The key was the ability to concentrate with abandon for the few seconds required to track the target, or to stick on the leader's wing and bomb with him as an element. The concept of element attack was one that evolved in our wing, and it proved to be both accurate and effective in terms of maintaining mutual support and element integrity.

As pilots gained combat experience, there was a natural tendency to become complacent, particularly in the supposed low-threat route packages. It was not uncommon to fly with a seasoned veteran who unwittingly set his flight up for a loss because of a complacent attitude. Complacency developed gradually, but it had a rather sudden and dramatic way of curing itself in combat. Staying alert was something I harped on constantly in briefings and pilot evaluations. I was always looking for new ways to illustrate the danger of complacency to help pilots learn the lesson before the North Vietnamese taught them the hard, ultimate way.

All of the pilots I flew with and evaluated were highly motivated, but they were also human and needed reminding. Being the "burr under the wing saddle blanket" had its challenges, but the rewards were worth it.

A Special Challenge

In January of 1967, we were short of F-105 pilots in our wing, but we had a surplus of pilots assigned to staff support positions. The commander decided to train several of these pilots at Takhli and asked me to develop a program to accomplish the task. It was an unorthodox thing to do but an interesting and exciting challenge to tackle.

Only three pilots on the staff were qualified for our in-house training program. I was their ground school instructor, flight instructor, weapons instructor, leader, and mentor all rolled into one enchilada. One had flown combat in Korea, but I had to start from scratch with the other two. We called it the 355 CCTS, and it turned out to be a gasser.

The program was based on an ambitious, exhaustive schedule. The trio of pilots completed ground school at Takhli in two weeks of intensive study and went on to an air base in Japan for a checkout in the F-105 before returning to Takhli for weapons training and preparation for combat.

When the pilots returned current in the F-105, we began a ten-hour training program that concentrated on aerial refueling, tactical formation, low-level navigation, and weapons delivery. Not many people thought it could be done, but with sheer determination and lots of luck, the program succeeded. In less than six weeks, we had transformed three frustrated staff "wienies" into happy and productive F-105 pilots.

Stan/Eval Staff

Staff Sergeant Cass Satterfield was my administrative backbone on the wing staff. He looked after the stack of paper it took to keep track of some 100 pilots flying combat. Captain Randy Plumb did a superb job as the weapons officer. He had a marvelous sense of humor and was a constant source of encouragement. Typical of Randy, he took the blame when bombs or fuses went haywire and very little of the credit when things went smoothly.

Major Ted Tolman was our chief "tactics consultant" in the 354th Squadron. He was a sharp, aggressive pilot, with so many good ideas that we recruited him to replace Randy as weapons officer when Randy completed his tour. The stan/eval pilots assigned in the squadrons did the daily coordination and liaison work, and each made a unique contribution to the accomplishment of our mission.

As pilots completed their tour, many returned to peacetime flying assignments and the "real world" of standardization and flying regulations. Before each pilot's departure, I flew an evaluation flight check with them to update their required annual proficiency and instrument flight checks. This was done as close to their departure date as our complicated schedule would permit, but sometimes I had to fudge a little to meet the requirements. Nonetheless, I felt comfortable that I was satisfying the spirit of the regulations. I was confident that anyone who had completed 100 missions in the F-105 was qualified to fly anything, anywhere in the world. The pilots completing a combat tour in the 355th Tactical Fighter Wing arrived at their next unit ready to fly with a minimum of fuss and paperwork.

7

VIET TRI FERRY

FOR THE FIRST TIME, I was going downtown, barely 30 miles up the Red River from Hanoi. An integrated strike force of almost ninety aircraft would depart from four different bases and converge on the same target from two directions at precisely sequenced times on target (TOT) measured to the second. In less than ten minutes the entire strike force would be in and out and on their way back to the tankers, jinking like wild birds with afterburners roaring. This was the big league and all of the players were pros, including the North Vietnamese.

It was my fourteenth mission. Going into the briefing room I felt an extra edge of anxiety, but I was pleased to finally be on the first team. We had planned the mission carefully and I felt well prepared. I was looking forward to seeing Thud Ridge and celebrating my first mission into the Red River Valley.

The target was the ferry slips located on the Song Lo River where it joined the Red River at the town of Viet Tri. An easy place to find but a well defended, difficult target to hit. The target photo we were given showed multiple AAA and automatic weapons sites surrounding the ferry slips on both sides of the river, but only one site was marked as being occupied.

On this mission, we would join forces with the 388th Wing from Korat as a combined strike force and follow them to the target. We were supported by our own Ironhand SAM-suppressor Weasel flights and two flights of F-4s from Ubon for MiG cover.

Random Flight

I was Random Two in a four-ship strike flight led by Major Gordon Mickelson. Mick was fussy as hell, but he knew what he was doing, and anyone who flew with him respected his ability. He was very experienced in the F-105 and had a good head on his shoulders.

We would be the last flight into the target. This was a mixed blessing, depending on how much ammunition the AAA gunners had left by the time we got there. As a wingman, I was a "chopper," flying an aircraft loaded with six CBU-24 canisters filled with hundreds of baseball-sized antipersonnel bomblets. My job was to attack and neutralize the flak sights surrounding the target. The spinning blue bomblets formed a hail of explosive terror, which served to discourage the gunners.

The North Vietnamese had their own brand of discouraging weapons, the SA-2 radar-guided surface-to-air missiles. To counter the SAM threat, we employed defensive formation tactics using QRC-160 radar-jamming pods to mask us from the enemy radar and confuse the defenses. Our strike flights were supported by Wild Weasel aircraft equipped with sophisticated radar-sensing equipment and anti-radar Shrike missiles, used to attack and suppress SAM sites. The combination worked to improve our chances of surviving but, if a SAM was launched at us, we had to see it coming to have a decent chance at beating it. We could outmaneuver a SAM if we saw it come off the launch pad or spotted it in-flight in time to take evasive action. By necessity, we spent a lot of terrifying moments "taking it down" to the deck to defend against SAMs that may not have been a threat, but we had to rely on the launch light. The SAM threat was intimidating, disruptive and complicated our bombing problem enormously.

In late 1966 the supply of QRC-160 jamming pods was limited. There were usually only enough pods for one to be mounted on every other aircraft. So, on this mission, the leaders got a pod and bombs, and the flak "choppers" got bomblets.

Everything was normal coming off the tanker. We headed northeast from Channel 97, a Tacan navigation site in northeastern Laos, and started a gradual descent 1 mile behind the F-105 flight ahead of us. One of our F-4 MiGCAP flights was tucked in slightly high and behind us over my right shoulder. As we crossed the North Vietnamese border, Mick called, "Green'em up, Random!" I felt my pulse quicken as I adjusted my equipment, took a swig from my water bottle, and armed the aircraft.

The strike force checked in on the radio, and the force commander from Korat took control of the mission. Ten flights of F-105s spaced a minute apart. The radio crackled with tense and choppy chatter. Out of the corner of my eye, I noticed the lights on my radar-warning equipment starting to wink at me. Seconds later, a frenzy of SAM warning calls from the flights preceding us confirmed that the defenses were ready and electrified my senses. My mouth and throat were dry so I took another swig of water.

Everything was happening much faster than I had imagined. We were in a slight descent and had stabilized at 600 knots airspeed. I was on Mick's right wing in combat spread formation and working my butt off to stay there. The force commander called that he had reached the loop in the Red River. He was just south of Yen Bai and turning south toward Thud Ridge for the run-in to the target. We were just ten minutes behind him, and I knew we were committed.

Thud Ridge

Suddenly, we burst out above the sculptured foothills west of the Red River and into the valley that spread before us. It was a patchwork of green irrigated fields and narrow dirt roads. Nothing appeared to be moving. The countryside was deserted, and the valley looked angry and menacing.

We were level at 2,000 feet. At that height, the ground swept by quickly beneath us. The dense air in the valley was moist, and the condensation vortices twisting off our wing tips left beautiful white streamers as we turned hard to parallel Thud Ridge to the target. I was on the inside of the turn and struggling not to overrun the leader. My throttle was all the way back, and I was pulling hard on the stick, but I was so far forward that I felt like I was going to the target backwards. Mick finally rolled out, and I jammed the throttle forward and stabilized in position.

Thud Ridge wasn't as big as I had imagined. I was looking for something the size of the Rockies, a mountain we could hide behind to completely shield ourselves from the surveillance and attack of the enemy radar. We streaked past the highest point on the ridge (5,223 feet) and headed for a small saddle. From there, the ridge sloped downhill toward the airfield at Phuc Yen. Curiously, it reminded me of a one-way arrow pointing down the valley toward Hanoi.

The instant we passed the notch in the ridge, my SAM launch light came on and stayed on. I tried to call it out on the radio but there was too much chatter, and I had forgotten my damned call sign in all the commotion. The radio cracked, "Taking it down. SAM at two o'clock and closing!" The strike frequency was jammed, but I heard the force commander call that he was pulling up for the target.

Mick pushed over in a slight dive to get closer to the ground for cover. I was on the inside of the maneuvering turns and all over the throttle trying to stay in spread formation. It was tough to keep Mick in sight when he turned toward me. We were already in the weeds, and I felt like I would drag a wing tip if I got any lower.

Mick signaled me to move across into left echelon formation in preparation for the bomb pass. As I stabilized, I saw a J-shaped lake coming up on our right. It was our pull-up point and I knew we were only seconds away from the target. The radio chatter was frenzied and ominous.

When Mick started his pull-up, I stuck with him like cheap underwear. I felt confused, frightened, and way behind the power curve. We topped-out upside down on our backs at about 12,000 feet in a right rolling turn for a 45-degree dive angle at the target. I looked down and saw the river, Viet Tri, exploding bombs, and towers of billowing smoke. The weather was crappy and the scene was chaotic.

I hung in the arc of my roll for a second or two looking for a flak site. There was plenty of flak but all I could see was fire and smoke on both sides of the river. I rolled in and started down the chute behind Mick. Glowing, red goofballs spewed up through the smoke and past the nose of my aircraft. *It was aimed at me, and the bastards were trying to kill me. What a crummy way to welcome a frightened rookie!*

I stabilized in the dive. The ground was coming up fast. As my sight moved across the southern bank of the river I decided to hit the area where most of the flak seemed to be coming from. At least four sites were still firing from an area ringed with fires from the previous "chopper" flights. Not bad for flak sites that were supposed to be unoccupied. Red goofballs kept streaming by, but I held the aircraft steady until the pipper touched the center of the target area and then pickled the CBUs and pulled off hard to the left. I hoped that Three and Four were right behind me.

I stroked the afterburner, started jinking and looked for Mick desperately. I spotted an F-105 slightly high and about a quarter of a mile in front of me. *It had to be Random.* I was supersonic and closing quickly. I pulled back the throttle and checked hard to move back into spread formation.

Mick barked, "Random Two, Lead. Have you closing starboard side. They're tracking you, move it around, old buddy!"

In less than a minute, we were out of range of the AAA guns but still vulnerable to SAM attack from the rear. My launch light blinked on and off erratically. Our egress route over the low foothills guarding the Black River had a deadly reputation as a favorite hunting ground for MiGs lurking in the haze below.

Random Three and Four moved into position about 1,500 feet to the left of Lead. I finally settled down enough to clear the six o'clock position of Lead and the element. We had regained flight integrity with four sets of eyeballs searching for bogies. Random flight was smoking out at warp speed, but it seemed like we would never cross the Black River into relative safety.

The radio was still jammed with short, cryptic calls, but the situation was easing. Mick called Red Crown, "Random crossing the Black outbound with four chicks, looking for our post-strike tanker. Random, go to channel ten and check in." I was exhausted, relieved, wringing wet, and ready for a smoke and a long swig of water.

Once we found the tanker, post-strike refueling was easy, and the rest of the recovery was normal. We had gotten in and out of a dangerous target and done our job without a scratch. It was my first mission downtown and I was thankful to be on my way home. I looked forward to adding a red stripe to my campaign hat. I had been shot at, but I wasn't hit, and I couldn't wait to get on the ground to buy a round at the stag bar. My Package Six initiation ticket had been punched over Viet Tri.

I was tired but I felt exhilarated. *Hell, I might even go to town and really celebrate—tomorrow's schedule would determine that.*

Sitting on a JCS Target

The wing spent the next week anxiously sitting on a new JCS target (51.10)—a large fuel storage area near the airfield at Phuc Yen, north of Hanoi. The weather up north was terrible, but our headquarters at Seventh Air Force in Saigon kept moving the mission back rather than executing on a secondary target in Laos or in the southern route packs. The mission crept from morning to afternoon to morning, waiting for the weather to break in Hanoi.

Sitting and doing nothing but replanning brought out the worst in everyone. The pilots were getting nervous and edgy. There was a lot of uneasy talk among the crews. They were beginning to question the purpose of what we were doing in light of the targets we were hitting and the significant losses we were suffering. In my diary, I noted "The consensus is that we can't keep this up much longer—the election results should have some effect—wishful thinking."

My first Rest and Relaxation (R&R) was scheduled for the middle of November. I was looking forward to a break, but the idea of stopping and starting again bothered me. Judging by some of the guys I watched return, it took longer and longer to recover after each succeeding R&R. In fact, a couple of pilots never returned from a fifty-mission break with their families in Hawaii. After a week in the sun, they reasoned that their safety was more important than their careers and chucked in the towel in spite of the consequences.

The weather over Phuc Yen did not improve, but we continued to stand down and sweat out the mission. Seventh Air Force was anxious to hit the fuel storage area, but we would have settled for anything. Tension filled the air. One of our pilots who had been downed and rescued by the Navy took one look at the schedule board and decided he had had enough of combat. He hung up his spurs, went to Bangkok to think it over, and didn't return to fly again.

Diversion Flights

On 11 November headquarters decided to hit the target, in spite of the weather. The frag order called for the main strike force to come from the west minutes behind two flights that would approach from the east over the coast to check the weather and divert the defenses. The 354th Squadron was tagged to lead the diversion flights. Don Asire took one flight to the outskirts of Hanoi northeast of the target while the other flight went to a secondary JCS target on the northeast railroad.

The weather over the target was stinko—low overcast, ground fog, and poor visibility. The main strike force got the word in time to abort safely, but the second diversion flight was not recalled, and their leader, Major Art Mearns, was shot down and listed as missing in action. We didn't know who at Seventh Air Force was responsible for the diversion strike tactic, but it was a bum idea from the outset. Even if the weather had been better, the diversion flights were naked as jaybirds and defenseless in a high-threat environment.

We continued to sit on the same target but the weather stayed lousy. After a week of getting up at zero-dark-thirty for a predawn mission to a high-threat area in marginal weather, even the fearless began to get touchy. Each day, it got tougher to get ready, face the anxiety of knowing you might get your ass shot off, and then not go anywhere.

We eventually struck JCS 51.10 successfully, but paid a hell of a price.

New Director of Operations

Colonel Harold I. "Sam" Hill reported in as the new director of operations, replacing Colonel Bowman. Colonel Hill was my new boss, and I spent a lot of time those first few days briefing him as well as getting to know him. He turned out to be a *full* colonel all right, and he didn't mind sharing his views on most any subject. I learned to be a good listener and to appreciate the old saw that "senior colonels were entitled to their eccentricities."

Colonel Hill wore metal caps on his leather heels, and you could hear his distinctive stride the minute he entered the building. He also wore prescription sunglasses in the office, so it was hard to see his eyes when he talked to you. In my journal, I noted that he was *"a little self-conscious, nervous, overbearing, and will have a hard time filling Colonel Bowman's shoes."* In other words, he struck me as an ambitious colonel who was faced with the challenge of replacing someone who was respected and doing a super job. Colonel Sam Hill had his work cut out for him.

Weather cancellations continued, and flying came close to a standstill. For the first time since my arrival, several of us took a day off and went to town to shop and see what kind of mischief we could find. We started with a tour of the market in Takhli village. It was a mistake. The sight and smell of the food displayed there was enough to kill even the heartiest appetite.

I had a cast iron stomach and was looking forward to a spicy meal of hot beef, peppers, and Podjarka at the Villa Tropicana but my buddies were hesitant. I finally convinced them to try the Thai menu, but they drew the line on a dessert, which was billed as the specialty of the house. It was a candied fruit that resembled a large, swollen testicle with a soft, clear center.

After dinner we checked out the ladies at the Takhli Villa. The one we called "the Body" was entertaining at the bar and already taken. We settled for a couple of drinks, a hot bath and massage, and took a taxi back to the base before the peppers hit bottom. Wow! Thank goodness it was the night before my first break for rest and relaxation.

It was 16 November 1966. I had flown fifteen missions in two weeks and stood down for another week sweating out bad weather. I was ready to relax.

Gooney Bird Express to Malaysia

My first R&R was a tour de force of Malaysia led by our wing commander and a company of nineteen. Colonel Scott borrowed the base flight C-47, an aging twin-prop transport from the 1930s. He insisted on flying the airplane himself, and was at the controls when we landed at Kuala Lumpur, Malaysia, our first destination.

We were greeted by the air attaché and a half-dozen aides who were standing beside a brightly decorated bus, which we dubbed the "Manchurian Express." The airport was large, and the terminal was obviously brand new and very modern. Our vintage Gooney Bird looked conspicuously awkward sitting alone on the sprawling concrete ramp. Colonel Scott seemed ill at ease, and I thought, "surely, they hadn't gone to all that expense just for our distinguished party."

The air attaché explained that the airport had been totally remodeled in anticipation of a visit by President Johnson, who was expected sometime after the first of the year. We were surprised, but we had heard rumors that the president was going to visit Southeast Asia and perhaps even announce our presence in Thailand. Colonel Scott looked relieved but may have felt slightly deflated. We joked about it as we boarded the gaudy bus for the ride to the hotel.

We wheeled away from the airport with the attaché and commander leading the way in a shiny black sedan with the Manchurian Express close behind. Military police stationed along the route snapped salutes as we passed. Our driver's face reflected the urgency of his charge as we lurched and honked our way through the crowded streets of the capital city.

As we approached the Hotel Merlin in downtown Kuala Lumpur, it began to rain with a vengeance. Our luggage was strapped to the top of the bus and was getting soaked in the downpour. When we came to a stop in front of the hotel, we were inundated with bellhops eager to save our clothes and earn a handsome tip in the process.

Lieutenant Ed McCaffrey and I were assigned to room together. When we unpacked our B-4 bags, we found what we suspected. Our precious R&R civvies were soaking wet and needed ironing. We considered going to the bar in our flight suits but decided that American fighter pilots didn't need that kind of international exposure. Instead, we used the good old Yankee dollar and sent our clothes out for emergency service with an obliging house boy. In less than an hour, we were standing at the bar in damp but neatly pressed clothing.

After a couple of drinks, we were set for an extravagant dinner and a night on the town. Kuala Lumpur had its share of exotic nightclubs, so we picked a bar that offered hot baths and full body massages. A bath would have been relaxing, but we had more on our minds than rubber duckies. Later, I found myself alone with a lovely young lady who insisted her name was Suzy Wong. It was an interesting ploy, which I didn't necessarily buy, but I didn't let that spoil the evening.

Our next stop was Singapore. It was very similar to Kuala Lumpur, except the weather was hotter, and the British air base we used was austere compared to the airport that awaited our thirty-ninth president. On our way into the city, we passed an old fortress prison. It was surrounded by walls covered with mildew, and the place looked decrepit. I felt sorry for the poor souls, whoever they were, who had to endure it.

Our hotel was modern and air-conditioned. It was on the main avenue overlooking the waterfront and the view was spectacular. I felt like staying there and enjoying room service, but the call of intrigue was simply overpowering.

The first stop on our itinerary was a tour of the famous Tiger Balm Gardens. The path through the gardens led up a steep hill past brightly colored figures set in scenes extolling the healing powers of Tiger Balm and commemorating the inventor. The weather was oppressively hot and sticky, and the tour wasn't really very interesting, but we were determined to reach the top of the hill for a rest and a view of the city.

As we talked, a group of young men approached us carrying rocks and clubs as weapons. They made it clear that they disliked Americans, and it looked like they intended to prove it with a couple of unwelcome fighter pilots. We were surprised but clever enough to make a hasty retreat to the safety of the taxi. As we ran down the hill under a hail of rocks and bottles, I told Mac to jink, and we both started laughing so hard, I thought we would collapse before reaching safety.

We jumped in the car and sped away under a shower of rocks that pummeled the roof of the taxi. Back safely at the hotel, the enraged driver insisted that we pay him for the damages. After an ugly argument, we paid him the fare, scattered some loose change beside the curb, and ran for the security of the lobby. We escaped but had become prisoners of our own caper. We didn't leave the hotel again until the morning call for the bus to the airport.

Our last stop was the island of Penang, located off the west coast of Malaysia, just 5 degrees above the equator. The island was smaller than both Kuala Lumpur and Singapore and unbelievably hotter. We were driven to a quaint little hotel in old Georgetown, a small city near the center of the island. Our driver and host was a sergeant in the Royal Air Force and a fascinating person. He tactfully told us that during his off-duty time he doubled as the town's chief of police and a procurer of young ladies, a convenient combination in a town where prostitution was strictly forbidden.

I had come down with a terrible cold and felt absolutely rotten. A group of Australian school teachers were staying at a nearby hotel on the beach, so I opted for some sunshine and the ocean. Both helped my cold, but the Aussies turned out to be by far the best medicine.

After four days of sweltering heat and chasing, I was thankful that the commander decided to skip Bangkok on the return flight and head straight for Takhli. When we landed and I caught sight of the F-105s, I was rudely reminded of my daily flying duty. It had been a short respite but we were back, and the war was still a reality.

I hadn't brought back any souvenirs but several of the base personnel had bought out every store in Malaysia. They gloated over their bargains as they laid them out for a cursory inspection by the customs officer. They were welcome to their bargains as far as I was concerned. I needed a couple of aspirin and the bed in my air-conditioned trailer.

Radar Bombing

The wing was still sweating out the same targets—JCS 19 and 51.10—and the weather forecast was not encouraging. Predictably, the crews had grown more restless, raw nerves abounded. Colonel Hill spent most of his time pacing the hall between the commander's office and the Tactical Operations Center (TOC), asking for updated forecasts and scorning the answers.

I kept myself busy doing routine paperwork and briefing new replacements. Even though the likelihood of flying was low, I had trouble getting on the daily squadron mission schedules. The scheduling officers were coveting their limited sorties and made all sorts of excuses. The story I got from the 333d Squadron was the most incredible. They had the audacity to suggest that I would end up going to Route Pack Six too often. I thanked the scheduling officer for his concern but assured him that I was willing to take the risk and reminded him that my safety was strictly my business. He got the point but gave me a look that said, "Screw you and the horse you rode in on!"

When I took my frustration to Colonel Hill, he listened but his answer surprised me. He was unpredictable. "Fine, Bell," Colonel Hill said impatiently. "A break will give you the time you need to work on a project I want done right away. Get whatever help you need and figure out how we can use radar to bomb targets in this lousy weather. Seventh is about to go nuts and it would be a great initiative on our part."

I discussed the idea with Randy Plumb and several others. We concluded that it would be very difficult to hit targets in North Vietnam on radar with any accuracy. The F-105 radar-bombing system was designed to deliver nuclear weapons against large strategic targets where 1,500- to 2,000-foot errors were acceptable. Going after point targets in North Vietnam with hard bombs using radar would be extremely risky and potentially inaccurate. It could be done, but it would take balls, and someone in Washington would have to be willing to take the political heat for collateral damage.

We reported our preliminary conclusions to Colonel Hill and he threw us out of his office. Fortunately, the weather took a turn for the better so he lost interest, and I was off the hook at least temporarily. Ironically, General Ryan, the Commander of Pacific Air Forces (PACAF), would ask me the same question a few months later. He was not so easily dissuaded.

I finally clawed my way onto the 354th schedule, only to oversleep and miss the briefing. The mission was canceled because of weather so nothing was lost, but it was an embarrassing way to restart after a ten-day layoff.

Three new pilots needed a local area checkout and refresher flight in the F-105, so I quickly planned a training flight and got the pilots and airplanes together. As usual, time was short, and I only had an hour to tell them everything I usually included in an eight-hour briefing. We covered the most important points and headed for the airplanes.

In the rush, I forgot to put on my G-suit. I thought I had everything, but when I got to the airplane and the crew chief noticed my G-suit was missing. I couldn't believe it. I ran back to the squadron building and startled Sergeant Perry. He was terribly embarrassed and couldn't believe that we had both overlooked the G-suit. We were both frantic. In his haste, Perry tripped over a box of .38 caliber ammunition and scattered rounds all over the floor. I finally got myself together and back to the airplane just in time to start engines.

The mission went surprisingly well, considering how it started. We accomplished everything necessary to get the pilots recurrent in the airplane. After the debriefing, I was exhausted but hadn't forgotten that it was Thanksgiving and the club was serving turkey. It was dusk when I walked back to my trailer. I was feeling lonely and hoping that turkey and dressing might warm my spirits.

When I arrived at the club, the dining room was still crowded. I ordered turkey, but the Thai waitress answered with a frown of disappointment, "No hab white meat, Major." That was the final straw. I settled for a hamburger steak and went to my trailer to have a drink and sort through a screwed-up day.

Three days later, I finally got back into action over North Vietnam, but just barely. Ironically, I was assigned to an eight-ship Sky Spot mission with the 333d Squadron. On the command of Milky Control, we dropped forty-eight 750-pound bombs through an overcast on a suspected truck park just inside Route Pack One. During the debriefing in the squadron, I couldn't resist needling the squadron scheduling officer about his concern for my potential overexposure in Package Six. "Bob, an eight-ship Sky Spot is a long way from downtown Hanoi," I said. "But keep trying, I'm willing to risk flying with you." I smiled and he laughed, but the point found its mark.

I made the 333d schedule again the next day, assigned to fly Colonel Scott's wing. As mission commander, he was set to lead the strike force against JCS 19 or 51.10, but the weather turned out to be a problem again. We ended up reverting to another Sky Spot and a recce mission in Route Pack One.

It was my first flight with Colonel Scott. One of the purposes was to perform a standardization check on the commander so he could evaluate my approach to the job and judge how well I did it; sort of a check on the checker by the boss.

I was impressed with Colonel Scott as a pilot and leader. Although he lost his temper taxiing out to the arming area and tried to force an wayward C-47 off the taxiway, he cooled down once we got airborne. There were some rough spots during the join-up with the Sky Spot airplane, and I covered them in the evaluation of the mission during the debriefing. He told me he liked my approach and dismissed the flight without further discussion. My credibility with the 333d Squadron began to improve immediately.

The next day we were fragged again to hit JCS 19 but wound up with a weather divert to the Barrel Roll area in Laos. It was an interesting mission, flown under the close control of a FAC and my first one logged as a noncounter. Only missions flown over North Vietnam counted toward the magic 100.

We were directed to bomb a heavy troop concentration of Pathet Lao prior to an offense by Laotian government troops near the Plaine des Jarres. The FAC marked the target with a smoke rocket, and we rolled in seconds later. The defenses in Laos were usually light, but we had been surprised before by the Pathet Lao. The little buggers were tenacious and put up some wicked ground fire when they were angered.

Our bombs were right on target, and the area erupted with secondary explosions. The FAC sounded jubilant over the radio, "Beautiful, give me more of the same. The good guys are jumping up and down!" We finished with two strafing passes and headed home.

In Laos it was hard to tell how well we were doing, and even harder to determine who was winning. I hoped that we had done some good that day for somebody.

The next day was a no-fly day for me, so I decided to visit the flight line and see what the ground crews were doing. The airmen broke their backs keeping us in the air, and most of the pilots went out of their way to give them the extra support they needed.

One crew chief complained that he was seldom able to check his mail because the post office was closed during his normal time off at night. I was surprised. My schedule was hectic, but I always found time during the day to check my mail, so I had never experienced the problem. That night, I decided to check out his story.

Sure enough, the post office had never gone to war. The officer in charge, who turned out to be an impervious second lieutenant, was operating under stateside, nine-to-five hours. The next morning, I tried to convince him that he was there to support the troops, but he didn't see any compelling reason to change.

Colonel Scott solved the problem in a matter of minutes with a rather one-sided call to the air base support group commander. As of that moment, every supporting element on the base was put on a twenty-four hour, around-the-clock operation to match the pilots and ground crews. The personnel office, pay and finance, the legal staff, the post office, and even the base exchange found themselves on extended work hours for the duration.

For the next couple of days, I made it a point to check on the lieutenant at the post office. He looked a little stressed and strung out, but he knew better than to complain to me. He didn't respond to NCOs or majors, but he had gotten the unvarnished word from the boss and knew that I had blown the whistle.

I received my first, long-awaited care package from home: cigarettes, an assortment of canned Mexican food, and a six-pack of *Snappy Tom* bloody mary mix. Cigarettes were available and very inexpensive at the Class VI store, but the Mexican food was a real treasure. My folks knew what I missed most and kept me supplied with regular shipments. Packages came so often that the lieutenant at the post office suspected I was the Southeast Asia distributor for Ashley's canned enchiladas and bloody mary mix.

8

IRONHAND IN SIX-
ALPHA

WHEN THE NORTH VIETNAMESE introduced the SA-2 SAM into their defenses in the summer of 1965, it had a dramatic impact on our tactics. Until that time, our fighters had the option of staying above the effective range of the AAA guns until they were ready to commit to a target. With the introduction of radar-guided SAMs that could reach altitudes of 60,000 feet at supersonic speeds, the limited safe haven that we enjoyed over enemy territory was eliminated.

Despite months of warning, we had to react rather quickly to the SAM threat. Immediate changes in tactics were employed by the combat units but longer range changes in our strategy and weapons systems were needed on a priority basis. One of these changes was the modification of fighter aircraft with equipment to locate and destroy SAM radar sites.

Ferret aircraft were used against enemy radar as early as World War II, but the development of electronic warfare equipment for modern fighter forces had suffered due to a lack of priority. The introduction of the SA-2 missile gave new impetus to the need for specially equipped fighter aircraft to counter the SAM threat. These aircraft and crews were called Wild Weasels and their mission was code named Ironhand.

The Weasels started out in the F-100F aircraft and gradually transitioned to specially modified F-105F aircraft. Before their development was complete, the Weasels would ultimately use modified versions of the F-4 and a remanufactured F-105G aircraft.

Each of the Weasel aircraft had a two-man crew—pilot and EWO. The pilot flew the aircraft from the front seat, and the EWO operated the sophisticated electronic sensing and warning equipment from the back. Our F-105F Weasel aircraft carried two Shrike antiradiation missiles that could be launched individually against ground radar sites posing a threat to the strike force.

Ideally, the Shrike missile was designed to guide on the radar energy emanating from a AAA or SAM site and destroy the radar transmitter, rendering the site ineffective. Practically, Shrikes were not 100 percent accurate, and they were seldom launched under the optimum conditions envisioned by the designer. Consequently, more often than not they turned out to be better markers than hitters. In addition, it was difficult to evaluate the effectiveness of the Shrikes because of three factors: employment restrictions, uncertain launch range, and the defensive reaction of the SAM site.

For political reasons, we were not allowed to simply hunt for SAM sites and strike them with our Weasel aircraft. Granted, the Weasels were a valuable resource and in very short supply, but we argued that they were designed and best equipped to hunt and kill radar sites and ought to be used primarily in that role. Instead, we were told to limit their use to a complementary role to protect the strike force by suppressing the enemy radar. When a SAM site posed a threat to the strike flights, the Weasels were allowed to seek out and attack the site.

Consequently, the Weasel mission was a terribly difficult, agonizing, and often frustrating one to accomplish. There were too many F-105s, F-4s, and SAM sites, not to mention AAA and MiGs, involved in the action around a typical Six-A target, for the Wild Weasels to accomplish their mission effectively, given the ground rules imposed on them. God knows, some talented and valiant people did the best they could under some unbelievably difficult conditions.

The Shrike missile had to be fired within its maximum range envelop to reach its target, and despite the sophisticated equipment on board the F-105F, range to the enemy radar site had to be determined by the Weasel crew based on experience and judgment. Even if the Shrike was launched within its range envelop, it was difficult to determine when, if, or why the ground radar signal stopped. The North Vietnamese were clever devils, and they learned early on to detect a Shrike launch. Tactically, that gave them the option of shutting down their own search or guidance signal to avoid swallowing the explosive impact of an in-coming missile. They understood the proverb about pride going before the fall.

On one occasion, we took a bold initiative and launched what could only be described as an unorthodox Ironhand mission. Alone, two Wild Weasel aircraft flew toward the Hanoi defensive ring from high altitude and at maximum range. When enough SAM sites came up to make the contest interesting, the Weasels fired four Shrike missiles at several unsuspecting SAM sites in and around downtown Hanoi. The Shrikes hit some sensitive radar targets and the effects were devastating. The North Vietnamese cried foul, and the Weasels went back to escort duty.

Major Leo Thorsness planned and led the mission. Leo was an agressive Weasel pilot and a staunch advocate of hunt and kill tactics. With a single stroke, he had successfully demonstrated the effectiveness of a technique we knew would work effectively. He was later shot down and held as a prisoner of war. For his sake, I hoped that the North Vietnamese didn't realize who they had.

There were days when I felt that we should have loaded all of our F-105s with Shrikes and launched a massive hunting expedition against SAM and AAA sites. The North Vietnamese would have crapped in their pants and had to double the size of the chains holding the gunners to their positions in the AAA batteries.

It is difficult to describe an Ironhand mission, particularly the range of feelings one experienced in the span of a half-hour spent dueling with enemy defenses as a member of a Wild Weasel flight. The mission was grueling, dangerous, and hairy as hell. Not everyone got a "chance" to fly with the Weasels but anyone who did came away exhausted, often terrified, and always full of respect for the guys who did it everyday for a living.

Spitfire Four

I got my first Weasel opportunity on my twentieth mission. It was an Ironhand mission in support of our long-awaited strike against JCS 51.10, a fuel storage area near the airfield of Phuc Yen in the outskirts of Hanoi. I was Number Four in a Wild Weasel flight, dragging six 500-pound bombs at low altitude on the end of a 600-mile per hour daisy chain.

Dive-bombing a heavily defended target required dedication, skill, and concentration. Being able to improvise as a bomber in a Wild Weasel flight was next to impossible; just trying was a formidable challenge.

As a Weasel flight, we knew we had our work cut out for us, but I couldn't know how hairy it would be. We were going to a JCS target we had been sitting on for over two weeks, and everyone was tense and stale. Our wing was tagged to lead the composite strike force, and we would precede them into the target area to suppress SAMs and radar-guided guns. I hoped the North Vietnamese gunners were as out of practice as we were. The weather was forecast to be marginal but Seventh Air Force was under enormous pressure to get us there one way or another.

Halfway through the briefing, we had to re-form the flight because only one F-105F Weasel aircraft was available for the mission. Leo Thorsness and his EWO, Captain Harry Johnson, would lead in the Weasel aircraft with three D-models flying as bombers. The other pilots had a little experience on Ironhand missions, but this was my first turn in the barrel. It would be difficult for three bombers to stay with a maneuvering Weasel in a high-threat area and remain poised to deliver bombs accurately. My element leader, a wizened veteran, looked grim but determined.

I knew we were in deep yogurt when we turned down Thud Ridge toward Phuc Yen. The weather was hazy with broken clouds at about 5,000 feet, absolutely the worst and most vulnerable conditions for an attack by SAMs. Number Three and I were stable and looking through the flight toward Thud Ridge. We were on schedule, just five minutes ahead of the strike force. When the force commander called "Crossing the Red," I felt a tingle go up my back. Warm adrenaline shot through my system, and I began to feel close to panic-stricken, but under control. "We're finally going to do it," I thought resolutely. "And someone is going to get hit, sure as hell."

As we approached the foot of the ridge, the AAA guns started shooting, and the radar-warning gear blossomed. The SAM launch light blinked once and came on solid. Someone called "SAM launch, one o'clock," and the next thing I knew, we were in a hard, four-G turn away from me. I was able to stay with Three but lost sight of Spitfire Lead and his wingman. A split second later Three reversed the turn into me, and I had to slide high across his tail to keep from hitting him. I was breathing hard, gulps of dry oxygen parched my mouth, and my pulse was pounding.

Spitfire Lead marked a site and called for one of us to bomb it. "Crap, I'd hit it if I had any idea where it was or what I was doing," I muttered sarcastically.

The radio was jammed with calls and their tone was frantic. Someone called, "Take it down, take it down!"

I looked straight ahead in time to see three smoke trails coming straight at me, about 2,000 feet away and closing rapidly. A salvo of three SAMs had barely missed Three but had me bracketed. I froze. Two missiles split and flashed by my wing tips, but the one on my nose went right over the canopy and exploded, violently rocking the tail of the aircraft. I thought I'd had the schnitz, but the airplane came out of the fireball without a scratch. Miraculously, I was still flying and everything in the cockpit looked normal.

Spitfire Lead called, asking if anyone was in position to put bombs on the SAM site. I searched frantically for the SAM site, but I was confused and frightened as hell, and it was all I could do to keep Spitfire Three in sight, much less bomb something. Someone called another SAM launch, and seconds later another volley of three streaked by the right side of my airplane. "Who's suppressing who," I thought out loud. "The bastards will be out of missiles before we get our bombs off."

I was holding on by the skin of my teeth with six 500-pound bombs still on the bomb rack, and burning fuel like crazy. My face and head were soaking wet. I knew I was low on fuel but I couldn't get a second free to look in the cockpit to check the fuel gauge. My helmet and mask kept slipping down on my face under the high sustained G-loads. The front of the helmet pressed down over my eyes, blocking my vision. I tried holding it up with my left hand, but it was no use, the lining was too slippery. *Damn this helmet anyway!* We were in a terrible jam, and I felt like I had drawn the short straw and about to get the bloody wiener.

During a brief pause in the action, I peaked at the fuel gauge. *Son of a Bitch!* I was 2,000 pounds below the 10,000-pound bingo and gulping fuel going in and out of burner. "Spitfire Four is bingo minus two," I called, trying to sound as cool as possible. I knew Lead wasn't ready to leave, and I hadn't dropped my bombs yet.

My call must have prompted Three to check his fuel and punch off his wing tanks. "Heads up, Four. Tanks now!" They tumbled off with a puff of fuel and damn near hit me. I eased off on the G and punched mine off quickly. I was tempted to pickle the bombs as well but decided to keep them. I didn't have the foggiest idea where we were or what had become of Spitfire Lead, but I felt obliged to hit something.

Emergency beepers started wailing on Guard Channel. At least two aircraft were hit and down. In the confusion, I lost sight of Three. He had rolled in on a target, and I had missed it. When I spotted him, his bombs were gone, and he was pulling away from me. In desperation, I lined up on a road and pickled my bombs hoping to do *some* damage. I was disgusted, but I could have sworn my airplane said thank you.

"Spitfire Four, bingo minus four," I called as a reminder.

"Say *again*, Four. This is Lead!"

"Rog, Four is bingo minus four." I only had 6,000 pounds remaining.

"Spitfire flight, let's get out of here. Three, take Four back to the tanker. I'll pick you up on the way out, over!" Lead called frantically.

We were right on the deck in the valley east of Thud Ridge. Three turned to the west and started a slow climb. I thought we would never get over the ridge and across the Red River. Someone called "Launch, take it down," and back we went down into the ground fire. We were pinned down and forced to turn south toward Hanoi to skirt the ridge and get out of the cross fire. It was a risky thing to do, but the SAMs had us between a rock and a hard place.

Three turned to avoid going over Phuc Yen and started a cautious climb for the foothills west of the Red River valley. It was a dangerous place to expose ourselves to radar, but we didn't have a choice. It was a calculated risk, but we were burning fuel we would need to reach the tanker. Sure enough, the launch light came on and Three screamed, "Take it DOWN Spitfire!"

We made a carving turn back down to the cover of the small, rolling foothills. The afternoon sun and haze made it difficult to see much in any direction. We were doing better than 600 knots and weaving in a scissors maneuver to avoid being hit. "Grit your teeth and pray," I said to myself as the amber launch light blinked twice and came on steady, glowing brightly.

An explosion of a pair of fireballs on a hillside at our ten o'clock position startled me. The radio crackled, "Scratch two SAMs low at ten o'clock, Spitfire. Four, Lead here. Fuel state?"

"Spitfire Four has forty-eight hundred pounds and sucking."

"Roger, Four. Better go for altitude buddy, and find a tanker. This is Spitfire Lead, over."

Spitfire Three motioned for me to take the lead, and as I slipped past him, I pulled the nose up into a zooming climb. The airplane was clean except for the centerline bomb rack so I pickled it and crossed my fingers.

The next few moments lasted a lifetime. We were climbing away from the threat and looking straight into the sun; a perfect setup for MiGs and SAMs. Until we could get out of range, we were at their mercy. Spitfire Three was off my right wing about 2,500 feet and slightly ahead, so we had some cover for our six o'clock, but we were sitting ducks if someone wanted us. The launch light continued to flicker on and off, adding to the pucker factor.

After an eternity, Spitfire Lead called that he had us in sight, high at twelve o'clock. "Might as well go for it, Four. It looks clear from back here. See you later at Channel Forty-Three, this is Spitfire."

I was at 25,000 feet and climbing fast. The fuel gauge showed just under 3,000 pounds remaining. My only chance of getting the airplane back was to climb to an optimum cruise altitude and stay there until I was within "gliding" range to the closest recovery base. Udorn was located in the northern part of Thailand just a few miles south of the Laotian border. It was my only hope of making it back without a tanker.

We were scheduled for post-strike refueling, but finding a tanker quick enough to be helpful looked futile. I would burn more fuel getting to a tanker than I had in the first place. It was a crappy situation, but I had no one to blame but the luck of the draw and the North Vietnamese gunners.

Spitfire Three decided to join Spitfire One and Two on a post-strike tanker in case they were needed for search and rescue. At least three aircraft were already down, and the rescue teams might need top cover. It could turn into a long afternoon for the strike force. The radio chatter sounded desperate. I suspected that our strike flights had taken a number of hits in the target area, and my suspicions would be confirmed later.

I leveled off at 35,000 feet over the middle of Laos. It was as high as I had been in the F-105 since training. There was just under 2,000 pounds of fuel remaining, which was "minimum fuel" for landing under *normal* circumstances. Thus far, Friday, the second of December 1966, had been anything but normal, but I was praying for some improvement.

Seventy miles out of Udorn, I eased the throttle back to idle and started a maximum range descent. The weather report was good, and I spotted the base easily from about 50 miles out. At long last, luck had taken a turn for one of the good guys.

I checked in with Udorn Tower and asked for their surface winds and landing instructions. They advised me that several F-4s were inbound with battle damage and asked for my fuel state. As I descended to 15,000 feet, the fuel flow to the engine started increasing noticeably, and the fuel remaining seemed to hang up and then drop just slightly below 1,000 pounds. "Udorn Tower, Spitfire Four is thirty miles north with one thousand pounds and no battle damage, request a minimum fuel approach, over."

"Roger, Spitfire Four. Traffic at Udorn is landing southeast. We have two flights of F-4s ahead of you with heavy battle damage. Use caution and be prepared to hold over the field for F-4 barrier engagements, over." Suddenly, lady luck had turned the other way again.

"Roger, Udorn. Spitfire Four has the field in sight and will follow the F-4s. Be advised I am down to emergency fuel, over!"

"Roger, Spitfire. Call ten-mile final," the tower said calmly.

If I hadn't been so low on fuel I might have enjoyed watching the air show. Eight F-4s with various states of battle damage were trying to get on the same runway at nearly the same time. I hoped like hell they all made it because I was in no position to hold or go elsewhere. For me, it was Udorn or make parachute letdown.

All of the F-4s landed safely, but three of them had to take a barrier with their tail hooks to stop because of brake failures. What a pickle! I was on the glide path 5 miles out, and the runway suddenly closed. "Spitfire Four, this is Udorn Tower. We have three F-4s in barriers, approach end, midfield, and far end. Go around, over!"

I had less than 500 pounds of fuel and was in no position to make a go-around. At low levels, fuel gauges were not accurate, and the amount of fuel consumed in a go-around varied, but it was always enormous. I could flame-out at any minute, and I damn sure didn't want to punch out of a perfectly good F-105 at low altitude within sight of an airport. Landing on a congested runway was my best option. At worst, I would have to thread my way through the disabled F-4s and settle for minimum damage if I clipped one. I had a minimum weight aircraft, a drag chute, and tail hook, so I decided to go for the runway and hope for the best.

"Tower, Spitfire Four is going to land. Clear the runway ASAP. I'll save the hook for the far-end barrier, over!"

"Spitfire Four, the runway is *closed*, repeat *CLOSED. Go Around!*"

"Tower, Spitfire is at two miles with three green. I have the F-4s in sight."

With only 300 pounds of fuel, I would be lucky to make the runway, a go-around was out of the question. The F-4 at midfield appeared to be free of the barrier and on the right side of the runway. I planned to land long enough to clear the F-4 at the approach end and deploy the drag chute just as I touched down. If the drag chute failed, I would hold the arresting hook up until I passed the midfield barrier, try to stop with maximum braking, and as a last resort, put the hook down in time for the last barrier. I couldn't figure out what to do if the F-4 in the far-end barrier wasn't moved before I got there.

The ground crews were still working to clear the runway when I touched down just beyond the F-4 hung up in the approach-end barrier. My drag chute worked, but I had to swerve to miss the F-4 sitting crippled midway down the runway. The crew was still in the cockpit, and I saw some big eye-balls as I veered past them with a couple of feet to spare. I was able to slow down enough to turn off the runway but the next problem was finding a place to park on the crowded ramp before I ran out of fuel. The engine was running on fumes and I just barely made it.

The recce wing commander at Udorn met my airplane. We had a "father and son talk" about paying attention to tower instructions, and then he drove me to the command post for a mission debriefing.

I was the only F-105 that recovered at Udorn that day. The rest were damaged F-4s, and their crews had long faces as we met outside the debriefing room. They looked tired and demoralized. The F-4s had taken a real beating; two aircraft lost, and a half-dozen more damaged.

The intelligence officer told me that Korat had also lost a bird in the target area to a SAM. There was little hope of getting the pilot out, but a Rescap was in progress. Worse, he added that post-strike reconnaissance revealed only minor bomb damage to the target. That meant we would be going back to JCS 51.10, probably by morning. Suddenly, my mood went sour.

All I needed was full internal fuel and a drag chute, and I would be ready to depart Udorn. I was looking forward to the short flight back to Takhli. It was dusk and I hadn't made a clean, lightweight takeoff since leaving Nellis. I decided to show the guys on the ramp what a lightweight, slick Thunderchief could do.

The takeoff felt spectacular. The afterburner pinned me back in the seat, and the airplane leaped off the ground in less than 4,000 feet and was off to the races. Without bombs and external tanks, the F-105 was a nimble airplane. As soon as I cleared the field boundary, I eased the nose down and let the airspeed build to just below the Mach number. The airplane was as solid as a rock, so I settled back for a carefree ride home at treetop level, a rare treat and as much fun as you can have with your clothes on.

Leo Thorsness waited until I returned to Takhli to gather up Spitfire flight for a let-your-hair-down debriefing. Leo was a pro at "Weaseling," and he wasn't a bit bashful about pointing out mistakes, including his own. We had made plenty that day, and it was obvious that Leo was not happy.

"Guys, that was awful, the worst I've seen," was Leo's greeting as we sat down around the table in the 357th operations room. It was late, and it got much later before it was over. "We lost flight integrity before the first SAM warning and things went to hell fast after that," Leo went on. "We're lucky we're not all in the Hanoi Hilton right now! Damn it Three, you and Bell never were in position. You fell out in the first turn and stayed behind the rest of the way. You were easy targets for SAMs or MiGs, and you're lucky you didn't get hammered." Three's face started to drain, but I knew Leo was right so I kept my mouth shut.

Leo was just getting started so I let my mind drift back to the mission briefing when the trouble started. "What do you think, Ken? You've been mighty quiet," Leo asked in a stern voice. It took a minute to collect my thoughts, but I finally realized that it was my turn to speak my piece as Spitfire Four.

"It was my worst mission, and the lousiest job I've ever done on the wing, that's for damn sure," I said knowing everyone agreed. I went on to say that I did not feel adequately prepared for the difficulty of the task, but I didn't know a better way to get ready to fly with the Weasels than do it the first time and learn the hard way. That was the unvarnished truth, but not hardly music to Leo's ears.

The Wild Weasels were a proud bunch and certainly used to taking hits, but Leo seemed to have little patience with errors on the part of wingmen and less tolerance for criticism. He kept pressing me, so I finally let him know where I stood.

"Yeah, we messed up all right, but we really screwed ourselves before we ever got started," I said as politely as a new guy ought to. "Trying to keep three D-models loaded with bombs in tactical formation with a maneuvering Weasel is plain dumb! Hell, doing it with two-and-two is hard enough. I know I've got a lot to learn, but I'd like to meet the guy who can fly number four in a three-on-one Weasel flight and do much more than just hang on. As far as I'm concerned, we *were* asking for it, and I agree that we're damned lucky we're not being interrogated in Hanoi right now, end of speech."

Leo came right back. "Great speech, Ken. But what can we do about it if we only have one F-model, stay home?" I didn't have a good answer, and I could see the discussion was going nowhere, so I apologized and suggested we call it a night. Leo and the others agreed, but we challenged ourselves to give the concept of a three-on-one Weasel flight some critical thought. It was an unworkable combination.

I thought about that mission all the way home that evening, never dreaming I would go back to the same target in a strike flight just two days later. I had done several things wrong, and I knew I needed more than luck to survive again. I needed to learn from my mistakes and improve the way I had flown that mission.

After the debriefing, I made a beeline for the 354th Squadron personal equipment room. It was late, but I knew Sergeant Perry would be waiting. He never closed up until the last pilot was back safely.

"Sergeant Perry, we've got a problem," I said. "This helmet is too loose when it gets sweaty, and we need to shrink it or squeeze my head into a size smaller. Whatever it takes, I'm not going back to Six-A with blinders on. If I get hit, I want to at least see what hit me."

"It's your head, Major," he said with a smirk as he started to strip padding out of the liner. "It's not shaped like a standard helmet."

After more than an hour of cutting and fitting, we decided to go to an undersized helmet with minimum padding. I tried it on, and it felt like my head was in a form-fitting vice. "That's great, it fits perfect," I said. "It hurts now, but I'll get used to it in a mission or two while I'm enjoying seeing what the hell I'm doing."

Sergeant Perry laughed, "I hope you never need this helmet for crash protection, Major. It won't save your brain, but it will damn sure hold your head together for the medics." I laughed and added that surviving a crash was not first on my priority list.

Sergeant Perry put the finishing touches on the helmet and stuck it back in my bag and hung it over my parachute and G-suit on peg number 8. We turned out the lights and left together.

Back to JCS 19

The next morning the strike force went back to the same area to hit an adjoining target, JCS 19, in the outskirts of Hanoi. I didn't make the schedule, so I watched and listened as the strike force launched at first light.

Don Asire was the force commander. Don tried his best to get to the target but was forced to turn back because of bad weather. Undaunted, the flight led by the 357th Squadron commander tried to sneak in under a cloud deck but ran into some low-flying metal. He got hit and lost the use of one rudder pedal, while his element lead took a hit just behind the cockpit. Both made it home with help from the tower and an anxious SOF (Supervisor of Flying). Results, two more damaged aircraft, and the weather was still ahead by a wide margin.

I had to settle for a training flight with Captain Harry E. Higgins. If Hank hadn't been such a great fighter pilot, he could have made millions playing a tough gunslinger in movie westerns. He was big and burly and short on words. He had a chipped tooth and a scar above his upper lip from an old football injury. When he laughed, the scar made his mouth appear to snarl just before he broke a broad smile. Hank Higgins became a good friend and close adviser. He had a long record in fighters and was a walking encyclopedia of sage sayings about the F-105 and flying in general.

Before I went to bed, I made an entry in my journal about the prospects for the morning mission.

Saturday, 3 December 1966.
Seventh Air Force changed the frag again. All week it's been execute and hold on 19 and 51.10, but tomorrow Seventh will execute on the secondary target with a 15-minute alert to switch back to the JCS target. Now they're going either/or. What next?

The answer came early. It was Sunday, the fourth of December. We got our salt tablets with breakfast and another shot at JCS 19 or 51.10. The mission had all the earmarks of another white knuckle disaster.

9

MiGs Everywhere

Sunday, 4 December 1966.

Detroit flight was a total disaster. Every mission over North Vietnam is different, and each one is memorable, but Detroit flight may stand as the low-water mark of my tour. It exemplified the chaos that results when flight integrity and mutual support are lost and not regained. We violated every principle of fighter warfare, broke every rule of judgment, made every mistake we could possibly make, yet, we returned to tell about it.

To add to our trouble that day, Detroit flight had the good fortune to encounter sixteen MiG-17s right over the target. The details of this encounter, including all of our glaring errors, were carefully documented and included in a classified study titled *Red Baron Report*. Even a casual student of air warfare would conclude that Detroit flight had their collective heads "up and locked" but somehow mustered the grit to make it home and laugh about it.

It was my twenty-first mission and second trip to the infamous JCS 19/51.10 target complex near the Phuc Yen MiG base near Hanoi. I was flying with the 333d Squadron again and on the brink of understanding the danger of staying in Package Six-A too long.

Captain Gerald Hawkins was leading Detroit flight. Hawk had a lot of time in the F-105, but he was brash and unpredictable. Captain Ron Scott was Detroit Two. Ron was a quiet, dependable wingman. Lieutenant Colonel Ben Murph was Number Three and my element leader. Murph was a gruff, no-nonsense guy who was relatively new to the F-105 and working his way up the experience ladder toward a job as squadron commander or operations officer. As individuals, Detroit flight had plenty of talent, but it was the first time any of us had flown together.

A thorough flight briefing was the key to a successful mission. There was no such thing as a normal mission over North Vietnam. Consequently, an abbreviated flight briefing that relied on "use standard procedures" was usually a blueprint for failure, perhaps disaster. When I heard a flight leader say, "You have the tail numbers and target data. Start engines at four-zero, check in on squadron common before taxi. Everything else is standard procedure, any questions?" I knew we were in for some surprises and an exciting mission. That's how Detroit flight started out against a pair of tough JCS targets on a sultry Sunday afternoon wrought with danger.

Detroit was the first bomber flight into the target behind the Ironhand flight and the mission commander leading the flak suppression "chopper" flight. As we turned down the ridge, the radio chatter increased, and it sounded like the Wild Weasels had their hands full. Moments later, a series of monotone MiG warnings from Motel control blanketed the radio. The strike force was headed straight down the valley toward Hanoi at 1,000 feet off the deck.

Because the weather was marginal, we were prepared to go to either target, based on the judgment of the mission commander. Our flight path was on a line that split the two targets; the railroad yard at Yen Vinh on the right, and the fuel storage area at Phuc Yen on the left. Detroit was in a left-echelon formation set up for the pull-up and right-hand roll-in on the rail yard, the closest target.

At the last minute, the mission commander decided to pass up the rail yard and hit the fuel storage area at Phuc Yen. Detroit flight was right on his butt and didn't have enough time to react properly. The mission commander called "Pulling up," and before our formation could switch sides with the echelon, Detroit Lead started a sharp, turning pull-up to the left. As Number Four, I was jammed on the inside of a steep, climbing turn toward the element.

As we climbed for the roll-in point, the horizon blossomed with orange bursts of flak and streaming SAM trails. The flak was heavier than I seen before. The chopper flight had started fires that raged with enormous clouds of smoke and dust, but the gritty little bastards on the guns were still firing.

I was forced to slide by Detroit Three on the inside of the pop-up. I could have drifted higher and fallen in behind him but that would have been suicide. A high, stationary target was duck soup for the AAA gunners. As I went by Three, I assumed he would follow me down the chute to the target, but I didn't use the radio; it was already jammed with overlapping calls and threat warnings.

At the apex of the pull-up, I rolled inverted and pulled the nose of the aircraft down through the horizon to a steep dive-angle toward the target. As I rolled the wings level, I caught a glimpse of an airplane that should have been number Three, but wasn't. Instead, a silver MiG-17 was in close formation off my right wing tip. *What the hell was he doing!?*

We were diving through 11,000 feet and still above the heaviest flak layer. The pilot of the MiG must have been confused but he stuck with me. *Brazen bastard, I hope he follows me down the chute and gets a taste of the flak his gunners on the ground are dishing out.* I looked back down at the ground rushing up, and that was the last I saw of him. Getting bombs on the target required undivided attention. If a MiG pilot had the balls to tag along for a shot at me in that environment, I figured he was welcome to it. Meanwhile, I had a rack of bombs to deliver.

Bombing Through a MiG Formation

My dive-bomb pass was stable, but I couldn't spot the fuel storage area for all the flak coming up and gray smoke obscuring the target area. A constant stream of red fireballs flashed past my nose. I could see the flak sites, so I decided to bomb one. Just as I released my bombs, the sight filled up with MiGs, a formation of them. Lead called, "MiGs all under us!" They were in flights of two crossing from right to left in a close, trailing formation. It looked like we had interrupted an air show. They must have flushed from Phuc Yen figuring we were going to hit the air base and were on their way up to engage us.

Through my windscreen, it looked like it was raining bombs and some were starting to hit and explode under the MiGs. I chuckled as I imagined the shocked reaction the MiG pilots must have been having. "What a way to hit MiGs," I thought. "I hope my bombs get at least six of the bastards."

The situation presented a rare opportunity to attack the MiGs with an advantage. I was tempted to break left to press the attack, but I pulled up hard and turned out to the right, as planned, behind another F-105 I thought was Detroit Three. He was headed for the ridge and I assumed that he had passed me in the dive and was following the lead element. We needed to reestablish flight integrity in order to defend ourselves and perhaps attack the MiGs as a two-ship element. We were strung out and extremely vulnerable to SAMs and to the MiGs, which were up in numbers I had never experienced before. It was a unique opportunity to bring our guns to bear on the enemy.

At the bottom of my bomb pass, I had heard someone call, "Clean 'em up and bringing her around to get the MiGs." It sounded like Detroit One, but I wasn't sure, and it was difficult to interpret "bringing her around." I suspected that Hawk had decided to break left to engage the MiGs but the rest of Detroit flight appeared to be headed to the right toward the ridge.

Moments later, the anguished calls of Detroit One made it clear that he had turned left with the MiGs and had bitten off far more than he could chew. "I've got MiGs everywhere, there goes one head on. Oops, I think I've been hit!"

Detroit Three answered, "Roger, what's your position and altitude?"

"I'm going two-four-zero right on the deck. I'm getting hit several times, I think. I got cannon balls going all around me!"

Detroit Three shouted back, "Come on, get up out of there Detroit!"

"I can't! I got a whole bunch of'em behind me!"

There was a short pause before Three responded. "Okay, Detroit, there's a MiG turning south here."

"Okay, it's an unfriendly," Detroit One affirmed pathetically. Seconds later he declared emphatically, "Okay, Detroit, let's get out here to the southwest!"

We were already out of there as far as I was concerned. I was terribly confused, and a rapid succession of radio calls between Detroit Three and myself would only serve to confuse and frustrate me further. I was convinced that I was closing on Three, and I kept telling him that, but he insisted he couldn't see me. "Detroit Three, this is Four. I have a tally. Continue your turn, I'm at your eight o'clock, one mile out and closing."

"Roger, Four, still don't have you," Three responded angrily.

By coincidence, the airplane I was chasing did everything I asked Three to do to, but something seemed fishy. It took a few anxious minutes to figure out that we were chasing our own tails in a stupid mix-up and didn't realize it. Except for Lead, Detroit Two, Three, and Four had come off the target as planned but in a different order. We were going out Two, Four, and Three. Detroit Two was out in front without a leader and didn't acknowledge any radio calls. He must have been petrified. He was alone and trying desperately to out-turn an airplane he thought was a MiG closing in for a kill off his left wing. "I've got one on my ass I can't get rid of," someone called frantically on the radio. When I heard the call, it sounded like Two and I suspected that I was the MiG he was trying to outmaneuver.

It was an airborne version of the comedy classic, "Who's on First." Detroit Two thought Detroit Four was a MiG, and Detroit Four assumed that Detroit Two was Detroit Three. Detroit Three thought Detroit Four was Detroit Two, and all the while, Detroit One had gone in the opposite direction with sixteen MiGs in hot pursuit. It would be impossible to restage, but it actually happened.

Meanwhile, back in the MiG furball, Detroit One was on the deck and streaking for the safety of the foothills. The radio was saturated with calls as Barracuda, Rainbow, Texas, Ford, and Cactus flights entered the target area. In between "BREAK, BREAK, BREAK," and "TAKE IT DOWN," Bonecrusher control flooded Guard Channel with a series of MiG warnings.

In the midst of it all, someone had the audacity to call, "Get you one of those MiGs, boss. There's about eight of them down there swarming around like flies." Boss must have been an F-4 flight leader.

Three had taken control of Detroit flight and was trying desperately to round up Two and Four and somehow locate Detroit Lead amongst all of the confusion. "Detroit Four, this is Three. Do you have me?"

"Rog, Three. Four has you!"

"Where's Two?"

"No idea."

Detroit Lead finally called over the Black River leaving the high-threat area. Seconds later, Detroit Two broke his silence and checked in on the radio, "Two's at the Black, I had one on my ass, but I finally shook him." We were still confused, but we were all alive and headed out in the same direction. The next step was to find each other and get back to a post-strike tanker.

Just as the situation was starting to look better, Detroit Three lost all of his navigation equipment and needed assistance. Detroit Lead followed with the news that his engine was vibrating and "just about to come apart!" *Talk about being snakebit, what else can happen?*

"Detroit, let's get out of the area. This is Lead. Go to button two and check in, over."

"Detroit check!"

"Three."

"Four."

"Two's on, negative tallyho!"

We were headed west and approaching the Laotian border. I was with Detroit Three, and we were trying to get oriented in order to join on Detroit One and hopefully find Two. Lead thought he had taken some hits in a head-on pass with a MiG-17, and the condition of his aircraft was uncertain. The situation was tense, and it soon got worse. "There goes the engine. So long, you guys. I got flameout," Detroit One radioed rather matter of factly.

Detroit Three stuttered, "Roger, squawk May Day, and let us know just before you bail, Detroit One."

"Roger, I'm going to stay with it for a long time to see if I can get the damned thing started!"

"Stick with her dad, stick with her," Three repeated resolutely. "Four, do you have Three? What's our bearing to Channel Ninety-Seven?"

"Four is at your seven o'clock, a quarter-mile back. We are forty-four east of ninety-seven."

"Who's forty-four east of ninety-seven?"

"Detroit Four, over!"

Our radio transmissions were saturating the strike egress frequency, so we switched over to Guard Channel to cope with the emergency. When we checked in on Guard, Detroit Lead called, "I got her fired back up, hot doggies!"

Hawk had restarted the engine on the emergency fuel system, and it was running smoothly for the time being. We were approaching Channel Ninety-Seven in northern Laos. Detroit Three called Bonecrusher and asked for assistance. "Bonecrusher, Detroit declaring emergency. Detroit One has flamed out once and gotten it restarted. Advise Red Crown to set up for a possible Rescap. Detroit flight will need a tanker."

"Roger, Detroit. Bonecrusher will relay to Red Crown. Detroit One, your position?"

"He's swinging ninety-seven and heading direct for Channel Thirty-One. Detroit Four, this is Three. Give me a bearing on ninety-seven."

We needed a tanker in case Lead bailed out and we had to cap him. He was south of us at 28,000 feet and making a beeline for an emergency recovery at Udorn, with 4,000 pounds of fuel remaining. We still hadn't located Detroit Two, and Three was concerned about him. "Detroit Two, Three here. Do you have a tally?"

"Detroit Two has a flight of two at three o'clock. Four, rock your wings if you read me."

I rocked my wings but there was no acknowledgment. Detroit Two had someone in sight but it wasn't us, and I hoped he could find a tanker on his own.

Post-Strike Tanker

Detroit Three was having a difficult time trying to gather up our remaining flock and get to a tanker. His navigation equipment was down, and he had lost his heading indicator. "Four, why don't you come on up here and take the lead, over," Three called with resignation. As I slipped by him, he finally saw me. "Fuel state, Detroit flight? Three has a thousand."

"Two, twelve hundred and still no tally."

"Four, one thousand."

Red Crown gave us an emergency vector. We were low on fuel, so I asked Crown for the closest available tanker. The airways were jammed with calls from the rest of the strike force, and as usual, the post-strike refueling tracks were rather hectic.

I finally spotted a tanker. He was slightly low at our ten o'clock position about 5 miles out and closing. I pointed him out to Three and started a descending turn to join him. As we approached the tanker, I saw a single F-105 trailing the boom, and I knew intuitively that it was Detroit Two. Sure enough, we had finally found our lost wingman.

After a minute or two of radio gymnastics, we established contact with the tanker, and I slipped into the refueling position with 800 pounds of fuel remaining. We each took on fuel and departed the tanker as a flight of three headed for home. Detroit flight was almost history and I felt relieved.

Hawkins made it to Udorn safely and returned to Takhli after a thorough inspection of his airplane revealed no damage and all systems as operable. We met in the 333d Squadron building after an extended and somewhat embarrassing intelligence debriefing. Our faces were grave as we gathered to dissect the mission.

Murph was visibly upset. His square jaw was set, and the muscles in his cheeks rippled. He lit into Two and chewed his ass for losing sight of Hawk in the target area and continuing on his own without a word to anyone. Next, I took some heat for turning inside Murph during the pop-up, but the bulk of his criticism was reserved for Hawkins. Detroit had done a crummy job, and Murph was livid. As far as Murph was concerned, Hawk was through as a flight leader and would have to work like hell to get back on the mission schedule. You could hear a pin drop.

I was thankful just to be back to talk about it, so I excused myself to let the 333d wash their dirty linen privately. They knew how I felt. If the pre-flight briefing had been as thorough as the post-flight debriefing, we might have avoided some of the mistakes we made on the mission. We were lucky that no one got hammered, and we all knew that luck wasn't the key to survival.

After a quick stop at wing headquarters for a peak at my in-basket, I was off to the stag bar and a rendezvous with a couple of soothing martinis. The place was buzzing, and Detroit flight was the topic of conversation. "Well look who's here," said someone at the bar. "It's Detroit Four. Let's say hello, fellas."

"Hello ASSHOLE!" the bar replied in unison.

I ordered a "deep dish olive pie" and braced myself for the ribbing.

The next morning came very early again, and it turned out to be another "double pumper." We had hoped for a change of pace, but Seventh Air Force was determined to get to JCS 19/51.10. So we were headed back downtown at first light. As usual, the weather was doubtful.

Coming off the tankers, we were diverted to another target due to weather. It was a dandy—a railway bridge at Yen Bai about 60 miles northwest of Hanoi. Yen Bai was a dogged little town situated in a prominent loop in the Red River and known for layers of barrage flak.

I was Gigolo Three in a four-ship flight carrying 750-pound bombs. A new, relatively inexperienced but alert lieutenant was flying my wing.

The weather was crummy, but the flight leader found the bridge and we hit it, dropping a span. Just as expected, the ground guns were active. Relentlessly, the AAA gunners pumped flak at us with two layers of gray 57mm barrage fire and a black umbrella of 85mm bursts. Coming off the target, Gigolo Four got hit in the tail, but the damage was minor. It was his first encounter with flak but he made it home okay with a timely lesson on the value of jinking.

During the mission debriefing, the intelligence officer told us that word had come in from Seventh Air Force that we were going back to JCS 19/51.10 "until we destroyed both targets, even if it killed us." His somber tone was alarming, and it was easy to figure out who "us" was. It sounded like someone at headquarters thought we were loafing.

For the next eight days, both F-105 wings tried in vain to strike JCS 19/51.10. On 7 December, I noted in my diary that *I expected at least a raid on Haiphong to commemorate the Day of Infamy, but no—still sitting on JCS-19.* Before it was over, the warning from the intelligence shop would prove to be closer to fact than speculation.

Kingpin Three is Down

On 8 December, our wing made it to the outskirts of Hanoi before having to yield to the weather. In the process, every MiG at Phuc Yen flushed, and we got in a heck of a fight that cost us our 354th Squadron commander.

Don Asire was Kingpin Three leading the element in the force commander's flight when he got jumped by MiGs and forced down into the ground fire. At very high speed, he tried to punch off his wing tanks, and one would not jettison. Out of control at desperately low altitude, Don apparently hit the ground trying to fly his crippled airplane. Kingpin Four reported losing sight of Three, hearing a short beeper, and that was all.

All hits were hard to take but I felt especially stunned over the loss of Don Asire. He was a close friend, a devoted commander, and a very sensitive person. It was a senseless loss of a beautiful airplane and thoughtful leader. The idea of hitting a two-bit rail yard and lousy fuel dump in rotten weather just to satisfy the ego of some limp-dicked civilian analyst really enraged me. Don Asire was special, but he was just one of many who answered the call so I "sucked it up" and got ready for the next mission.

I knew that Gene Conley would move over from the 357th to take command of the squadron, and I thought back to our meeting in the stag bar when Don had told Gene that he deserved his squadron. What a tragic prophecy.

After several more false starts, we finally made it to JCS 19 on 14 December and put the railroad yard out of business. We had paid a heavy price in terms of emotional stress, morale, and aircraft losses during those first two weeks of December, but the pilots were determined not to break under pressure. In spite of the load, their spirit was remarkably resilient.

While leaving the target, Fosdick Three took an Atoll missile right up the tailpipe. Captain Spade Cooley and his flight were climbing out over the foothills just west of the Black River when a MiG-21 nailed him. It was Spade's first trip downtown, and it was a beauty. His aircraft exploded in a burst of flame, broke in half, and started tumbling. Miraculously, the ejection seat worked, and he was able to get out, but he was down dangerously close to Hanoi.

An Air Force rescue team made a spectacular rescue despite a company of North Vietnamese soldiers who were combing the area. By shear guts and selfless valor, a Jolly Green rescue helicopter was able to pluck Cooley from a small mountain clearing surrounded by enemy and fly him to safety. It wasn't until he stepped down on the ramp at Udorn that he realized his back was seriously injured.

Spade was airlifted home for surgery and months of recovery, but his ordeal, and the determination of the team that rescued him epitomized the spirit of our effort against JCS 19/51.10. Like the intelligence guy said, "It damn near killed us!" For the twelve-day period, our losses totaled ten aircraft down, seven crewmen killed or missing, five captured, and three crewmen recovered by USAF helicopter.

Tactical Pod Formation

Although our QRC-160 radar-jamming pods were in short supply, we learned to make the most of their ability to jam and confuse the North Vietnamese ground radars. We employed the pods in mutually supporting formation tactics, which proved to be effective against the ground defenses but still flexible enough to allow us to maneuver to the target.

Essentially, we flew a standard, tactical spread formation with 2,500 feet between the elements horizontally and separated vertically by as much as 1,500 feet. A flight of four aircraft carried either two or four pods total, depending on the target and pod availability. Theoretically, if all the pods worked properly and the flight maintained a spread formation with overlapping jamming coverage, a flight of four F-105s would look like a square-mile of reflected energy, a blob of light, to a ground radar operator. A box of radar clutter that big moving at 600 knots toward a target left little doubt that it was a flight of F-105s, but the trick for the SAM site was to figure out which part of the box had an airplane in it.

The QRC-160 pods were originally made for use as Soviet bomber simulators in mock raids against our own U.S. air defenses in the late 1950s. The pods were never intended for rugged use in actual combat conditions, surely not repeated use in the environment they were experiencing aboard the F-105. Consequently, the QRC-160 pods were a precious few, and they required constant maintenance and tender-loving care.

The original pods were manufactured by General Electric, but the Hughes Aircraft Company ended up with the contract to support the existing pods with spare parts and to manufacture additional pods in sufficient numbers to keep up with attrition.

The replacement ALQ-170 pods were supposed to be carbon copies of the originals, but something got lost in the translation from General Electric to Hughes Aircraft. The new pods didn't perform very well and balloons starting going up in high places in Washington.

At Takhli, we asked for help and got it in the form of Hughes Technical representatives and some very extensive maintenance procedures. We even had a visit in December from the chairman of Hughes Aircraft, Dr. Allen Puckett, who came to see firsthand what we were talking about. His visit helped and no doubt demonstrated an important corporate commitment to their product, but it was the undying dedication of our own maintenance troops that finally spelled success with the jamming pods. The few that we had worked well, had a significant impact on our tactics, and most probably reduced our loss rate.

During our strikes against JCS 19/51.10, we noticed a marked increase in the use of MiGs by the North Vietnamese Air Force. The shift from SAMs to MiGs was a welcome change, but it took us a while to figure out that it was a response to the effectiveness of our jamming pod formations and a good omen as far as our survival was concerned. The increased use of MiGs required some tactics changes on our part, and it in no way lightened the threat of AAA guns. But everyone looked forward to the opportunity of shooting down MiGs. It added a touch of class and chivalry to an otherwise nasty and relentless struggle.

The U.S. Navy was quick to see the new opportunities that the heightened MiG activity presented, and they sent a team from their carrier task force to Takhli to propose a novel idea. The Navy wanted to use F-105s on normal strike missions as MiG bait for their "last, real fighters," the F-8

Crusaders. In order to mask the caper, the Navy planned to operate with the Air Force in Route Package Six-A and offered us corollary hunting rights in their Package Six-B—no real bargain.

Their briefing was received with keen interest at our level, but we knew the concept they proposed would require approval far above our pay grade. It represented a great show of interservice cooperation, and the surprise could have netted some MiGs initially. But I sensed that the concept would never stand the scrutiny of Seventh Air Force. There were too few MiGs and too many aspiring aces. Sure enough, the war continued in compartments, and the Navy's initiative was lost in the shuffle.

Later, we would learn that an Air Force plan for a bold MiG sweep was secretly hatching at the 8th Tac Fighter Wing at Ubon. In less than a month, our jamming pods would be used in support of Operation Bolo.

The effectiveness of the jamming pods on ground radar and the increased threat from MiGs served to spark another innovation in our strike tactics, one we had the authority to implement on our own. Well, almost.

The General Electric 20mm M-60 Gatling gun in the nose of the F-105 was a formidable weapon. At a firing rate of 6,000 rounds per minute, we could expend our load of 1,012 rounds of armor-piercing and high-explosive ammunition in ten seconds. The gun was respected by the North Vietnamese pilots even though the F-105 could not turn in a tight, maneuvering fight with a MiG.

The awesome firepower of the M-60 cannon made a difference in the aggressiveness of the MiG pilots and the defensive employment of the MiGs used to intercept F-105 strikes. Just the chance that a MiG might find itself cornered in front of an F-105 for one growling second of 20mm firepower had earned the deserved respect of the North Vietnamese.

Ironically, the F-4 and F-105 each had the air-to-air weaponry the other needed for kill balance. The F-4 needed a gun to go with its turn capability at close range, and we needed a missile we could use to surprise MiGs at longer ranges.

The F-105 could carry the short-range, heat-seeking Sidewinder air-to-air missile. On missions when we expected to encounter MiGs, the shooters, numbers one and three in the flights, carried two Sidewinder missiles on one of the outboard wing pylons. The trouble was that two missiles were probably twice as many as we needed on any mission, and we paid heavily in terms of increased drag and fuel consumption to carry them.

The Sidewinder was designed for use at high altitude and was not intended to undergo the high speed friction and heat loads associated with flight at 600 knots on the deck. To our dismay, we discovered that most of our missions took the Sidewinder far beyond its design limits, and that many of the missiles we fired were probably damaged earlier beyond usefulness. Consequently, it made sense to carry fewer missiles and properly use the ones we carried rather than drag them home for the missile shop to discard in the junk pile. As a last resort, some of our more enterprising pilots started firing Sidewinders at hot ground targets in hopes of getting some use out of the aging missiles.

After repeated missions, scorched Sidewinders were returned to the missile shop for a thorough checkup. Missiles that were returned to service were sent to the paint shop for a cosmetic touch up. In an effort to return the missiles to showroom condition, one of our painters sprayed paint over the infrared sensing window of the warhead fuse by mistake. Fortunately, his error did not go undetected, because it could have been disastrous in terms of blind missiles or early detonation. The overzealous painter got a strong lecture and enough paint thinner to correct his error.

In order to save expensive missiles and reduce unnecessary drag, we decided to modify the Sidewinder pylon missile rack to a single rail. The concept was nicknamed "Slim Jim," and Colonel Broughton, our vice wing commander, assigned the project to me on a priority basis.

We made the modification to the rails in our shops at Takhli, and I flew two test flights with the new configuration to check the vibration response of the single rail and document the revised fuel consumption data. In a matter of days, our base shops had modified several missile pylon racks, and I put together the paperwork needed to take the modification forward to Seventh Air Force for review, approval, and forwarding to Thirteenth Air Force in the Philippines.

Administratively, our airplanes belonged to the Thirteenth Air Force, and they were very covetous regarding the peacetime rules governing aircraft modification and configuration. The change we had made on our own needed documentation, test, and the ultimate approval of the Air Force F-105 system manager, notwithstanding that it would come after the fact. We realized that our combat innovation might be viewed as bending the system, but we felt justified in going ahead, expecting approval.

To test the single-rail modification under close to combat conditions, I flew a test mission with a Nail FAC in Laos against a battalion of Pathet Lao he said were hiding in the deep jungle. We used a damaged missile that came off the rail smoothly and flew stable. *"You can't miss the trees,"* I noted sarcastically in my journal. The test was a far cry from bagging a MiG in a dogfight, but it gave us the aerodynamic confidence we needed to employ the system.

We began flying with Slim Jims over North Vietnam on a daily basis before we had approval. Eventually, I would have to sell the idea at headquarters, and I hoped to be able to grease the skids in Saigon without upsetting too many rice bowls. I wasn't looking forward to that day in the barrel.

Two More Planes Down

The 355th Wing experienced only two noncombat, operational aircraft losses during the nine months that I was there, and both occurred in the space of a week in December 1966. The first one happened during a test flight for a recurring write-up for engine compressor stalls on an F-105D, S/N 58-1160.

I had flown the airplane a few days earlier but could not duplicate the malfunction. On a subsequent combat mission, the problem showed up again, so the airplane was returned to maintenance for more investigation.

On a test hop the next afternoon, airplane number 160 roared down the runway; seconds after liftoff, the engine compressor stalled, the fire light came on, and the pilot ejected. From his open parachute, the pilot watched the airplane crash into an irrigated field below him. Before he touched down, swarms of Thai peasants were busy removing the wreckage.

By the time the base fire truck and emergency crews reached the scene, the only piece of the airplane left for salvage was the damaged engine. Even the ejection seat and a lap belt that was suspected of malfunctioning had been taken. In flying safety terms, we had suffered a double loss and were faced with a dilemma. We had lost an aircraft and most of the evidence needed to find out what had happened.

Because Vern Frye was an experienced maintenance officer, he was appointed to head up the accident investigation. Vern was at his wit's end when he returned to the trailer late that night from the crash scene. All of the important evidence was gone except for the engine, and it was buried in the middle of the klong (swamp) out of reach of the heavy lift equipment. What a predicament!

On a lark, I told Vern to solve the problem with money. Given enough Baht, Thai villagers could do anything. I suggested that we park a flatbed trailer on the levy road beside the field, with a promise to reward the bearers of a J75 engine handsomely, and leave them to their own devices.

The ransom worked. The next morning a battered jet engine was found loaded on the flatbed and ready for the trip back to the base for evaluation. We thought we knew what the problem was, but the accident investigation team needed the evidence. Vern thought I should be recognized for my ingenuity, but the story didn't make any of the USAF flying safety periodicals, and it was just as well.

The next day, I was back on the mission schedule with the 354th Squadron. I flew a noncounter in Laos with a wingman the squadron wanted evaluated. He was the only lieutenant in the wing with a record of difficulty, dating back to his training at Nellis. He could do everything but fly formation and put bombs on the target. That didn't leave much we could count on.

The flight went all right until we got to the target. *"He panicked when we rolled-in on our backs. His bombs were short, and he broke the wrong way coming off the target. I had to bust him."* The squadron didn't like the outcome anymore than I did, but we all knew the kid desperately needed retraining before he busted his ass and took someone with him. It was his last mission, and word spread through the wing like wildfire. I was a hard-nosed bastard. It didn't surprise me, but I did feel lonesome.

That night I ran into Major Ted Tolman at the bar. Terrible Ted had just arrived from Nellis. He was a wiry down-easter from Maine and an aggressive, hard-hitting pilot.

Ted knew the kid I had busted, and he listened intently as I told him what had happened. His narrow eyes flashed under his dark, bushy eyebrows. "You're a hard-ass all right, but you did him a favor," Ted said with a rasping bit of cutting humor. "Now tell me who's got balls in this wing and who are the pussies?" Ted hadn't mellowed. Something told me that the North Vietnamese were going to notice his contribution to the war effort.

The next morning, I flew a strike mission against a highway river bridge in Route Pack Five with the 357th Squadron. It was my twenty-sixth counter and it felt good to round the one-quarter mark of the tour, but I was getting stale flying on the wing of every Tom, Dick, and Harry. I needed a change of pace, so I welcomed a trip to Saigon to brief Seventh Air Force Headquarters on our Slim Jim proposal.

On the way to catch the T-39 Scatback courier, I picked up a copy of a Bangkok paper. I was shocked to read the headlines, "AMERICAN FIGHTERS BOMB VIETNAMESE CITY." The press had seized on some propaganda that we had bombed residential areas in Yen Vinh instead of the rail yard. JCS 19 had cost us dearly, and now we were accused of killing civilians. *Bum rap! Considering the weather, the flak, and all the MiGs that were up, it's no wonder some of the bombs were off the mark. The bastards deserved it.*

I snuffed out my cigarette and headed across the ramp for a seat on Scatback Delta. The afternoon sun reflected off the ramp, and the heat was stifling. I was upset with the press but there wasn't a damn thing I could do about it.

We flew nonstop to Tan Son Nhut and landed just after sunset. What a shock. The ramp was congested, and the field looked like a war zone. We taxied to a deserted revetment and unloaded quietly in the darkness. I jumped in an unmarked pickup with a Vietnamese driver and asked for a ride to operations. He could have been a Viet Cong for all I knew.

With some difficulty, the driver explained that he had been told to take me off-base to a nearby hotel in Saigon. It troubled me, but I had no choice; I was at his mercy. As he drove clumsily through the dimly-lit, littered streets toward the gate, I was stunned by the conditions I saw. Every Air Force headquarters I had visited before was like a country club, and in my naive experience, I expected the same at Tan Son Nhut. The fact that a war had been going on for years had escaped me, and I felt like an idiot.

As we jerked through the streets of Saigon, the harsh reality of the war in Southeast Asia really began to sink in. The gruesome pictures in *Life* magazine were coming alive before me. For the moment, I had forgotten about the 355th Wing in Thailand and the morning flak over Hanoi. All that seemed distant in the middle of a war torn, dirty city.

The Hotel Ariega was another sobering disappointment. Even in the midst of all the squalor, I somehow expected to find an island of opulence remindful of what had once been Saigon, the Pearl of the Orient. From the balcony of my room on the fourth floor, I could look down on the alleys surrounding the hotel. Shots rang out sporadically, and it seemed incredible that fighting might be going on in that neighborhood. Where could I get a good steak dinner in the face of all that? It was a selfish and irrational thought, but I hadn't had a bite since breakfast.

There were three other bunks in room 409. They belonged to three Army officers who lived in the hotel and were involved in the skirmish outside. I couldn't get over it. *I had landed in the middle of a real war movie with real soldiers, real bullets, real Viet Cong, real rats and devastation, and no steaks or pretty girls!*

There was no central latrine in the hotel, so I took a leak against the wall in the corner of the room. As I watched my urine run down a trough and out a spout onto the alley below, I thought about the irony of the war and the events that had brought me to it. I went to bed and thanked God for my country and the safety of my cozy trailer in Thailand.

Early the next morning, I tried to arrange for transportation to Tan Son Nhut but met with no success. There was no telephone service to the base and the young Vietnamese night clerk was absolutely zero help. He was indifferent and surly, and I'm still not sure he wasn't a Viet Cong moonlighting in a government hotel. He finally gave me directions to the base, so I set out on foot armed with a bag of briefing charts and a heart full of worry.

After a brisk walk through the slums of Saigon, I arrived at the main gate of the base out of breath but thankful. The Vietnamese military police at the gate were as discourteous as the boy at the hotel, but I assumed that they were good guys. After a slight delay, I worked my way through their bureaucracy and caught a ride to a drab building marked Seventh Air Force Headquarters.

I had an appointment with Brigadier General Edward McGough, the director of out-country operations for Seventh Air Force, who had a reputation for being both receptive and reasonable. After an initial meeting with his staff, I was ushered into his office and he greeted me warmly.

General McGough had a busy schedule, so I got right to the point. I described the Slim Jim project and illustrated the modification with pictures of our test installation. General McGough liked our proposal and said he was surprised that we weren't already flying with the single-rail Sidewinder. I had to confess that we were, and he smiled smugly. We discussed the air war over North Vietnam briefly, and then he had to duck out to attend a staff meeting with Lieutenant General William Momyer, Seventh Air Force Commander. General Momyer's nickname was "Spike," but he looked like "General" might suit him better.

General McGough's staff drafted a message to Thirteenth Air Force that did not reflect the same enthusiasm for the project I had detected in his reaction to my briefing. The message endorsed the Slim Jim modification in principle but left a lot of room for logistics bureaucrats to drag their feet.

I thanked the staff and asked for help in rescheduling my return flight to Takhli. It was barely midmorning and I had accomplished my objective. My flight was scheduled for the next day, but I didn't relish the idea of killing a day and another night in Saigon or the Hotel Ariega.

While I was waiting for an answer from Scatback Operations, one of the staff officers took it upon himself to explain what he did and how a Frag Order was written. He was a major who headed up the Alpha Team in the Frag Shop, and he epitomized the frustration and defensiveness I had heard attributed to the fraggers.

I asked him about the wooden nameplate he took from a side drawer and put on top his desk. He explained that the headquarters staff was on duty twenty-four hours, and in order to accommodate the congestion of people in the small offices, each of the shift chiefs shared the same desk but

had a separate drawer for their papers. I tried not to laugh and to be atten-
tive, but it wasn't my morning for staff minutia. I asked him for directions
to the Officers' Club, and excused myself for a spot of early lunch.

The Officers' Club was anything but inviting. A large sign crudely
printed from a stencil hung outside the door, "Check Your Weapons Before
Entering the Club." A red 55-gallon drum filled with sand was positioned
horizontally under the sign with a half-moon opening large enough for the
muzzle of a weapon. Once again I was reminded of the proximity of the
war, and I felt a little naked not having a weapon.

As in most Officer Club bars, there were some familiar faces, so I joined
them for what proved to be a long afternoon. The food was unattractive but
edible, the drinks were cheap, the air was heavy with cigarette smoke, but
the company was delightful and worth the unpleasant conditions. We
talked and enjoyed some animated fun, but I couldn't help but notice that
the Army officers around us just sipped their drinks and stared blankly at
the ceiling.

Word came back that my Scatback schedule could not be changed, so I
settled in to enjoy more stories out of the past and prepare for another
evening at the Hotel Ariega. My companions had heard about the Ariega
and confided that it was reserved for out-of-country pilots who were naive
enough to come to Saigon in search of pleasure. We laughed and later that
night someone was kind enough to find me safe transportation back to the
Ariega.

The same night clerk was on duty when I arrived at the hotel, and I read
him the riot act about his manners and the importance of an early morning
wake-up call. He had the temerity to ask if I would like a girl for the night.
I told him there wasn't that much Scotch whiskey in Scotland but the point
was totally wasted.

The next morning was a rerun of the previous day, with the addition of
a first-class hangover. I overslept so I threw my things in my B-4 bag and
headed out on foot for Tan Son Nhut. The clerk was still dozing on a cot
under mosquito netting, clad only in G.I. underwear and wearing rose-col-
ored glasses.

The sun was just starting to come up on the back streets of Saigon and I
was upset, late, and frightened. If anyone approached me, I decided to
act like my B-4 bag was a satchel charge armed to go off if I dropped it.
I looked in vain for a familiar uniform and a ride to the base, but there
were none.

I finally arrived at the main gate only to find myself facing a maze of
barbed wire and a platoon of angry looking "White Mice" South

Vietnamese military policemen armed with machine guns. It was the morning rush hour, and the guards were checking identification papers and observing the predominantly civilian crowd which pressed for entrance.

I must have stood out like a sore thumb in my rumpled uniform with my "satchel charge" in hand. After looking me over carefully, the guards waved me through with total indifference. I was tempted to give them a street-side lecture about "fighting for their roachy asses over Hanoi" but decided not to. I was thankful to get through the gate and be on my way to Scatback operations.

I came close to missing the flight, but a friend of mine was the aircraft commander, and he delayed long enough for me to make it. One of the other passengers was the new chief of the public information office at Seventh/Thirteenth Air Forces. He was on his way to visit our bases in Thailand to see firsthand what was going on. He seemed like a good head, so I let him have it with my unvarnished views on Tan Son Nhut, Saigon, and the Hotel Ariega.

When I got off the plane, I kneeled down on my hands and knees and kissed the ramp. Randy Plumb met me and listened to my story over breakfast. Randy dubbed me "the President of the Seventh Air Force Fan Club." I laughed sarcastically and headed to the trailer for a shave and fresh underwear.

Later that morning, I reported the outcome of my visit with General McGough to Colonel Broughton. He seemed pleased, but he warned me that I might have to go to Thirteenth Air Force and PACAF Headquarters in Hawaii to sell Slim Jim, as well as a couple of other "minor modifications" we had come up with to enhance the war fighting capability of the F-105.

Marines South of the DMZ

The morning after I returned from Saigon, I flew a mission that was diverted to support a company of U.S. Marines in trouble southwest of the DMZ. It was unusual because we were not supposed to engage in the war in South Vietnam, and it was ironic because the memories of the chaos there were still fresh in my mind. It was the only mission I flew over South Vietnam.

We were under the control of Cricket in Laos and sent to support some Marines on an emergency basis. Had our presence over South Vietnam been reported, it could have caused some serious political consequences in Washington, but the Marines were desperate for help, and we were the only air support available.

We crossed the DMZ and tried to contact the Marine command post on their radio frequency, but they couldn't hear us. The radio was jammed with urgent calls for help, which were frustrating because the Marines didn't realize we could hear them. Cricket tried third-hand to vector us to their position but the effort was futile. Finally, we dropped our bombs on the mark of a local forward air controller and hoped for the best. The bombs exploded in a thick stand of jungle but apparently went unnoticed. The frenzied radio chatter from the ground continued for several minutes and then subsided as we headed west for home plate.

I was proud of Cricket for having the grit to divert us, but I couldn't get those Marines off my mind. It seemed like another horrible page in the book of futility that our ground forces endured daily.

On return, the weather at Takhli had turned nasty. We didn't have enough fuel to go to Korat, so we opted for two-ship formation approaches in the weather. I was the element leader and had to fly the gauges all the way to touchdown. My landing was a controlled crash, but we were home safe without any damage, and I was ready for some rest and quiet reflection.

That afternoon, I took a well-deserved nap in my trailer only to awake in a drenching sweat. It was midafternoon, and the main power had failed, leaving us without air conditioning in the trailers. It was 93 degrees with 105 percent humidity. It reminded me that we were in the jungle, and my thoughts returned the cries of the desperate Marines. Their fate would remain a mystery.

Element Bombing

It was the twentieth of December 1966, and the Bob Hope USO Christmas Show was scheduled for that afternoon. Understandably, everyone was more interested in seeing the show than flying, so I volunteered for a morning mission with the 354th Squadron. It was a rare opportunity to lead an element with Lieutenant Glenn Gidel on my wing. I had trained with Glenn at Nellis, and he was one of the sharpest wingmen in the outfit.

The target was a well-defined road segment in Laos, and it was an opportunity to demonstrate a new bombing technique that I had developed and was trying to implement. Rather than roll in singly and dive-bomb one at a time, I felt it would be better to roll in and bomb as elements of two, a technique I called "element bombing." It was easy to do if the element leader was an accurate dive-bomber. Tactically, it meant being able to put two loads of bombs on target accurately in much less time, with reduced exposure to enemy fire.

Before the mission I briefed Glenn carefully, and he seemed eager to try. All he had to do was stay on my wing during my dive-bomb attack, clear my six o'clock position, and pickle his bombs when he saw mine come off the rack. It was a wingman's dream as far as execution was concerned; in, off, and out quickly with a minimum of fuss and danger.

With the help of a Nail FAC we found the target quickly and rolled in as a two-ship element. The pass was ideal. We dropped a beautiful stick of twelve bombs, which hit the target dead center. It was a demonstration of element bombing at its best, and it worked perfectly.

On the way home, I heard a loud bang during the descent and felt the airplane shudder abruptly. It felt just like I had taken a direct hit in the aircraft midsection. We were over Thailand and out of range of enemy guns, but it was conceivable that a MiG might have followed us out with some crazy notion of treachery. No one in the flight looked disturbed and Glenn was in position to see anything unusual. The gauges in the cockpit looked normal, but I kept hearing the oil-canning sound of bending metal, like a giant beer can being crushed under pressure.

When the fuel warning light came on, I discovered the problem. The vent on the fuel tank in the bomb bay had malfunctioned, and the bomb-bay tank was collapsing under increased atmospheric pressure as we descended. It was an unusual malfunction and the results were startling, but it was easy to correct once I realized what was happening. I moved the fuel-tank selector switch to the bomb-bay tank position to recycle the vent shut-off valve, and the problem gradually subsided.

I landed without further incident, but my beard had grown a quarter of an inch and I had some brown pucker marks in the seat of my flying suit. The crew chief was less than thrilled because he was faced with the tough job of replacing a bomb-bay tank instead of attending the long-awaited Christmas Show. He changed the tank in record time, with lots of help from his buddies on the ramp, and they all made the opening number.

The Bob Hope USO Christmas Show

After years of watching the Bob Hope USO Christmas Show in newsreels and on television, I was finally going to see one live. At first it was hard to believe that I was actually standing in the heat of the afternoon jungle sun watching the real Bob Hope read cue cards and make wisecracks that only he could make funny.

Along with some other dignitaries, Senator Stuart Symington was sitting in the front row, wearing a suit and tie. He looked hot, flushed, and very uncomfortable. The Thai jungle provided an unusual setting for a Christmas show, but it was a piece of home and the men were enjoying it immensely.

Bob Hope looked older and more strained in person, but the jokes, the wit, and his timing were as fresh as ever. Miss Universe drew her share of whistles and cat-calls from the ogling airmen but they got the biggest kick out of Joey Heatherton, a sexy young starlet who was dressed for the occasion. She did a couple of song and dance acts between the comedy routines, but her talent didn't really matter. It had been months since most of the guys in the crowd had seen an American girl, much less one that pretty.

Senator Symington was finally overcome by the heat and had to be helped to a first-aid station. I was worried about Bob Hope and several of the other performers who were really sweating, but they keep right on going for over an hour without pausing. Everyone was enjoying the show and very appreciative of the personal effort Bob Hope was making so unselfishly. He was truly a class act, a part of America brought to the front lines to remind us of home and what we were fighting for.

Miss Anita Bryant was the featured singer. She sang *The Battle Hymn of the Republic* for her grand finale. When she began to sing, a hush came over the crowd. For more than five minutes, she held them spellbound in the palm of her outstretched hand with each inspiring word. Tears filled my eyes. It was a beautiful rendition and she got a standing, cheering ovation. As I looked around me, I was almost overcome by the open sensitivity of the American airmen. To a man, they were smiling proudly, with tears streaming down their cheeks. It was a remarkable sight and a reminder of what our nation stood for.

After the show, Bob Hope and Senator Symington were driven to the Officers Club in a fancy Jeep for an all-ranks party, which was a smashing success. I continued to be amazed at their stamina. We all longed to be home in time to see clips of the show on Bob Hope's Annual Christmas Television Special, but that wasn't even vaguely possible.

When the stage was cleared and the last C-141 roared off for the next stop on the USO tour, it was back to business as usual. By sunup the next day, the Bob Hope Show was just a pleasant memory etched in the hearts of some very dedicated, homesick airmen.

The sortie rate began to tail off in anticipation of a rumored Christmas bombing lull, and I used the time to catch up on some paperwork. By Christmas Eve it was official. The U.S. would observe a forty-eight hour bombing pause, with the exception of missions over Laos. For some reason, Laos didn't share the same diplomatic grace that North Vietnam received, but that didn't matter. The stage was set for a well-deserved, if not welcome, break at Takhli. The pilots didn't want it, but the ground crews needed a chance to rest and let their hair down.

F-105 pilot Maj. Ken Bell, USAF.

Pilot hooch at the Royal Thai Air Force Base at Takhli, Thailand, home of the 355th Tactical Fighter Wing.

Rescue photo that would have been used for identifying the author had he been downed.

Smoke billows from the start cartridge of a flight of F-105 Thunderchief fighter-bombers as they fire up for a mission.

An F-105 on a refueling boom. The difficult maneuver was performed going in and returning from North Vietnamese targets.

En route to a target, two F-105s leave a tanker.

Target photos show the Viet Tri ferry and pontoon bridge complex (left), the author's fourteenth mission, and the Ha Gia railroad bridge (below, in box), his thirty-eighth.

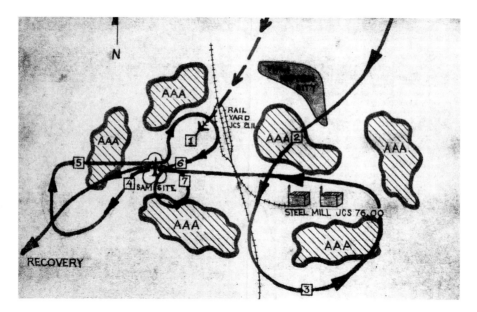

Ken Bell was Maj. Merle Dethlefsen's wingman on March 10, 1967, when Dethlefsen won the Medal of Honor during the first strike on the Thai Nguyen steel mill. Bell received the Silver Star for gallantry. This diagram was part of the after-action report.

"Flame-out!" On May 3, 1967, Bell's plane ran out of fuel while on a desperate search for a downed pilot. In this painting by Mike Machat, Col. Jack Broughton waits his turn while Bell refuels on the boom of the tanker.

FLIGHT LINEUP CARD

94/2971

CS		SE	TAXI	TO	TOT	SIF
BEAR		1247	1257	1314		4
1	BELL	413	B21			
2	SHEEHY	748	86			
3	FERGUSON	181	A20			
4	LAWRENCE	336	A7			
	PIOWATY					

TOR 6000   NWLO 175   TOS 185
LS 111   2M   MAX REF 155   X
SAR 14   P364.2 S 282.8
CROWN/SANDY/JOLLY GREEN
MIG GATEPOST
SAM NORTH WESTERN

	CS	ARCT	FL
A	BR 42	1430	120
A	Post Strike		
R	BR 61	1555	210

1st WAY 620   1635   150
P.S. WAY 1645   230
2nd WAY 153   130
P.S. WAY 1645   250

TGT ICS 9.10 RAP   CODE ROSE
HECTIC PORK RANDOM
COORD 21.23 26   106.65 58
ELEV 35   WINDS P   C
ALT STG 2963   S 14/5

TGT SQ69 R.R'VD   CODE TARNISH
COORD 21.35 20   105.57 25
ELEV   WINDS P
ALT STG   S

TGT R.78 II   CODE NURSE
COORD 1824/05 10 T 1833/05 33
ELEV   WINDS P 28/7
ALT STG 2958   S 23/5

BORD
VIOL GUM DROP
EXEC PRESIDENT 1G600 WONDER BREAD
CANX STEVENS ADAM ALLEYWAY BASE TIME
TOT
CHG DECADE
RECALL SWAGGER STICK
WX CITIES
SUCESS SORREL
UNSUCC LUCKY STRIKE
DIVERT PUMPERNICKLE

DO Form 1, Jan 66

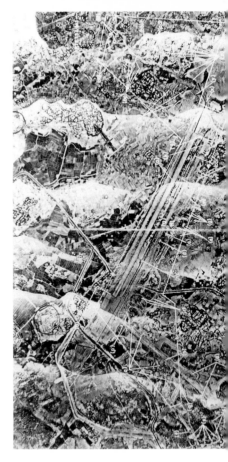

On June 13, 1967, Major Bell was a flight leader during the first strike on Kep airfield. From left, the flight lineup card, a target photo, and the result as headlined by *Stars and Stripes*.

U.S. Jets Blast 6 MIGs on Ground

SAIGON (UPI)—U.S. warplanes darted past thunderstorms over North Vietnam Tuesday to blast six more MIG jets on the ground, a pair of ammunition dumps and two main rail lines, spokesmen said Wednesday.

The Americans drove straight into the country's industry-rich Red River delta and ranged up and down the southern panhandle in 97 raids, dropping hundreds of tons of bombs in attempts to short-circuit the movement of war materiel south.

Over South Vietnam, meanwhile, other U.S. jets bombarded the communists in 493 sorties, but the price was another plane.

Officials here said communist groundfire probably hit the plane, an F100 Super Sabre which crashed 14 miles southeast of Pleiku.

The pilot was killed, spokesmen said.

For the first time in nearly a week no American planes were downed over north Vietnam, despite the thunderstorms

PACIFIC STARS AND STRIPES

AN AUTHORIZED PUBLICATION OF THE U.S. ARMED FORCES IN THE FAR EAST

Vol. 23, No. 166   ★★★ EDITION   Friday, June 16, 1967.

Security Council Kills Russ Mideast Demands

Compiled From AP and UPI

The United Nations Security Council Wed...

The 100th mission! Bell is congratulated by (from left) his wingman, Lt. Paul Sheehy; Col. Jack Broughton and Lt. Col. Nelson MacDonald; Col. Bob Scott; and his fellow pilots of the 354th Squadron.

F-105 Losses in Southeast Asia

The air war over North Vietnam devastated the F-105 fleet through stea attrition. Of the 833 Thuds built, 382 were lost from 1965 to 1972. The los were not all directly related to combat, but were losses nontheless. Brol down by year, they occurred as follows:

YEAR	COMBAT	OPS	TOTAL
1965	60	8	68
1966	111	16	127
1967	87	15	102
1968	34	12	46
1969	14	5	19
1970	7	3	10
1971	1	—	1
1972	7	2	9
	321	**61**	**382**

The Christmas Eve party at the Takhli Villa looked more like a wild New Year's Eve orgy than a celebration of the yuletide season. Nearly every bar girl in Thailand must have come to stake her claim on the proceeds of the evening. By the time I got there, the bar was a sea of shouting drunks who had long since let more down than their inhibitions. "Come on in, Major, the water's fine. These sharks won't bite," they welcomed me as I stood looking shocked in the doorway.

I was certainly not a prude but what I saw repulsed me. The mood of the party was irreverent and hardly in keeping with the spirit of the Christmas season. It was in sharp contrast with my naive expectations for a traditional Christmas Eve celebration, and I resented it. My reaction might have been different if I had been there from the start and brought up to a party pitch gradually.

After a couple of drinks, I excused myself and caught a taxi back to the base. Let's face it, I was old-fashioned when it came to having a traditional Christmas, and I wanted to be alone to suck my emotional thumb and enjoy my memories. I could do that best in my trailer with some traditional music and a few nips from a cozy bottle of Scotch whiskey.

I missed my family and close friends and felt a little homesick. It was my third Christmas away from home but the first one in combat. I read the Bible, opened my presents, and gave myself the day off.

I thought about the guys who were in Hanoi as prisoners and felt guilty about feeling sorry for myself. I wondered what a bombing lull really meant to the North Vietnamese and got angry thinking about how they might take political advantage of one of our most sacred days. While we cooled our heels they were no doubt replenishing their supplies.

By late afternoon, I felt terribly sentimental and lonesome, so I went to the stag bar for some company. The place was jumping. I joined some friends, rolled the dice for a couple of beers, had a big dinner, and decided to go back to my trailer to go to bed early. The day after Christmas would come soon enough and dawn would mean back to the business of warfare.

Our first mission after the pause was directed against targets in Route Package Five northwest of Hanoi. We were cautioned not to fly within 10 miles of the capital city. The briefer stressed that it was an extra political restriction, but it was music to my ears.

Our flight was assigned to bomb a railroad bridge over the headwaters of the Red River just south of Lao Cai on the Chinese border. The target was close enough to Red China to warrant extraordinary care to avoid navigation errors. A dispute with Hanoi was one thing, but incurring the wrath of Peking was quite another—the analysts in Washington would be livid.

We intercepted the Red River north of Yen Bai and turned northwest toward Lao Cai. The radar-warning gear indicated that we were being watched by SAM radar but were not in immediate danger. The flight leader pushed up his throttle and began a gradual, weaving descent up the river valley.

The valley narrowed to a gorge as we approached the border. I was Number Four, but I watched the coordinates of our position on my Doppler navigation display carefully. The flight leader pressed on, looking for the railroad bridge. We passed over several small villages, but I didn't see one that looked like it might be Lao Cai. We were two minutes past our estimated time-on-target, and I sensed that we were getting into trouble.

"Lead has the target, twelve o'clock, five miles." I glanced down at my Doppler. Damn! We were only 10 miles short of the 23d parallel and across the Chinese border. I started to say something but didn't, hoping that my Doppler was in error.

The leader popped up, and we rolled in on a short railroad bridge spanning the narrow gorge below us. Our bombs hit their mark, the bridge dropped, and we left quietly and unceremoniously. We didn't encounter any defenses but I felt like Chairman Mao was looking over my shoulder.

When we debriefed, the intelligence officer asked if we had stayed clear of Hanoi, but he didn't mention Red China. We pointed out the coordinates of the bridge that we thought we had hit, and the intelligence officer almost collapsed. On closer inspection of the map, he convinced himself that we were mistaken, and he changed the coordinates of the bridge in the strike report (OPREP) to coincide with those of a target inside the North Vietnamese border. Sometimes the reports out of intelligence were as inaccurate as their estimates.

We held our breath for a couple of days, waiting for the big Red shoe to drop. But apparently the Chinese government didn't have the lines of communication with their remote areas that we gave them credit for, or they just chose to not make an issue of it. My guess is that by the time someone in authority found out about it, the episode had been overtaken by events, or lost its political impact. In any case, the bridge in China was my last mission flown in 1966—the next day was New Year's Eve.

After my experience on Christmas Eve, I decided to celebrate New Year's Eve in the stag bar and stay within stumbling distance to my trailer. As it turned out, I was right about the stumbling part but a few feet short on the distance.

I had a little too much to drink trying to settle a argument that was really none of my business. Colonel Broughton, who only came into the stag bar on special occasions, got into a one-sided discussion with a liaison pilot from the Fighter Weapons School about the tactics the Wild Weasels were using. The major had some ideas about flying Weasels that didn't exactly square with those of Colonel Broughton.

I should have kept quiet, but for some damn fool reason, I jumped in on the visitor's side and let the whiskey do the talking. It was a dumb thing to do, but not near as dumb as my decision to try walking home on my own afterward. Somewhere along the way, my gyros tumbled, and I made an unexpected landing in the gravel. I touched down nose wheel first, just short of my trailer. What a lulu! Sometime later, I made the following note in my diary:

> I vaguely remember falling flat of my face about 2 A.M. on my way home from what turned out to be an ugly evening, a New Year's Eve party in the club. Morning broke to find the left side of my face all but removed by gravel, what a mess. Vern Frye thought I was dead and fetched Dr. Frank Carbone. He patched me up, but I couldn't make the commander's reception. My QRC pods left without me to go on the Big F-4 Mission. I went to see Colonel Hill in the afternoon to find out if I still had a job on the wing staff—he didn't know but he knew Colonel Broughton was angry. What a way to start a New Year!

10

"QUEEN FOR A DAY"

NINETEEN HUNDRED SIXTY-SEVEN got off to a rip-roaring start once I recovered from my New Year's Eve crash. My ego was bruised, but worse, the left half of my bulletproof mustache was missing.

I apologized to Colonel Broughton for my actions in the stag bar, and he and Colonel Hill gave me some new guidance regarding my job as chief of Stan/Eval. I appreciated their renewed support and felt good about starting over with a clean slate.

My mustache was recovering, but the pains in my head and neck were beginning to worry me. I wouldn't even risk getting a Thai haircut for fear the shoulder massage might kill me. Dr. Carbone took some X-rays that revealed nothing serious. He suggested I stay off the flying schedule for a few days and give mother nature a chance to heal the damage. There was plenty of paperwork to catch up on, and I had a training program to put together for our in-house 355th combat crew training course. The commander had approved the program and wanted it implemented on a priority basis.

Operation Bolo

On 2 January 1967, a combined force of forty-eight F-4s from the 8th and 366th Tactical Fighter Wings flew a mission called Operation Bolo. It was much bolder than the MiG sweep concept proposed to us earlier by the Navy and more attractive, because it didn't depend upon real F-105s for MiG bait.

The concept behind Bolo was unique and straightforward, but the operational timing was difficult, and the planning turned out to be very intricate.

Two strike forces made up of six flights of four F-4s each would simulate a normal F-105 strike using similar formation tactics, radio call signs, and the radar signature of our jamming pods to masquerade the operation. Normal mission support would be provided by F-105F Wild Weasels and B-66 ECM aircraft, including MiG warnings and electronic intelligence from the College Eye and Silver Dawn aircraft.

The objective of Bolo was to deceive the North Vietnamese ground radar network and exploit weaknesses in their command and control system in hopes of flushing up MiGs from four bases for a battle royal.

The rules of engagement were streamlined for the occasion. Because the F-4s would be the only aircraft in the target area that day, they would have the rare but short-lived, advantage of operating in a missile-free environment. If an aircraft target appeared on radar in front of the first three flights of F-4s it was presumed to be a MiG and could be engaged without visual identification.

Timing and tactics were paramount. Six flights of F-4s from the 8th Wing would masquerade as F-105s and lead the attack flying over land routes from the northwest toward Hanoi: three flights straight down Thud Ridge toward Phuc Yen coupled with three flights out of the west aimed directly at a new airfield near Hoa Loc, some 15 miles west of Hanoi. Simultaneously, six flights of F-4s from the 366th Wing out of Danang, South Vietnam, would simulate an F-105 strike against the northeast railroad. The F-4s would come from the east off the Gulf of Tonkin and fly down MiG Ridge, hoping to attract MiGs from Kep in the northeast and from Cat Bi Airport near the Port of Haiphong. Short intervals between all of the flights were included to purposely stretch out the mission and tax the fuel endurance of the MiGs to their limit.

Security measures were extraordinarily tight. The F-4 wings needed to borrow our QRC-160 pods in order to simulate the F-105 radar signature and perform the mission. We were ordered to stand down and I was directed to chaperon our pods to Ubon and brief the F-4 crews on their installation and use. I was curious as hell and anxious to go, but because of the battle damage I sustained at the New Year's Eve party, Randy Plumb had to make the trip in my place.

Colonel Robin Olds, the commander of the 8th Fighter Wing, planned and led the mission. The initial flights of F-4s from the 8th Wing executed the Bolo plan beautifully, but the weather turned out to be a discouraging factor. A solid overcast of clouds, with tops at 7,000 feet, covered the entire target area, starting at the mountains west of the Red River and stretching east throughout the valley to the Gulf of Tonkin.

Olds Lead decided to proceed above the overcast. His flight pressed down Thud Ridge as planned, and had actually overflown Phuc Yen and doubled back when the first MiGs were encountered. At last, the North Vietnamese took the bait, and the aerial battle began to unfold. The fight lasted barely fifteen minutes, but when it was over the F-4s from the 8th Wing had bagged seven MiG-21s, plus two "probables." The North Vietnamese fighter force from Phuc Yen had suffered a devastating and decisive blow.

Due to bad weather along the coast and confusion over the mission execution order, the F-4 flights from the 366th Wing did not close the eastern arm of Bolo. The leader of the 366th force orbited short of the coastline, awaiting an order to proceed and hoping for some improvement in the weather. His decision to delay was unfortunate, because the 366th missed the very opportunity that Bolo had anticipated. Several flights of MiG-17s fled the battle over Phuc Yen and recovered at Kep unscathed. The MiGs were low on fuel and would have been ripe prey for an attack by F-4s armed with missiles free to fire without visual identification and the advantage of surprise.

The 366th continued to orbit until they reached the minimum fuel required to return to their tankers. Frustrated, they began the long trip back to Danang without even the scent of a victory.

Overall, Bolo 1 was a success. Despite the mix-up, the 8th Wing waged a decisive air battle on their own with excellent results. News of the outcome spread quickly. Seven MiG kills in one outing was good news and provided a boost for morale everywhere. The *Stars and Stripes* gave Bolo headline coverage. Jealously, we felt that we could have done as well under similar circumstances, but we were delighted for the 8th Wing and the significant success of their mission. Actually, the more nimble F-4 with its advanced intercept radar and air-to-air missiles was better suited for air-to-air combat than the faster F-105, but as Thud pilots we liked to think that the Thunderchief was invincible and could do it all.

Visiting dignitaries were a dime a dozen at Takhli. Hardly a day went by without an official visit by someone eager to see what was going on. Officially, we weren't stationed in Thailand, so visitors had to slip in secretly to rub shoulders with real combat pilots and get a firsthand look at the war up north.

Each of our distinguished visitors received a thorough briefing, which always included an invitation to fly a mission in the back seat of an F-model. "The best way to appreciate what we are up against," Colonel Scott would conclude, "is to have a look for yourself." The visitors usually blushed and pretended not to take him seriously, but he meant what he said and always made it clear that his offer was genuine.

We didn't have any takers among our high-ranking visitors, but when the word got around that we were giving dollar rides in the high threat area, a young Air Force combat photographer took us up on our offer. He wanted a credible story, and he had the guts to put his life on the line to get it. When he landed he was a little green around the gills but he had some incredible combat footage.

On the fourth of January, we received word that Dr. Harold Brown, the secretary of the Air Force, planned a visit to Takhli to inspect our operation and pin on some medals, "gongs" as they were referred to in combat jargon. There had been persistent rumors that LBJ himself might come to the base when we were officially declared present in Thailand, but Secretary Brown was by far the biggest fish to come our way on the celebrity circuit. A visit by Secretary of Defense Robert McNamara had also been rumored, but he had political trouble enough on the front lines in Washington without risking an appearance before the troops flying out of Thailand.

Preparations for Secretary Brown's visit began immediately. Hundreds of Thai laborers worked like ants to transform the base into a jungle paradise. There was an overnight facelift of the grounds around the old wooden structures that faced the flight line. An arch was added over the path that lead from the ramp to the entrance of the Tactical Operations Center, a complex of small windowless, frame buildings that were interconnected and set up on stilts for protection from the jungle.

The finishing touch in the renovation was the addition of a stone-lined pathway that lead through a garden of transplanted banana trees to the steps of the TOC. Functionally, nothing was changed, but it looked pretty and gave us something different to talk about.

When a dignitary visited the base, we hung a hand painted sign across the top of the gateway saying "Welcome *General or Mr Whoever* to the 355th Tactical Fighter Wing." The signs were easily removed and replaced as often as two or three times a day, depending on the density of visits. At peak load, there were probably half a dozen signs in the paint shop in various states of readiness, with enough calligraphy work to keep one painter busy on a full-time basis.

En route from their airplanes to the TOC for a welcoming briefing, all dignitaries were taken through the honored gateway. Without exception, they all noticed their signs, and you could tell that it pleased them. Luckily, none of them ever looked back over their shoulders at the reverse side of the sign. It read "Queen for a Day" in very small but distinct letters. Foolish perhaps, but it was our way of demonstrating a defiant sense of humor. The prank seemed appropriate because it dared to lampoon the ego of high-ranking dignitaries.

On their departure, we reversed the process, and the men in the wing who knew about it thought it was hilarious. It was a small reward for the time we spent doing show-and-tell briefings for a few people who had an ancillary interest in our mission and a primary interest in logging a day in-country in order to qualify for one month of tax-free combat pay.

The first few weeks of the year were very difficult for me. Pressures were mounting, and I was sick with a high fever but didn't have sense enough to ask for help or just say "to hell with it" for a couple of days and get the rest I needed.

The wing was sitting on JCS 51.10 again, and it was frustrating because we all knew that there was nothing there but dust and a nasty flak trap. Aside from combat, I was faced with putting the finishing touches on our in-house training program and getting our trainees in the air before their currency in the F-105 expired. In the office, I was under my own pressure to finish a long overdue White Paper on tactics and reconcile a deteriorating relationship with Colonel Hill.

Gradually, Colonel Hill had become more and more difficult to deal with. He was loosing his grip on his job, and it seemed like he was running scared. I couldn't appreciate his position fully, but I began to feel a little guilty about the anger I held toward him. He was stuck between two powerful and proud men, the wing and vice wing commanders, Colonel Scott and Colonel Broughton, and he simply couldn't stand the pressure.

With each mission flown, Colonel Hill realized that his days were numbered and that he would ultimately be forced to overextend himself or quit altogether, alternatives that were not attractive. The pressure was relentless, and Colonel Hill vented some of his frustration on me, and I had to take it.

As always, there was the constant gnawing inside me to be a part of a squadron and away from the vagaries of a staff job, as valuable as the work was to the mission and the effectiveness of our aircrews. In my diary I lamented, *"This wing job is a very lonely job indeed—I would love to belong somewhere."*

On the sixth of January 1967, I finally got our three trainees airborne on a practice mission, which included heavyweight refueling on a tanker at one of the combat anchors. Lieutenant Colonel Bill Norris, Major Bud Catron, and Captain Joe Abbott were pilots on the wing staff who had volunteered for F-105 upgrade training. They had just returned from being checked out in the airplane but had not received in-flight refueling training. I grew a head of gray hair watching them learn to refuel on Green Anchor 41. Joe Abbott never did get on the boom but it was a beginning.

Bill Norris and Bud Catron were more experienced pilots than Joe Abbott and they adapted to refueling quickly. I recalled my own difficulty on the boom and realized that Joe just wasn't quite mentally ready for aerial refueling. I hoped that he would improve with more practice but Norris and Catron had passed the first test and were close to being combat ready.

After a four-day bout with a rare strain of jungle fever, I was back in the saddle and airborne again with my trainees for a proof-of-the-pudding refueling mission on a Papa tanker equipped with probe-and-drogue fuel transfer equipment. Talk about risky training. I was leading a flight of pilots who had never seen a drogue before, and they were practicing for the first time over enemy-held territory in Laos. The safety guys at Thirteenth Air Force would have lost their minds. I was anxious as hell, but the trainees surprised me and did an outstanding job without a bobble. The mission was a success, the guys were ready, and I wanted to get them into combat while they still felt confident.

It took almost a week to get final approval and enough airplanes for a flight we could devote to getting our fledgling pilots into combat. The commander insisted that I lead the flight and use another experienced flight leader in the number three position. Consequently, I had to cut Joe Abbott and let him wait for another mission to make his combat debut. Joe was disappointed, but we both understood that it was a wise decision. I described the mission in my diary in some detail:

> *Carbine Flight (354th Squadron) 2 + 45 Hours*
> The Pride of PACAF, 355TFW, hung its ass way out and let me take my most promising up-graders, L/C Norris and Maj Catron, over to the lower route packs on a fragged mission. Briefing and departure were delayed an hour unbeknownst to us while the squadrons had a pissing contest about who would be charged with the sorties. The 354th lost the argument but won the day with their attitude. Catron was late for the briefing and, by flight check-in time, two aircraft had already aborted.
> We left the ground with Catron on my wing as #2 and a single-ship element leader. Norris got the spare and met us on the tanker as Carbine #4. Perfect rendezvous and smooth refueling.
> Dropped through an overcast to find Echo and Cricket Control saturated with Army, Navy, and Air Force radio calls. It was hairy. Dodging aircraft, I got my bombs off on a suspected truck park along with #3 and Norris. Catron's bombs did not release but we finally unloaded him using the right pickle button (I suspect) and proceeded to snoop along Route 8 in Route Pack Two for the counter. The element beat us back to Channel 89 at Nakhon Phanom but we recovered without further incident. Norris and Catron logged Big #1 and Norris surprised me with his candid evaluation of the flight during debriefing. He had spotted several errors that #3 had made and he didn't hold back his punches. In short, he had done a much better job than his experienced element leader.

Although they made mistakes, both Bill Norris and Bud Catron did a good job and had justified my confidence in them and in the training program. We had some fine tuning to do, but they were finally on their way, and I was proud of them.

That afternoon, it was Joe Abbott's turn to fly. I had hoped for a two-shipper into Laos, but we had to settle for an air combat training (ACT) mission closer to home. Joe was disappointed again, but he didn't let it show. It was a chance to practice refueling and to fly one-on-one with me before trying it real-time on a mission up north.

Joe Abbott was not a born fighter pilot, but he was giving the transition training everything he had. I knew he needed extra help, and I admired his guts and determination.

Tactics White Paper

The evolution of fighter tactics is a dynamic process, and the first evidence of stagnation and danger in an organization is an unwillingness to consider change. Pilots live and die by instincts developed through the repeated use of tested procedures, and there is a tendency to want to do it the way we always did it because it was comfortable or it worked fine in the last squadron the pilots were in.

Clinging to low-level tactics, born out of years on alert with nuclear weapons in the late 1950s, reaped some enormous losses over North Vietnam a decade later, due to restrictive mission routing and an unprecedented concentration of defensive ground fire. High speed at low altitude had a very useful place in the F-105 tactics book, but it had to be balanced with other tactics and certainly not used exclusively or with predictable regularity.

Tactics within the entire strike force had to be carefully coordinated. In order to be effective as a team, the flight leaders, the Wild Weasel crews, and the F-4 supporting flights had to work together and know what to expect. When both F-105 wings were employed together or in concert against the same or adjoining targets, the frag order directed one of the wings to designate a mission commander for the combined strike forces. Consequently, coordination between the strike wings and all of the supporting elements was especially important. The complexities of multiple mission alternatives and the uncertainty of weather made force coordination very difficult. Therefore, some form of a published, versatile tactics doctrine was all the more important.

Late in 1966 and at periodic intervals starting in 1967, tactics conferences were conducted among the participating wings to affect closer coordination and evolve tactics better suited to the threat, our changing capability, and the tactical environment. The privilege of hosting these conferences rotated among the Thailand-based wings, and the results were always outstanding as well as entertaining.

The Red River Valley Fighter Pilots Association had its start at one of the earliest of these tactics conferences, thanks to the initiative of Colonel Scrappy Johnson, the director of operations of the 388th Wing at Korat and a close friend of mine. Scrappy came by his nickname honestly, and through his leadership, the River Rats became a close-knit group whose number continued to grow into a vital organization, which is even stronger today.

As far as the 355th Tactical Fighter Wing was concerned, we had plenty of combat tested procedures, but we needed to examine our tactics in order to develop and publish a doctrine that we could understand and use as a guide for mission planning and force coordination. This job fell within my staff function of standardization and evaluation.

By late January 1967, I had flown forty missions and had successfully conducted a mini in-house training program, so I had some ideas about improving our tactics and enhancing our effectiveness and survivability. Most of my ideas were based on common sense but a couple of them bordered on revolutionary, and I knew I would need to be clever and very convincing in order to sell them to the F-105 old guard. I decided to try the time-honored strategy of "you had a good idea that I took the time to develop."

Before I had completed the first draft of the White Paper, I discovered the trap of confusing tactics with policy. As much as policy needed changing, it was simply outside the control of our fighter wing and I had to learn to accept that.

For example, as cruel as it may sound, it made a lot of sense to strafe a water buffalo pulling a plow or wagon. They were slow, easy to track, and a short burst of 20mm high-explosive rounds would literally disappear them; they were in one frame of film and gone in the next. Seventh Air Force spotted some being hit during a routine review of our gun-camera film and questioned it immediately. We argued that a water buffalo was as valuable to a North Vietnamese farmer as a John Deere tractor is to an American farmer but the "SPCA office" at Seventh Air Force held sway and we were ordered to spare the buffaloes.

Bombing dikes was another example of a policy change we tried to sneak up on unsuccessfully. The control of water was essential to the agricultural economy of North Vietnam. Earthen dikes were used almost exclusively to control the rivers and retain heavy runoff from the highlands. Compared to most of the targets, dikes were easy to spot, relatively easy to hit, and difficult to defend. An assortment of time-delay bombs and mines would have been an excellent deterrent to their repair, and the results would have had a devastating effect on the morale and economy of the country.

Bat Lake, in one of the lower route packs, was a classic example of a water supply that screamed to be destroyed from the air. Its distinctive shape, from which it inherited its nickname, made it so visible that we used it routinely as a rendezvous point for missions. It backed up mountain head waters for a large agricultural delta, and a few well-placed bombs would have flooded thousands of acres of rice fields, a major highway, and the only railroad linking North Vietnam with the war in the south.

Repeated requests to hit the dam at Bat Lake were denied by higher headquarters on the basis of policy. It was frustrating, but we had to abide by it, so we reconciled our feelings humorously. Even though we were denied an important target, we reckoned that we kept an excellent rendezvous point for lost or disoriented F-4 pilots.

North Vietnam was a small country about 1 percent the size of the United States. In its largest dimensions, it measured about 400 miles north to south, 380 miles east to west, and covered an area of 50,000 square miles, about the half the size of Colorado. On a map, the country resembled a small pork chop, bounded on the east by the Gulf of Tonkin, to the north by China, and to the west by Burma and Laos. The terrain was characterized by a series of jungle mountain ranges and fertile valleys oriented northwest to southeast, with three main rivers emptying into the Gulf of Tonkin.

Politically and geographically, there weren't many ways to approach North Vietnam, and once you got there, there wasn't much to hide behind. Everyone knew where the important targets were, and there were only two ways to approach them: from the southwest over land or from the south and east over water.

Given that a strike force going to the Hanoi area required the support of twelve to fifteen KC-135 tankers, our time-on-target and intervals between strikes were dictated to a large extent by the amount of time it took to turn around a fleet of tankers requiring almost 200,000 pounds of fuel per aircraft. Adding our requirement for maximizing the number of daylight hours available for search and rescue in case of a shoot-down, further restricted our already limited flexibility. Consequently, our strikes were somewhat predictable and anyone who knew geography, had a watch, and knew what time the sun came up could figure out within thirty minutes when we were coming and what target we were gunning for.

Because of our predictability and the concentrated defenses of the North Vietnamese, we had every reason to study tactics and innovate ways to improve our effectiveness. It was a tough problem, but finding the answers held the keys to our survival and longevity.

Jamming Enemy Radar

There were three ways to survive in a high-threat defensive radar environment: hide, maneuver, and jam. Hiding and maneuvering were natural fighter pilot skills, but most of us were new to the art of electronic warfare, and we had to learn to work against radar and look for ways to make the best use of our QRC-160 jamming pods. Fortunately, both F-105 wings approached this problem differently.

The 388th Wing at Korat preferred to approach the target at high altitude and attack from close formation in a quick succession of dive-bombing flights. By relying on the mutual jamming support of the wing formation, the vulnerability of individual flights to heavy AAA and ground fire was reduced during run-in, at the risk of having to operate for a short time in the most lethal part of the SAM envelope. The North Vietnamese responded by firing salvos of SAMs at the attacking formation, hoping to provide terminal guidance during a chance break in the jamming.

Our wing preferred to go in low and fast in trailing flights, using jamming in conjunction with terrain masking. This combination provided a great deal of flexibility, but it also required precise timing and almost continuous maneuvering by each flight and the element leaders. It could also be employed with a number of other variations, depending on the terrain, target characteristics, and differing bombing techniques.

We soon learned to combine each wing's tactics and maintain our own preference for terrain masking. By starting in at high altitude and descending gradually as we penetrated the enemy defenses, we could add another dimension of uncertainty to the defensive problem. Using normal tactical spread formation techniques, we entered enemy radar surveillance with our jamming pods turned on and providing mutually supporting jamming coverage between the flights. On ground radar, we probably resembled a maneuvering box of jamming energy.

As we approached the target area, individual flights could adapt to the conditions they encountered—weather, flak, SAMs or MiGs—and use bombing techniques tailored to the situation. Flight integrity and mutual jamming support were essential for this tactic to succeed.

This combined technique was known as the QRC pod formation, and it was adopted quickly by our wing. Variations in the pod formation were inevitable but they were welcomed as effective ways of keeping a dogged enemy off balance.

Most importantly, both wings used different techniques to cope with the electronic threat, and this served to confuse the defenses. Even though the North Vietnamese knew we were coming, they didn't know in what order, thus they had to guess how to defend against us. If they guessed wrong, we all had a better chance of getting to the target without being hit. If they guessed right, only one wing really caught hell.

Our external fuel tanks usually went dry about the time we crossed the Red River on the way into the target. Individual flight leaders decided whether to retain the empty tanks and drop them later, if necessary, but I preferred to jettison the tanks early under stable conditions. With clean airplanes, we were prepared for any eventuality and could concentrate on the run-in to the target.

Invariably, when flights got into trouble in the target area, the first thing they did was punch off the tanks, and that was the worst time to do it, for a host of reasons. The F-105 was durable and very forgiving, but there was always a risk that a jettisoned fuel tank might strike the aircraft and severely damage a control surface. This risk was pronounced during high-G maneuvering flight, and we suffered several unnecessary losses because of it.

I preached getting rid of the tanks while the flight leader was still in control of the situation. As far as I was concerned, the only thing an empty tank provided was extra weight and increased drag. Understandably, the maintenance folks preferred not to have to replace tanks on a quick turnaround, but they were good at it, and we had literally acres of extra tanks standing by to do their bit for the war effort.

To pilots and ground crews, I became known as "Punch tanks, ready now, Bell!" It was a deserved reputation.

Putting Bombs on Target

The proof of our pudding was how well we put bombs on target the first time. With rare exceptions, dive-bombing was the only way to deliver bombs accurately and survive. The ideal dive attack began at 10,000 feet above the target in a steep 45-degree dive angle, and ended at bomb release, pointed straight down at 5,000 feet, with the pipper on the target. It was the real commitment part of the mission, a ten-second moment of truth when nothing mattered but tracking the pipper to the target. Consistency and speed made for accuracy and survival, but everything else tilted in favor of the ground gunners for those crucial few seconds.

To increase our odds, we constantly searched for new ways to confuse the defenses and concentrate our destructive power more quickly. On every mission, the force commander met with the flight leaders to discuss the target and improvise tactics. Given that accuracy required consistency during the dive attack, the task was to vary ways of getting the strike force to the roll-in point for the commitment to the dive-bomb pass.

Criss-cross bombing, simultaneous attack, and element bombing were tactics that were introduced in the White Paper, and I hoped would become part of our tactics doctrine. Each new technique was developed as an adaptation to the threat, and I tried to use my position on the wing staff to nurture and coordinate these changes with all three squadrons.

Criss-cross bombing was easy to adapt to our low-level run-in technique. At the pull-up point, each strike flight alternated a left- or right-turning climb in order to roll-in on the target from opposing sides and complicate the defensive problem. The scissors effect gave the ground gunners a decision to make, and while they were making it, we hoped to be in, off, and out of range.

Element bombing was an effective way to put bombs on the target with the least amount of exposure. Dive-bombing in formation pairs turned several things in our favor. As a flight of four, our vulnerability to ground fire was reduced because the opportunities of the AAA gunners were cut in half and a good element leader could place twelve bombs on target at once. In addition, wingmen were not as apt to get lost pulling off the target. Despite its advantages, element bombing was slow to catch on but it ultimately sold itself throughout the wing.

Simultaneous attack grew out of element attack. It applied the same bombing technique to flights of four and groups of several flights, typically six. With a one-second delay between elements, a flight of four could be in and off of a target quickly and never lose flight integrity. This allowed succeeding flights to bomb the same target in quick succession, with obvious advantages. The concept of simultaneous attack caught on gradually in our wing, but it was implemented early by the 388th wing as a matter of necessity in their preference for attack from a high-altitude, massed formation.

Once the bombs left the airplane, getting home safely became our primary objective. Typically, egress meant jink to avoid being hit, light the afterburner, re-form the flight, and head for the nearest exit but don't relax. The toughest part of the mission was over, but we were still vulnerable to attack from the rear by SAMs and MiGs, and it was easy to expose ourselves unnecessarily.

Because we were accustomed to exiting the target area in a defensive posture, we seldom looked for targets of opportunity, even though we had enough firepower left to be effective offensively. I didn't like taking unnecessary risks, but leaving a target in the heart of North Vietnam with unexpended ammunition bothered me.

Ted Tolman agreed that we were missing an opportunity to exploit the egress phase of the mission. Even though our job was to put bombs on the target and return safely, it seemed that we could make better use of the time we had in the target-rich area around Hanoi. Why not take the offensive and shoot at something worthwhile on the way out of the high-threat area? We were good at armed reconnaissance in the lower route packs and occasionally got our butts shot off for nothing there, so we reasoned that we might as well do it where the odds of finding something worth destroying were much higher.

We coined the phrase "offensive withdrawal" to describe the phase of the mission we wanted to transform. Although the term "egress" aptly described what we were doing, it had the connotation of "getting the hell out of there," and psychologically it sounded defensive. Ted and I figured that pilots might be inclined to be more aggressive if we labeled egress as offensive withdrawal and flew it that way.

The notion of armed reconnaissance during withdrawal from the JCS target area had an electrifying effect on most of the pilots. I thought Ted and I might be burned at the stake or banished from the stag bar, but it was a sound idea and represented a positive change in our tactics and doctrine.

We decided to test the concept ourselves and perhaps sell it gradually on its own merits. We found plenty of rolling stock to strafe and several guys, including Ted, killed MiGs coming back from targets downtown. However, convincing most pilots that offensive withdrawal had merit proved to be a slow process, even though we were positive that the concept would pay dividends. If nothing else, it would serve to demonstrate a more determined and aggressive attitude to the North Vietnamese at a time when our national will was in real question.

Some of the changes we suggested in the White Paper were not revolutionary. Every day we worked with the tankers and B-66 support aircraft that were stationed with us at Takhli, but we seldom, if ever, saw the crews on the ground other than socially. It didn't take a mental giant to figure out that we might do a better job as a team if we talked to each other professionally before each mission. The stag bar was a great place to discuss what went wrong on a flight, but the briefing room was the place to plan ahead and avoid costly errors.

Everyone seemed surprised but pleased with the idea of asking the tanker and B-66 crews to attend our mission briefings as an integral part of the strike team. The support crews welcomed the chance, and the results were predictable, immediate, and gratifying.

The tactics White Paper was received with mixed reactions. The command section, which helped in its formulation, agreed in principle with the paper but asked me to try it on the squadron commanders and report their reactions. The commander knew that the squadron commanders wouldn't appreciate even the appearance of a staff wienie messing with their prerogatives as commanders and tacticians.

Colonel Hill, who had supported the paper from the outset, backed it enthusiastically until he got wind that the squadron commanders were uneasy; then he dropped it like a hot potato. Overnight, his approval turned to indifferent contempt, and I knew I was in for some rough treatment as a *persona non grata*.

The squadron commanders were more than uneasy; they were almost hostile in their unwillingness to accept what they perceived as a threat to control or dictate the tactics employed within their squadrons. While they liked some of the tactics I was suggesting, they were very skeptical about how changes would be introduced and supported. I agreed with their concern and tried my best to temper their misgivings but I was not very persuasive.

The flight leaders and pilots were more receptive. At least they were willing to listen, and many of them expressed an eagerness to try some of the ideas, given the opportunity. Everyone, including the squadron commanders, agreed that we needed to make changes in our tactics and operate from a documented and coordinated doctrine as a common point of reference.

The evening after I met with the squadrons I was having dinner in the club, feeling let down and lonesome. Gene Conley, the new commander of the 354th Squadron, joined me. Gene and I were good friends, and he sensed that I felt somewhat betrayed and very disappointed.

Although Gene did not support all of my ideas, he complimented me on my willingness to think creatively. He reminded me that it was my duty to prod the consciences of the squadrons. "Be patient, Ken. A measure of success often comes in slight attitude changes or in millimeters, but seldom in miles or very quickly," Gene added as a comforting note of encouragement.

Gene and I finished dinner and went to the stag bar for a shooter. He was enjoying his new job as a squadron commander, but he felt badly about the way Don Asire had bought it and somewhat hesitant about inheriting the 354th Squadron under such tragic circumstances. Gene was a quiet leader, and he had respected Don, but he was determined to put his own mark on the squadron. Tragically, the dark shadows of fate would fall on Gene's path just three days later.

PACAF Management Inspection

The wing had been hitting targets in Route Pack Six all week. For four days, the morning and afternoon missions from both Korat and Takhli had enjoyed excellent results against tough targets, with no losses. We all wondered how long it would continue.

I had been on the ground for a week, putting the finishing touches on the tactics White Paper and preparing for an inspection team from PACAF. I missed flying and wasn't looking forward to a staff inspection in the midst of combat. Given a choice, I would have much preferred facing the North Vietnamese gunners.

In addition, we were notified that another group of QRC-160 experts was in-bound from North American Aviation, and Colonel Hill had assigned me the duty of escorting them. Thanks to Sergeant Satterfield, the stan/eval shop was ready for anything.

When the PACAF inspectors arrived, I was pleasantly surprised. Both were majors and well known for their straightforward approach to flying fighters. One had been the operations officer of my training squadron at Nellis, and the other was one of the first pilots to check out in the F-105 and a longtime friend of our wing commander. We reminisced over a cup of coffee, as Randy Plumb introduced them to our approach to managing weapons and weapons checklists.

Major Bobby Bond was assigned to inspect my office. He was from the PACAF standardization office and he agreed that the role of stan/eval in combat was to review and broker tactics changes and make sure that the occasional numbskull who managed to slip through training didn't bust his ass and ruin an airplane in the process. His message was clear and refreshing, "Minimum paper and maximum tactics."

Bobby asked if he could fly a combat mission. "What would you give?" I fired back quickly.

"A million bucks and a bottle of cheap whiskey," he answered, expecting that his request would fall in the category of too hard to do.

"I'll try under one condition," I surprised him, "a promise that you won't mention my name at Headquarters PACAF as a candidate for your replacement."

He agreed, I got Colonel Scott's blessing, and that afternoon I took the inspector up north for a live combat evaluation. Bobby was anxious at first and a little rusty at flying wing, but he settled down quickly and did an outstanding job. The flak was light, we put our bombs on target, and the mission went in the books as a counter.

After we landed, my visiting wingman was ecstatic, and I had a hunch that we would pass the inspection with flying colors. After a night in the stag bar, the visiting inspector went back to PACAF headquarters tired, but with a smile on his face, never to mention my name as a likely replacement.

No one at Takhli on the morning of 19 January 1967 would forget what happened when Lieutenant Colonel Bobby Wayne, the feisty commander of the 357th Squadron, and his wingman Lieutenant Bob Abbott, finished their tour together and made a 100-mission pass in close formation, going supersonic. They came in low, right above the buildings, and the shock wave hit the base like a bolt of lightning.

I was having breakfast in the club and thought at first that a bomb had gone off on the flight line. The waitresses dropped their trays and lay sprawled on the floor whimpering. By the time I got to the door to see what had happened, the celebrating flight was lined up for a third pass, but even lower.

When I got back to my trailer, I found the maid crouched in the corner, frozen with terror. The shock wave had knocked everything on the wall across the room, including my radio. Even the light bulbs had burst, and Water Buffalo was sure she had been hit by something deadly and evil.

Colonel Scott was furious when he met Bobby Wayne at his airplane. He looked stern and his welcome was subdued. The pilots assembled there were stifling smirks behind pious faces. Colonel Wayne said he was just under the Mach and blamed it on his wingman, but Abbott pleaded ignorance.

The Thais started cleaning up the damage while Colonel Scott had a private one-on-one with Bobby Wayne in his office. The base personnel were highly incensed, but later that afternoon, the 357th threw a double-barreled 100-mission party. It was a knock-down, drag-out affair, which lasted until early morning. Fun was fun but Wayne and Abbott had enjoyed the first and last supersonic flyby.

When I got back to the room late that night, I found a package from the post office. It was my monthly shipment of Mexican food from El Paso. I loved the stuff, but I didn't have a way to prepare it in the trailer. My old buddy Bill Egan suggested that I save the canned goods until there was enough to prepare a meal in the club for anyone suffering from jalapeno withdrawal. In the meantime, we would continue to satisfy the hot section of our taste buds with Thai beef and peppers. Compared to a standard Thai

pepper, the hottest jalapeno pepper on the Mexican border ranked somewhere between hospital food and mild salsa picante.

A Week for Bridges

With the headquarters inspection complete, I resumed flying. On the twentieth and twenty-first of January, I flew consecutive missions against two of
the toughest targets in Package Six-A, the Ha Gia and Bac Giang railroad
bridges. The North Vietnamese defended them like they were the last two
bridges standing in Southeast Asia.

The only railroad and parallel truck route linking Hanoi with the industrial center of Thai Nguyen crossed the Song Cong River at a village called
Ha Gia, just 15 miles north of Hanoi. The railroad bridge was east of the
village, and the target photo showed at least twelve large gun positions surrounding the area.

I was Rainbow Four in a relatively inexperienced flight from the 354th
Squadron. Rainbow Two was a sharp lieutenant making his first trip to Six
Alpha, and I was giving Rainbow Three a check-ride as a new element
leader.

> *Friday, 20 January 1967.*
> Nothing like a morning mission to 6A to take the sleep off your
> teeth. We got to the tanker late, and as the last flight on target, had
> to makeup time on the run-in. Let down through an overcast to the
> Red River and found a lost, lonely F-105 who joined on us. Run-in
> visibility down Thud Ridge was crappy. One SAM came up unguid-
> ed at twelve o'clock. Flak started early and continued heavy at all
> levels. In the pop, I floated high and wide and damn near got it from
> a close burst of 85mm—thought it had me. Rolled in shallow, trig-
> gered the gun by mistake and dropped long on the bridge obscured
> by smoke. Our flight bombs dropped the span! More flak! Jinked
> back up the north side of the ridge and out for post-strike refueling.
> Home and best landing ever. SMMMOOOTH!

We had dropped the Ha Gia Bridge but made some mistakes in the process.
We talked things over during the debriefing and realized that Rainbow
flight had been a learning experience for all of us. We lacked confidence in
each other at first and made some stupid errors, but as the flight progressed
we solidified as a team. We had gone out green and came back a fighting unit.

The mission had been tiring, and I was tempted to go to the trailer for a
nap, but I couldn't resist stopping by the office for a peek at the PACAF

inspection report. Sergeant Satterfield showed me a copy of the draft report we had received, and it gave us high marks in every category. My spirit was uplifted.

Satterfield told me that Colonel Hill was anxious to see me. I reported to his office hoping to find him in a buoyant mood, but not so. Without mentioning the outcome of the inspection, he glanced over his dark sunglasses and reached for his out-basket. "Bell, these need your immediate attention," he said sharply and dismissed me. I left with a stack of QRC-160 reports that needed evaluation before the contractor on-site study team's arrival.

To hell with it! I threw the papers on my desk and headed for the trailer. After a long, refreshing nap, I went to the club and joined three pilots whom we called the "333d stooges" because of their offbeat and burlesque humor. We rolled for drinks, ate dinner, and had a hilarious time until the schedule for the next day was posted.

Both morning and afternoon missions were against JCS targets. I drew the afternoon mission, a strike against a bridge on the northeast railroad with over-water refueling. The day had all of the ingredients necessary for disaster. We hadn't lost an airplane for almost a week, and everyone was edgy.

The morning mission ran into a buzz saw going to the rail yard at Thai Nguyen. Gene Conley was the mission commander leading Waco flight, the flak- and SAM-suppression flight ahead of the strike force. The weather was marginal, and the defenses were poised and ready to retaliate.

When the strike force reached the target, the flak was heavy and the radio was saturated with SAM calls. Waco flight was waging a gallant fight against the defenses but was outnumbered. The skies over Thai Nguyen had erupted into a caldron of boiling flak and gunfire. SAM sites were firing volleys of missiles, and a mushroom of smoke shrouded the area.

The strike flights began to roll-in despite the intense fire and confusion. In quick succession, a stream of F-105s dove toward their target through the blistering canopy of gunfire. "Waco Lead is down!" someone called in shrill anguish. In the heat of battle, Gene had taken a direct hit by a missile; only an ugly ball of orange smoke marked the explosion. No beeper, no chute, and the attack raged on for nearly twenty minutes without noticing; but for Waco Lead the war was over.

News of Gene's fate spread quickly. He had been the 354th Squadron commander less than two months, succeeding Don Asire, who had gone down under similar circumstances. The 354th was snakebit. Gene had completed two previous combat tours in South Vietnam and was one of the most respected leaders in the wing. His loss was a terrible shock to all of us.

On my way to the afternoon mission briefing, I saw Phil Gast walking down the flight line road toward the 354th Squadron. He was in a hurry, and from the determined look on his face, I sensed that he was on his way to take command of the squadron. He had just been promoted to lieutenant colonel and was an odds-on favorite to inherit the squadron. Phil had paid his dues on the staff. He was competent, ambitious, and eager to command.

When I reached the TOC, my suspicion was confirmed. Colonel Scott had acted quickly to minimize the emotional blow of Gene's loss to the squadron. It was the opportunity Phil needed but certainly not his choice of circumstances.

The outcome of the morning mission had cast a pall over the wing and set a somber stage for the afternoon mission. The last place on earth I wanted to go was the northeast railroad.

Bac Giang Bridge and MiG-19s

The bridge at Bac Giang was designated JCS 18.23. It was a vital link in the heavily defended railroad and highway system between Hanoi and China. In less than 80 miles of railroad there were at least 1,000 active flak sites, maybe more. We had been there before, and the idea of going back set my adrenalin flowing. It was a forbidding target in one of the toughest locations in North Vietnam. Just getting to the northeast railroad meant going the long way around over water, with extended refueling over the Gulf of Tonkin.

Unlike Ha Gia, the bridge at Bac Giang provided a crossing for both the highway and railroad on the same structure. The bridge crossed the Song Thuong River just northwest of the village about 8 miles southeast of Kep Airfield, an active MiG base. The area was ringed with an assortment of guns and automatic weapons. The target photo showed six occupied AAA batteries intermixed with smaller automatic weapons positions. Several SAM sites were also active in the area. A trip to Bac Giang was not billed as a stroll through the daisies.

I was Shark Four in a strike flight from the 357th Squadron. To get to the over-water refueling tracks, we had to fly east across the width of Thailand and Laos in order to coast-out near the DMZ. It was a long flight, and it gave us too much time to think about the odds we were facing. Just the thought of refueling on the over-water Brown or Black Anchor tankers had a demoralizing effect on me.

By the time we got to the tankers, my butt was aching. We cycled through the boom twice to fill the tanks and dropped off heading north. We were the last flight in the strike force behind Panda the Ironhand flight;

Dallas, Buick, and Flapper. Each aircraft carried two 3,000-pound bombs armed with delay fuses, a Sidewinder AIM-9 missile, and a QRC-160 jamming pod. With a 650-gallon drop tank on the fuselage centerline, we were fully loaded.

As we flew north, I could see the entire coastline of North Vietnam, the Gulf of Tonkin, and the large Chinese island of Hainan. The coast was beautiful. Cynically, I wondered if it might one day be an exclusive international resort area. Approaching the Port of Haiphong, I could see a carrier and ships operating to the east of Yankee Station, and I thought about the Navy pilots who had come to Takhli. It would have been an ideal mission for the F-8 Crusaders to follow us in, using us as MiG bait.

Large, afternoon storm clouds marked the northern coastline. The weather en route to the target looked threatening. As we approached Cam Pha Harbor, the enemy air defenses began to track us on radar. Judging by the strobes on the RHAW gear, we must have been under the surveillance of every radar site in the northeastern quadrant of North Vietnam.

We turned west at the southern tip of the Elephant Ear Island and started a descent to our run-in altitude. The force commander began threading his way through the heavy cumulus buildups toward the target. The radio cracked with SAM and MiG warnings. The Weasel flight was already in the target area and engaged with several SAM sites.

Shark #4, 21 Jan 1967—#39.
The last man across the target, God that's lonesome! We turned in from the sea and it looked bleak and sounded worse thanks to the Wild Weasels (Panda). Punched the tanks and pressed in. Passed over a beeper which was probably our MiGCAP Bass #3. When we started the pull-up, I sighted two MiG-19s under us heading north. In the confusion, Shark #2 turned the wrong way, forcing us wide and shallow on the bridge, which was already down. 85mm flak was intense. I had to give up and pickle my bombs on the edge of town. We got organized on the run-out but they shot at us from those beautiful islands north of Haiphong. The Ironhand flight was in deep yogurt, Ed Dobson brought home some 23mm hits from a MiG. Eight of us finally got on Brown Anchor 57 for gas. Long mission (3 + 45) and lots of war stories. Col Scott met us in debriefing looking very concerned.

The intelligence officers zeroed in on me and wanted to know all about the MiGs. I reported that I had seen two silver MiG-19s with North Vietnamese or Chinese markings. They were headed north at moderate speed, in a climbing turn toward us, and attempting a desperate head-on attack. Both aircraft fired a short burst and passed out of sight off my right wing at about 2,000 feet range. I last saw them as I rolled in looking for the target. They were in a turn descending toward the airfield at Kep and probably short on fuel.

The debriefing officers reminded me that the intelligence estimate for the North Vietnamese Air Order of Battle did not include any MiG-19 aircraft and suggested that the aircraft might have been MiG-21s. I assured them that the aircraft I had seen were not MiG-21s or smaller MiG-17s. In reply, the intelligence officer insisted that MiG-19s would have had to come from bases in Red China and warned me that the political implications of my OPREP report could be far reaching.

I stuck to my story. The aircraft I saw were MiG-19s; they were silver not camouflaged; they were marked with a red star on a yellow background; they engaged and fired at us; and then headed north toward Kep. I didn't pretend to know where they were based or whether they were Red Chinese.

The debriefing officer looked at me like I had asked him to eat a dead fish. As I parted, he warned me that I was likely to hear from the intelligence shop at Seventh Air Force later that night. Colonel Scott, who had listened to the debriefing quietly, looked stern but seemed satisfied.

During the flight debriefing in the squadron, we talked about the opportunity we had lost so awkwardly. Regardless of their origin, we would never get a better opportunity to engage MiGs. They were surprised, on the defensive, probably low on fuel, and anxious as hell to get on the ground.

Our flight leader reminded me that our mission was to hit the bridge and worry about MiGs later. He was right but I couldn't get the encounter out of my mind. A classic school maneuver would have put us in a perfect firing position. In less than thirty seconds, we could have been in their six o'clock position with our missiles on the way and guns blazing. It would have been all over before the MiGs made it to the traffic pattern at Kep.

The telephone in my trailer had been installed for a month, but it never rang until the night after my reported MiG engagement. I was sound asleep and a little out of sorts by the time I finally got the right end of the phone to my ear. "General Philpott is on the line for Major Bell, Shark Four. Is this Major Bell?" the operator queried. The intelligence debriefing officer was right, my report had reached Seventh Air Force, and the staff was in a dither.

Brigadier General Jammie Philpott was the director of intelligence on General Momyer's staff at Tan Son Nhut. I had never met him, but he didn't mince words and got right to the point. "Are you sure the aircraft you encountered were MiG-19s, or could they have been MiG-21s or 17s?" he asked abruptly. I answered with the same story I had given the debriefing officer, but General Philpott wasn't satisfied. "Is there *any* chance that the aircraft you saw were not MiG-19s?" he asked firmly.

"Yes Sir, they could have been F-100s with Vietnamese or Chinese markings," I said respectfully.

"That's ridiculous, Bell," General Philpott shot back. "Why would two of our own aircraft be flying over North Vietnam with enemy markings and make a firing pass on F-105s?" I agreed that it was stupid notion but it didn't help. He was very upset with my report and threatened to change it himself, based on the accepted intelligence estimate.

With all the respect I could muster, I answered his ultimatum. "Sir, if you're certain they weren't MiG-19s then go ahead and change the report, it's your choice." I felt certain that the aircraft I had seen were MiG-19s but I was willing to let the intelligence community call the shot as long as they were willing to take responsibility for the report. General Philpott grumbled something profane and hung up abruptly. I went back to bed with the uneasy feeling that I had not heard the last word regarding the incident.

Several days later, we were notified to be ready to relocate our jamming pods to the F-4 bases on short notice. It sounded like another MiG sweep was in the wind. On 23 January 1967, Bolo 2 was executed but did not succeed. The weather was perfect for SAMs and AAA, but the MiGs stayed on the ground. Too bad, there might have been some MiG-19s in the fray, maybe even some misguided F-100s marked with red and yellow stars.

Special Treatment for Special People

In late January, a special team arrived from the USAF Military Personnel Center to discuss future duty assignments, a subject near and dear to fighter pilots. We were eager to hear what they had to say and hoped to gain some insight into what the Air Force had in store for us after combat. Most of us wanted flying assignments where we could make the most of our combat experience. I had put my bid in for a reassignment to the Fighter Weapons Center as an instructor.

A colonel who was the team chief opened the meeting with some remarks about the latest revisions to personnel policy and how they related to returning pilots. He assured us that every effort would be made to assign us to jobs that would profit from our experience, and then handed the pointer to a major to cover the specifics.

The major was a rated personnel specialist who had been helpful in arranging my reassignment to fly F-105s, so I had reason to have confidence in him. "The Air Force appreciates the difficult job that F-105 pilots have been doing against incredible odds, and we have been directed to use special care in selecting your next assignment," he said proudly. "The reason that we have come here today is to make certain that we know exactly what you want in order to best match your desires with the needs of the Air Force. As far as we are concerned, you guys are special, and we intend to see that your next assignment gets special attention."

After the briefing, I talked with the personnel officer long enough to assure myself that he knew I wanted to go back to Nellis, and then I headed for my trailer. Their special people pitch had satisfied me.

On the way back to the trailer, I stopped to check my mailbox. I unfolded a message and couldn't believe my eyes. It was a telegram from the office of rated assignments at the Air Force Personnel Center, alerting me for an assignment to the Air Staff in the Pentagon upon completion of my combat tour. The message concluded, "Report to the Deputy Chief of Staff for Research and Development, Directorate of Operational Requirements, Defense Division [AF/RDQSD] on or about 1 July 1967." What timing. I didn't understand the alphabet soup describing my future job title, but I knew I had been done in by another sweet-talking personnel wienie.

Keeping up with the awards and decorations process in the wing was an enormous administrative headache. Each mission flown produced a new set of combat actions worthy of special recognition. The risks and opportunities for daring action were unprecedented. Daily, crews displayed courage that was truly above and beyond the call of duty.

Each squadron had an officer in charge of preparing the paperwork for awards and decorations, and they were constantly inundated with recommendations from flight leaders. The review process was arduous, and squadron-appointed award boards worked overtime and late at night in order to reduce the backlog. At times, the paper workload was so great that it was easy to get discouraged, and most of the awards officers felt "overworked, under loved, and poorly paid."

As with any large administrative process, there were some oversights as well as a few exaggerations and abuses. It was difficult to describe succeeding actions without resorting to repetitive and hackneyed phrases. New superlatives had to be created. In jest, I noted in my diary that "Write-ups have gotten so out of hand that someone is going to have to miss a bridge and empty the ocean with one bomb" in order to get proper recognition.

The awards officers complained of pressure from the top to process certain recommendations more quickly than others. But in the end, those who deserved recognition received it, and those who contrived it were soon found out. On balance, the awards and decorations process was much like a self-righting buoy, it bobbed along with the swells and valleys but it never went under.

Old Green, My First Bicycle

Even though everything on the base was within easy walking distance, I decided to splurge and buy my own transportation. I made several trips a day between my trailer and the flight line, and a bicycle would help save a few precious moments. The likelihood of keeping a bike more than a month was slim due to thievery, but with combat pay and all, I figured I could afford to invest in someone else's long-term transportation system for the time being.

> Bought a bike at the Thai BX, had more fun buying it than anything, cost me $3.00 extra for a small stand. It is English racing green with a blue plaid seat cover.Great transportation and good exercise. I must miss my days as a kid because I've grown attached to this skinny Japanese Greenie.

The Thai BX sold a standard Japanese bicycle for about thirty dollars. It came in two colors and a choice of accessories: kick stand, seat cover, speedometer, luggage rack, headlight, and wheel reflectors. I opted for green, the kick stand, and a heavy-duty locking chain.

Even though bicycles were common on base, I felt conspicuous pedaling around like a proud kid on Christmas morning. However, in a matter of hours, I became accustomed to the bike and began to feel like a part of the landscape. Others had warned me about the affinity Thais had for idle bicycles, so I was careful to lock the bike to something solid whenever it was not in use.

The theft rate was incredibly high, and several bizarre attempts to steal Old Green would fail before I found myself back at the Thai BX investing in a replacement, the second of a total of three bikes eventually lost to the Thai system. Preventing theft seemed almost futile, but we tried all sorts of innovative ways to discourage the crafty bike thieves.

One of our pilots had a large metal sign printed and riveted to the top of his luggage rack. On both sides, it read in large, block letters: "IF YOU SEE A THAI RIDING THIS BIKE—HE STOLE IT." Sure enough, the bike was stolen and probably ridden out the main gate with the sign in full display. The Thai guards on the gate most likely couldn't read English, or if they did, they were probably offended.

11

TEXAS LEADER TO
THAI NGUYEN

ON 29 JANUARY 1967, I flew my first mission against a JCS target near the industrial city of Thai Nguyen. It was the first in a series of missions that would be etched in my memory forever. Anyone who flew over North Vietnam during the 1966–67 time period will remember Thai Nguyen for the ferocious and tenacious character of its defenses. Just the mention of Thai Nguyen still quickens my pulse and stirs sinister feelings. The railroad yard, the power plant, and the steel mill were some of the best defended and most sought after targets of the war. Thai Nguyen was Ploesti revisited.

My first trip to Thai Nguyen was against JCS 21.11, a railroad classification yard just south of town. Lieutenant Ed McCaffrey and I were both flying wing in Opal flight, led by Lieutenant Colonel Danny Salmon, the squadron commander of the 333d Lancers. We were the first flight into the target carrying CBU-24 bomblets for flak suppression, and Colonel Salmon was the force commander. It was a dress rehearsal for a flight I would lead against the same target just five days later.

> First time Mac and I had flown together. We're fragged daily now to 6A, so we're all getting a tad spooky. The call sign Opal being my birthstone and it being Sunday spooked me even more. Mac didn't like the fact that we were in the same flight at all.
>
> Run-in across the Red was normal until Tico #1, the Ironhand, literally knocked himself out of the air with his own tanks. A 450-gallon tank took off the horizontal slab [elevator control]. Larry Biediger and Honey Bear Silva both had good chutes but no SAR. The turn south at Cho Moi was grim with low visibility looking right in the sun. They started shooting early, we popped and I had a beautiful vertical CBU drop on a big flak site. Both Lead and I hit it. The big 100mm guns were firing from the south. Mac thought I was hit

172

on the run-out. No MiGs, no SAMs, and NO SAR! The wing found out they had a loss when the Weasels landed. Heads rolled.

The command section was upset about the circumstances surrounding the loss of Tico One, the leader of the Wild Weasel flight. When I got back to the Tactical Operations Center, everyone was uptight, and Colonel Hill was in a flying rage. Seventh Air Force had called asking about the loss, and the duty officer referred them to Tico Two for the details. He told them exactly what had happened, but Colonel Hill felt that we could have avoided the embarrassment of telling headquarters the part about the tanks hitting the horizontal elevator and causing the airplane to go down. In his anger, Hill fired the duty controller and scowled at everyone in the room as he stomped out of operations center. "Thank goodness he's going on R&R," someone muttered as the door slammed behind him.

I felt terrible about the incident in the TOC and worse about the tragic loss of the Weasel crew. I poured a quiet drink in my trailer and thought about what had happened. It bothered me. Two guys were down and probably scared as hell in the hands of the enemy. One poor guy had been fired for doing his job honestly, and the whole command post staff was on edge, waiting for the next shoe to drop.

Ironically, I heard on the news that night that three Apollo astronauts had been killed in a fire aboard the spacecraft during a test at Cape Kennedy. For a few moments, my thoughts shifted back to my days in the Gemini program and the times I had watched from the Cape as our Titan launch vehicles lifted our astronauts into space. The thought of losing someone during a test on the launch pad had never entered my mind.

It was Sunday night. Tragedy and fate had worked overtime that day.

Texas Leader

Thursday, 2 February 1967: Major Gordon Mickelson called me into his office in the 354th Squadron and told me that he was going to schedule me to lead a flight against the railroad yard at Thai Nguyen the next morning. He wanted to know if I was ready. I told him I would need a good wingman and strong element leader. "How about Paul Sheehy and Randy Plumb," he answered, with a hint of an approving smirk on his face.

Mick planned to lead the mission, but there was a chance that Colonel Broughton might take over at the last minute if he found out that Glenn Gidel, his favorite wingman, was flying his last mission. "If Glenn Gidel has the balls to go to Thai Nguyen flying your wing on his 100th mission, I'm sure as hell ready to lead a flight up there just to see what happens," I said with determination as I left Mick's office. Mick was a tall, skinny guy with tired, deep-set eyes and a serious manner, but he had a good sense of humor and knew what we had to do to get the job done.

As soon as the schedule was posted I rounded up Texas flight and headed for the mission planning room. On the way, I thought about the significance of our flight call sign. *Surely a kid from Texas could remember this call sign—it was ironic.*

I went to bed early but had a hard time sleeping. I was very nervous, and the thought of leading my first flight to Thai Nguyen kept rolling around in my head. It was a lot of responsibility, and I wanted to do everything right, including bringing everyone home. My mind kept clicking over all of the procedures I would have to remember as a flight leader. The more I tried to relax the harder it got.

I heard Vern sneaking around his end of the trailer trying to be quiet, so I got up and we had a long talk about home and our families. When I finally went back to bed it was midnight and only three hours until time to get up. I couldn't sleep then for fear of oversleeping and missing the morning briefing.

It was amazing to me that we could think straight at 3:00 in the morning, but we used to do it morning after morning for days on end. After coffee and a greasy egg, we arrived at the morning mission briefing, only to be greeted with the news that the weather in the target area was stinko, and the mission would be delayed and combined with the afternoon mission. I was thankful that it was delayed rather than canceled, but I couldn't help think about the sleep I had lost unnecessarily. We were told to check back in five hours, so I slipped off to the trailer for a cat nap.

On our return, the lineup had changed but the weather had improved, and it looked like we would be able to get to the primary target. Some flights had been rearranged because Colonel Broughton had decided to fly with Glenn Gidel and let him lead his 100th mission against a secondary target. In the shuffle, Mick Mickelson wound up as the force commander going to the railroad yard—JCS 21.11.

After the weatherman finished his briefing, the intelligence officer hurried into the room. "Gentlemen, I have words. You have been executed on October, the primary target. Good luck," he added as he moved to the screen to discuss the intelligence estimate of the defenses. The target code name stuck in my head. *A kid from El Paso on his first trip downtown as a flight leader, leading Texas flight against a heavily defended target code named October—my birth month. It had to be more than coincidence. I was getting superstitious and the conditions sounded ominous.*

I could feel my anxiety building during the briefing. We were the last flight scheduled into the target area behind the Ironhand, Flintstone, Dagger, and Detroit, so timing was critical. I had been in exactly the same position just five days earlier on our first strike against this target, and the memory of the flak from the big 100mm guns was still fresh in my mind. Someone has to be the last flight over the target, but I was determined to be so close to Detroit flight that the ground gunners would get caught between loading and shooting.

We were carrying six 750-pound bombs with .01-second delay fuses, two inboard 650-gallon fuel tanks, Sidewinder missiles, and jamming pods. I finished the walk-around inspection quickly and climbed into the cockpit. As soon as I started the checklist, I settled down and felt much better. We started and taxied out on time for a 1320 hours takeoff to the south on runway 18. Our TOT was scheduled for 1506 hours, a little later than normal and certainly not ideal for search and rescue operations if they were needed.

My confidence continued to grow once we were airborne and on the way to the tanker. I had a visual tallyho on Detroit flight ahead of us and everything was going smoothly. I must have checked and rechecked our timing a hundred times. My mind was clicking and really focused on what we were doing. I was calm and able to keep several steps ahead of the sequence of events.

I spotted our tanker at our one o'clock position, about 10 miles out and slightly high at his assigned altitude of 17,000 feet. Almost simultaneously, Randy Plumb called a visual on the tanker over the radio. We were closing fast and in good position.

The tanker rendezvous was a critical point in each mission because of timing. It was essential for the strike force to drop off the tankers together with full tanks at a precise point and time. An integrated strike force of some thirty-six aircraft had to leave the tankers with enough fuel to complete the mission and return to the post-strike tankers with adequate reserves.

Each flight had a precise drop-off point and time as part of the coordinated mission plan. Consequently, the last flight to the tankers had the least amount of time to refuel and make the drop-off with the rest of the strike force. The tanker navigators were always willing to help, but it was the responsibility of each flight leader to figure out the timing for the drop-off.

Orange Anchor

"Texas flight, I have the tanker in sight. Go channel nine, two-twenty-nine-five, and check in for refueling," I barked over the radio.

Texas Two and Three checked in, but Four was not on frequency and apparently having difficulty. It was a very crucial time in our rendezvous, and I let the problem distract me when I could least afford to.

"Texas flight, this is Orange Anchor Four-Four. We are at the ARCP [air refueling control point] and ready to start a turn to the north. How do you read, over?" Instinctively, I asked the tanker to standby while we sorted out our radio problem with Four. I should have continued normally with the rendezvous and waited until we were in formation with the tanker to solve the problem, but I let it distract me. The few seconds I delayed initiating the tanker's turn caused us to overshoot the rendezvous and cost us several precious minutes we couldn't afford to lose.

"Texas flight, Orange Anchor Four-Four here. We have you at twelve o'clock, closing fast, over!"

"Roger, Orange Anchor Four-Four. Start a hard port turn now," I shot back over the radio. "Texas flight, hold on tight," I warned the others, as I started maneuvering to undo the fix I had gotten us into. We had gone past the tanker and had to double back in a wide turn to join on him. It was a heads-up-and-locked error a rookie flight leader would make, and I knew it could cost us dearly.

When we finally settled down on the wing of the tanker we were seven minutes behind schedule, with less than ten minutes until the planned drop-off time for the strike force. We were in a first-class crack. My heart was pounding as I moved into position behind the tanker to start refueling. The tanker commander realized that we were going to be more than socially late and volunteered to take us as far north as he could before turning back.

My mind was racing. We could make up the time if we cut the refueling short but that would only compound the problem. It was a cardinal sin to arrive late over a target, but to get there late and low on fuel was just plain suicide. We had no choice but to refuel and leave the drop-off point a little late.

With the help of a super-boom operator, we refueled all four aircraft and recycled through the boom for a fuel top-off in eleven minutes flat. Texas Three was coming off the boom when I heard Flintstone Lead, the force commander, call, "Dropping off and greening up." I called Mick and told him we were running late, and he advised me to make it up on the run-in. Texas Four finally moved onto the boom for a two minute top-off. I checked the clock and held my breath. After what seemed like an eternity, Four began to vent fuel signaling that his tanks were full and we were ready for drop-off.

"Texas flight is off Orange Anchor, thanks for the extra help. Texas go to strike frequency and check in!"

We had four minutes to make up in order to close up in proper position behind the strike force. Four minutes equated to 40 miles behind, a big gap and tough to make up, even at 600 knots. It would give the gunners more than enough time to reload, and was way too long to expect the Ironhand flight to hang around in the target area suppressing SAMs.

I had two choices: go faster and burn more fuel, or cut the corner on the turn to the final run-in and risk early exposure to radar from our flank. I decided to try a combination of the two and pushed up the throttle. We began to close slightly and by the time the strike force called "Turning at Cho Moi" we had made up half the time with two more minutes to shave.

The weather in the valley was rotten, but there was a hole in the overcast right over a familiar loop in the Red River. I saw the river and gritted my teeth as I started a turn to cut off the strike force. "Texas Three, keep your eye on our three o'clock, I'm cutting the corner," I called as I looked over my left shoulder at Randy Plumb.

"Roger, Texas Lead, you're covered!" The external tanks were not dry, so I decided not to drop them and pushed up into minimum afterburner as we skimmed across the northwest peak in Thud Ridge. It was 1504 hours on the cockpit clock and we were just two minutes from pay dirt.

Within seconds I heard Flintstone flight call rolling in on the target, and the whole Thai Nguyen area erupted with ground fire and flak. The foundry smoke stacks just north of the railroad yard were on my nose so we were right on course, but I wasn't close enough to distinguish the target well enough to start a pull-up.

Sweat was streaming down my face as I strained to find the target. The ground never did look exactly like the map or the target photos, and that, coupled with our speed and all the action in the target area, made target acquisition extremely difficult.

Detroit flight called rolling-in so I started my pull-up, hoping the extra altitude would help me find the target. It did but I managed to string out the flight in the cross-over to the echelon formation for roll-in. Three and Four were really humping.

The railroad yard looked untouched except for several fires just to the south around the 100mm-AAA-gun emplacements. The flak suppression may have worked for the earlier flights, but the devils were shooting like hell when we reached the perch. I rolled in on the target. My dive angle was slightly shallow, so I pressed the release altitude slightly lower to compensate for the error and put the bombs on the target. I pulled up hard to the left toward the ridge and started jinking. The little buggers were tracking us and I was worried about Texas Two getting hit.

After a few long seconds, Texas Four called "Off the target." I was relieved and looked back to count noses. Just as I did I saw a flash of fire explode under Three.

"Texas Three is hit in my right drop tank," Randy called calmly but deliberately. Before I could respond, Rainbow Three, one of the F-4s in our MiGCAP, called that he was hit and heading for the foothills west of the Red. Trouble had struck quickly.

With our MiGCAP hurting and gone, we were the last flight out of the target area behind the Ironhand. I wanted to get the flight gathered up quickly and assess our damage. Randy's right drop tank was opened up like an exploded banana, but there was only surface damage to the wing. The airplane was flying all right with some extra rudder trim, so we headed for the tankers. It was a shame to drag a damaged wing tank home, but we couldn't risk the uncertainty of it's trajectory if it was jettisoned. It was a case of leaving well enough alone in order to minimize the risk of doing more serious damage to the airplane. For once, an expendable, empty drop tank had served a useful purpose.

The last surprise of the mission was the weather on recovery at Takhli. The visibility had dropped quickly due to haze and a late afternoon thunderstorm. We were forced to split into two elements to make instrument approaches for landing. When we finally touched down, I felt totally relieved and couldn't wait to get to the bread truck for a cigarette and a relaxing ride to debriefing. We were just in time to watch Glenn Gidel's 100-mission pass and join in the reception party.

What a way to end the day, my spirits were soaring. On my forty-fifth mission, I had finally achieved my goal and emerged as a combat flight leader. I had been baptized under the fire of the infamous little city of Thai Nguyen. My hometown newspaper reported the story this way.

> SAIGON, Feb. 4.—Air Force Maj. Kenneth H. Bell of El Paso led a wave of F-105 Thunderchiefs Friday in a bombing run on the railroad complex adjacent to the Thai Nguyen Iron and Steel Works north of Hanoi.
>
> Bell, 35, led one of the bomber flights that crossed from Thailand to unload 750-pound bombs onto the railroad.
>
> The Defense Department said 20 railroad cars were destroyed and the rails were out in several places.
>
> MAJ. BELL is the son of Mr. and Mrs. Bliss B. Bell, 1137 Baltimore drive. He graduated from El Paso High School and attended the University of Texas at El Paso.
>
> "We are proud of him," said Mrs. Bell upon hearing the good news. "It's nice to hear he's doing fine. We had not heard from him for sometime."

Bless my dear, sweet mother; she never missed an opportunity to remind me to write home. When I received the clipping, I wrote a loving reply, which respectfully chided her about the purpose of UPI News releases and hometown newspapers. She didn't buy a word of it, and she let me know it.

Joe Abbott's First

The next day I flew with the 333d Squadron and took Captain Joe Abbott, our third homegrown trainee, on his first combat mission. I was Number Three in the flight, with Joe on my wing. The flight leader was the wildest guy in the squadron. He flew like he was the only pilot in the war. As far as he was concerned, no one else or any of the rules mattered.

Joe hung in there but had a very difficult mission. He didn't get his bombs off on the first pass, broke the wrong way, and got too low and slow over the target. It was no wonder, he was trying desperately to fly in the big leagues with minimum training and getting little, if any, help from the flight leader. I did my best to gather him up and get him home safely.

At the debriefing I really had it out with the flight leader and his squadron commander. I had earned my stripes under fire, and I let them both know in no uncertain terms that I thought the flight leader had conducted himself like an irresponsible hooligan and ought to be grounded until he came to his senses. I could tell from Joe's eyes that he agreed but didn't dare say so.

Colonel Hill agreed with my assessment but was angry about the way I had handled it. I got a lecture about my role as a flight examiner on the wing staff and the hazards of appearing to preempt the prerogatives of a squadron commander.

Rumors persisted that there would be a bombing lull the next week during the Tet holiday. I was scheduled for an R&R to Bangkok so the timing was perfect. I was beginning to feel and act like a martyr, and I needed to adjust my attitude. Sometimes I wondered what kept me going back up north, day after day, to face the enemy. It had to be self-discipline, a sense of duty, or an unwillingness to quit in front of the other pilots. It sure as hell wasn't the pay, raw guts, or bravery.

12

"In Between"

BANGKOK WAS ONE OF the most fashionable watering holes in Southeast Asia. It was a beautiful city; anything was available at a price, and old friends had a curious way of popping up in the most unlikely places. Randy Plumb and I decided to join forces for a first-class week of rest and relaxation in Bangkok during the second week in February. It was my second R&R and first of several in Bangkok.

We reserved a suite of rooms at the Hotel Siam Inter-Continental and hired a car and driver at Takhli for the entire week. After a dusty trip south out of the jungle we cleaned up and hit the city with a vengeance. Our agenda was ambitious: cocktails and luncheon at the Hotel Erawan, swimming and happy hour at the Siam, cocktails and a beef fondue dinner in the Cat's Eye Lounge at the Hotel President, a show at the Club 99, and whatever after hours entertainment fortune might bring our way. Given enough time and energy, our daytime contingency plans included visits to the floating market, several temples, and an inside tour of a downtown snake farm where venom was collected for use in snake bite serums.

As it turned out, we visited the snake farm during our first "morning after" with big heads and queazy stomachs. Against our better judgment, we accepted an invitation for an arm's length inspection of some of the most deadly reptiles in Southeast Asia. We watched in horror as a veteran snake handler nonchalantly uncovered large, tangled piles of sleeping vipers for our amusement. The combination of snakes, slithering terror, and punishing heat was sobering and not the least bit amusing. The shock did cure my hangover, but it was a visit I knew I would never repeat.

Our driver, Lek, started out strong but caved in by midweek. He appreciated the pay but our pace was too much for him. He wanted to spend more time with his relatives in the big city and less time burning up valuable fuel looking for a perfect hot bath. After a few days on the chase, we gave Lek the evenings off, and I settled for a comfortable seat at the bar in the Cat's Eye Lounge to chat with Subhanee, a delightful cocktail waitress, whose native beauty was absolutely enchanting.

During my last evening at the Cat's Eye, the normal rustle of the bar was rudely interrupted by a loud disturbance. It was the unmistakable voice of Major Al Hamblin, one of my most illustrious classmates from West Point, making his way through the bar looking for a seat and perhaps a familiar face. I knew Al was flying F-4s at Cam Ranh Bay with the 12th Tactical Fighter Wing but our chance meeting that night in Bangkok came as a complete surprise. Al was a roughshod cowboy from Wyoming, with a zest for life and a loud, raucous sense of humor.

We greeted each other with a look of astonishment and settled in at the bar to catch up on old times. Before we had finished our first round of drinks, we were surprised again when Bill Egan came into the bar quite unexpectedly. By a chance coincidence, we had a rare opportunity for an impromptu class reunion, and we made the most of it. Reminiscence quickly turned to war stories punctuated with flying hands and boisterous laughter. Too quickly, the evening faded into dawn as rest gave way to recreation.

Late the next morning, Randy and I departed Bangkok. The cashier at the Siam presented us with a hotel bill for a whopping 2,353.10 Baht, the equivalent of $120. It seemed high but, for five days of high living out of earshot of combat, it was a bargain.

Back at Takhli, the mood of the pilots had grown dark and restless. The Tet bombing halt was weighing heavily on their nerves. The uncertainty was the worst part. No one liked getting shot at, but not knowing from day to day what the risk was going to be was even worse. Sitting around chafing, and doing nothing was bad medicine for morale, even under the best conditions.

On 15 February, Tet was over and the lull finally ended. Newspaper headlines heralded the news, "U.S. Resumes Bombing in North Vietnam." Morale in the wing began to improve immediately, and within two days we were back in full stride. Two pilots and a Wild Weasel crew completed their 100 missions, the first Weasel crew to finish successfully in the F-105F. The celebration coupled with my rest gave me a fresh outlook on my job.

My first day back at work was very encouraging. It started with a near perfect mission I flew with a new captain who had come to the war much like I had, via the technical Air Force. He was low on fighter experience but was bright as hell and a sharp pilot. Under the control of a FAC, we clobbered a new highway construction project in northern Laos and had so much fun in the process that we lost track of our fuel and had to squeak back to Takhli on fumes.

That afternoon I reported to Colonel Hill in the command post. I expected the worst, but he was relaxed and greeted me cheerfully. "Welcome back, sport," he quipped with a lighthearted smile. I was dumbfounded. Perhaps both of us had profited from my time away on R&R. Whatever the case, I decided to let it signal a new beginning in our relationship.

Professor Henry Higgins

Colonel Hill flew with the 357th Squadron and was influenced by the pilots in the squadron and their commander. Bobby Wayne had been fiercely independent and very leery of the stan/eval function of the wing staff. But Ben Murph, who had replaced Wayne, was more understanding even though he was still skeptical of my motives and the need for stan/eval in the first place. Consequently, I was forced to develop an arm's length working relationship with the 357th squadron in order to satisfy Colonel Hill and still get my job done.

To bridge the gap, Colonel Hill assigned one of the top pilots in the 357th Squadron to act as my assistant and watchdog. On the sly, Colonel Hill and Colonel Murph agreed to give Captain Hank Higgins the additional duty of assisting me on the staff. It was a crafty move but one that I welcomed because it gave me some help I needed and lent Hank's credibility to my effort in the squadron.

Hank "Henry" Higgins was a long-time F-105 pilot and an acknowledged expert in the art of flying and delivering weapons. He was stubborn and sometimes cantankerous, but he usually knew what he was talking about and was a pleasure to work with. I was nearing the fifty-mission mark of experience and had become confident that I could match credentials with even the most knowledgeable of old heads.

By design or by accident, Hank Higgins and I made a good pair. We inaugurated our partnership by flying a mission together. He was leading the flight, and I was flying his wing to check him out as an instructor pilot. We were executed on JCS 43.11, an army barracks in Package Six-A, but the weather was bad, and we were diverted to work with Hillsboro Control for a formation bomb drop on a target just north of the DMZ. "Just a couple of flight examiners out for a good time," I noted in my diary on return.

After the bomb drop, we worked our way down under the clouds to strafe a road target near Mu Gia Pass. Several other flights had found the same target, and we came close to shooting down an F-105 in the congestion. Not far away, a new SAM site at Vinh came up and started firing missiles. Magnum Three, a Wild Weasel from Korat, took a direct hit and went down near the city. No recovery effort was made, and both crew members were taken prisoner. It was a lousy way to end the mission.

That night I started drafting letters to everyone I knew who might help me avoid an assignment to the Pentagon. I stressed the Air Force's heavy investment in my training, and the need to take advantage of my recent combat experience. Purposely, I played down my technical experience and the investment the government had in my engineering education. I was hoping to appeal to sentiment rather than reason.

Ironically, I had just gotten a wonderful letter from my old boss in the Gemini program, encouraging me to return to a management position and discouraging my future in the flying Air Force. After giving it some thought, I noted, "If only I could stomach a career in the technical Air Force, I'm sure there would be plenty of opportunities for promotion."

To the tension of daily flying, I added the worry about my next assignment.

The next morning, I rudely discovered it was Sunday when I rushed into the 333d Squadron and found a priest celebrating Mass in the briefing room. It shouldn't have surprised me because I was scheduled for my usual Sunday outing with the 333d against a JCS target in Route Pack Six-A; a double target near Viet Tri. We had a choice of hitting the army barracks or a railroad yard, depending on the weather and the mood of the defenders. Some choice; I felt like attending the service and asking for last rites just in case.

The mission was scrubbed at the last minute and we wound up in Laos working with an Air America Firefly FAC against some enemy vehicles and troops dug in at the base of a big mountain. Pulling out, we had to come uncomfortably close to the mountain, but we hit the target and got some good secondary explosions, which pleased the FAC and made the effort worthwhile. The mission wasn't a counter but it was rewarding because we could see the results, and we got an instant scorecard.

My fiftieth mission was especially memorable because I witnessed what could only be called a weather miracle. Minutes after we arrived over Route Pack One, the solid layer of clouds that greeted us began to clear very quickly. In less than five minutes, we were able to see the entire valley south of Dong Hoi. The road that traversed the valley was lined with vehicles, the first concentration of trucks I had seen in months of tiring road reconnaissance.

For once, the weather had worked to our advantage. The drivers were probably watching in shocked disbelief from the cover of the neighboring trees. We reported the action, asked for additional fighters, and went to work attacking the stalled convoy.

Vern Frye, the flight leader, split us into elements to bomb the road north and south of the convoy to seal off their escape routes. Ted Tolman took his element to the left to make a northern cut while Vern and I pulled up to hit a bridge to the south. I was so excited that I lost my concentration and made a sloppy dive-bomb pass. Vern dropped the bridge, but my bombs hit long in a big clump of trees, hopefully among a band of astonished drivers.

Among the four of us we had 4,000 rounds of 20mm ammunition to expend on the trucks, and we made the most of it. It reminded me of the World War II gun-camera films we had seen in training, minus the trains and locomotives. For a few moments, we threw caution to the wind and enjoyed multiple, low-level passes on the hapless convoy. For once, we had some worthwhile targets and they were undefended. We made strafing passes until our ammunition was expended. When we finally headed home, a dozen trucks were destroyed and more were burning, but over half of the vehicles were left untouched. As we departed, several more flights checked in on the radio asking for clearance and directions to the convoy. It had been a mission to remember.

That afternoon I caught a ride on Scatback Delta to Tan Son Nhut. I was going to Seventh Air Force headquarters to represent our wing at a conference on armament requirements and the use of excess weapons.

I purposely chose a hotel other than the Ariega in a different part of Saigon, but the squalor was still almost overpowering. Living conditions were wretched. Outside my hotel, there was a family of six Vietnamese living in a discarded television packing box. The children were playing with rats, and the scene was replete with ducks, dogs, filth, and poverty. I felt sorry for the children, but they were laughing and seemed happy. Nevertheless, their living conditions were abominable.

The conference was unusual. The main subject of discussion centered on using a greater variety of weapons against targets in North Vietnam. Specifically, Seventh Air Force had storage facilities full of weapons that were not being used, and they were looking for ways to employ them effectively. We employed five different sizes of hard bombs regularly, but there was still a variety of bomblets and air-to-ground rockets that were not being used, and they were stacking up in warehouses all over Southeast Asia.

We discussed the use of white phosphorus fire bomblets as an effective weapon against ground gunners. Someone suggested that a white phosphorus bomblet might have an added psychological effect because Buddhists especially feared death by burning. As much as I liked to neutralize ground gunners, I had to empathize with the Buddhists and suggested that we stick with fragmentation bomblets. Hot, flying metal was intimidating enough for the average soul.

The conference soon bogged down and made very little progress. During a lull after lunch, I sarcastically asked if we were going to eventually discuss the use of nuclear weapons. "If anyone is interested in fire bombs, nukes are dandies," I said humorously. "And they will suppress a lot more than flak," I concluded, to the amazement of the group. They finally laughed but decided to call it quits for the day.

After another inconclusive morning, the conference ended abruptly, so I jumped on a C-130 bound for Udorn. I spent the night swapping stories and sipping Scotch with the host recce pilots in the 20th Tactical Reconnaissance Squadron and made it back to Takhli the next morning.

It didn't take long to brief the front office on the results of the conference. There was a wide variety of new weapons on the shelf around the Air Force, but they were either untested or no one had the guts to use them. Consequently, the conference was all talk and little action. I excused myself and headed for my mailbox, some breakfast, and a fresh change of underwear.

Letters from the Fourth Grade

I received a large package of letters from children in the fourth grade class at Fairmount School in Golden, Colorado, just west of Denver. Their teacher had been a friend of mine during my graduate days at the University of Colorado. As a surprise, she had each of her pupils write a letter encouraging and thanking me for what I was doing in the war.

They were beautiful letters, innocent and very direct. Most of the children sent their pictures and asked for one of me and my airplane in return. They wanted to know how I liked war and who I thought would win. Almost without exception, they expressed fear and sorrow about Vietnam and hoped I wouldn't have to stay too long.

Each letter was a masterpiece of its own in expressing genuine, caring love. I read each one carefully and was moved by their simplicity and purpose. Their message was a fresh breath of air from America, and I felt proud to have been singled out and remembered by this class.

I saved all of their letters. Here are a few samples exactly as they were written, spelling and all.

Dear Major Bell,

I am in Mrs. Deines room at Fairmount school. I am in grade 4. I am 9 years old. How are you doing? Do you know yet, who will win the war or, when it will stop? What city are you fighting in?

Mike Koeltzow
January 9, 1967

Major Bell,

I'd like to know a few things about Viet Nam. Is Viet Nam a very lonely place? Do you like it there in Viet Nam? I wouldn't!! I'd hate to be in a place where they're having a war! Some of my friends are writing to Major Egan. Mrs. Deines said you were very good friends. I'm very anxious to meet both of you. I hope you can visit our room some time. If you can I hope you can tell about you and your job. If you want to know what I look like, here I am. [Picture attached]

Carol Gott
January 9, 1967

Dear Major Bell,

Is it forest country over there? How are you? All right I hope. I hope we win don't you? I can imagine how noisy it is and muddy. Do you think you could visit us some time? I sure hope so.

Sincerely yours,
Joe Lee

Dear Major Bell

What does your airplane look like? What is the name of it? Have you ever shot down another airplane? Have you ever fought on the ground? Have you ever bombed anyplace?

From, Cole Young
Jan. 9, Fairmount

Dear Major Bell,

Mrs. Deines told us about you! Before I go any further, my name is Diana. I am ten years old. I have a friend in the army like Mrs. Deines! His name is Raymond Andrews and he runs a tank! What kind of food do you eat? (fried snake skin and roasted grasshoppers?) Do you think you'll send me a picture of you? Here is a picture of me: I hope you won't stay long in Viet Nam!!!! Have you ever had any visitors? I bet it is lonely there!! Do you like to fly? (I would, if I knew how to drive!) Guess what instrument I play? [a cello]

I'll be seeing you!!!

                                        Your friend,
                                        Diana Sue Cooper

P.S. I hope you come and see us!!!!!

                                        Jan 10, 1967

Dear Major Bell

Have you been in Viet Nam very long? What is the name of your
plan? How many missions have you flown? Have you ever been on
TV on the news? In our school there are about 400. Have you ever
been bit by a snake? If you have what kind was it and was it very
bad? I will inclose my picture.

I hope you come home soon.

                                        From Arthur Ohanian

I couldn't send them each a picture so I autographed a large one and sent it
to the class with a small American flag I had carried on a mission. I borrowed a typewriter and wrote the class a letter that I hoped would answer
their questions.

                                        March 1, 1967
                                        355TFW, Box 1679
                                        APO San Francisco 96243

Fourth Grade Class
Fairmount School
Golden, Colorado

Dear Fourth Graders,

During the course of fighting a war, particularly an air war in the very hostile skies over North Vietnam, emotions are charged, goals sometimes
clouded and courage is taxed to the limit. Your letters, so warm and innocently straight forward, are a righting force which serves to sharpen our
focus and bring everything back into the proper perspective. Simply, we are
here so that you may continue to study and grow into our future America,
out from under the shadow of fear which is a way of life to children your
age here in Southeast Asia. You are our investment in the future. Your free-

dom to write encouraging letters is our stake in this conflict. Thank you very much.

The airplane I fly is an F-105 "Thunderchief" fighter bomber. It is a wonderful airplane and when history records the trail it has blazed in Southeast Asia it will find it's place among such names as "Spad," "Lafayette Escadrille," "Mustang," and "Sabre Jet." It is a single pilot, single engine supersonic fighter, capable of speeds up to Mach 2.0. It is the fastest airplane in the world at sea level and the breathtaking roar of a flight of "Thunderchiefs" at tree-top level will sound a note for freedom for years to come over the rugged jungles of Vietnam.

As for myself, I am a professional soldier, I have been expertly trained as a jet fighter pilot and I enjoy my profession very much. On the personal side, I am a bachelor, I have never been bitten by a snake, I find the jungle very beautiful and interesting and I do miss my family and friends who I have left behind. God willing, I will return to our precious United States soon and I will make every effort to come to Fairmount School and meet all of you personally. Until then, I hope you enjoy the pictures I have enclosed in deep appreciation for your letters. In return, I only ask that you continue to honor your country, your family, your education and your teachers who are making great sacrifices in order to properly prepare you for your responsibilities as adult Americans. As a symbol of that responsibility, I am enclosing a small American flag which flew with me on my 51st mission over North Vietnam.

> Your good friend,
> Kenneth H. Bell, Major,
> USAF

The kids are all grown now, but I'll bet they still remember the fourth grade in Fairmount school, their teacher, and the fighter pilot they once encouraged.

New Target Policy

For months, we had been chafing to hit targets that were critically important. The Port at Haiphong, the airfields at Kep and Phuc Yen, and the highway/bridge system around Hanoi itself were untouched and vital to the military and economic survival of North Vietnam. The target list was controlled by the political winds that blew in Washington, and changes were slow and usually unpredictable.

At long last, two important targets were added to the list. On 24 February 1967, we received a message designating the steel mill and power plant at Thai Nguyen as primary targets—JCS 76.00.

We asked intelligence for the latest target information and began detailed mission planning at once. For the next two weeks, we waited to hit JCS 76.00. Both the morning and afternoon strikes were prepared to go, but the weather would not cooperate. The strike force tried several times to get to the target only to be foiled by weather. Pressure and tension mounted daily. By the first of March, I noted that "They're bound to know we are coming by now, the flak and headlines ought to be sensational when we finally get there."

The Navy was claiming limited success with radar bombing in their A-6 Intruder and that added to the pressure we were facing. Colonel Scott asked me to dust off our radar bombing procedures and identify a nucleus of pilots who could carry out the mission. If the weather didn't improve soon, he was apparently considering going ahead with radar bombing on his own hook.

Hank Higgins, Ted Tolman, Randy Plumb, and I began to study the problem. The F-105 fire control system was designed to deliver nuclear bombs at night and in bad weather, but it was not capable of the accuracy required to put conventional weapons on politically sensitive targets without risking collateral damage.

Dutifully, we tried to find a way to get more out of the system, but we all knew that a decision to deliver bombs on radar would be political and not technical. It could be done if someone was willing to accept higher losses and corollary damage in the target area. We had no idea that our study had top priority in Washington, or that we would get a four-star push in a matter of weeks.

To break the monotony of the radar study, I volunteered for an Ironhand mission. It was my fifty-fifth mission, and it had been some time since I had flown with the Weasels.

The target was JCS 21.10, a small railroad marshaling yard near Vinh on the southern coast of North Vietnam. The Weasels were interested in a new SAM site that had become operational in the area and, I had a special interest in seeing what the railroad yard looked like on radar. Our study group had selected that yard as a test target in the event we were asked to demonstrate our prowess at radar bombing. Vinh was a formidable target, but it was a safe distance from Hanoi, and its coastline would be easy to distinguish on radar.

I was Number Two in a four-ship Ironhand flight. Our job was to go in ahead of a single strike flight to see if we could coax the SAM site into coming up so we could attack it with a one-two punch before it had a chance to launch any missiles. We wanted to use a combination of Shrike missiles and bombs to knock out the radar and destroy the site. It was a bold, cunning plan, based on exploiting the inexperience of a new, hopefully unsuspecting SAM site.

We approached the site in a gradual descent from the south with the ocean on our right. The weather favored the SAM site. A low, solid overcast covered the area. It was a treacherous setup for a game of cat and mouse with deadly missiles. The site started toying with us before we got within missile range. The launch light blinked on and off several times, but the lead Weasel pressed the attack, hoping to get his Shrikes off against the SAM-search radar.

I glanced back and forth at my ground-map radar. We were tracking straight down the coastline, but my radar picture wasn't good enough to pick out Vinh or the rail yard. We were playing Russian roulette with a SAM site and I didn't have time to fine tune the radar. My eyes swept the cloud deck below us for anything that resembled a SAM in flight. The radio chatter was reserved but tense; Number Four sounded particularly nervous.

The leader of the strike flight behind us decided to call it quits, but his element wanted to press the attack in spite of the weather. It was no use. They were vulnerable as hell, and without visual contact with the ground their weapons were useless. We called it off but continued toward the site long enough to cover the departing strike flight.

Lead pulled up and headed west for the mountains. It was a precarious moment. We were heading away from the SAM site, and the launch light came on solid. There wasn't much we could do but bend the throttle. The bastards had us. All they had to do was fire a salvo. It was a situation all Weasels dreaded. We jinked hard and looked back at our six o'clock for missiles.

Time stood still until we got out of range of the SAM site. For some reason, they didn't fire any missiles. Perhaps they didn't have any. If so, we had played a clever game of blind man's bluff and come away with a standoff. Relieved, we unloaded our 500-pound bombs on Route Two in the foothills and headed for the tanker, intact and a little wiser.

For the purposes of the radar study, the mission was useful. I was distracted by the activity of the SAM site, but the radar data we gained would be helpful if we decided to come back on a radar bomb strike. The contrast of the coastline on the radar was as good as expected, but the reflective definition of the rail yard was poor, and picking it out of the clutter would have been chancy. The river south of Vinh showed up well enough for use as a radar timing point, but the probability of pinpointing the rail yard with time-released bombs would have been very low.

On balance, the mission was successful. The Weasels gained some valuable information about a new SAM site, and I gained some insight into the vagaries of radar bombing. The next step was still uncertain.

When I returned to my office, there was a note on my desk asking me to attend a meeting with Major General Hank Kucheman from the Air Staff in the Pentagon. He was scheduled to arrive the next morning and was interested in new operational requirements. I guessed that he might be my new boss and wanted to talk about my resistance to an assignment in Washington. Or perhaps he was the guru of radar bombing. Either way, I was in trouble.

General Kucheman was levelheaded and easy to talk to. He wanted to discuss our operational problems openly and hadn't come to talk about assignments or radar bombing. He had been in the 354th Squadron during World War II and presented an original Bulldog patch to the squadron commander during a break in the briefings. When he left, he promised to take our message back to the Pentagon, but the look in his eyes said he would rather stay and fly some missions.

Minutes after General Kucheman departed, the TOC got word that we had lost an airplane over northern Laos. The flight was strafing a remote target in Package Three, and Number Two was hit with heavy 37mm ground fire. The airplane crashed in Laos and the pilot, Major Ralph Carlock of the 357th, was reported killed. It was the airplane I had flown over from McClellan. A good friend was dead, number 274 was down, and I still had forty-five missions ahead of me. I wondered if I would make it.

Visit with Scrappy

We needed to coordinate some new ideas with the 388th Wing, so I flew over to Korat on a beautiful Sunday afternoon to visit with Colonel Scrappy Johnson. Scrappy had been the operations officer in the first fighter squadron I was assigned to after flying school. He was a personal friend, and as his nickname implied, he was action-oriented.

Scrappy and a few of his troops met me at the airplane and gave me a warm reception. We went to his office and talked about everything we had been doing. I hadn't seen Scrappy in several years, so there was a lot to catch up on.

There were half a dozen tactics changes that needed to be coordinated, and in each case, the group readily accepted my recommendation. I told them about our radar bombing study, and we discussed the subject in detail. They agreed to look at it from their perspective, but they shared our concern about F-105 system limitations.

We also needed their coordination on a cockpit display change we were recommending for the airplane. The QRC-160 pod control lights were difficult to see and needed to be relocated. We had already made a successful prototype installation at Takhli and were ready to take action to implement the change, with Korat's backing. Even though they had separately come up with a different solution to the problem, they agreed to endorse our proposal.

Scrappy invited me to stay and enjoy a quiet evening at their club, but I had to return my airplane for the morning mission. He took me back to the flight line for my departure. As I taxied out, I saluted Scrappy and lowered the canopy as my aircraft passed his staff car. Characteristically, he stood smiling with a cigar gripped between his teeth, a picture of rugged confidence.

Scrappy Johnson was a solid, first-class leader and I admired him. He was concerned about talk of a growing rift between our wings and wanted to overcome it. I shared his concern, but I was convinced that any friction that existed between us had its roots in Takhli. It disturbed me, but I hoped that my visit that day had been instrumental in bringing the organizations closer together.

On 6 March 1967, we heard a rumor that an official U.S. government announcement acknowledging our presence in Thailand was imminent. The word spread like wildfire, and one version even had President Johnson himself making the announcement during a personal visit to one of the Thai bases.

Within hours, the switchboards were jammed with calls from the press seeking confirmation. We didn't know any more than they did, but their calls confirmed one thing. We were in for a media blitz, the likes of which we could hardly imagine.

For the next two days, the international press corps began to arrive *en masse*. By sheer coincidence, we appeared to accommodate them by launching twice on JCS 76.00 at Thai Nguyen although both strikes returned with unsuccessful results because of weather. The pressure to do something spectacular was building rapidly.

13

JCS 76.00 THE HARD WAY

THE RISING TIDE OF pressure to strike the steel mill at Thai Nguyen finally crested on 10 March 1967. In the two weeks since the target was first fragged, the wing had tried eight times to get there without success. Seventh Air Force was under the gun politically from Washington, and aircrew tension increased daily. We were tired of mission planning and strained with anxiety. The North Vietnamese had more than sufficient warning and time to shore up their already impressive defenses.

On that fateful day, I was assigned to fly with the Ironhand flight as Lincoln Four, a call sign that would be etched in my memory. I knew when we walked into the mission briefing room that we were going to the target regardless of the weather.

> What a mission. The Wing briefing was a political master-piece. Phil Gast was the mission commander. Col Scott briefed that we would proceed to the target regardless of Korat's decision on the weather. Prior to takeoff, we were directed to deliver weapons on target—period. It was the day that LBJ himself would reveal our presence in Thailand and announce a major policy change regarding targets such as the steel mill. Tension was everywhere and I was #4 in an Ironhand flight, one minute ahead of our strike force and right on the heels of the Korat birds.

Lincoln Flight

Our flight met the night before the mission in the wing planning room. We had a tough job to do and we knew it. Sandwiched in between the two strike forces, we would inherit an enraged enemy in a chaotic scene without

193

the benefit of surprise. With our own strike force breathing down our necks, there would be no margin for error or time to reconnoiter for the attack. We were between the proverbial rock and a hard place.

Two of the most experienced Wild Weasel crews in the wing were assigned to Lincoln flight. Major Dave Everson and his EWO, Captain Dave Luna, would lead the flight with Captain Bill Hoeft hauling bombs in the number two aircraft. Major Merle Dethlefsen and his EWO, Captain Mike Gilroy, were in the number three F-model, and I was flying the number four spot. Each of us had over fifty missions with plenty of experience in Package Six, including several trips to the Thai Nguyen area, not counting weather aborts on the steel mill. The mission would be difficult but we were prepared.

The forecast was not encouraging, but all we could do was hope and pray for the best, so we headed for our trailers for a few hours rest.

The next morning the mission was put on hold to wait for a break in the weather. After a tedious five-hour delay, we finally received an order to take off just before noon for a 1550 hours time on target. Minutes later, Lincoln flight was the first flight airborne behind the tankers. We were on our way to the steel mill and there was no turning back.

We tagged up easily with our tanker and waited nervously while the rest of the strike force formed and began the prestrike refueling operation. We were monitoring the radio transmissions between our mission commander, Phil Gast, and the 388th force commander from Korat. The calls were clipped and a little anxious, but it sounded like everything was falling into place for a max effort. The 388th would lead the force into the target; a force totaling some seventy-two aircraft, including two flights of Weasels, and four flights of F-4s providing MiGCAP.

The force commander called "dropping off" the tanker and one minute later we joined him. We were finally on our way to JCS 76.00, and I was doing it the hard way, as a wingman with the Ironhand flight. Deep inside, I sensed that one of us in Lincoln flight was not coming home.

We crossed the dog pecker, a familiar landmark in the Red River, and headed for the turning point at Cho Moi. The weather looked surprisingly good to the south and east of the ridge, only scattered clouds with hazy visibility. The 388th had arrived over the target, and the radio was jammed with calls on the strike frequency.

After we turned south, there was absolutely no doubt about the target location. Thai Nguyen was ablaze with AAA fire and a large column of black smoke covered the area. The 388th was in the thick of it, and we were a minute away from the most intense barrage of ground fire I had ever seen. Several SAM sites were up and tracking us but their threat paled in comparison to the guns. The defenses were ready and Thai Nguyen was a boiling mushroom of ugly, black flak.

Our flight was in combat-spread formation heading southwest at 2,000 feet altitude. Lincoln Three and I were on the left side of the lead element in a line-a-breast formation. Just prior to reaching the target, Lincoln One started a wide sweeping turn to the right toward the railroad yard southwest of Thai Nguyen city. Dave Everson was headed straight for a SAM site through the center of an enormous concentration of ground fire. He was diving into the very jaws of hell and I said to myself, "We'll never make it!"

Lincoln One and Two disappeared into the boiling cloud of flak, and within seconds the gruesome whine of beepers flooded the radio. It sounded like both aircraft had taken direct hits from the 85mm guns and at least one of them was down. Neither aircraft responded to radio calls from Lincoln Three. We were surrounded by exploding flak, and it looked as if our fate was certain, the gunners had us. I said a prayer and tried to concentrate all of my attention on Lincoln Three.

We were west of the steel mill, and Lincoln Three started a left turn to swing around to reattack the same SAM site that the lead element had been after. Halfway through the turn, the strike flights began rolling in on the steel mill. The ground fire under us intensified so much that I could hardly see the target for the layers of flak. It looked as if we were making a large pylon turn around a black ball of smoke. Every gun and SAM in North Vietnam must have been located at Thai Nguyen that afternoon. We continued the turn and started boring in on the SAM site.

My SAM launch light came on solid. I strained, but I couldn't spot a launch site or any missiles coming up at us. I was watching Lincoln Three, expecting him to launch a Shrike so I could track it to the site and set up for a bomb pass. As I rolled out of the turn, the radio cracked with a menacing MiG warning, "Lincoln Four, MiG at six o'clock and firing!"

Instinctively, I looked back over my right shoulder. Sure as hell, I had a MiG-21 cornered at my six o'clock position. He was shooting, and my right wing started to sparkle as some of his rounds found their mark. I wanted to break into the MiG but I didn't have a choice. Lincoln Three was pressing the attack on the SAM site and I had to stay with him.

I pushed the mike button down to warn Three, but before I could say anything, the sky surrounding me turned orange and black and my airplane rocked violently. The ground gunners had found our range and had opened fire again. The MiG behind me either broke off, got hit, or lost sight of me. Paradoxically, the gunners on the ground had solved my problem with the MiG, but their big guns were tracking me. I gritted my teeth and pushed over hard to change altitude and gain airspeed.

When the smoke cleared, Lincoln Three was at my ten o'clock position and the MiG was gone, but my right wing had been damaged. The right leading edge flap was blown down forcing the airplane into a left turn because of added lift from the right wing. I was able to hold the wings level with cross-controls but it added a difficult complication I didn't need at that moment. I moved the flap lever down, hoping to extend the left leading edge flap to a symmetric position, but it would not budge because of my airspeed. I had to settle for cross-controls and hope for turns to the left.

Lincoln Three launched a Shrike and called out a SAM site at twelve o'clock. I saw the site but I was too low and close in to make a decent bomb pass. "Pull-up left, I'll try a right roll-in," I radioed to Lincoln Three. Merle lit his burner and started up as I followed. We couldn't get high enough for a good dive angle, so I rolled in and tried to compensate by pressing lower than the normal release altitude. I pickled long but it was impossible to see where the bombs hit. Between the flak, the difficulty I was having with my flight controls, and the confusion of the battle, I was lucky just to stay with Lincoln Three.

When I sighted him again, Merle had pulled up to the left to reattack the site from the east. I reset the armament switches and the gun sight to GUNS GROUND for strafing and tried to cut Three off in the turn. The situation was frantic. We were maneuvering wildly through the target area trying to protect the strike force and I had worked up a drenching sweat.

The radio was swamped on the strike frequency. Our lead strike flight had come off the target and was rejoining when they engaged four MiG-17s. In the short fight that ensued, the element leader, Captain Max Brestel, bagged one of the MiGs with his cannon. "I GOT ONE, I GOT ONE," Max repeated excitedly over the radio.

"Shut your fucking mouth and get another one," someone radioed anonymously, providing a profane touch of humor to an otherwise tense situation.

As usual Max had the last word, "Hey, Lead. I think I got the second one, too."

"Roger, let's rejoin and head west," his flight leader radioed calmly.

The last strike flight was coming off the steel mill when we rolled in to strafe the SAM site for the last time. I had fallen behind Three and was afraid of loosing sight of him. My fuel was getting low, but I was forced to use afterburner just to keep up. Just as I pulled the trigger to fire on the site, I heard Lincoln Three call, "off and up, left of the site." I fired a burst at the target with the gun. The cannon growled, and I looked up in vain for my leader.

All of a sudden, it was very lonesome over Thai Nguyen. There wasn't another airplane in sight, and I was headed east away from the egress route. I decided to roll in for another pass on the SAM site and pull out heading west for the ridge. The radio chatter confirmed that the last strike flight and the F-4 MiGCAP were ahead of me. "Lincoln Three, Four has lost tallyho," I called woefully.

"Roger, Four. Lincoln Three heading two-eight-zero at three thousand feet crossing the ridge. Say your position, over?"

"Leaving the target area about ten miles behind you. Still no tallyho. Give me a couple of turns, over!" Lincoln Three made several turns trying to find me, but it was no use. He had troubles of his own, and I was looking into a hazy, afternoon sun and limping slightly with wing damage. Thanks to me, we were separated and the potential consequences could be devastating.

We had made four passes on the SAM site, probably lost two aircraft in the process, and we were coming out separately and vulnerable to attack without warning. I was scared stiff and began to wonder if all the crap was worth the effort. If you were lucky enough to make it home, there were always more targets and more flak from angry gunners.

The plight of two of our MiGCAP F-4s from the 8th Wing was unfolding on the radio, and it snapped me back to my senses.

Cheetah Four had flamed out and was about to go down in a high-threat area. Incredibly, Cheetah Three was trying to push Four out to a safer area for bailout and a possible recovery. Cheetah Four had put his tail hook down, and Three was behind him, pushing on the hook with the windscreen of his aircraft. It was hard to believe, but I was hearing it happen real-time.

The aerial nose-to-tail, high-wire trick worked. In the process, Cheetah Three also flamed out, but not before both aircraft were over Laos and in a much better position for search and rescue. After an unbelievable ordeal, all four pilots were recovered by Air Force Jolly Green helicopters and returned to their units to fly again.[*]

Because of my battle damage, I decided to recover at Udorn. I limped in to the field and landed at dusk. When I taxied into a parking spot on the ramp, I saw Bill Hoeft standing by his airplane with a broad smile on face. It was a miracle. I thought surely he was down and on his way to the Hanoi Hilton. Bill gave me a encouraging thumbs up as I shut down the engine.

---

[*]10 March 1967, 0800Z, F-4C, 64-0839, 433TFS/8TFW, Cheetah-3, JCS 76.00, Thai Nguyen Iron Works, Capt. J. R. Pardo A/C, 1st. Lt. S. A. Wayne, ejected over Laos and recovered with minor injuries by USAF helicopters. 0803Z, F-4C, 63-7654, 433TFS/8TFW, Cheetah-4, JCS 76.00, Capt. E. D. Aman A/C, Capt. R. W. Houghton, ejected over Laos and recovered by USAF helicopters.

He was a quiet, studious guy, not the type you would expect to find flying F-105s, but he had plenty of grit and character.

Quite a crowd had gathered around Bill's airplane to inspect the damage. The left side of the fuselage was peppered with hundreds of shrapnel holes, and hydraulic fluid was still dripping into a huge pool on the concrete ramp. The airplane had taken a direct hit by an 85mm round in the left wing, just outboard of the landing gear. A large, gaping hole in the wing spoke for itself. It was 4 feet in diameter, and nothing short of a miracle had held the wing together. The airplane looked like a total loss to me, but it would live to be repaired and fight again, briefly.

Bill Hoeft said that Lincoln One had not been so lucky. "They took a direct hit in the nose and the airplane disintegrated, just disappeared in pieces," he said somberly. "I heard a good beeper but I don't know if either of them got out," he added expectantly.

I confirmed Bill's account of the action when we talked with the intelligence debriefing officer at the command post. It had been a tough mission and the enemy was waiting and well prepared. Lincoln One had done what he was expected to do in the face of overwhelming odds. We suspected that Dave Everson and Dave Luna were en route to Hanoi, probably wounded but alive and lonesome as hell. A few days later, Radio Hanoi confirmed that they were both prisoners.

The maintenance people at Udorn patched up the holes in my airplane and rigged the leading edge flaps so they would stay down in flight. The airplane was cleared for a one-time flight to Takhli at reduced airspeed. Bill Hoeft had to wait for a hop in a transport, but I gathered up the rest of our F-105 stragglers and led them home that night. We were a ragged bunch.

After we landed at Takhli, I was surprised and relieved to find Merle Dethlefsen and Mike Gilroy sitting in the intelligence debriefing room. We went through a thorough debriefing and tried to piece together a very significant mission. It was difficult to describe or comprehend all that had happened during our mission as Lincoln flight, but we knew that we had survived some extraordinary conditions and built a lasting bond in the process.

The next day, the strike force went back to Thai Nguyen. The steel mill was severely damaged, but the stiff defenses continued to take their toll. The wing lost three more aircraft and three pilots were down without hope of recovery, one from each squadron.

JCS 76.00 proved to be an expensive target. When the dust settled on the steel mill at Thai Nguyen the second day, we had lost a total of six aircraft in two days of vicious fighting: one F-105F Weasel, three F-105Ds, and two F-4Cs from the 8th Wing. Thankfully, the F-4 crews were rescued, but five of our guys would spend the next six years in captivity as prisoners of war. Four were repatriated and came home alive, but Captain Joe Karins paid the ultimate price at the steel mill.

When the press got wind of the action over Thai Nguyen, we were inundated with a frenzy of reporters seeking interviews. They wanted all the details, including the extent of our losses. We were eager to talk to the press after so many months of silence, but at the same time, most of us were somewhat guarded.

One of our pilots gave a rather attractive, young reporter more than she had ever bargained for. Ted Tolman was returning to the debriefing section when he was confronted by the eager reporter, just off the flight line. "What was it like, Major?" she asked. "Did you get to the target and how were the defenses?"

Ted seized the opportunity with his usual flamboyance and intensity. "Madam," he said gruffly and very deliberately, "I've just returned from a life-and-death duel with a North Vietnamese gunner, and the gunner lost!" Ted's eyes darted back and forth as he glared at the reporter through his dark eyebrows. When he broke into a roar of laughter, the reporter's look of shock turned to amazement and then delight, as she realized she had quite a story.

Medal of Honor

Almost a year later, Major Merlyn H. Dethlefsen was awarded the Medal of Honor during a ceremony at the White House. Merle was sighted for conspicuous gallantry during the action he had taken as Lincoln Three over Thai Nguyen. I was privileged to attend the ceremony as one of his comrades in arms.

After the ceremony, a few of us met with President Johnson to exchange a few brief pleasantries. I shook his hand and introduced myself as a fellow Texan. The president smiled and greeted me warmly, but he seemed frail and somewhat distracted. I wanted to ask him a question about the war, but he smiled and I moved on quickly.

As I watched President Johnson chatting with the others, I thought back to the rumor of his visit to Takhli and wondered how he might have reacted to being our most distinguished "Queen for a Day." He probably wouldn't have noticed.

14

A Quiet Sunday

THE NEXT FEW WEEKS were the most draining period of my combat tour. Pressure was building from the top to bomb something, regardless of the weather. Washington opened another JCS target at Thai Nguyen, the thermal power plant, and wanted immediate results.

On 12 March 1967, in response to the "fly or else" pressure from Saigon, I noted in my diary:

> Colonel Broughton took the boys to Viet Tri in the soup and missed the whole damn target. Captain Dave Nichols took a SAM hit in the gut but got the bird back to Udorn leaking fluids everywhere. The damage reminded me of Bill Hoeft's airplane after Lincoln flight.

The new "weather is no longer a factor" policy was senseless and demoralizing. The prospects of dodging SAMs in weather were futile and utterly discouraging. Morale ebbed as low as it had ever been in the wing.

To add to my personal load, I received a letter from a girl I loved very much and had once intended to marry. I would have sacrificed anything for her love, but I foolishly let her down and she married another man. She had tried corresponding with me as a friend, but I was too proud to let her know how deeply I was hurt or how much I regretted losing her. Instead, my reply was angry and mean spirited.

I stared at her letter for an hour before I found the courage to open it. I knew it would be her final reply. "Sorry we can't continue writing," her postscript ended poignantly. She knew me much better than I knew myself and had decided to call it quits, even as friends. The finality of her letter hurt me deeply and put me in a melancholy tailspin. Cherished memories flooded through my thoughts and left me feeling empty, with a horrible sense of frustration and loss. "If only I had it to do all over again," I thought. "I'll never recoup any of it now. God help me start anew."

Ed McCaffrey and Gene Haggerty flew their 100th mission together. They had a big party and left the day after. Part of my heart and most of our wing-lieutenant talent left with them.

I don't think Mac thought that he would ever finish. He was all smiles when he climbed on board his flight to Bangkok. His sights were set on one thing—marriage. He was engaged to a pretty stewardess he had met at Nellis. Six of us had done the town in San Francisco before splitting for combat. We enjoyed champagne and caviar at the Mark Hopkins Hotel and had a "we'll meet back here when it's over" nightcap at the Yankee Doodle Bar, a renowned World War II watering hole for pilots. Mac was on his way back to San Francisco and I envied him.

That afternoon we lost another airplane and pilot to ground fire over an obscure target in Laos. My emotions had been on a three-day roller coaster ride and I wanted off, but I sensed that something was in the wind that was terribly important.

CINCPACAF

General John Ryan, the Commander-in-Chief of the Pacific Air Forces, arrived on 13 March 1967 with an inspection team from Thirteenth Air Force. They were determined to find a way to deliver bombs at night and in bad weather.

I briefed General Ryan on the preliminary results of our study group. Although he seemed pleased that we had taken the initiative to study the problem, he wanted a better answer, faster. Right on the spot, he formed a Tactics Working Group, and I was appointed the chairman. General Ryan wanted an answer in one week.

The Tactics Working Group began work immediately. We brought in two more participants from the squadrons to round out our experience, but decided to keep the group small in the interest of finishing quickly.

Once again, we soon found ourselves up against the design limits of the aircraft systems, and concluded that we had to recognize those limits and work within them rather than spend time trying to reshape reality. If there was a way to improve on a 1,500- to 2,500-foot circular error probable (CEP) with hard bombs, it would have to be based on pilot skill or something outside the built-in parameters of the weapons system.

The characteristics of a target and its surrounding topography were most important in terms of radar performance, hence target choice was critical to the predicted outcome. We knew that PACAF and Washington would not appreciate limitations in target selection, but we were determined to report the facts as we found them.

Ultimately, we knew we would be asked to demonstrate the results of our study, and none of us wanted to recommend something we couldn't live with. As the report worked its way up toward PACAF headquarters, there would be ample opportunity for embellishments, so we guarded against including anything that might come back to haunt us. We stood a good chance of getting screwed with our own study, and we were determined not to provide the screwdriver.

Our findings were documented in a rather large study report that we planned to carry forward to the headquarters with an accompanying briefing. The report concluded that the F-105, using radar and the other features of the aircraft weapons system, could deliver bombs at night and in bad weather against very selective targets, provided we were willing to accept reduced accuracy and increased losses.

When we made our report to Colonel Scott, we recommended that we fly a practice mission first, in order to gain current experience and add credibility to the report. That took big balls but it was the only reasonable way to proceed, and we thought we might learn something. Colonel Scott agreed and talked to Seventh Air Force. Within hours, we had a reply and a target, the thermal power plant at Viet Tri. What a way to practice!

After a last minute addition to the frag order, we were officially directed to execute our first all-weather strike of the war against a target in North Vietnam. Both wings would fly two missions, one in the morning for practice, and one in the afternoon against a fragged target. The order sent us into utter chaos and everyone went in opposite directions. As the author of the report, I felt obliged to volunteer for both missions.

We did the detailed mission planning and then cloistered ourselves in Colonel Hill's quarters to talk about the intricacies of the mission. Meanwhile, a team in the 354th Squadron was busy finishing the study report and reproducing enough copies to accompany us on the inevitable post-action briefing cycle. We finally retired to our quarters. Exhausted, I made an entry in my diary.

Late, 18 March 1967
The morning will bring the most important mission we have yet to fly. It will violate most of the principles which have been established and most of the ones our tactics committee recommended for radar bombing but we are going to hit the power plant at Viet Tri with a flight of three at low level in spite of the weather. Colonel Salmon, myself and Randy. It could be my most decisive mission to date. Korat, the lucky bastards, drew the power plant at Thai Nguyen.

Tomorrow could be an Air Force Cross Day!

After a rushed, early morning briefing, we took off for a practice mission in Laos. It was Sunday, 19 March 1967, and we were Gainful flight. Danny Salmon was leading, Randy Plumb was Number Two, I was Three, and Ted Tolman was the hot spare flying in the Number Four position.

The plan was to penetrate the clouds over a target in Laos where a FAC could observe our radar bomb delivery and report the accuracy of the weapons. We would drop 500-pound retarded Snakeye bombs using a simple radar technique called "lay-down bombing." At the last minute, our departure was delayed due to a donnybrook on how many Snakeyes we could carry safely. The frag called for six bombs on each aircraft, but there was a serious safety question about clearance on the bomb rack.

In order to escape the bomb blast in a low-level, lay-down delivery, we had to use high-drag bombs to increase the separation distance between the aircraft and the impact of the weapon. Snakeye bombs had four drag plates that opened like an umbrella into the windstream after release to provide rapid deceleration and sufficient aircraft separation. We were relatively inexperienced with Snakeye bombs and concerned that one of the front bombs on the rack might strike and detonate one of the rear bombs prematurely. At 600 knots airspeed, fractions of a second were critical. We decided to adjust the timing between bombs on the multiple ejector rack (MER) to provide for safe separation and loaded six bombs on each aircraft.

Once in the air, we got to our rendezvous point with the FAC only to learn that he was too busy to handle us. Colonel Salmon decided to divert to Route Pack One and find a target on our own.

We cleared the mountains between Laos and North Vietnam and started a gradual descent heading east toward a solid layer of clouds. The shoreline provided an excellent radar reference point, but the SAM warning equipment started blinking soon after we entered the overcast. It was hard to believe that we were actually practicing a difficult, new mission for the first time over enemy territory. I could have cut my tongue out for suggesting it.

We broke out of the clouds right above the shoreline. We were 500 feet above the water and an angry offshore wind was whipping rows of breakers onto the beach. The water was gray and forbidding. Lead turned back to the west under the clouds and started toward Mu Gia Pass. The visibility was terrible and it got worse as we got closer to the mountains. Enemy radar was tracking us and I was petrified.

Colonel Salmon finally found a suitable radar target on a road junction in a narrow valley, and we dropped our bombs together on his command. Twenty-four Snakeye bombs rippled off the racks and disappeared into the murk below us. The bombing system worked, but it was impossible to tell how accurately. We lit the burners and started a max-performance climb through the clouds, hoping to avoid the mountains and enemy missiles. I held my breath. In a matter of minutes, we would be safely on top and out of there.

On the way home, we heard Warhawk flight from Korat practicing on the west side of Mu Gia Pass in the Doghouse area. The weather there was equally bad, and they were having a difficult time. On their last pass, Warhawk One hit the top of a hill and was probably killed instantly. Miraculously, the other aircraft in the flight pulled up in time and returned to Korat to prepare for the afternoon mission. It was a horrible loss and a grim way to set the stage for a Sunday afternoon trip to Viet Tri and Thai Nguyen. I felt sick all over. Warhawk One was Lieutenant Colonel Joe Austin, an upperclassman at West Point, who was an All-American lacrosse player and captain of the Army national championship lacrosse team.

JCS 82.17 At Viet Tri

The plan for the afternoon mission was daring as well as sobering. Two power plants in North Vietnam would be attacked simultaneously at low level by two flights of F-105s when the enemy least expected it. A flight of three aircraft from each wing, supported by two KC-135 tankers, would constitute the entire afternoon strike force, the only eight airplanes operating in the skies over Laos and North Vietnam. For an afternoon, we had the war to ourselves, and everyone else stayed home to watch and wait.

We were Advent flight and our tanker was Orange Anchor 46. Our TOT was precisely 1505 hours. After an initial radio check with the tanker, we planned to operate in total radio silence, with all nonessential electronic equipment turned off except for the search and ground map radar in the lead aircraft. Even the QRC-160 pods would remain on standby until the run-in to the target.

We would navigate using time-distance procedures and the leader's ground map radar for terrain clearance and initial target detection. The power plant was located just to the south of Viet Tri, in the crotch of the juncture of the Song Lo and Red Rivers. Depending on the weather, we could use a prominent sand bar in the Red River as a radar release point or as a visual identification point to start the timing to release the bombs seconds later over the target.

Our route took us from the tanker drop-off point to the Channel 97 Tacan station in northern Laos, where we would start our descent on a northeasterly heading for the next checkpoint at the Black River. From the Black River, we would push up to 600 knots airspeed and continue the descent trying to hold no more than 1,000 feet above the terrain. At 600 knots, the target was exactly five minutes and eighteen seconds from the Black River, and the release point was ten seconds after the radar freeze point at the sand bar. We had everything figured out to the split second, everything except the weather and the exact location of the sandbar.

On the way out to the airplanes, we went over the last minute details and tried to reassure each other that we could pull it off with luck and agility. We had had very little rest and we were exhausted, but once I got into the cockpit it was business as usual. It was my sixty-first mission, and I hoped it wouldn't be my last.

Advent #3, 2 + 30, Low Level, JCS 82.17 Viet Tri
Tension set in early. Had a rough lunch. We still weren't planned properly for the most crucial mission I have flown so far. Ted Tolman dropped back to spare from our original 3-ship line-up. He got us all go-pills which finally hit me on the tanker. We were tight with fear but there weren't going to be any aborts and Ted knew it. Randy Plumb was the only one thinking straight on the way to the tanker. I had one real scare when it looked like Lead had radio failure and I might have to take over the flight and lead the mission.

When we left the tanker, I watched as it disappeared over my shoulder. Now we were committed. We left Channel 97 and nosed into thick clouds at about 12,000 feet on a gradual let down. We descended to the Black River and miraculously saw it through a break in the clouds—we were slightly left of course. The Vector radar warning equipment was absolutely quiet, the silence was eerie.

We made our final turn to 075 degrees and the valley was a bowl of soup. We were in solid weather letting down on time and distance and I said a prayer. On a time hack, the target lay dead ahead for 2:00 minutes and nothing but weather—it was getting tight! We broke out at 1,000 feet with 15 seconds to go and there it was right on the nose. Flak below us, one small correction to the right and "pickle"—we were short. Red goof ball flak started everywhere and we broke hard right to depart! We had surprised the bastards on a quiet Sunday afternoon.

On the break, I became the leader but my turn wasn't tight enough. The SAM launch light came on and I couldn't decide whether to go up and into the clouds. We were really "pumping" hard. I bit the bullet and hit the soup. When we broke out on top, I hoped a MiG was following us because I really wanted one. The closer we got to 97 the more we used the radio to congratulate each other. What an exhilarating feeling when we reached the tanker and realized we had made it! I said a prayer of thanksgiving. I couldn't get home fast enough.

We got quite a reception on the ground—we were kings. Colonel Hill met Salmon and there were lots of handshakes, whiskey, debriefing, and more whiskey. Thinking back on the target, when we broke out I said to myself "there it is boss" and I felt like a lone eagle swooping in on an unaware prey. WE MADE IT!!

The public information guys gave us a bottle of Crown Royal and we started a party. Rumor spread that we are going to be recommended for the Silver Star!

Ironically, the code word for SAM warning that day was Sandbar. There were several SAMs launched but they were not a serious problem. We were low and fast, and the SAMs were fired too late to be a factor. Our worst problem was the location of the sand bar that we had selected as our timing point. It had shifted enough to throw our timing off and cause our bombs to hit slightly short of the target. We did do some damage to the buildings surrounding the power plant complex, but the results were disappointing compared to the effort we had put into the mission and the extraordinary risks we had taken.

The 388th Wing did a little better at Thai Nguyen, but their post-strike report was also less than glowing. Unfortunately, someone at headquarters jumped to the premature conclusion that our first attempt at radar bombing had been successful when, in fact, we had only used our radar for terrain clearance during descent to the target and as a reference to start the manual timer to deliver the weapons.

Regardless of the results, it had been a day to remember. Two, tough, demanding missions flown in one day, and the second was the first of its kind against North Vietnam in the F-105. After almost two days of planning, five hours of flying, endless debriefings, and too much whiskey, I was absolutely exhausted. We had more drinks and another celebration in Colonel Hill's quarters before I finally had sense enough to leave and collapse in my trailer.

Briefings at Seventh Air Force

Word spread quickly that we had gotten to Viet Tri "on radar," and Seventh Air Force as well as PACAF wanted to know all about it. We sent out a detailed operations report combining our study and mission results in one message to all interested parties, including General Ryan. But as expected, several high-ranking staff officers requested personal briefings.

I spent the next two days in Saigon discussing radar bombing with the Seventh Air Force operations staff. I briefed Major General Gordon Graham, the director of operations, and his assistant for out-country missions, Brigadier General Ed McGough. Neither was particularly enthusiastic about the concept of using the F-105 in an all-weather bombing role over North Vietnam, but both men realized that General Ryan had it high on his agenda and would not be easily dissuaded.

A decision was made to brief General Ryan as soon as possible. I was told to go back to Takhli and standby for a trip to PACAF headquarters in Honolulu. The wheels of getting an executive appointment started grinding, but CINCPACAF was a busy man, and his staff guarded his time carefully. It would be several weeks before I would finally have a day in court with the staff at PACAF Headquarters.

In the meantime, we tried our best to discourage a *carte blanche* application of radar bombing, but we were fighting a losing battle. As it turned out, our mission to Viet Tri had set the stage for a decision to form a prototype unit called "Ryan's Raiders," a new group of crews trained and specially equipped to perform all-weather, interdiction bombing in the F-105F aircraft.

15

SON TAY ARMY BARRACKS

I RETURNED TO TAKHLI from Saigon on the evening of 22 March 1967, to resume flying and wait for orders to see General Ryan at a later date. The weather was still bad in the Hanoi area, so we had diverted our strikes to the lower route packages. On one mission to the Mu Gia Pass area, fighter congestion was a serious problem, even with the help of Cricket control. I noted that "The pass was heavy with haze, clouds, F-4s, and F-105s." It was like an old-time aerial circus, with all of the excitement but none of the fun.

During the last week of March 1967, Captains Frank Buchanan and Kevin Duff finished their tours and joined forces for a bashing good 100-mission celebration. The ranks of experience in the 354th Squadron were thinning. I was becoming a seasoned flight leader, but many of the pilots in the squadron were fresh out of training. Many of the squadron veterans were either captured, dead, or on their way home with 100 missions completed.

The Army supply depot at Son Tay was a very sensitive, well-defended target. We were ordered to bomb the warehouses in the northern section of the complex, but the rest of the area was strictly off-limits. Intelligence stressed that we should avoid hitting the other buildings or anything resembling a hospital. We didn't need a reminder about hospitals, but we didn't understand the sensitivity about the other buildings in the complex, particularly the troop barracks.

After further questioning, it was clear that the intelligence people knew more than they were willing to share. The target photos were only two weeks old, so we sensed that something was especially important about Son Tay. The secrecy was frustrating but not unusual. The intelligence community often marched to the beat of a different drummer.

We finished our flight briefing, suited up, and headed for the airplanes. Ready or not, I was going to Package Six on Easter Sunday afternoon with the 333d Squadron as the deputy mission commander. Before we left the ramp, the mission commander was forced to abort due to a mechanical difficulty, so I inherited the awesome responsibility of leading the mission.

I was Fearless One, leading three strike flights scheduled on the target behind an identical strike force of F-105s from Korat. We were supported by a composite force of F-4 flights from the 8th Fighter Wing carrying bombs and providing MiG cover. The weather was forecast to be low, broken clouds with poor visibility, a rotten combination for pinpointing a target or spotting SAMs.

The armament crews had chosen the occasion to decorate our bombs like easter eggs. It shouldn't have been a surprise but it seemed paradoxical at the time, and it disturbed me. Somehow Ho Chi Minh and Easter didn't go together, and the contrast spooked me. Aside from their unusual decorations, the 750-pound bombs clustered on the belly rack of the aircraft looked as clumsy and lethal as ever.

We crossed Tacan Channel 97 and headed northeast, straight for Son Tay. The final leg to the target would take slightly less than ten minutes in a gradual descent to clear the mountainous terrain guarding the Red River valley. Ten miles west of Son Tay, our inbound route crossed the Black River and then passed between a prominent peak and a large reservoir. The peak was 4,252 feet in elevation and an excellent reference point for the target. I thought surely it would be easy to see above the haze.

We stabilized on the final run-in heading, and I called the flights to green-up their aircraft. The weather didn't look very promising. The foothills and valley beyond the Black River were filled with thick haze, which was dirty gray with hues of yellow and orange. It looked ominous. Unfortunately, the weather forecast was accurate.

Fifty miles from the target, my radar warning equipment blossomed with potential SAM threats. We were about 20 miles (two minutes) behind the Korat force and skimming along just above the haze layer. Our three flights were bunched up in a fairly tight V-formation and extremely vulnerable. I could see straight down to the ground below us, but only the treacherous haze was visible ahead of us.

Judging from the radio chatter, the mission commander leading the force from Korat ahead of us was not able to see much either. My pulse quickened and pounded in my temples. It was my first trip as the Takhli mission commander. My mouth was parched, so I took a couple of long swigs from my water bottle. The pressure of leading eleven other pilots into a dangerous combat situation was taking its toll but I had no choice, we had to proceed.

I let the aircraft have its head and nosed down gently into the haze. The forward visibility was one-half mile or less. We were on course and only two minutes from the target, but still no sight of peak 4252. I heard the Korat leader call that he had overshot the target and was doubling back to roll in. "Damn," I thought. "We'll be right on top of them in the target area, this is going to be some show."

I spotted the Black River coming up under my nose. Suddenly peak 4252 loomed out of the haze and filled my windscreen. We were slightly south of course and barely seconds away from hitting the peak dead center. I turned hard to the left and gritted my teeth. Somehow we all made it, but things were happening too fast. I was almost panic-stricken and looking desperately for Son Tay.

Seconds later I spotted the target area, a scene of pandemonium. We were too close and too slow for a decent bomb pass, so I called for afterburner and swung out wide to gain speed and altitude. The radio was jammed with calls. To add to the chaos, one of the F-4s in Nelson flight had taken a SAM hit and was down. The terrifying wail of their beepers flooded Guard Channel.

At the top of the roll-in, I could see blue sky above me but smoke and haze shrouded the target. The other two flights were still with me, so down we went into the murk, twelve strong in formation, to fling ourselves at the target. The north end of the complex was barely visible. The accuracy of seventy-two bombs depended solely on my judgment and ability.

Just as I pickled, I was horrified to see a flight of F-4s come into my sight picture. They were very low and right over the target. There was nothing I could do or say, but instinctively I called "Heads up" and pulled out hard to miss them. Our bombs went everywhere, but we didn't hit an F-4, and I hoped like hell we hadn't hit the hospital.

As we were leaving the target area, a crippled MiG-17 flew by in the opposite direction. He was trailing black smoke and looking for a place to land. I was tempted to follow him for the kill but opted instead to gather up my flight and head for the tankers. I was physically and mentally exhausted and fed up with flailing around in haze. We were lucky not to be plastered on the side of a bloody peak, and it was time to count our blessings and return to prepare to fight another day.

All the way home I cussed myself for continuing into the target. The weather was terrible, and we had everything to lose and very little to gain.

During the debriefing, an examination of the camera film from the number four aircraft in my flight revealed a potential tragedy. A single 500-pound bomb had struck the hospital in the barracks complex. Colonel Hill was irate and tried to pin it on us until we reminded him that we were carrying 750-pounders. The errant bomb must have come from one of the F-4s, but we all felt a sense of responsibility. As the mission commander, I felt particularly bad, but I was also thankful that our bombs hadn't accidentally struck the F-4s in all of the confusion and mayhem.

To the best of my knowledge, there were never any repercussions from the hospital bomb incident, but I did learn several years later that the complex at Son Tay had been a suspected prisoner of war camp. In retrospect, I was thankful that we hadn't hit the barracks, but I would have appreciated knowing more about the target on the way into Son Tay that hazy Sunday afternoon.

After a five-day break for an R&R in Okinawa, I returned to flying in early April. It took a couple of missions to tune myself mentally and physically, but I found the groove quickly. The weather was still lousy, so we had to muck around in the outer route packs looking for targets of opportunity. On one mission, we set up an orbit over a valley east of Son La, hoping to attract a MiG training flight, but all we got was constant attention from the enemy Fansong radars tracking our position from SAM sites.

I took advantage of the lull in flying to move my office into the new wing headquarters building that had just been completed. Compared to the TOC, it was a large, sprawling complex, but lacked all of the charm and nostalgia of the old teak-wood structure. The new building was made of cinder block with unimaginative square lines and was painted dark green. Inside, you could have been in a standard Air Force Air Operations Center anywhere in the world, and I had to occasionally remind myself that we were a combat unit deployed in the jungles of Thailand.

Randy Plumb finished his tour with quite an air show and a knee-walking party. We all hated to see Randy leave, but he had done a superb job and he was ready. Ted Tolman took over his duties in my shop as the wing weapons officer. We gave Ted a desk of his own, but he didn't like sitting there any better than I did.

Stateside Visit

On the afternoon of 7 April 1967, I was summoned to Colonel Scott's office and told that I had reservations on the evening Pan Am flight from Bangkok to San Francisco. The purpose of the trip was to present a number of configuration changes we had made to our aircraft to the system manager at the depot in Sacramento so that engineering changes could be approved and included in the aircraft specifications.

Colonel Scott also wanted to take advantage of the trip by setting up a radar-bombing briefing for General Ryan in Honolulu during my stop there, either going or coming. All in all, it would be about a ten-day trip, and I had precious little time to get ready.

I had just returned from an R&R, and I didn't welcome another extended break in flying. I told Colonel Scott that I appreciated the opportunity to relax on a short trip home, but I'd seen some strange things happen to guys under similar circumstances, and I didn't want to go home until I had finished my tour. I wanted to stay in a combat stride, finish my missions quickly, and get on with whatever followed next, including an assignment to the Pentagon if that's the way things shook out.

Colonel Scott listened impatiently and finally told me I was burning up precious time on a closed matter. He felt that I was the best spokesman for the configuration changes and his mind was made up. Furthermore, he was certain that General Ryan would expect me to present the results of our radar-bombing study since he had commissioned me personally to lead the study several weeks earlier. I got the point and rushed out of Colonel Scott's office to collect my things and catch the afternoon C-130 flight to Bangkok. On the way out the door, the admin sergeant handed me a round-trip ticket to San Francisco with connections to Sacramento.

I landed at the Don Muang Military Airport and hailed a cab for the international airport. It was a short drive, and I arrived at the commercial departure terminal with less than an hour to spare. Pan Am Flight Number 1 was on schedule for a 9:00 PM departure.

During the check-in process, I came within a whisker of being arrested for being in Thailand illegally. When I arrived at Takhli in October of the previous year, I had neglected to go through customs and have my passport properly documented. At that time, customs procedures were the very last thing on my mind, but they loomed as all important to the agent checking papers for the Pan Am departure from Bangkok.

Officially, I had never entered Thailand, and to make matters worse, I had traveled to Malaysia on an R&R trip, and the only entry on the visa page showed me entering Penang in November 1966. I had to agree that the appearances were indeed incriminating, and I could see how an impersonal customs agent might conclude that I didn't care much about formal immigration procedures.

After an escorted visit to the privacy of a back office and some polite calls to officials downtown, my military identification card and travel orders sufficed to satisfy the agent, but I returned to the boarding line a more understanding and sensitive American fighter pilot.

Next, an attractive Pan Am agent noticed that my immunization record was out of date. I took a variety of shots at Takhli on a regular basis, but I had never taken the trouble to have my shot record updated. The young lady politely pointed out that I would need typhoid and cholera boosters in order to enter the United States. Unfortunately, the U.S. embassy downtown was the closest place I could go to receive the shots at that hour.

My flight was boarding so I did the next best thing to going downtown. I excused myself and sought the privacy of the nearest men's room. There, I updated the record and callously forged the signature of Dr. Carbone, our trusted squadron flight surgeon. I hoped Frank would understand that it was in the line of duty, but I never tempted his professional conscience by telling him the story.

When I returned to the boarding line, keeping a straight face was difficult, but thinking about how Colonel Scott might react to the news that I had missed the flight because of my own negligence made it easier to look stern. The agent waved me through, probably thinking that any country willing to send me to do their fighting deserved an epidemic of cholera or typhoid fever.

Pan Am Flight Number 1 was an around-the-world flight that originated in New York on its eastward journey. The flight arrived in Bangkok from Rangoon, Burma, and was destined for stops in Hong Kong, Tokyo, and Honolulu, before finally terminating in San Francisco. The flight schedule from Bangkok to San Francisco called for twelve flying hours, twenty-four clock hours, two sunsets, one sunrise, and two calendar days en route.

By coincidence, I was traveling with Sam Nelson, who was a test pilot for Republic Aircraft. Sam had been at Takhli demonstrating a company-sponsored change to the F-105, called the "pilot recovery system." It was a modification to the flight control system that would allow pilots to nurse a damaged aircraft back over friendly territory before ejecting for a safe recovery. Under the skilled hands of a test pilot, the system could be used to actually land the aircraft, but that was not recommended by Republic or the Air Force.

Sam, the company project manager, and I sat in adjoining seats in the coach section of the airliner. The seats were spaced to accommodate the average Asian traveler so we were quite cramped. We had a lot in common and plenty to talk about and time seemed to pass quickly, at first. In those days, stewardesses were generous with liquor on international flights, and there was no such thing as a no-smoking section. We settled back for an enjoyable trip home, laced with war stories, booze, and plenty of cigarettes.

The late evening sun set during the flight to Hong Kong and rose again during the leg between Tokyo and Honolulu. None of us had slept much, and the rigors of the trip were beginning to show. Breakfast was a welcome change from Scotch whiskey, but I needed some exercise, a shower, and sleep more than I needed nourishment. We were only halfway through the flight, and I knew it was going to be a grueling test of endurance.

Sam and the project manager decided to take a twenty-four hour break in Hawaii and encouraged me to do the same, but my orders did not allow for variations in itinerary. I had an important date with the F-105 system manager in Sacramento, and I had to press on. There was a slight chance that I might receive a call in Honolulu to report to PACAF headquarters instead of proceeding, but I knew it was slim.

The last leg to San Francisco took an eternity. We came in over the Golden Gate Bridge just as the sun was setting, and the sight of the city brought tears to my weary eyes. Walking out of the passenger tube, I was relieved to be out of the cramped airplane, but my knees felt like jelly.

The U.S. customs agent waved me through without so much as a look-see and, in a way, I felt disappointed. The sights and sounds inside the San Francisco airport struck a patriotic chord in my sentimental heart as I made my way to yet another passenger ticket counter. A short commuter flight was all that stood between me and a clean, cool, motel bed.

Sacramento Air Materiel Area (SMAMA)

First thing the next morning I reported to the office of Colonel James T. Johnson, the F-105 system manager. He was an outgoing, impressive guy, and he didn't stand on ceremony. His desk was fashioned to resemble the instrument panel of an F-105, and his desk chair was an adaptation of an actual ejection seat taken from the cockpit of an airplane. The office was designated the "Thunderchief Tepee," and a sign on his desk read "F-105 Spoken Here!" Based on the enthusiastic welcome I received, I concluded that I had found the right office.

We sipped coffee and went over the proposed changes one at a time. In less than thirty minutes, Colonel Johnson approved the entire package of a dozen changes and asked me to stick around to go over the technical details with his engineering staff if need be. By noon, I had accomplished my task and was on my way back to the motel. Things went so smoothly that I asked myself why I had gone to all the trouble of coming to Sacramento in the first place. Based on my experience with Thirteenth Air Force, I expected a protracted bureaucratic fight but met with nothing but cooperation. The process was gratifying and a credit to the leadership and forceful management of Colonel Johnson, whose style was truly unique and refreshing.

I had completed three days of business in one morning, and I was faced with the dilemma of deciding what to do with several days of unexpected leisure. I hadn't planned to spend any time with my family or friends because I wanted to get back to the war and finish up my tour before going home to El Paso.

Although I wanted to see my parents, I didn't want to put them through the ordeal of seeing me home safe and then having to send me off to combat again in a matter of days. On the other hand, I knew they would be hurt if they found out that I had come so close and not bothered to visit or at least call. Somehow, I found myself on the horns of a guilty dilemma.

I decided to call my parents and discuss the situation with them. Perhaps I underestimated their strength, but I was worried about how they might react to the sudden shock of just a telephone call, much less a visit. They were both in their late seventies and fairly strong, but my mother suffered with an aneurysm in an artery leading to her brain and often became quite faint. Somewhat reluctantly, I placed the call.

Thank God for understanding parents. They both sounded fine and understood my predicament. Although they would have enjoyed a short visit, they urged me to enjoy myself on the beach for a few days, return to the war and win it, and then come home for a proper homecoming. They knew me, and they were willing to wait faithfully for two months more to enjoy a lasting and genuine reunion. Their advice was unselfish and loving.

Honolulu Bound

After three days with friends in Manhattan Beach, I returned to San Francisco to catch Pan Am Flight Number 2 back to Honolulu. The reservation clerk told me that the computer was down and that there had been a mix-up in reservations. Consequently, Pan Am could only guarantee my seat as far as Honolulu. That suited me because it gave me an opportunity to visit PACAF headquarters and present the results of our radar bombing study, provided the results were still relevant.

Sure enough, I was bumped in Honolulu and provided with a beach-front, ocean-view room at a local hotel, courtesy of Pan American Airlines. It was a colossal confluence of fate, luxury, and the coincidental needs of the Air Force.

I spent the next few days walking the halls of PACAF trying to see General Ryan and briefing anyone who would listen. His staff seemed interested but they made it clear that General Ryan's mind was made up. He had already directed his staff to implement precision radar bombing on selected targets by fighter aircraft, and had taken measures to form and equip a specially trained unit to do the job on a regular basis. With that advice, I rolled up my briefing charts and headed for the hotel to make the most of the beach and night life.

Pan Am finally found me a seat to Bangkok after several days and nights of luxurious living on Waikiki Beach. The girls were pretty and the tourists were interesting to watch. It was hard to believe that they would pay a beach boy to go up a lone palm tree in front of the hotel and drop a battered coconut to the sand hour after hour. The beach boys took turns, but the tree and the coconut never changed.

Bangkok Immigration

The immigration officer at Bangkok studied my official business passport carefully. I was in uniform and the picture had been taken in mufti. Worse, I had been stamped out of Thailand only ten days earlier, but there was no record of my entry. The officer had a curious look on his face, but after a prolonged stare, he validated my visa without questioning me. I was pre-pared for an argument but gladly tucked my passport in my pocket and headed for a taxi. Later on I took time to read the fine print on the visa.

> Bangkok Airport Thailand.
> Permitted to stay 15 days from the date of arrival. Holder must leave the kingdom not later than 2 May 1967 unless previous appli-cation for extension has been made in person to the local immigra-tion office. Offenders will be prosecuted. Signed by an immigration officer and dated 17 Apr 1967.

As it turned out, I didn't make it out of Thailand by the second of May and no one came looking for me. Someday, I want to return to Thailand, just to see if I can get back in without a valid passport. When I do, I will be careful to carry an up-to-date shot record.

When I reported back to Colonel Scott, the only thing that surprised him about my trip was the fact that I had not taken full advantage of the time available to me at home. He was familiar with Colonel Johnson's man-agement style and had guessed exactly what General Ryan would do about radar bombing. I didn't bother to tell him about my scrape with the immi-gration authorities in Bangkok.

16

KNIFE LEAD TO HANOI

THE FIRST DAY BACK from the States I was scheduled to lead a strike against a new JCS target, an Army barracks in the suburbs of Hanoi. Talk about going in cold turkey. I felt a little shaky and very disorganized at the mission briefing, but Ted Tolman was flying the number three position and that was comforting.

Ted had a way of propping me up when I was down. He had enough confidence for both of us and I knew I could count on him. We both got a good laugh about our call sign. We were Bashful flight. "I'll bet there's some ass-hole on the staff at Seventh who does nothing but think up call signs," Ted said gruffly as we left the briefing room.

Before we took off, the primary mission was scrubbed due to weather, and we were redirected to bomb the Quang Khe Ferry in Route Pack One. As much as I liked going to Hanoi with Ted Tolman, I must admit that I welcomed the opportunity to tune-up my reflexes on an "easy mission" before returning to the high-threat area.

Leaving the tanker, there was some confusion with Cricket Control about our target assignment, but we were finally cleared into Package One and it felt good to be back in the saddle. The weather in the target area was perfectly clear. There wasn't a cloud in the sky, and the southern coastline was beautiful. I could see details that I had never noticed before.

The Quang Khe Ferry crossed the large mouth of the Nguon Nay River where it flowed into the Gulf of Tonkin. The ferry was a frequent target and was marked with literally hundreds of the bomb craters. There were so many craters that it was difficult to pick out a good target, but we rolled-in and put our bombs on a sandy road that traversed the pock-marked approach to the ferry. We encountered light ground fire, but there was no flak so we made two strafing passes for good measure and headed home.

That afternoon I received a Distinguished Flying Cross for a mission I had flown in January when we downed the Ha Gia railroad bridge on the dreaded northeast railroad. The ceremony was hastily arranged for the convenience of a visiting dignitary, a three-star general from Washington whom I didn't know or recognize. In my diary, I noted, *"Lt Gen Somebody gave me a DFC today."* He was very thoughtful and mentioned that he had read the account of Lincoln flight over the steel mill at Thai Nguyen earlier in March. He didn't know the outcome of the recommendations for awards, but he was impressed and urged me to keep up the good work. I thanked him, but I wasn't sure I wanted to face the perils of Linclon again for any amount of recognition.

The next day my vacation was over. The wing was fragged to hit a tough target on the northeast railroad, an ammunition depot at Bac Giang, designated JCS 47.21. I was Detroit Two in Colonel Broughton's flight. Memories of an earlier Detroit flight combined with the perils associated with the northeast railroad set a grim scene in my mind. My heart went on double pump the minute we left the tanker.

Colonel Broughton had intermittent radio problems, and the weather was rotten. I felt that we should have turned back, but the wing from Korat was ahead of us and had somehow gotten through to the target. We pressed on, but a serious navigation error put us several miles north of the target and directly over Kep Airport. Without warning, the antiaircraft guns ringing the airport opened up, and we were surrounded by large bursts of flak.

In desperation, Lead started a climbing turn, hoping to follow the railroad south to the target, but the flak was so bad we were forced to roll-in on a section of track, hoping to hit anything that might be crippling. I pickled my bombs on a AAA battery and headed east to catch Broughton. I could barely see his airplane through the smoke and haze, and I could hear the bursts of flak as they exploded around us. The guns were tracking Detroit flight.

Somehow we made it back to the water with only minor damage, but finding our tanker in the weather was a hassle. By the time I got on the boom, the airplane was so low on fuel the engine was sucking vapor. As the tanks began to fill, I thanked God and thought about the stupidity of having to jump out of a perfectly good airplane over the Gulf of Tonkin because of fuel starvation. All the way back to Takhli, I promised myself I would never fly another Detroit flight.

Knife Lead, Force Commander

I flew my seventieth mission on 25 April 1967 on a daring strike against a new target designated JCS 82.24, a transformer site that provided most of the electrical power to the city of Hanoi. It was a small target and difficult to see from the air at high speed and under pressure. From the single target photo we were provided, the transformer station was barely distinguishable from an adjoining village located in the northern suburbs of Hanoi.

The site was not shown on a map so the photo was the only reference I had to go by. The target was a small, dark square in the marshy suburbs of Hanoi, just north of the junction of the Canal Des Rapides and the Red River, and 1 mile south of two road bridges crossing a narrow, man-made canal. At best, finding the target was going to be a dicey maneuver.

Knife flight would lead the force, carrying CBU-24 bomblets for flak suppression. Five strike flights with 3,000-pound bombs, a Wild Weasel flight, and our F-4 MiGCAP would follow us into the target. After discussing the size and location of the target, we decided to fly down the east side of Thud Ridge in trail formation, with one minute between flights. The separation would give each flight leader a better opportunity to look for the target and react to the situation.

After engine start, I checked in as Knife Three but moved up to take the lead position as Knife Lead when the force commander was forced to return to the parking ramp with aircraft problems. We reorganized the flight in the arming area and took the runway for takeoff.

I was thrilled and excited. As an unexpectant flight leader, I had inherited the best team I could hope for to do a difficult job. Captain Gene Eskew was flying my wing, Captain Bill Hoeft was leading the element, and Lieutenant Paul Sheehy, with the eyes and reflexes of a hawk, was flying the number four position. We had flown together often, we had confidence in one another, and we had plenty of experience in Route Pack Six.

The weather in the refueling area was worse than expected. The tanker crews did their best to find a clear spot for refueling, but the clouds were everywhere, at all altitudes. At one point, I considered aborting the mission because of the weather, but we kept after the tankers and finally made it to the drop-off point with full tanks and in the proper flight order.

Over the Tacan station at Channel 97, I started a descent and headed northeast for the loop in the Red River. The weather didn't look any better over the foothills leading to the valley. To make matters worse, the mission commander from Korat had been delayed by the same bad weather and was late on target. I was out in front and all alone, making the decisions. I was nervous as hell and the weather indications were rotten, but I pressed on in spite of repetitive queries from the trailing flight leaders to reconsider.

I spotted the loop in the river through a hole in the broken clouds and headed due east for the ridge. Our external fuel tanks were dry, so we jettisoned them and pushed up to 600 knots airspeed.

The weather improved slightly as we turned down Thud Ridge. Halfway to the target, the clouds broke wide open and so did the defenses. In a sinister way, the scene was beautiful. We were streaking in at 2,000 feet with blue sky above us, a clear valley before us, and Hanoi right on the nose.

"Knife, two MiGs at two o,clock, level, one mile," Gene Eskew radioed from the left side.

Almost simultaneously, Bill Hoeft called, "Knife, we have four bandits at ten o'clock moving to nine. Slightly high at one mile."

I spotted the enemy aircraft and they were all MiG-17s. At our speed, they didn't pose a threat to our flight, but I warned the flights behind us. "Knife Leader has MiGs on both sides fading to six, heads up on the ridge!"

For a few seconds, I watched the MiGs carefully. It was a sight an artist could use for a painting. Both formations were in tight echelon and trying to attack us from either side, most likely under ground radar control. Because of our speed differential, they began to fall back quickly.

As if commanded by a single voice, both MiG formations turned toward us desperately trying to press the attack. In their turns, they fanned out in a spread formation and simultaneously dropped their external fuel tanks. It was a magnificent sight, and for an instant I almost felt sorry for them. They were too late for Knife flight and they knew it. I was tempted to engage them, but I pressed on toward the target, making gentle turns to keep them in sight.

As we got closer to the target the air filled with SAMs. The radio was jammed with warnings, but most of the SAMs were in front of us, easy to see and evade if necessary. I wanted to jink, but I held a steady hand on the stick and started an easy turn to the left to correct back to course for the transformer station.

From the radio chatter, it was clear that the MiGs had tried to convert their attack on the flights behind us. Even though they were not particularly effective, MiGs were a distraction and somewhat disruptive. I called the other flight leaders, urging them to press on in spite of the MiGs, knowing we would need all of the eyeballs and firepower we could muster to find and destroy the target.

Crab flight was the last flight in our strike force. I was relieved to hear Crab Lead call, "Leaving the loop, pushing up, and dropping tanks." The strike flights were carrying two 3,000-pound bombs, one under each wing, with a 650-gallon tank on the centerline station of the fuselage. The centerline tanks looked like big bananas, were a nuisance to carry, and sometimes were unpredictable when jettisoned. I sensed from the tone of Crab Lead's voice that he was uptight and concerned that something might go wrong with his flight.

We were about a minute away from the pull-up point, and I was still searching for the target frantically. The valley was a patchwork maze of water and small farming communities. I was looking for some sign of regularity and the slender canal that led to the target in the photo. The ground gunners around Phuc Yen joined the SAM defenses with their persistent and ever present barrage of flak. The ugly bursts were layered and detonated very consistently several thousand feet to the left of us.

Bill Hoeft spotted the target and called it out. I thought I saw it too and started to pull-up. There were plenty of guns firing on the ground, so selecting a flak site to bomb would be easy.

As I passed through 10,000 feet, just below the top of the pull-up, I identified the target and decided to bomb it instead of the neighboring flak sites. The transformer site was more difficult to see than I had imagined, so I figured we might as well try to hit it with bomblets rather than gambling on another flight finding it at all. Although small, CBU-24 bomblets covered a wide area and were very effective against vulnerable targets standing above ground.

As we rolled-in and started down the chute, it looked as if we could hit the transformers as well as several of the surrounding flak sites with the wide coverage of our weapons. Twenty-four bomb canisters loaded with several hundred bomblets could cover a lot of real estate.

I had a perfect dive-bomb pass and pressed the pickle button when the pipper centered on the target. In a matter of seconds, Knife Four called, "Off the target." I looked back over my shoulder at the ground as I pulled up in a high-G turn. Our bomblets were exploding all over the target area in a sparkling circle of fire a mile in diameter. The transformer site was right in the middle. Lights out Hanoi.

I was so relieved and proud that I forgot about the flak and SAMs for a second. I heard the next flight call "Rolling in," and hoped like hell at least one 3,000-pounder would find its way to the center of the transformer site. A direct hit would put it out of action for months, and would be good insurance against having to come back again.

Our flight re-formed and started jinking out along the Red River toward Viet Tri. I had a hunch that we might find some MiGs trying to sneak up behind the last flight in the strike force, so I turned back toward the ridge. So far, the mission had overcome incredible odds, and I felt buoyant enough to take on all six MiGs at once or one at a time.

I spotted a flight of F-105s streaking down the base of Thud Ridge. There weren't any MiGs behind them, but the flight looked like it was in trouble. Then, screams over the radio told the story. "Crab, take it down, TAKE IT DOWN," pierced my headset. A volley of SAMs was streaking head-on toward their formation. I felt helpless.

In a desperate attempt to evade the SAMs, Crab Lead pushed over sharply and the flight tried to stay with him. The wingmen had to pull extremely high negative-G loads to maintain formation. They were very low and forced to reverse controls quickly to avoid hitting the ground. Pulling extremely high positive-G loads under those conditions at high speed could induce an oscillating motion in pitch, called a "porpoise maneuver," a condition that could get out of control quickly and result in structural loads far in excess of the aircraft limits.

Crab Two bottomed out close to the ground and pitched up violently. Both 3,000-pound bombs broke loose from the wing pylons and smashed against the underside of the aircraft, seriously damaging both wings. "Crab Two is hit, I'm getting out," a voice said desperately over the radio. A split second later, his aircraft hit the ground with the full force of 600-knots momentum and exploded in an enormous fireball.

I watched helplessly and felt a huge lump form in my throat. We had lost Crab Two and one of our best young pilots, Lieutanant Bob Weskamp. What a horrible loss! As the force commander, I felt responsible, frustrated, and angry as all hell.

The other flights made it to the target, but Crab had to pickle their bombs in order to regroup and survive. I turned Knife flight in behind Crab, covering their six o'clock. They were vulnerable and easy pickings for MiGs returning to Phuc Yen. As soon as all the flights were out of the target area, I turned west across the valley for the foothills, and we were on our way back to the tankers.

Against stiff defenses, we had found an obscure target, bombed it, and lost a young pilot in the process. I was emotionally and physically exhausted, but I was proud of the job we had done as a team and especially proud of Knife flight. When we greeted each other on the ground we were drained, but it was obvious that we had experienced a new level of camaraderie, which was exhilarating.

The results of the mission were discouraging. Our camera film revealed that our CBUs had hit all around the transformer site and on top of several flak batteries, but the damage was difficult to assess. Unfortunately, in the confusion of battle only one of the strike flights put bombs close to the target. One frame of film did show a single 3,000-pounder hitting within 25 feet of the transformers, but the extent of damage was not clear. It didn't take a space scientist to figure out that we were going back to JCS 82.24.

During the mission debriefing, we discussed the loss of Bob Weskamp, and someone mentioned that his brother had been flying one of the tankers we used on the mission. What a jolt and tragic turn of events. I wondered if I had the courage to face his brother and thought about what I would say. There was no way to explain Bob's loss except to say that unfortunate things like that happen in the heat of battle. No explanation in the world would have eased the grief for his brother and family.

That evening, Radio Hanoi announced that their "Valiant MiG pilots had foiled a savage attack on an important transformer site in the outskirts of Hanoi." The announcement added that the United States had lost one aircraft in the raid and that First Lieutenant Robert L. Weskamp had been apparently killed while ejecting from his F-105 north of Hanoi. Several days later, a Bangkok paper carried a front page picture showing Bob's body laid across the wreckage of an airplane, with a caption praising the courage of the North Vietnamese defenders. The callousness of the Hanoi press enraged and disgusted me.

Ironically, the mission with Knife flight signaled the start of an all-out campaign to destroy the transformer site, and our losses began to mount quickly. In the next five days, we tried five times to reach JCS 82.24 and lost four aircraft and six crewmen in the process, one aircraft to a SAM and three in one mission to a MiG-21.

Box Lunch Over the Northeast Railroad

Several missions later, we were diverted to strike a rail yard on the northeast railroad. My wingman was flying his first mission into the high-threat area. It was a long mission (three plus fifty-five hours), and against my advice, he insisted on taking a box lunch. I assured him that he would not have time or an appetite for lunch once he got a look at the action awaiting us on the railroad but he insisted.

On the way into the target, I had to constantly signal my wingman to keep up with us. We were extremely vulnerable, and he was lagging back in a dangerous position. "Four, move it up," I urged him repeatedly.

"Rog, I got you," he responded, sounding very cool and nonchalant.

"What the hell," I thought. "He's gonna get his ass shot off eating his lunch and never know what hit him."

The entire strike force arrived over the target at the same time and rolled-in together. Incredibly, two trains were in the yard and another pulled in just as we started bombing. We plastered the yard without running into each other, but the force commander took some friendly hits in his tail from our own CBU-24 flak suppression. He survived but his voice went up an octave or two in the process.

Once the shooting started, my wingman changed his attitude. He moved up and stayed in position like a veteran. For the rest of the mission, he stuck to me like flypaper. I couldn't shake him. Leaving the tanker, I thought about the box lunch, but I couldn't tell if he was eating it.

After we landed and met in the line truck, it was obvious that Four had gotten sick in the cockpit and had been forced to use the box lunch as an emergency container. It was a disgusting mess, and I was tempted to say "I told you so," but I kept my mouth shut and saved my criticism of his formation-flying technique for the debriefing. He looked embarrassed as hell, and I had serious doubts about his longevity.

Of all my missions and exciting experiences, I'm fairly sure that was the only box lunch to log a counter over North Vietnam.

That afternoon, 30 April 1967, we suffered a staggering series of losses on the way back to JCS 82.24. Before the strike force got to the Red River, we lost two aircraft out of the Wild Weasel flight to a MiG-21 and were forced to abort the mission to provide rescue support for the downed crewmen. In the process, a MiG-21 (probably the same one) downed the Number Four man in one of the flights providing Rescap for the crews downed earlier.

In less than an hour, we had lost three aircraft. The force commander had his hands full trying to direct rescue operations to recover four of our men before the enemy could capture them. Carbine Four, Carbine Three, and Tomahawk Four were down in order, and it was a race against time to recover them.

The rescue effort was a chaotic scene compounded by hazy weather, late afternoon light, and some unfortunate equipment malfunctions aboard the rescue helicopters. The Carbine Three crewmen, Major Leo Thorsness, and his EWO, Captain Harry Johnson, were in sight on the ground, in communication with rescue forces, and ready for recovery, when the effort was aborted because one of the rescue helicopters developed engine problems.

The location of Carbine Four, Lieutenant Bob Abbott, was not pinpointed early enough to attempt a recovery, and darkness suspended the attempts to rescue Tomahawk Four, Captain Joe Abbott. (Only a tragic coincidence, the two men were not related.) The rescue commander told Joe Abbott to take cover for the night and assured him that the rescue forces would return at first light the next morning.

After an all night planning session, we sent a combination Rescap and MiG sweep force back early the next morning, but it was not successful. We were too late. Leo Thorsness, Harry Johnson, and Bob Abbott had been taken prisoner by the time we got there, and the whereabouts of Joe Abbott was not certain. Joe's loss hit me especially hard because I had a personal stake in his training.

We heard a weak radio call from someone on the ground responding to repeated calls for Tomahawk Four, but it was probably one of his North Vietnamese captors trying to bait a trap for a flight of MiGs lurking in the foothills. All four men spent the next six years as prisoners of war and were repatriated in 1973. They paid a high price for an aborted mission to an obscure and damaged transformer site in the outskirts of Hanoi.

The last time we went after the Hanoi transformer site, the commander of the 354th Squadron, Lieutenant Colonel Phil Gast, led the force, and I was his deputy, flying the number three position.

Phil had over ninety missions, and he was pushing himself hard. He was normally cool but that day he seemed edgy and terribly nervous. He knew that if he could fly his last ten missions in Route Pack Six it would enhance his combat record and his reputation as a professional, but it was also an added risk that might not be worth taking. Phil was on a fast track in the Air Force, and he wanted to maintain all of the momentum he could muster.

By sheer grit we got as far down the valley as Phuc Yen before the weather forced us to jettison our bombs and head back empty handed. We had plenty of fuel so we made an afterburner, supersonic departure from the Red River and popped up through the soup to rejoin with our post-strike tankers. We would return safely but the mission was a failure, and Phil was naturally disappointed.

After we landed, there wasn't much to talk about except all of the effort we had devoted trying to hit a single transformer site. Valuable resources had been squandered on a difficult target that had probably sustained sufficient damage during the first strike led by Knife flight, but we couldn't be sure of it.

Phil dismissed our flight and asked me to meet him in his office to discuss a matter privately. When I confirmed that the 388th Wing was planning to host a special dining-in and weapons conference at Korat, he looked disappointed. He was planning his own 100-mission dining-in for about the same time, and he didn't want anything to interfere with it. In particular, he didn't want our commander to use his party as an excuse to turn down the conference at Korat and appear to fan the flames of wing rivalry. I shared his concern; his timing was bad and the results could be embarrassing.

17

WABASH
CANNONBALLS

IN THE EARLY MORNING hours of 3 May 1967, we were tired and frustrated. We had made repeated attempts to destroy the transformer site near Hanoi, with only limited success. We had taken some cutting losses in the process and had seen the attempts to rescue four of our best crews fail when they should have succeeded. Our combination MiG sweep and rescue mission, as exciting and refreshing as it was, had been foiled by the weather, and hope of rescuing Tomahawk Four was growing dimmer by the hour.

Our frustration continued. After hours of planning, the morning MiG sweep mission was delayed only to be ordered to go at the last minute. As expected, the weather was terrible, and the MiGs sat it out safely on the ground, so the strike force returned to try again in the afternoon. Ted Tolman and I were in charge of all of the special flight planning, and we were worn out but willing to try anything that might work to get us off of top-dead-center.

When Colonel Broughton landed we put our heads together and came up with an interesting plan. We would use one flight of F-105s to provide our own MiG cover on a mission that would have the appearance of another strike against the transformer site. If the weather broke and we got through, so much the better. If not, we could divert the strike flights to alternate targets and use the cover flight to locate the position of Tomahawk Four and troll for MiGs simultaneously. In either event, we would have one flight of clean F-105s poised and ready for a MiG fight if the North Vietnamese adhered to their operational pattern.

Ted and I went to work planning the details while Colonel Broughton talked to the boss and Seventh Air Force. After a few last minute changes and a flurry of phone calls, headquarters reluctantly agreed to let us fly the mission.

Colonel Broughton led the cover flight as the force commander. I was flying his wing, and Ted Tolman was Three with Paul Sheehy on his wing as number Four. We were Wabash flight leading five other flights, tired but eager for a fight. The mission code word for MiGs was Hurdy Gurdy, and the Wabash cannonballs were armed and ready to face the music, red eyed and grinning.

Halfway down the ridge, we had to abort the strike mission because of bad weather. On command, the force turned in place to go to their alternate targets. Wabash flight headed for the foothills, eager to look for MiGs and make a last, desperate attempt to locate Tomahawk Four. Joe Abbott had been down for almost three days, and his trail was surely getting cold and lonely.

When we reached the foothills, Wabash flight split into two elements and started to fly a racetrack search pattern. After several turns, we received a very weak beeper signal that responded to our initial command but faded quickly. We continued the search for almost thirty minutes without success—no beeper and no MiG interceptors. We had worked our way down to low altitude and I was burning fuel like crazy. I was tempted to suggest that we concentrate on finding MiGs but I kept my mouth shut. Finding Joe Abbott was important but I sensed that we were flailing away at low altitude for nothing.

Wabash Lead sent Three and Four back to the tanker for fuel. It was necessary to split our coverage in order to continue the search effort. Without the support of the element we were more vulnerable to attack and far less effective as MiG hunters. Lead was determined to find Joe Abbott or MiGs, and I was obliged to hang on and do my job as a wingman. I kept glancing at the fuel gauge and wondering what we were going to do if we did get tapped by MiGs. Low on fuel, we would be asking for a fight we couldn't finish.

"Wabash Two, fuel state?" Lead asked.

"Roger, Wabash Two is bingo-minus-five [2,500 pounds of fuel remaining, about twenty-five minutes of flying time]. Suggest we punch tanks and save some drag, over." Without our drop tanks we would not be very useful for subsequent rescue cover, but I sensed that we needed to save fuel in case we ran into trouble looking for a tanker.

"Roger, drop tanks, ready now," and away they went to the foothills below. Both the airplane and I breathed a sigh of relief.

Lead was cutting it close and I was getting nervous. When I reached 2,000 pounds of fuel remaining I called it, and we started back to the tanker. With luck, I could make an emergency recovery at Udorn if we missed the tanker, but I didn't have enough fuel to screw around in the process. When Wabash Lead asked for a vector to the closest tanker, there was total silence. Suddenly, not a soul could hear us and we were left to fend for ourselves. Even Wabash Three and Four had apparently disappeared and were silent.

We started an immediate climb and headed for the Red Anchor refueling rendezvous point that had been assigned to us during the mission briefing. I had 1,500 pounds of fuel remaining, and the fuel flow meter indicated that I was burning 6,000 pounds per hour, 100 pounds per minute. At that rate, we had about ten minutes to wake up the airborne control net and find a tanker able to help us.

Wabash Lead switched to Guard Channel, and we turned our transponder beacons to the emergency squawk position. Suddenly, we had more help than we could use, including some from our own Number Three man.

"Wabash Lead, this is Three. We're outbound from the tankers heading zero-four-five for the search area. Have you at twelve o'clock on a DF* steer, over." We were heading southwest so Ted's report was encouraging. But we couldn't see the tankers, and our range to them was uncertain.

I checked our position, and we were over the Plaine des Jarres in Laos, the headquarters of the enemy Pathet Lao Army. My fuel was dropping steadily. At just below 1,000 pounds, I reported my fuel state to the leader. He wasn't exactly fat either; he only had 200 pounds more than I did.

We started receiving urgent radio calls from Red Crown and Ethan Charlie, two airborne command posts; from Brigham Control; and from points as far away as Udorn Tower in Thailand. Several tankers also tuned in trying to help us, but the net effect was zero. Lead finally lost his cool and gave a stinging all-points lecture about radio discipline, and the radio got quiet quickly. I was trying to save fuel, but my gauge was knocking on 500 pounds.

"Wabash Lead, Two is at five hundred pounds and hurting," I called with all the cool I could muster. My call prompted another open-mike lecture from Lead on the stupidity of two perfectly good F-105s going down over Laos because someone at a radar console couldn't get their thumb out of their butt long enough to find us a tanker.

White Anchor 66

"Wabash flight, White Anchor Six-Six has your beacon at ten o'clock, forty miles. We're heading north at twenty-four thousand, turn left to zero-niner-

---

*Radio Direction Finder. It uses a needle in the cockpit to point to the transmitting radio and show a bearing to the station.

zero degrees and you should have us at your one to two o'clock position and closing, over."

We turned and started a gradual descent as Wabash Lead froze the airways again, "EVERYONE EXCEPT WHITE ANCHOR SIX-SIX SHUT UP!"

I only had 200 pounds of fuel, and I was looking so hard for the tanker that my eyes were burning. "Wabash flight, White Anchor Six-Six has a visual. You're slightly high at twelve o'clock, less than five miles and closing fast, over."

We crossed over the tanker and Lead started a steep turn to the north to join-up, but the tanker was slower and we overran him. When I finally spotted the tanker, he was at our seven o'clock position and 1,000 feet below us. I had to do a high yo-yo maneuver to keep him in sight. My fuel gauge was bumping zero, and I could feel the engine beginning to surge. I was within seconds of a flameout.

I pulled the nose up and over in a tight left turn to try to drop in behind the tanker. I moved the throttle but there was no response, the engine was spooling down at 65 percent and I was out of fuel. I punched my mike button, "White Anchor, toboggan. Go down, GO DOWN. I'm flamed out!" I felt helpless. I was still overrunning the tanker slightly and too far ahead of him to drop down into the trail position. It was difficult to stay above him and keep him in sight. I was desperate, "Come on fellows, give me a chance and toboggan, get the nose DOWN!"

Finally, the tanker pitched over and started to accelerate. I eased down into the refueling position behind him. For a split second, I was in perfect position and steady behind the boom. I held my breath and said a prayer.

The boomer began to align the refueling boom nozzle with my receptacle just as the tanker began to inch away slowly. I thought, "Come on, boomer. Stab me now." The tanker slowed down slightly and the gap between us stabilized. Split seconds seemed like hours, and I felt myself tense up all over.

"Looking good, Wabash Two. Hold her steady, boom coming out now. Boomer has a contact and CONNECT, over!" The nozzle moved into the receptacle, and the locking latches closed with a sharp clunk. I almost went limp.

The boom was locked into the receptacle, and my aircraft was being towed as the tanker began to pass fuel. "Hallelujah, praise the Lord and that beautiful boomer," I shouted out loud to myself. "We did it!"

When fuel started showing on the fuel gauge, I went through the air start procedure, and the engine came back to life quickly. At 500 pounds, I hit the boom disconnect switch and moved out to the side to let Wabash Lead have a turn. Within seconds, he was in position and taking fuel. After

Lead got enough fuel to make it home, I moved in again for a top-off and we dropped down and headed for Takhli.

The feeling that came over me as we left White Anchor 66 was a combination of embarrassment, joy, pride, relief, thanks, and humility. I was so proud of the tanker that I could have kissed the whole crew on both cheeks, especially the boomer. They had stuck their necks way out for us and done a superb job under enormous pressure. The fuel they gave us reduced their own reserve and put them on the ragged edge of making it back safely.

"White Anchor Six-Six, this is Wabash. Good show, old buddy. Leaving your frequency. Thanks a bunch, see you at Channel Forty-Three. Wabash go button three and check in, over!"

"Wabash Two, roger."

The force of what we had done hit me halfway home as we were descending for a landing. In a way, I felt foolish because we had really done it to ourselves, but I was relieved that I wouldn't have to explain the unnecessary loss of an airplane.[*] The thought of spending time as a prisoner of war because I had failed to speak up when I knew we were putting ourselves in crack was enough to make my skin crawl. "Shake it off and count your blessings," I thought. "Skill and cunning had won again, but only by the skin on my rosy red ass."

We tried to submit a commendation for the crew of White Anchor 66, with a special recommendation for an Air Medal for the boomer, but their detachment commander discouraged us. I was shocked when he explained that the recommendation might result in a reprimand rather than a commendation because it would reveal the fact that the crew had overextended themselves beyond the limits set in their operating procedures.

The detachment commander apologetically suggested that we limit our thanks to a pat on the back and perhaps a personal letter of appreciation in the interest of keeping the episode out of official Strategic Air Command (SAC) review channels. It was hard to believe but we decided to think it over.

A few days later, I discussed the matter with Colonel Broughton, and we decided to submit the commendation anyway. We were convinced that the crew deserved official recognition, and we were willing to test the wrath of SAC headquarters to see that they got it. I figured they would appreciate our effort even if they did get their knuckles rapped, and the process might serve to air out a system that sounded a bit too autocratic and stuffy in the first place.

------

[*]The aircraft, F-105D S/N 62-4329, was subsequently lost by the 354th TFS during a crash landing at Takhli on 5 October 1967.

We submitted the commendations but they disappeared in the system. Suffice it to say, the courage and resourcefulness of White Anchor 66 over the Plaine des Jarres that afternoon will live on in the annals of war as a memorable accomplishment.

In all of the commotion of our refueling fete, it was sobering to learn that Major Charles Vasiliadis, my old buddy and one-time trailermate, had been shot down not far from where we had been refueling. The intelligence debriefer added that Vas had a good chute and the rescue operation was in process, but the outcome was still uncertain.

Within thirty minutes we were told that Vas had been recovered by a Jolly Green helicopter and was on his way to a hospital with injuries to his left leg and hip. During the ejection, he was trying to hold the aircraft straight with the rudder pedal, and the force of the ejection seat jammed his leg under the instrument panel, nearly severing his leg and breaking his hip. It was a serious injury that was not uncommon during ejections from damaged F-105s with hydraulic control system problems.

Vas was treated at the emergency hospital at Korat and airlifted to Kadena Air Base on Okinawa for hospitalization and rehabilitation. Vas was indestructible and I wondered when I would see him again. Little did I know that it would be a surprise visit during an unexpected stopover at Kadena.

The next morning I flew another mission in the vicinity where Carbine and Tomahawk had been shot down. In vain, I tried to locate their position and listen for some evidence of a beacon but there was nothing. For an instant, I thought I heard a weak beeper, but it was probably my imagination or a North Vietnamese soldier trying to bait a trap with a worn out beacon.

During the mission, the weather went sour at Takhli, and I had to recover at Korat. The 388th Wing had a penchant for unusual mascots and their newest was an Asian honey bear cub they had affectionately named "Thud." I was leery of bears, but Thud looked friendly enough to want to cuddle. My host assured me that honey bears were gentle by nature and encouraged me to get to know Thud a little better. After all, he reasoned, a bear with a nickname like Thud couldn't be all bad.

Against my better judgment I reached down to pick up the cub, and suddenly he was all teeth. Before I could react, Thud had a grip on my forearm with his mouth and claws, and he wasn't being playful. He growled, and I instinctively jerked my arm out of his grip, tearing open a small wound that was not serious. A large Band-Aid stopped the bleeding, but my confidence with small bears was irrevocably damaged.

Later I learned that Thud turned out to be an Asian black bear, and he grew to several times the normal size of a honey bear. Alas, I had been the victim of another clever plot by Major Lash Lagrou, the 388th's champion practical joker. I chuckled because I knew it would make a great a war story, one I could embellish and tell over and over.

More Losses

During the first week and a half in May our losses continued to mount heavily. Lieutenant Jim Shively took a direct hit right over downtown Hanoi and had to eject immediately. Within minutes, he was being paraded down the main street of Hanoi as a war criminal, with full coverage by the international press.

In Route Pack One, Captain Mike McCuistion went down flying the wing commander's airplane, tail number 105. Only a handful of pilots in the wing were authorized to fly that airplane, and Mike wasn't one of them. Colonel Scott hit the ceiling but he simmered down when he realized that his anger was foolish and insensitive. The aircraft had taken a direct 37mm hit on a strafing pass. It was unfortunate, but it could have happened to anyone.

The rescue attempt for Mike was a failure. While he waited desperately on top of a hill for recovery, forty precious minutes were wasted in a senseless argument between rescue forces over who had jurisdiction, the Navy or the Air Force, for the recovery. The delay gave the North Vietnamese the time they needed to locate Mike and send him on an agonizing journey toward years of captivity in Hanoi.

On 12 May 1967, Captain Earl Grenzebach was hit by heavy automatic weapons fire during a strike on a JCS target at the Nguyen Khe storage area in Package Six. In an instant he was hit and out of the airplane, but a rescue attempt was not feasible. Regrettably, Earl became another MIA on a growing list of losses.

The next morning the weather was bad in the Hanoi area, so the wing took a breather flying missions in the lower route packs.

The 354th Squadron used the break to let Major Ed Sutton earn his spurs as a flight leader on an armed reconnaissance mission along the southern shore line. I was Number Three in the formation, acting as his instructor and check pilot. Ed seemed nervous, but he had his act together.

The weather was overcast when we arrived in the target area but it broke up very quickly. To our surprise, we spotted three longboats about 200 yards offshore headed for the beach. They were loaded with ammunition and trying to use the cover of the clouds to reach a surface rendezvous.

The air was calm with a very light onshore breeze, perfect for a school-book strafing pass. We were out of range of the AAA guns and too low for SAMs, so we could relax and concentrate on accuracy. If the boats were armed their guns were out of sight and certainly no match for our 20mm Gatling guns.

We fanned out in two elements and rolled-in on offset axes. On the first pass, Ed Sutton's gun jammed so he pulled his element up to cover us. I rolled in to the south parallel to the coastline and started tracking the boat closest to the beach. An instant before the pipper centered on the target, I pulled the trigger and the gun answered with a deep growl. The boat exploded in my gun sights, and a geyser of water and smoke shot up in front of my aircraft. As I pulled up for another pass, I saw two halves of the boat sinking very quickly.

I made several more passes on the other boats, but they didn't sink and there weren't any secondary explosions. I had to settle for one confirmed "longboat victory" and two probables. Ed Sutton was frustrated and disappointed, but he had earned his flight leader orders.

MiGs Over the Rail Yard

That afternoon the weather broke in Six-A, and we finally caught up with some MiGs over JCS 19, a railroad yard near Hanoi. Banner headlines in the Monday, May 15, 1967, edition of *Stars and Stripes* read "7 MIGs Shot Down in Hanoi Air Fight." The newspaper story gave the following account of the action.

> SAIGON (UPI)—U.S. Air Force pilots, stung by the loss of three jets during raids on Hanoi Friday, launched a massive "MIG sweep" over the Communist capital Saturday and downed seven of the Communist fighters and probably two others, a U.S. spokesman announced.
>
> The Air Force F105s and F4Cs, again flying from Thailand, caught the MIGs while on strike missions in the Hanoi area. All were MIG17s, the workhorse of the Communist air defense system.
>
> The spokesman said the F105 Thunderchiefs destroyed five of the 17s and probably two others. The Phantoms knocked down two more. They flew from the 8th Tactical Fighter Wing at Ubon, the 355th Tactical Fighter Wing at Takhli and the 388th Tactical Fighter Wing at Korat.
>
> There were no immediate reports of American losses in Saturday's raid.

Saturday's kills brought to 58 the number of MIGs shot down by U.S. aircraft over North Vietnam. Communist fighters have downed only 16 American planes.

By the time the story ran in a subsequent issue of the *Seventh Air Force News,* the number of confirmed kills had grown to ten. At Takhli we had contributed three kills to the tally and were proud of the pilots. Lieutenant Colonel Phil Gast, Major Bob Rilling, and Captain Charlie Couch had each scored a victory over the heavily defended rail yard and we had a whale of a party to celebrate the occasion.

A few days later, I flew a mission under some very unusual circumstances. Late at night and at the last minute, I was asked to take Colonel Scott's place on the schedule as the force commander for an early morning raid on a JCS target. Colonel Scott was recovering from surgery on his nose, and the wound was bleeding badly.

The mission briefing was scheduled for 0345, and several of us overslept due to the gaiety of the previous evening. The Tactical Operations Center didn't get the word on the schedule change and awoke Colonel Scott when no one showed up at the mission briefing as the force commander. I was late, but I made it just in time to receive a masterful ass-chewing by the commander. He was still drowsy and very much out of sorts.

Undaunted, we continued with the mission. As we taxied out in the dark, the Weasels wound up in the arming area one aircraft short and absent a leader. After a confusing radio discussion between me, the supervisor of flying, and the command post, we decided to leave the Weasels behind and leap off as scheduled. Thank God the mission was scrubbed on the way to the tanker. We split up into flights to go to our alternate targets, and we all returned unscathed but weary and a little wiser about partying too late the night before a mission.

The next day we got off to a better start but the primary mission was aborted again, and my flight was diverted to work with a Firefly FAC near Sam Neua in northeastern Laos.

The FAC marked the target, and we rolled-in to bomb it by elements from opposite sides of a high orbit. Low, puffy clouds covered the area, so it was difficult to distinguish the smoke marker and the exact location of the target, but our luck took a turn for the better.

The defenses were light and our bomb damage was outstanding. The FAC was excited when he reported the assessment. In two passes we had destroyed the Pathet Lao Reserve Officer Training Center, a large storage area, an automatic weapons site, and a weapons storage area which was hidden in the karst. All of our bombs produced excellent secondary explosions.

On the way back to Takhli, I thought about the irony of a West Point graduate destroying an enemy ROTC headquarters. Contrary to the myth that ring knockers had little patience with reserves, I had a great deal of respect for our reserve officers, but I wasn't sure about the Pathet Lao. The more I thought it, the more I hoped the FAC's report was accurate.

Each mission milestone was significant and important in its own way. I had flown eighty-five missions and was approaching the magic number of ninety, the last ten missions—the "senior year" of combat. That night, I closed the day with this entry in my diary.

I am getting very covetous about the remaining missions, each one has to be savored. I feel that I am really in my stride and I hate to waste a step. Better watch out, I might also be getting "mission senile." I really admire my wingman, Paul Sheehy. He is me ten years ago—or, at least, where I wanted to be.

18

VENOM FLIGHT: THREE FOR THE PRICE OF ONE

THE TWENTY-SECOND OF May 1967 was a day to remember. It started with a mission plan that was as dangerous and chilling as any I had faced, and ended with a wild and woolly "practice fighter pilot reunion" that would set the standard for many to come.

Phil Gast was the force commander on the morning mission to JCS 50.96, the Nguyen Khe storage area just north of Hanoi. It was Phil's 100th mission. If he returned, he would be the first 354th commander in a succession of three to complete a tour successfully. Tragically, Don Asire and Gene Conley had gone down before him. As a grand gesture, the 354th Squadron volunteered to fly as a single strike force, sixteen pilots and aircraft, plus a flight of Wild Weasels. It was a 354th gaggle and a first for Takhli. Colonel Hill tried to keep Ted and me from flying the mission, but we volunteered, knowing the 354th couldn't fill the schedule without us.

The mission planners at Seventh Air Force came up with a clever plan to beat the odds with the weather. It amounted to three ways to bust your ass on one mission and was obviously the work of a well-intentioned staff wienie who had no experience over Hanoi and zero appreciation for the dangers of a solo reconnaissance mission.

To start with, the mission had three JCS target options: the infamous steel mill at Thai Nguyen (76.00), the storage area at Nguyen Khe (50.96), and a railroad siding at the Bac Mai Airport (54.06) on the south side of Hanoi. We were instructed to leave the tankers prepared to go to any one of the targets, depending on the outcome of the reconnaissance flight that would precede us.

An RF-101 photo recce aircraft was scheduled to make the rounds of the three target areas at low-level and select the one with the best weather. The timing was critical. The RF-101 would reconnoiter Thai Nguyen first, and then turn south to fly over Hanoi and evaluate the other two targets. If the weather in all three areas was questionable, the RF-101 would double back to Thai Nguyen for another look at the steel mill. Having run the gauntlet, the recce pilot would recommend a target to the force commander prior to our arrival at a decision point west of the Black River and approximately ten to twelve minutes from any one of the targets.

When the briefing officer concluded the briefing, he asked if there were any questions. From the back of the room, one of the pilots asked sarcastically, "How are they going to get the balls of that recce pilot into the cockpit?" The room broke up in loud but anxious laughter.

I was in Venom flight, the third and next to last strike flight scheduled into the target. We made an 0622 takeoff, seven minutes ahead of Newark and behind Shotgun, Renault, and Academic. Academic was the Wild Weasel flight, and Renault was the force commander. Two F-4 flights from the 8th Wing provided our MiGCAP, and an identical strike force from Korat followed one minute behind us. There was a lot riding on a lonesome decision by a brave recce pilot.

We used five KC-135 tankers in the Green Anchor refueling area. The prestrike refueling went very smoothly. We all dropped-off on time and within sight of each other. The plan was to run-in to the target low and in trail formation, with one minute separation between Renault and Shotgun, and two minutes between Venom and Newark. Venom's TOT was 0748 at either of the selected targets.

All three targets were important and would be heavily defended. The steel mill at Thai Nguyen was an "old friend," but the targets in the Hanoi area were new releases hot off the Washington hit list. They would be more difficult to find, and we planned to approach them from two different directions. We would come down Thud Ridge to hit the Nguyen Khe storage area but come straight across out of the western foothills for a strike on the railroad siding at Bac Mai. Each route was carefully planned to keep the run-in times nearly equal.

Minutes after leaving the tanker, we were surprised to receive a target designation from Red Crown. "Renault, this is Red Crown with words. Go Cardinals, repeat, go Cardinals. This is Red Crown, out."

The force commander acknowledged the message and had it authenticated. "Cardinals" meant hit the Nguyen Khe storage in the northern suburbs of Hanoi. It was a dangerous target, but it was a relief to have the problem simplified early.

The decision came so early that the recce pilot must have found the weather to be surprisingly good and reported it to Red Crown for a target decision at headquarters. In any event, the weather in the valley was excellent, and that was encouraging. It was a lucky break and probably made the operations planners look smarter than they were, but if it helped to keep the recce pilot's ass out of a crack it was a worthwhile coincidence.

When we turned down the ridge, the visibility was perfect. For a change, we could see what we were doing. Our odds could be better, but if the North Vietnamese were ready, the stage was set for a classic double-pump battle. I admired Phil Gast for leading the strike on his 100th mission, and I hoped it wouldn't turn out to be a decision he would regret.

We punched off the tanks and moved in low against the ridge for protection from radar. The Red River valley was silent. It looked like it was frozen in time and space. The scene was eerie. There were two faint strobes on the radar warning scope, but nothing to indicate the resistance we had expected. A few light flak puffs dotted the morning sky above Phuc Yen, and a lone SAM streaked up aimlessly. But the big guns were silent, and there were no ominous MiG warnings blanking the radio. It gave me an anxious feeling, like we were being watched by someone waiting for us to trigger a trip wire. Not much of a mission for a hero's send-off but it was a welcome change if it lasted.

We were at the foot of the ridge, and the defenses were still silent. It was either a clever trap or we had finally run the little buggers out of everything; ammunition, SAMs, and fuel for their MiGs. If so, we had paid a high price to deplete their resources, but it was rewarding to find that they also had limits. They were probably watching us in frustration, and Radio Hanoi would undoubtedly scream about the criminal acts of the American air pirates. Good for them, they deserved to watch and take it on the chin for a change.

With next to no resistance, we rolled-in and put our bombs right on target. It was like bombing on the range at Nellis, but I enjoyed it more and didn't feel the least bit guilty.

When I pulled off the target, all I could see were afterburners streaking up the valley. There was no flak at all, and the SAM sites were apparently out of missiles. I was tempted to relax but I still felt uneasy. A potentially dangerous mission had succeeded without a hitch under some uncanny circumstances.

Phil gathered up the force on the post-strike tankers. After refueling, we formed into a sixteen-ship formation for the return flight to Takhli and a series of squadron flybys. Three miles out, we moved into a tight diamond of four-ship diamonds.

"Takhli Tower, Renault is on initial with sixteen Bulldogs, over!"

"Roger, Renault, cleared for your one hundred-mission passes. This is Takhli Tower."

We made three passes; one in diamond, one in fingertip, and one in trail formation. They were all beauties, and our reception on the ground was impressive. The entire squadron turned out to welcome their triumphant commander. Only Phil Gast could have pulled it off so well. He had put his life and career on the line and returned a winner. Colonel Scott was all smiles.

Birth of the River Rats

After an unprecedented 100-mission celebration on the ramp and a quick debriefing, I jumped on board a C-47 to fly to Korat for a tactics conference and the "1st Red River Valley Fighter Pilots Reunion." Lieutenant Colonel Nelson McDonald, who would succeed Phil Gast as the 354th Squadron commander, and I, represented our wing at the conference. Everyone else stayed at Takhli to toast Phil at a special 100-mission party being held that evening in his honor. Intentional or not, the dining-in for Phil appeared to upstage the conference at Korat, and it was a snub that would not go unnoticed.

The relationship between our command section and the other wings stationed in Thailand was cool and aloof for reasons that escaped me. It was an unfortunate situation, and it was particularly evident when we arrived at Korat that afternoon. We were the smallest, most junior party to attend the conference and it was very conspicuous.

Colonel Scrappy Johnson and several of his pilots met us at the airplane with a festive welcoming parade, which included five elephants and a Thai military marching band. The 388th pilots joined in the parade with an assortment of makeshift musical instruments, and they were doing their best to beat out the rhythm of the marching music. Everyone was singing and clowning around. It was a scene typical of Scrappy Johnson's style.

Scrappy insisted that we ride the elephants to wing headquarters. The elephants were not full size but getting on them was a challenge. With the help of the Thai handlers, I found myself perched on top of a rolling pachyderm for a slow but exciting ride to wing headquarters. The tactics conference had all the earmarks of a gala occasion.

The two-day agenda was busy. It was a surprise to some who came solely to party, but the tactics conference was legitimate. It gave us a unique opportunity to exchange ideas, discuss problems, and work out new tactics that would make us a more effective fighting team. There were some beefs and petty differences, but by and large, the conference was an enormous success and signaled the way for more to come.

At a cocktail party that evening at the Officers' Club, business turned into fun and then some. A postscript on the conference program noted, "Dress for Events at the 'O' Club—White Short Sleeve Shirt and Dark Trousers." It was a formality required for the reunion dinner and not intended to last a minute longer.

The dinner followed the protocol of a traditional Air Force dining-in, with an added touch of special importance. Alongside the head table, a small table was prepared with a single place setting, including an empty wine glass. The chair at the table faced away from the audience as a symbolic gesture of the lonely plight of our fallen comrades.

Using a wine glass charged [filled] with water, we raised our cups in a toast to our fallen comrades. We vowed to continue to carry the fight to the enemy and to reserve an honored place at our table until the return of all those killed, missing, and captured. It was a solemn beginning to a raucous and memorable evening.

A motion was made to retitle the conference and all subsequent meetings as practice reunions until a reunion could be held that would reunite all members of the "Red River Valley Fighter Pilots Association." The motion carried unanimously, but no one there expected that it would take until July of 1973 for the first real reunion to be convened in Las Vegas, Nevada. There would be many more opportunities for practice reunions in the coming years.

After dinner, it was time for the "Fun and Games" item on the agenda. The games were fun at first but, as the evening wore on, they became more and more physical and less and less enjoyable. As a matter of fact, to an outside observer we might have appeared to be drunk and out of order.

Arm-in-arm fighter sweeps the length of the bar swept drinks and inattentive drinkers to the floor with regularity. The shout of "dead beetle" prompted merrymakers to hit the deck and freeze in position to avoid buying a round for the house.

Spilled drinks and beer set the stage for a new game called "carrier landings," which was borrowed from the Navy. With a large serving tray held tight against the chest, the object was to get a long run and leap forward at the takeoff point in order to land and slide on the beer-soaked floor as far as possible, using the tray as a makeshift landing gear. It was hard on chests, knees, and fingers, but it was particularly hard on the chins of those overzealous revelers who had the misfortune to touch down nose wheel first.

There was no published curfew that evening, but participants were urged to save themselves for a champagne breakfast the next morning in preparation for a noon departure to Bangkok. Some slept and some didn't, but everyone who had signed up for the morning flight somehow made it to the club in time to eat and load into the bus for the crowded trip to the flight line.

The sight of a plane load of hung-over fighter pilots sitting quietly, side-by-side, enduring a hot and bumpy flight in the back of an old C-47 Gooney Bird, was both humorous and nauseating. Only the memories of the night before, and the promise of the rewards of Bangkok could have possibly made the trip bearable. Otherwise, it was simply a grueling one-hour test of one's mental and physical fortitude.

We made it to Bangkok in various states of repair and jammed into cabs headed for the Siam Inter-Continental Hotel. There were twenty-five of us, and we all needed a room, a shower, a nap, a dip in the pool, a cold beer, and the refreshing sight of a pretty girl. The Siam held great promise of meeting all of those needs.

We were still milling around the lobby of the hotel, trying to sort out our keys and luggage, when Scrappy reminded us in a loud voice that the next scheduled event was "cocktails in the bar at nineteen hundred!" I grabbed my bag and went to my room to relax.

The cool, quiet room was a welcome relief but I wasn't in the mood for a nap. Instead, I went out to the pool for a dip and an early look at the girls adorning the water's edge. Airline stewardesses frequented the Siam, and they were known to make their choices early.

Several of our group were already at the pool and had several choice tables staked out for the afternoon. They were talking with their hands, so the war stories had already started. Bottles of cool Singha beer were crowded on each table. Pools of moisture collected under the bottles as a constant reminder of the suffocating heat and humidity. Swimming was the only way to beat the hot afternoon weather. The cool water refreshed the body while the mind prepared for the promise of a Bangkok evening.

By seven, the cocktail lounge was packed with international patrons. Businessmen, contractors, diplomats, journalists, and an assortment of professional people crowded into the bar to discuss business, talk about the war, and prepare for dinner. The gentlemen wore coats and ties, and dry martinis had replaced beer as the drink of choice. It was an elegant, suave setting for twenty or so River Rats who were refreshed and ready to make an impression.

We were too much for the Siam Lounge. Everyone there enjoyed our rowdy fun, but the manager drew the line on throwing empty glasses into the nonexistent fireplace. As a substitute, one of the guys decided to demonstrate the lost art of eating martini glasses, and we were quietly asked to leave the premises. As we left, it occurred to me that our only problem was that we were trying to *gulp* down life one day at a time among people who lived life with much less urgency.

I went to the President Hotel and found my usual stool in the Cat's Eye Lounge. Subhanee wasn't at work, so I had a couple of drinks and a double serving of beef fondue by myself in the dining room. After dinner, I went back to the Siam for an early lights-out and a good nights' sleep. The tactics conference had been a rousing success, but for me it was over.

The first mission I flew after returning from Bangkok was to JCS 51.61, a railroad siding at Ha Gia, 15 miles due north of Hanoi at the foot of Thud Ridge. Colonel Broughton was the force commander and I was his deputy, leading the element as Tico Three. Broughton's wingman was particularly weak and he asked me to keep a close eye on him. My wingman was sharp, but he was new and lacked experience. Between the two of them I had my work cut out for me.

Colonel Broughton had adopted me as his favorite element leader after our close call on the tanker a few weeks earlier. He told me he wanted me to keep him out of trouble during his last few missions, but I knew that would be next to an impossibility.

Sure enough, on the way to Ha Gia, we flew right over Yen Bay at low altitude and the guns there really peppered us. Lead started his famous super jink maneuver, but the gunners were tracking us and the flak bursts got closer and closer. Luckily, we outdistanced the guns before anyone got hit, but it was a close call that got our attention. I thought to myself, "We haven't started the run into the target yet, and we've already been shot at and damn near hit. This could be a hairy mission."

Either my instincts were wrong or the North Vietnamese were up to something. The valley was absolutely quiet when we turned down the ridge. It was a replay of Venom flight four days earlier and eerie as hell. We eased over to the east side of the ridge and let down just below the ridge line, hugging the mountains for cover.

When we passed the foot of the ridge, Lead popped up for the target. He made a very sharp pull-up, and someone in the flight accidentally pickled their bombs early. There wasn't any flak in sight, so I rolled over into a vertical dive and aimed my CBUs at the rail yard. The bomblets would damage the rolling stock and hit any AAA-gun sites lying low in the vicinity.

We pulled off the target jinking up the valley toward Thai Nguyen. We were in good shape except that Two was way out of position. "Tico Two, bring it up and get in formation. Keep an eye on him, Three!" Broughton barked angrily.

We turned left to cross back over the ridge and Tico Two fell even farther back and dangerously out of position. "DAMN IT, TWO, THIS IS LEAD. GET IN POSITION. DO YOU READ, OVER?"

"Roger, Lead, Two reads. Give me a little." I thought his request for power would bring Broughton right out of his cockpit, but it didn't.

"Tico Three keep a close eye on Two. He'll get his butt shot off way back there," Lead called, with a note of resignation in his voice.

After the mission Colonel Broughton looked angry when he stepped into the bread truck. His eyes were on fire, and the muscles in his jaw were quivering. The van inched its way along the flight line, and no one said a word. Broughton just glared at his wingman. The silence was intimidating. When we approached the squadron, he asked the driver to stop at his sedan. "Ken, you do the debriefing. I've got something hot at the office," Broughton said, as he swung out the door impatiently. He was still furious.

We stored our gear and went into the debriefing room to discuss the mission. I laid the cards right out on the table and zeroed in on what we had done wrong and what the wingmen had to do to improve. Four took the criticism in his stride, but Two didn't like what he was hearing and stomped out of the room angrily. Later he said he would never fly with us again. It was a shame. I knew if he didn't change he wouldn't make it through 100 missions and sure enough, he didn't.

When I returned to wing headquarters, I was surprised to learn that Colonel Hill had left hurriedly for an R&R in Hong Kong and would not return to Takhli. He had been quietly reassigned to the Seventh Air Force staff and replaced by Colonel Bob White, a renowned test pilot with a great deal of fighter experience.

No one knew much about Colonel Hill's departure except that it had been sudden and unannounced. Although I was surprised, I felt a deep sense of relief. I had watched Colonel Hill slowly buckle under pressure, and I knew that a change was inevitable. Frankly, the prospects of starting over with a new boss were encouraging.

On 27 May 1967, I met Colonel White and welcomed him to the office. I gave him an expanded version of the orientation briefing we gave all incoming pilots. He was relaxed, receptive, and very much at ease with himself. His confidence and calm presence were welcomed by everyone in the operations office. Within hours, we were accustomed to his style and felt like we knew exactly what we could expect.

Colonel White wanted to do some reading in his office, so I had time to sneak in a mission. The afternoon strike force was waiting for a weather go-ahead to launch for a strike on the northeast railroad at Bac Giang, but I was able to leap off early with a two-ship flight against a target in Laos near Sam Neua.

A new replacement pilot in the 354th Squadron was flying my wing on one of his first missions. We were carrying pods of 2.75-inch rockets instead of bombs and assigned to work with a Firefly FAC against a concentration of Pathet Lao troops holed up in a cave in some rugged karst mountains.

My wingman seemed very confident, flew excellent formation, and put his rockets "right in the hole," to quote the FAC. He turned out to be a crackerjack pilot, and his attitude was very refreshing compared to some of the other replacement pilots we had received that spring. Although experienced in other aircraft, they were older, more set in their ways, and reluctant to adapt to the skills needed for a difficult air-to-ground mission.

The afternoon mission got through to the Bac Giang rail yard on the northeast railroad. Apparently, the North Vietnamese had been resupplied. The strike force met with stiff resistance from both guns and SAMs. It was clear that the lull in defenses was over.

Captain Gordon "Buzz" Blackwood took a SAM hit over the target and ejected but was not recovered. As his nickname implied, Buzz was a colorful guy, and his loss hit the 333d Squadron and the wing like a ton of bricks. Bac Giang was a futile, two-bit target that seemed to swallow F-105s. It was a treacherous flak trap and it was senseless to keep going back, but we always did.

Mission Ninety, Threshold to Greatness

The ninety-mission mark was an important milestone emotionally and traditionally. Although the odds of getting shot down didn't change, it seemed as if pilots became a little less vulnerable with less than ten missions remaining.

Being in the nineties was like the last month of senior year all over again. You could begin to enjoy the fruits of graduation even though you weren't quite there yet. Guys with ninety missions stood a little taller and were the envy of those just starting up the mission ladder.

At ninety, we joined a highly respected nucleus of pilots who were expected to shoulder the full burden of leadership. Sometimes, with that much confidence and authority, it was tempting to become cocky or cynical. If you weren't careful, your mantle of experience could become a barrier rather than a bond between you and the newer guys, a condition quickly cured by the next burst of ugly, orange flak.

An unofficial wing policy allowed pilots to pick their last ten missions according to their appetite for danger. Colonel Scott had set quite a precedent for the wing when he flew his 100th mission in Route Pack Six and went back the next morning with very little fanfare. Although his example put pressure on everyone, the choice of missions after ninety remained the personal business of each pilot, no questions asked.

I let the wheel of fortune pick my ninetieth mission, and I came up as the force commander on a mission I could, and sometimes did, fly with my eyes closed—my old friend JCS 76.00, the steel mill at Thai Nguyen. I was Machete Lead, a call sign well suited to the savage nature of the target.

I was excited about going back to the steel mill and wanted to plaster it one last time. The time on target was very early in the morning, so we planned a dawn blitz attack with a few new wrinkles.

We would come in low and fast from the mountains to the north. The flights were briefed to join up in a jamming pod formation after leaving the tankers and stay closed in that formation until turning south at Cho Moi, 20 miles north of Thai Nguyen. I instructed the flight leaders to punch off the wing tanks crossing the Red River and anticipate pushing up to 540 knots for the run into the target.

I wanted my flight to be line-a-breast with the Wild Weasels and told the F-4 MiGCAP flights to cut the corner at the Red River and meet us in the target area. After turning south at Cho Moi, we would light the burners and split the flights into a pincer attack with two flights on each side of the axis. Machete was carrying CBUs to suppress flak, and the rest of the flights were dragging six 750-pound bombs with .01-second time-delay fuses, just enough to get through the roof of an industrial structure before exploding.

Everything went like clockwork until we turned south at Cho Moi. The Weasels were slightly ahead of us, and the radio chatter indicated that the SAM sites were awake and ready. We were only two and a half minutes away from the target, but the valley was socked in with a heavy layer of morning ground fog. We were too damned early, and the defenses were poised. The bastards were sitting there, cocked and anxious to launch SAMs at anyone foolish enough to test their defenses in that weather.

Reluctantly, I called off the mission. "Machete turning west, go secondary. The weather is lousy!"

We headed for Yen Bai to surprise the gunners there. Buckskin flight covered our six o'clock for SAMs, while we started a climb to the west. The timing worked out perfectly. We hit 20,000 feet just in time for an easy roll-in on the flak sites at Yen Bai. As always, they started shooting early, so we pickled a little higher than normal to throw off their aim and give our bomblets a little wider coverage.

When we pulled off the guns, Machete Three was torching badly. An orange sheet of flame the length of his airplane was streaming behind him. I thought he was hit, but it was only excess fuel that had vented and ignited in the afterburner. To add to the confusion, his radio calls happened to coincide with those of a crippled Navy fighter. We got it sorted out quickly but it cost me a few anxious minutes.

"Red Crown, this is Machete with words, over."

"Roger, Machete. Red Crown here, ready to copy."

"Machete *Station Wagon on Cleo, Sheboygan, with a Mile to Yen Bai,* over." (Coded shorthand for unsuccessful on the primary target due to weather, diverted to Yen Bai.)

"Machete, Red Crown copies. Cleared to three-zero-one-point-five for your post-strike tanker Green Anchor Three-One, good day."

In spite of the necessity to divert, I felt good about the mission and I was glad to finally be in the nineties. On the way back to Takhli, I decided to take the last ten missions one at a time, like all the others and trust in God and my skill to see me through safely. It was the thirty-first of May, and June was just around the corner.

19

THE MAGIC
NINETIES

ON THE FIRST OF June, I was scheduled to go to Route Package Six, but the weather was bad so we ended up on a very peculiar mission south of Dong Hoi in Route Pack One. Captain Charlie Couch was the flight leader and I was Number Three, covered by the wingman who had vowed several days earlier never to fly with me again.

We bombed a truck park and headed for the coast to investigate a large group of suspicious fishing boats that had been reported by an earlier flight. The boats numbered in the hundreds and stretched out for a couple of miles north and south just outside the breakers. I had never seen anything like it. Fishing nets were stretched out on the beach to dry, but there wasn't a soul in sight and nothing was moving.

We made several strafing passes and kicked up a lot of water but it was difficult to tell how well we were doing. There may have been some light small arms fire but the boats appeared to be empty, and those we hit didn't explode. If they were fishing, they were going about it in a peculiar and dangerous fashion.

After several passes, Charlie Couch re-formed the flight and headed home with potentially the greatest fish story ever told in combat. We were tempted to refuel and go back, but Hal Bingaman and Hank Higgins were flying their last mission and we wanted to be on the ground at Takhli to enjoy their passes.

Out of the blue, I received a message from Thirteenth Air Force directing me to stop flying combat immediately and report to the next class at Jungle Survival School. With only nine missions left to fly, the last thing I needed was an unnecessary trip to the Philippines to attend survival training. Someone on the staff at Thirteenth Air Force had finally caught up with me and was serious about me completing Monkey School. It was so idiotic that it was almost funny, but I knew I was on my way if I couldn't find a clever way to stall the headquarters.

Reluctantly, I recanted on an earlier refusal and volunteered for a trip to Taiwan to pick up two aircraft that had been sent to the Air Asia depot for repair. It meant four days of travel, but that was better than a month away for a week in the jungle eating rats and evading half-cocked instructors.

We sent a message to Thirteenth Air Force, stating that I had been ordered to ferry aircraft from the repair depot on Taiwan and was temporarily unavailable for training. It was a stopgap measure aimed at exploiting the delays of routine message traffic. By the time the message worked its way through the bureaucratic bog at Thirteenth Air Force, I could return from Taiwan, complete my tour, and be on my way home with a 100-mission patch on my shoulder.

On the second of June 1967, Major Bob Lindsey and I boarded a C-130 flight for Taiwan to pick up two F-105s. Bob and I knew each other from the Gemini space program, so I decided to catch up on old friends and make the most of the trip despite the untimely delay it put in my schedule.

About an hour into the flight, the pilot of the C-130 told us that we would have to divert to Clark Air Base due to a mechanical problem with the airplane. The news brought me up short. "It's a desperate plot to get me to the Philippines for survival training," I thought, hoping that no one on the staff at Thirteenth Air Force was that quick or clever.

We landed at Clark in a driving rain just after dark. The pilot was sympathetic with our plight and offered us two choices. We could stay overnight until the aircraft was fixed, or we could go to the Officers' Club for a bite to eat and take a chance on catching another flight that evening. In the interest of minimizing my exposure at Clark, I chose the latter, and within hours we were fortunate enough to be airborne and back on course for Taiwan.

The Air Asia facility was located on an airfield close to the island city of Tainan. The base was an armed camp of Nationalist Chinese Guards. To protect against aircraft theft and potential pilot defections, the Chinese used an elaborate system of colored cards and code numbers to allow aircraft to pass between several guard posts situated along the taxiways to and from the runway. We were warned to pay strict attention to our instructions, because the guards were trained to shoot first and ask questions later.

The Air Force procedures for ferrying aircraft out of Taiwan were equally complicated. We were required to have visual flight rule (VFR) flight conditions for departure and forecast at the destination, as well as air-sea rescue coverage for the over-water part of the flight. SA-16 amphibious aircraft from Clark had to be deployed along the route of flight in case we went down at sea. In addition, we needed tanker support to ensure that we would have enough fuel to cope with almost any known contingency.

Getting rescue Duckbutts on station with good weather and tanker support would require patience and intricate coordination, but it was better than the alternative of island hopping via the Philippines.

I took the bull by the horns and requested clearance for a nonstop three hour and ten minute flight to Takhli without tanker support en route. A full load of fuel on takeoff, including three external tanks, would give us enough range to make it, provided we dropped the external tanks as they went dry. It was an unorthodox flight plan, but it was worth trying. If we ran short of fuel, we could land at Danang, but I couldn't list that as a contingency because of another ferry rule prohibiting the emergency use of alternate airports in South Vietnam, the war zone.

After some verbal arm twisting and negotiations with the command post at Clark, our flight plan was approved and the wheels of progress were set into motion for an 0800 takeoff the next morning, good weather permitting.

Bob and I went to the Air Asia office to check over the aircraft records and accept the airplanes. We had hoped to pick up the two aircraft that had been damaged in Lincoln flight over Thai Nguyen in March, but only one of them was ready. I took the records for the aircraft that Bill Hoeft had been flying. It had been fully repaired and looked like new. The entire left side of the airplane, including the wing, had been replaced during the overhaul.

The aircraft I had been flying in Lincoln flight was not quite ready for delivery, but one of the technicians gave me a small bag of metal bullet casings that he had removed from the right wing. It was a thoughtful memento, which I appreciated very much, but I felt somewhat disappointed. I had a special place in my heart for that airplane and wanted the honor of bringing it back to combat.

After satisfying ourselves that the airplanes were ready, we walked back to base operations to check on the weather forecast for the next morning and then caught a cab for a hotel in downtown Tainan. Neither of us had been to the island before, so we checked into our rooms quickly and went out on the town shopping. I bought an engraved marble ashtray that I didn't need and tagged along with Bob while he bought gifts for his family.

In less than thirty minutes we had done the shops so we headed for a bar to relax over dinner. No one in the restaurant spoke English, so we pointed at items on the menu, hoping the waiter would make sense out of our order. We didn't get what we thought we had ordered, but we enjoyed a wonderful meal and plenty of laughter.

Early the next morning we checked out of the hotel and caught a taxi for the airport. The weather didn't look promising and our hopes for a departure were dashed when we talked to the forecaster. The weather was below minimums for departure and not likely to improve for several days.

We went back to the hotel to sweat out the weather. Our only choice was to initiate the same flight plan on a daily basis, even though it meant checking in and out of the hotel and getting up at an ungodly hour. I could only imagine what the SA-16 pilots were going through each day, getting the Duck Butts on station.

Finally, on the fourth morning the weather cooperated and we departed on schedule. I almost screwed up the number card code with the taxiway guards but recovered gracefully after receiving nothing more than a menacing stare. After takeoff, we gave each aircraft a thorough checkout and headed west for Thailand.

During the climb, we went into the weather at 10,000 feet, and when we reached our initial cruise altitude of 25,000 feet we were still in the soup. In order to get the best fuel economy, I set up a gradual cruise climb to hold a constant .86 Mach number, but the weather above was solid.

Thirty minutes into the flight, the centerline drop tank went dry, on schedule, but we were still in the clouds and unable to clear the space below us for a safe tank drop. It was a situation I had failed to anticipate. We had to reduce drag in order to stretch our fuel, but I could hear aircraft calls around us, and I didn't want to risk putting an empty 650-gallon fuel tank through the windscreen of an unsuspecting airplane.

We were out of range for help from a ground radar site, so I gritted my teeth and radioed Bob to punch off the centerline tank on my command. It was a calculated risk but we didn't have a choice. For two long minutes, I listened for startling calls around on the radio, but there were none. "Phew," I thought, "surely we'll be in the clear by the time the inboard tanks go dry."

Almost halfway home, we were still in the clouds and skirting around the southern edge of Hainan Island, when the inboard pylon tanks went dry. I hated to risk annoying the Red Chinese Air Force, but in order to save fuel, we had to fly a little closer to Hainan Island than was diplomatically allowable. Undaunted, we punched off the tanks, hoping they would go unnoticed on the enemy island.

The airplanes were finally clean and cruising efficiently. We were at 30,000 feet, and Bob had 9,300 pounds of fuel remaining. At a fuel consumption rate of 5,000 pounds of fuel per hour, we were slightly behind our flight plan, but it was too early to worry.

Papa Tanker

Fifty miles east of Danang, I had to make a decision whether to press on to Ubon and hopefully Takhli. Fuelwise, we were on the borderline, so it was a judgment call. I decided to press on and make a final decision in time to land at Ubon if necessary.

After we coasted in over Danang, I checked in with Hillsboro Control for clearance into Laos. To my surprise, Hillsboro asked if we needed fuel and offered to vector us to a tanker. I accepted, realizing that once we committed to rendezvous with a tanker we had to get fuel in order to make Takhli. It was a reasonable gamble.

Hillsboro gave us a vector for Blue Anchor 22 and cleared us to change to the refueling radio frequency.

"Blue Anchor Two-Two, Zephyr Lead on two-seven-one-zero. How do you read, over."

"Zephyr, Blue Anchor Two-Two, read you five-by. We are level at two-eight-zero heading three-two-five degrees. Have your beacon at three o'clock, fifty miles. Understand you're in-bound to Channel Forty-Three. How much fuel do you require, over."

"Roger, Blue Anchor Two-Two. Zephyr has you at twelve o'clock about forty miles. We are a flight of two. Each aircraft would like three thousand pounds, over."

"Zephyr, this is Blue Anchor Two-Two. We can spare about twenty-eight hundred pounds each and be advised we are a Papa tanker, over."

I was surprised that Blue Anchor 22 was a probe-and-drogue tanker, but I didn't give it a second thought until Bob called sounding somewhat distressed.

"Zephyr Lead, this is Two. Go squadron common [radio frequency 354.0], over."

We checked in, and I got a very shocking message.

"Lead, this is Two. What's a Papa tanker, over?" Oh-oh, we were in trouble!

"Two, this is Lead. Papa means drogue-equipped tanker, over."

"Roger, Lead. This will be my first time on a basket, can we make it back to Ubon? I have one thousand pounds remaining."

"Negative, Two. We are committed, you better make it good on the first stab, over."

What a jam! We had overflown two perfectly good refueling bases only to find ourselves hurting for fuel, and Number Two had never seen a refueling basket. I gave Bob a quick tutorial on the art of probe-and-drogue refueling and then moved into position behind the tanker to demonstrate the technique.

"Blue Anchor Two-Two, Zephyr is back on your frequency. Stabilized and ready to hit the basket, over."

"Zephyr, check noses cold and cleared into position."

I extended the probe and moved into contact with the drogue. I hoped my example would encourage Bob. I had my first run-in with probe-and-drogue refueling months earlier over the Pacific, and the memory was still fresh in my mind.

"Zephyr Lead has twenty-eight hundred pounds, moving out. Zephyr Two, it's all yours. Make it good, babes!" I knew the next five minutes would spell success or disaster and I was a bundle of nerves.

Bob moved into position and stabilized behind the basket. He started to move up slowly and I held my breath. The airflow over the nose of his airplane pushed the basket up and slightly to the left, but Bob compensated nicely. The next thing I knew, he was on the basket and taking fuel like an old pro. I could almost see him smiling through his oxygen mask. I was smiling too, and thankful. It was my careless overconfidence that had gotten us in this fix, and an unnecessary aircraft loss due to fuel starvation would have fallen into the category of blatant negligence.

We thanked Blue Anchor 22 for their help and took up a heading of 270 degrees for Takhli. The tanker crew didn't have any idea that they had just serviced a basket rookie, and I figured it was a story that didn't need telling. We were only thirty minutes from home and had a shot at getting on the next morning's schedule.

We landed with fuel to spare, but after pressing our luck to get back quickly I couldn't get the canopy to open when I parked the aircraft. It took the mechanics almost an hour to remove it manually. By the time they got me out it was 150 degrees in the cockpit. It didn't justify the risk we had taken en route, but I was thankful that we hadn't made an intermediate stop anywhere.

In a twist of irony, the aircraft that I returned was shot down on its next combat mission. It seemed like a terrible waste of a valiant aircraft, especially after all of the damage it had sustained over Thai Nguyen, and the extensive repairs that had been done by Air Asia.

On 7 June 1967, I flew a two-shipper with Captain Charlie Couch. It was my ninety-second mission and his ninety-eighth. We both decided to take a breather and fly a Sky Spot mission in the lower route packs. Sky Spot missions could be very boring, but any mission with Charlie Couch was usually interesting, just his radio calls were usually worth a chuckle. Charlie was a laid back guy from the country and sometimes unpredictable.

The mission went as planned, but the intelligence debriefing was a different story. We were both feeling our oats and decided to have some fun with the intelligence officer who was conducting the debriefing. He was a brand new lieutenant and far too serious and businesslike for a couple of veteran jocks.

We answered the routine questions very quickly. When the young lieutenant asked us for the results of our armed reconnaissance, we let our imaginations take over. Very matter-of-factly, we told him that we had encountered some MiGs and downed four airplanes. To our surprise, he wrote it down very carefully without expressing any reaction and asked calmly, "Were there any other unusual events to report from the mission?"

We made up a story about strafing a vehicle that looked like a mobile snack bar servicing North Vietnamese regular forces who were infiltrating to the south. To our amazement, he took that down too and asked us for more details.

Before it was over, we had concocted an outrageous story that the intelligence section put in the form of a normal Confidential OPREP-4 message addressed to several headquarters. We could hardly contain our laughter as we checked the message for accuracy. At that point, it was hard to tell who was pulling whose leg, but I felt certain the message was too ridiculous be sent out.

> Truck on Rt 1011, 1753/10550 RP I. M-61 vehicle was parked on the side of the road and was probably a mobile exchange snack bar or a traveling whorehouse because of the number of troops standing in line waiting for service. As strafing commenced, several objects were seen fleeing from the van. Pilots were prevented from flying lower than 10 ft to make more precise observations because modesty had to be taken into consideration. Guided muscle seen entering a cave, exploding on impact, no secondaries observed. Pilots feel they have broken the morale of the combat weary troops who were partaking of the pleasures included in the North Vietnamese Armed Forces Day ceremony.

The only thing the intelligence officer questioned was how we knew it was Armed Forces Day in North Vietnam. We told him that we had heard it on Radio Hanoi the night before but suggested that he double-check the information before releasing the message. As we left the building, we could hardly wait to share our story with the guys at the stag bar.

The next morning I found a copy of the message sitting squarely in the middle of my desk. It appeared to be an authentic information copy, identical to those I routinely received from our message center. I couldn't believe it had actually been dispatched, and could only imagine what the reaction of the recipients might be, including some in high places in Washington. I rushed to the message center to verify the authenticity of the message.

The sergeant on duty assured me that the message had been transmitted and showed me the authenticating date/time group that was stamped on the original document. He added that a separate OPREP message had been sent to the same addressees describing our MiG encounter and congratulated me on the victories. That did it, I smelled a rat. He was too reserved to suit me. I suspected and hoped that I had been the victim of an intricate prank engineered by Charlie Couch.

With a sly grin, Charlie maintained his innocence and the message center stuck with their story. I knew they were putting me on about the MiG report, because the public relations world would have erupted immediately. But I figured the message about the mobile whorehouse might take longer to attract attention. My only choice was to sweat it out and see what happened.

I flew the afternoon mission and returned to the intelligence section expecting to be met by a laughing, jeering crowd, but all was quiet and business as usual. I ran into Colonel Scott on the way back to my office, and he gave me a curious smile but that was it, nothing out of the ordinary. Apparently, what had begun as a practical joke ended as a hoax, and to this day I don't know what actually became of that message. I still have my copy and each time I read it I can't help laughing.

The next day Charlie Couch flew his 100th mission and put on quite an air show. I couldn't stay for the party because I was on the afternoon mission, a strike against a target on the northeast railroad. Colonel Broughton was scheduled to lead the strike in Flamingo flight and had selected me to fly the number three slot as his deputy.

During the mission briefing I had a queasy feeling that we were headed for serious trouble and secretly questioned my decision to go to a remote railroad siding close to the Red Chinese border on my ninety-fourth mission. Everyone felt that the mission would be scrubbed because of bad weather, and a sudden hush fell over the room when the briefing officer announced that we were on a primary hold status. Translated, we were going to the primary target, the only question was when.

Execute Parrot on Soda Pop

After a long forty-five minute hold in the cockpits, we were launched on the primary target, code name Soda Pop. Even though we had taken plenty of time to prepare, it seemed like we got off in a terrible rush and things went downhill quickly. It was a typical late afternoon mission.

The weather in the refueling area was terrible. The tankers were forced to move to partially clear areas outside their normal anchors for the refueling. It was difficult to find them and even harder to stay on the boom long enough to get enough fuel for the mission. As a result, we were twenty minutes late dropping-off, with a strike force that was disorganized and spread all over the Gulf of Tonkin. Mentally, I was prepared for the worst, but the same question kept running through my head: What am I doing here under these circumstances? Risk was one thing, but self-inflicted anxiety and destruction were quite another.

Colonel Broughton struggled to re-form the strike force before we reached Elephant Ear Island, north of the port of Cam Pha, for the turn west to the target. The railroad siding was in the small village of Bac Le, just 15 miles northeast of Kep and not far from the Red Chinese border. Our plan was to split the strike force east of the target and attack it simultaneously from opposite directions crossing north and south. Flamingo would be the first flight in on the target from the north with a mix of 750-pound bombs and CBU bomblets.

Hitting a target that close to the Chinese border required pinpoint navigation accuracy. There was a solid wall of towering thunderstorms along the coast, so we were forced to drop down under them to maintain visual contact with the ground. As we progressed, the weather kept forcing us farther to the north and closer to the border. The radar warning equipment lit up with SAM and AAA threats, and a stream of border violation warnings from Red Crown droned on the radio. I couldn't keep track of our position and fly combat formation at the same time, so I decided to relax and enjoy the ride, even if it meant an undiplomatic welcome to the People's Republic.

We intersected the railroad north of the target and headed south, following the tracks. We were under a layer of low-hanging clouds, and it looked like we were in for a classic World War II skip-bomb and strafing pass, if we ever found the target.

The air was thick, and white condensation streamers plumed off of our wing tips as we maneuvered back and forth just above the valley. Shafts of sunlight began to interrupt the sullen grayness of the afternoon as we worked our way south, desperately searching for the target.

After several minutes, I moved my element over to the right side of the formation in anticipation of a pull-up for the bomb pass. The weather was improving slightly, but it was still very much on the side of the enemy.

Suddenly, Lead pulled up hard into a steep climb, with his wingman tucked in tight beside him. I followed him up and started looking for the target. The sky was full of ugly flak, so I figured we had found something important and rolled-in, hoping to zero in on a flak site. Six guns from a battery situated on a small knoll just south of the village were blazing away, so I rolled-out in a steep dive and started tracking the pipper toward the center of the battery. Luckily, it turned out to be a perfect setup, and I pickled my bombs right on speed and altitude. "Flamingo Three off to the right," I called, confident that I had silenced another nasty flak site for at least an afternoon.

The strike force got split up in the heat of battle, but we somehow managed to outmaneuver the defenses all the way back to the coastline and rejoined prior to reaching the post-strike tankers. By the grace of God and no thanks to the weather, the entire strike force made it out without a scratch, and we had scored heavy damage to the railroad siding. According to a short news release in my hometown newspaper, "Bombs hit on the western approach to the rail yard, causing an estimated four cuts in the lines. Three cuts also were reported in the northern mainline approach." No mention was made of the route we used to get there.

The next day I flew number three for Ted Tolman on a raid to hit a railroad bridge south of Thai Nguyen. It was Ted's first time out as force commander, and I wanted to make sure he got off to a good start. I wouldn't have gone back to Thai Nguyen for anyone else under any circumstances. I had already stretched my luck too far over that grim little city.

10 June 1967—Dolphin #3—Mission 95—A/C #735
    Ted led a perfect mission as force commander. He was a little shaky at the mission briefing but it was his first. Colonel Smith was the tanker commander and they did a great job together. The weather was miraculously good. I tried to help Ted a bit on headings but he was right on the money. I thought he was going to be early on the target but we were right on time. Flak was light at first so I started to roll in on a new building complex with my CBU but they finally opened up so I took the element across the top and rolled in a little shallow on a flak site. Pulling off, the red goof balls got intense and were crossing in front of me. I began to doubt the wisdom of being there with a 90+ easy ticket at my disposal. We came out as a five shipper—picked up a lost soul from the 333rd. He did alright until we started to recce and then he gave us up for crazy.

During the debriefing, Ted looked as proud as I had ever seen him. He had won his spurs as a force commander on a tough target and brought everyone home successfully. The mission was especially gratifying to me because it illustrated the cooperative working relationship we had developed with the tanker forces and the rich camaraderie that existed between our units. It also turned out to be my last trip to Thai Nguyen.

Eskew's 100th

Captain Gene Eskew was one of the nicest and most respected pilots in the 354th Squadron. He was quiet and effective on the job and always willing to give his best. Gene had a ready smile and a quick sense of humor, glib but genuine, and sometimes vulnerable. He epitomized the nice kid on the block, and we all saw a little of ourselves in him. Everyone was pulling for Gene to finish.

Gene wanted Paul Sheehy to fly his wing on his last mission, but Paul was late returning from R&R so I filled in as his wingman. Gene had paid his dues and it was an honor to fly with him.

The mission started in Laos with a FAC-directed strike against a target near Ban Ban, a prominent village located in a rugged valley in the northeastern mountains. The FAC marked a Pathet Lao supply point just off a small road in a steep valley southeast of the village near Ban Xa. We made two passes and put our bombs and rockets squarely on the FAC's smoke, causing a series of secondary explosions.

The FAC was elated and asked us to make a strafing pass, but Gene declined. We didn't need to press our luck any further there with ground fire, and Gene wanted to save ammunition for his last whack at the North Vietnamese.

We popped up over the mountains to the east and dropped down to recce along Route 7, a winding road in the Song Ca Valley. It was a major supply route and often a lucrative target area because of the cover afforded by heavy mountain foliage.

Gene seemed determined to find a target worthy of his last firing pass in combat, and I began to get nervous. We were between two ridge lines, snaking our way through the valley at high speed. The North Vietnamese were clever at setting up gun positions in mountains on opposite sides of a valley overlooking an obvious target. They were also patient enough to wait for a flight to make a second or third pass before opening fire to better their chances of hitting an attacking fighter. The technique was as old as dirt, but the targets were irresistible and often deadly.

Gene finally spotted a flat opening in a side valley that had all the earmarks of a hasty truck park. Several vehicle tracks left the road and ended under some nearby jungle foliage. Gene decided to try it, but I was leery. It looked too inviting to me and I hoped it wasn't a setup.

We pulled up and rolled-in for a high-angle strafing pass. "Samba Lead in," Gene called as he started down the chute.

"Roger, Samba Two in with you," I called, as I followed in a close fighting wing position. I saw Gene's gun belch a stream of fire with trailing smoke, just as I pulled my trigger. My pipper was buried in the target when I felt my gun roar into action. The smell of burning cordite filled the cockpit. Our two-second bursts of 20mm rounds shattered the tree line, but it was hard to tell if we had caught any trucks or done any damage.

We pulled out hard to the left, and I could tell that Gene was finished. He wasn't going back for a second pass and I felt like cheering.

"Samba, let's swing around and check for damage on the climb out," Gene said as we prepared to leave the area.

As we turned, an A-1E aircraft in a vertical dive-bomb pass on a nearby target almost hit us. He was alone and putting on quite a bombing demonstration. On his third pass, the valley opened up with ground fire, and in a flash of fire his aircraft disintegrated—no chute, no beeper, and another victim of multiple passes against a setup target.

Gene's voice cracked as he reported the action to Red Crown on the radio. We had watched another tragic loss and there was nothing we could do but head home and wonder what might have happened if we had made a second pass.

"Samba, fuel check," Gene asked on the radio.

"Samba Two has eight-point-four [8,400 pound of fuel remaining], nose's cold," I responded, as I closed up the formation. We were only forty-five minutes away from Gene's 100-mission pass and a brilliant end to a hard-fought combat career.

Back at Takhli, we made two passes in close formation, and then I took the lead for a tactical pitch-up and landing. Gene wanted to do a victory roll in the traffic pattern, and he thought it would be more exciting if he did it from the wing position. It was a unique way to make a pass and it confused the tower, but it gave the crowd on the ramp something to talk about.

Ironically, Gene's drag chute failed after landing, but he managed to get the airplane stopped short of the barrier. His brakes were cherry red, so he parked in the hot brakes area rather than returning to the ramp. He took it in his stride and made a triumphal return to his parking spot in the back of a speeding pickup truck. As he approached the crowd, he was grinning from ear to ear and spraying champagne from an open bottle. The nice guy, Gene Eskew, had flown his 100th mission.

Broughton's Wheel

The last mission I flew with Colonel Jack Broughton was a humdinger. He was the force commander and I was his deputy leading the element in Bison flight. It was 12 June 1967 and my ninety-seventh mission.

We had been fragged to hit a target near Thai Nguyen but the Red River valley was socked in solid, so Broughton got permission to strike a target in the highlands west of Hanoi. The day before, he had found a remote army supply depot nestled in the mountains and damn near got his tail shot off trying to strafe it. He had a score to settle and was determined to go back and hit it with the power of a strike force.

The target lay in the bowl of a small valley at the base of some steep karst mountains 20 miles west of the Black River. The area was relatively secure from the threat of large guns and SAMs, but it was well within rangeof MiGs and located in one of their favorite trolling areas.

The plan was to strike the target with five flights of F-105s and put two flights of F-4s in an orbit east of the target to guard against a MiG attack. Bison flight would find the target, bomb it, and orchestrate the attack of succeeding flights from an orbit overhead, a tactic reminiscent of the wagon wheel attack used by Indians on the prairie. It was a dicey mission. Just finding the target again would prove to be a difficult task.

The mission briefing was grim. It was 0330, pouring rain, and obvious from the looks on the pilots' faces that they had doubts about the mission. The intelligence people had very little to offer, except for some outdated photographs. The weatherman so much as said we were crazy for even trying. Colonel Broughton did his best to sound upbeat but our spirit was lacking. I figured that once we got to the cockpits the troops would fall into line and settle down to business.

It was one of my last missions and I wanted to have some fun in spite of the circumstances. I put some water in an empty Beefeater's bottle and took it with me in the cockpit to the arming area. When the Catholic chaplain came to my airplane for a prayer I took a long swig and tossed him the bottle. Thank God he caught it and thank goodness for his quick sense of humor. He smiled, blessed the airplane, and gave me a thumbs up as he broke out in laughter. What a character. No one knew why, but he always wore white sneakers.

When the armorers finished, we eased up the power and taxied toward the runway. "Bison flight, Channel One, ... pins, canopy, lanyard, number one for takeoff," Broughton barked on the radio.

"Roger, Bison. This is Takhli Tower. Winds calm, temperature seventy-nine, altimeter two-nine-seven-seven, cleared for takeoff."

In successive flights, we rolled down the runway into the black sky of early morning. It was still raining and the weather was terrible. One by one, our afterburners cracked and glowed as we torched down the runway in single-ship departures. After takeoff, we used our radar to maintain trail formation and to help join up as flights as the weather permitted.

The tanker refueling tracks were also clobbered in with weather. The entire area was dominated by a wall of towering thunderstorms, a morning weather phenomenon peculiar to that part of Southeast Asia.

After an exhaustive amount of radio chatter, improvisation, and incredible luck, we found the tankers and started the long, tedious process of pre-strike refueling. It was the hairiest refueling I had ever attempted. Visibility in the clouds was zero-zero, and we were bouncing up and down so hard in turbulence that you could see the wings on the tankers flex. It was a miracle that we didn't lose several aircraft, including a tanker or two, trying to get enough fuel to get to the target.

After a treacherous twenty minutes of refueling, we popped out into an open area and headed for the target. The foothills below us were still dark and covered with a layer of scud and morning fog. Wherever we were, the target was no more than fifteen minutes away from us. On the map, the target was 60 miles from Channel 97 on a bearing of 070 degrees. Bison flight was heading east in a gradual descent, and our formation had finally settled down.

According to the map and photo, the target was marked by a three-way road intersection that formed a large Y at the base of a karst mountain, with the bottom of the Y pointing south. I hadn't been on the previous day's mission so I was at a disadvantage as far as locating the target was concerned.

"Bison Lead has the target area at twelve o'clock about five miles. Got it, Three?" Broughton asked.

All I could see were low-hanging clouds in a bowl surrounded by mountains. "Negative on the target, Lead. I'll follow you in, over," I said as reassuringly as I could manage.

"Green'em up, Bisons. Lead's in on the center complex in the Y," Broughton called, as we rolled in on the target. Short bursts of ground fire started flashing immediately, and I finally spotted the depot. It looked just like the photo but much smaller.

We were carrying a mixture of 750-pound bombs and CBU-24 bomblets; two aircraft in each flight had one or the other. Bison Lead's bombs started impacting just as I released my bomblets on a supply complex and a battery of guns east of the Y intersection. Every gun in the valley was shooting back, so our bombs were bound to hit something. Pulling off, we had to turn hard to keep from getting hit and also stay inside the small, clear area surrounding the target. We were forced to stay in a tight, predictable orbit above the target, a vulnerable situation that was fraught with danger.

As planned, we orbited as high as we could, while Bison Lead directed the rest of the strike flights in on the target. In between flights, we punctuated the attack with strafing passes, and then resumed the wagon-wheel orbit just above the range of the guns. It was a dangerous tactic. We were in a constant turn, and it was very difficult to stay in position out of the clouds without loosing valuable airspeed and maneuverability.

On our third or fourth orbit, Broughton rolled-in for a final strafing pass on a complex of buildings just south of the road intersection. The 37mm guns opened up with a vicious barrage. Halfway down the chute, Broughton took a direct hit in the tail section of his aircraft. The whole aft section behind the horizontal slab was damaged and on fire. Bison Two warned him, "Bison Lead, you're hit and on fire. Get out of that thing before it comes apart!"

Lead pulled out of the dive straight ahead and headed west. The guns were still tracking him, but he was out of range in a matter of seconds. I was about a half-mile behind him and trying to close quickly.

"Lead, Two. Fire's bad, parts are falling off. Better step out, chief," Broughton's wingman insisted.

I knew that Broughton would stick with the airplane as long as he could in order to put as much mileage between himself and the target as possible.

"Bison Lead, Three here, Channel Ninety-Seven is two-five-zero degrees at fifty miles, steer ten degrees left for a vector to Udorn. I'm coming up on your left wing," I called, as I took control of the situation. "Bison Two, take Four back to Red Anchor for refueling. Alert Red Crown we are heading for Udorn and may need Sandy and Jolly Green support, over," I barked as I pulled in for a close look at the damage to the lead aircraft.

"Three this is Lead. I've got a solid fire light, P-One flight control system is gone, P-Two system pressure is fading, and the utility pressure is holding but weak. What does the bird look like from there, over?"

He had major damage to the aft section of the aircraft just forward of the afterburner petals. Hydraulic fluid and fuel were leaking into the jet exhaust, but the fire had gone out, and smoke was trailing from the damaged area. I only gave him a fifty-fifty chance of making it back to Udorn, but I kept it to myself.

"Lead, we've got Sandys and Choppers on the way. I think you can make if we can get through this weather. Watch the P-Two and utility pressures, but don't put out the RAT [ram air turbine] unless P-Two goes to zero, over."

Even if Bison's hydraulic systems held out, the weather and mountainous terrain we had to cross presented serious problems. The elevation of the ground for the next 100 miles was around 4,500 feet, with one peak reaching as high as 6,800 feet. The weather was solid and covered most of the higher elevations. I could see a little light through the lower valleys, but I knew those holes could be very deceiving.

We could climb up into the weather, but with damaged flight controls, Lead couldn't risk the turbulence of a thunderstorm. My ground-map radar showed a solid wall of precipitation in front of us, so we needed to find a valley or get help from a ground-radar site in order to pick our way through the storms. Udorn was just over 200 miles away.

Limping into Udorn

My job for the next thirty minutes was to maintain control of the situation, stay calm, and try to encourage Bison Lead in an otherwise discouraging situation. Red Crown had been alerted and a flight of Sandy A-1 Spads was on the way. We could read one of the closest radar sites, but he was having difficulty identifying our radar return because of our altitude and the heavy weather.

Bison Lead was hurting, but he was holding his own at about 2,000 feet above the ground. The fire in his aft section had blown itself out, and the smoke had dissipated. We had no choice but to stick with it and start back one ridge at a time. About 10 miles from Channel 97, I angled left of course for a shot at a large valley I spotted on the map. At last, luck took a turn our way, and we broke out under the clouds just as we passed over Sam Neua. For some reason the enemy guns didn't start shooting.

Broughton was very ginger with his flight controls. He had to monitor the aircraft hydraulic system pressure every second or two, and time seemed to hang in a balance. I kept a close check on the fuel gauges and calculated the fuel to go versus the fuel remaining as often as Broughton checked his hydraulic pressure gauge. By my calculation, we had enough fuel to make Udorn at low altitude, but there wasn't much margin for error. A few extra turns to avoid weather would make a significant difference, and I damn sure didn't want to step out of my airplane because of fuel starvation.

One of the Sandy pilots checked in and said that he had a tallyho on us. We were about halfway to Udorn and he reported that the weather ahead was significantly better. What a relief, I took a deep breath and a long swig on my water bottle. It wasn't until then that I realized how tense I was. I had a death grip on the stick and throttle and I was wringing wet.

"Bison Lead, Three here. We've got it made if you can hold on for another fifteen minutes. How's your P-Two doing, over?"

"Roger, Three, holding just above one thousand with lower fluctuations as the hydraulic pump cycles. When should I deploy the RAT, over?"

I cautioned him again not to use the RAT until P-2 had failed completely. Pressure from the RAT would pump the utility system fluid overboard unnecessarily, and he could end up with three dead systems and no flight controls.

After a few more agonizing minutes, we reached the Thai border, and I breathed a sigh of relief. We weren't home free but the worst was over.

Udorn was expecting us. "Bison flight, this is Udorn approach control. We have a radar target thirty miles northeast squawking emergency. Change squawk to three-five-zero-zero and ident, over." Bison Lead resumed control of the flight, and I dropped back on his wing to act as a chase plane and keep him out of trouble.

"Udorn approach, Bison squawking thirty-five-hundred level at three thousand feet. What is the active runway, over?"

"Roger, Bison, traffic at Udorn is landing to the northwest. Winds are out of the west at twenty knots with gusts to twenty-five, altimeter is two-nine-nine-zero. You are number one in the pattern, emergency equipment is standing by. Call five miles out turning final, over."

The gusty crosswinds presented a new problem. The movement of the flight controls required to keep the aircraft aligned with the runway would put a continuous demand for pressure on the hydraulic system, which could deplete the pressure and freeze the controls without warning. It was a potentially dangerous situation, but the only alternative was to eject and lose a good aircraft.

At 5 miles, Bison Lead turned to line up with the runway. I suggested that he keep the landing gear up until he was 3 miles out. This would save the utility hydraulic system and still give him time to get the gear down manually if necessary.

"Bison turning a long final at five miles, Tower. Flaps set, going to hold the gear for a couple of miles. Confirm your barriers are operational, over."

"Roger, Bison. This is Udorn Tower. Three barriers are in operation, call gear down and locked."

I was flying Broughton's left wing and expected to land in formation if possible. I was getting very low on fuel and didn't want to risk a go-around even though I knew Lead might get into trouble on the runway. The risk of something happening was low compared to the chances of flaming out in a nose high attitude with less than 500 pounds of fuel remaining.

Lead was stable but slightly low on the glide path at 2 miles from the runway. Without thinking, he dropped the landing gear and extended the RAT. "Bison has three green, pressure is coming up, and the RAT is out." It was too late for lectures; I hoped the RAT wouldn't bleed off the remaining fluid before he could get the airplane on the runway.

I lowered my landing gear and moved in a little closer in formation. Lead was getting too low on the glide path so I called him and suggested that he "hold it up a little." He misunderstood the message and almost panicked. He thought I said his landing gear was up, and he went through some wild gyrations before he realized that I meant he was too low. By the time he got it sorted out, he was only feet away from a successful landing.

Bison lead touched down, but I didn't have room to land with him on the left side of the runway. There wasn't a choice, I was forced to make a go-around. I pushed the throttle forward gently and pulled up the landing gear. The fuel gauge indicated just under 300 pounds of fuel remaining. I was sweating out having enough fuel to get to a high, downwind position where I would have enough altitude to eject or continue the landing, depending on whether the engine kept running. It was an awkward position to be in, but I had been there before with my boss, Jack Broughton. He was agressive as hell, and had a knack for getting his wingmen into trouble, God love him.

"Udorn Tower, Bison Three on the go. Request closed. I'm below emergency fuel, over!"

"Roger, Bison Three, cleared for a closed pattern. You are number one, call turning base leg with gear down and locked!"

I rolled the wings level on a high downwind leg and looked back at the runway. Bison Lead was already on the taxiway, and all of the emergency equipment was following him. The runway was clear, and I felt I had a good chance of making it.

Without hesitating, I lowered the landing gear handle, dropped the flaps, and started a tight descending turn onto the base leg. The strong crosswind was blowing me toward the runway, so I had to compensate by pulling the turn even tighter, an uncomfortable and potentially dangerous position to be in. The fuel gauge was stuck at 300 pounds so I concentrated on lining the aircraft up for a good landing.

Purposely, I held it high and a little hot to make sure I could make the runway. If necessary, I could take the barrier in the event of drag chute failure. That was better than taking a chance on rolling up in a ball of fire and red dust short of the runway.

"Tower, Bison Three on final with three green and looking keen," I called with a silly touch of poetry. I felt like telling the whole world that I had cheated the odds and was going to make it. The runway numbers disappeared under the nose as I eased back the throttle, and the wheels squeaked on the runway.

After turning off the runway, I raised the canopy and released my oxygen mask, always a welcome relief to a sticky face. Even though it was still early, I was bushed, and the morning air felt delightful on my soaked body. As I taxied to the ramp to park, I tried to recount the number of times I had been to Udorn under similar circumstances. I couldn't recall exactly, but I hoped like hell this would be the last.

I parked beside Colonel Broughton's damaged aircraft. For the first time, his aircraft tail number registered with me. It was number 450 instead of number 338, his regular aircraft. Of course. Number 338 was laid up in the shop at Takhli with similar battle damage from the day before. Broughton was hard on airplanes, but I figured he had finally learned a lesson about orbiting a target.

The ground crew asked if I had any special problems. "No, just fuel and a new drag chute," I remarked as I stepped off the ladder and into the staff car for a lift to the command post.

I met Colonel Broughton inside the command post in the midst of an intelligence debriefing. He still had on his G-suit. His face was drawn, the imprint of his oxygen mask still fresh on his cheeks, and he was wringing wet with sweat. He shook my hand somewhat gravely as he expressed his thanks for my help. As we talked, he looked at me and made a statement I would never forget. Almost pitifully he said, "Ken, I don't understand it, I never got below ten thousand feet," lamenting the fact that he had sustained major battle damage for the second day in a row. For an instant I forgot myself and blurted back, "And you stayed in the same damned orbit for ten minutes and never got above three hundred and fifty knots, either. That's the bloody problem, Boss!" He looked shocked but it was true, and I think he appreciated my honesty.

When we completed the debriefing, the duty officer reported that my airplane was fully serviced and ready to go. As a conciliatory gesture, I offered to let Colonel Broughton take my airplane home, indicating that I would be willing to wait for the courier flight. He smiled and told me to go on. I think he needed the time to think. I saluted and jumped into the waiting staff car.

I inspected my aircraft and strapped into the cockpit. As I checked the operation of the flight controls, I couldn't help but notice number 450 sitting silently in a pool of fuel and hydraulic fluid. Sadly, the airplane looked as exhausted as I felt, and I wondered if it would fly again. As it turned out, it was repaired and flew a month later. On 13 July 1967, number 450 was damaged over North Vietnam and crashed in Thailand. Sometimes, the golden BB was just plain unavoidable.

I taxied to the runway wondering if I would ever see Udorn again. "Udorn Tower, Bison Three number one for the runway, pins, canopy, and lanyard. VFR to Channel Forty-Three, over!"

"Roger, Bison Three. Cleared on and off, have a good day."

After takeoff, I cleaned up the airplane and leveled off for a relaxing ride home. The jungle was beautiful from 200 feet above the trees. It was the only way to fly; low, and as fast as the speed of sound.

Bear Lead to Kep—Number Ninety-Eight

After months of anticipation, we finally struck the airfield at Kep on the afternoon of 13 June 1967. Until then, Kep had been off-limits because of its proximity to Red China. Its occasional use as a recovery base for Red Chinese fighters made it politically sensitive in the view of Washington. Consequently, Kep had become a sanctuary for MiGs operating from other bases throughout North Vietnam.

A constant source of frustration was flying past Kep on missions, knowing that we were vulnerable to attack from MiGs that could take advantage of its political immunity. Kep was a veritable safe haven in an area that witnessed some of the most intense aerial combat of the war, and was the scene of some of our worst losses. For that reason alone, I was pleased to take part in the first strike on that important airfield. It was my ninety-eighth mission and one that I greeted with high expectations. The thrill of making a surprise attack, and the lure of MiGs far outweighed the risk of being shot down only days before finishing my tour.

I was scheduled to lead Bear flight with Paul Sheehy on my wing and Lonnie Ferguson and Chris Lawrence in the element. The mission was primarily a 354th Squadron effort, and we put together a good team to do the job. Our objective was twofold: to destroy MiGs and put the airfield out of commission. To accomplish the task, we loaded six flights of F-105s with a mix of CBU-24 bomblets and 750-pound bombs, bomblets for the MiGs and hard bombs to crater the airfield. Even if the MiGs escaped, we were looking forward to busting up a lot of concrete.

We made an early afternoon heavyweight takeoff and headed east for the long way around, water route to the target. It was dreadfully hot, and the air was rough all the way to the tankers. Our flight was assigned to refuel on Brown Anchor 42, orbiting at 12,000 feet above the Gulf of Tonkin. The weather in the refueling area was hazy, and scattered domes of cumulus clouds had already begun to build on the strong afternoon convection. The weather to the north was forecast to be rotten, and it looked forbidding.

Leaving the tankers, the strike force headed north for the turning point just northeast of Haiphong Harbor. As we proceeded, the ever vigilant radar defenses along the coast of North Vietnam began to track us. It seemed paradoxical to fly a course that split a seam between the enemy and the U.S Navy operating off of Yankee Station. It was as if we were an airborne armada coming to the aid of our beleaguered forces. In a way, I envied the Navy pilots because they were seldom far out of sight of the carriers during their strike operations. However, to those who got into trouble with the North Vietnamese defenses, it was probably a tragic paradox of being so close yet so far away.

The weather looked grim as we turned west over the Ile de Madeline and started our penetration into the target area. A solid wall of thunderstorms lay across the course to Kep. We were forced to twist around towering cells in order to avoid the storms and maintain visual contact with the ground. I hoped that our movement coupled with the radar reflection of the thunderstorms would confuse the defenses and help conceal us from their coverage.

Surface-to-air missile and AAA gun radar warnings began to saturate the RHAW gear. It would have been impossible to see a missile coming up through the clouds, so I took a deep breath and concentrated on getting to the target despite the threat. I was nervous as hell but excited because I felt certain we would catch Kep by surprise, and the weather made it unlikely that they would be flying. If we could just see the airfield, it would be a turkey shoot.

Twenty miles east of Kep, the force split into two attack groups. Hectic Lead kept three flights on a steady heading, while I took three flights slightly north to form a pincer. When we got to the target, we planned to roll-in from opposite sides in close succession, Bear following Hectic. Therefore, it was imperative to maintain visual contact with the other force even though the clouds made it very difficult.

I spotted Kep through an open wedge in a giant cumulus cloud that was sitting right over the airfield. I held my breath hoping that Hectic flight would roll-in before I lost sight of the target. I was tempted to roll-in first, but I finally heard Hectic Lead call rolling-in.

After a very short five-second count, I rolled into a vertical dive to my left. "Bear Lead in from the north, heads up. It's a tight squeeze!" The congestion was dangerous, but it was beautiful to see twenty-four F-105s streaming down through a narrow canyon in a huge thunderstorm toward an airfield loaded with enemy aircraft.

I rolled the wings level and began tracking the pipper toward a cluster of MiGs in revetments along the southeast side of the runway. For the first time in a dive-bomb pass, seconds seemed to tick by like hours. It was a race to reach the release point before the clouds obscured the target. I was so intent on hitting the MiGs that I barely noticed a blanket of flak that began exploding over the airfield. The gunners were probably surprised and desperately firing a steady stream of barrage fire just above our release altitude. Orange bursts of flak radiated with an eerie glow as they exploded in the base of the clouds surrounding the airfield.

I released my CBUs and started a hard pull-out to the left. Bombs from the flights ahead of us were starting to hit the field, and the explosions looked spectacular. By a miracle, we had found Kep and scored a punishing blow, but it was going to be tough to get everyone out without taking some hits or colliding with another airplane.

As I pulled out, I tried to avoid going into the base of the thunderstorm. I pulled back hard on the stick and my G-suit almost cut me in half. I was straining to stay in a narrow valley of clear air between clouds at the bottom of the towering anvil. It would be impossible for the rest of the flight to avoid dishing out into the clouds. It was an unfortunate but unavoidable situation. I hoped we could somehow avoid a midair collision.

"Bear Lead. Two in the soup behind you with hung bombs, over." Paul's bombs had failed to release, and he was blind in the weather below me. My heart raced; Paul was in a dangerous jam.

"Bear Three and Four off and in the clouds. Checking port to clear you and look for a hole, over." The element was also in the clouds and Fergie had decided to make a check-turn to the left to avoid hitting us.

Quickly, I shot back, "Bear Lead steady one-one-zero at six-thousand. Ease it up out of the clouds, Two, and I should be at your twelve o'clock, over." I pulled back on the throttle to help Paul catch up with the increased drag of his bombs and prayed that he wouldn't hit me.

For the next few minutes, we were terribly vulnerable to attack from SAMs, and it was a helpless feeling. Sweat poured down my face, and I felt a flood of emotions coursing through my body; anxiety, fear, guilt, and loneliness. We had lost flight integrity at a very crucial point, when we needed it most. *What a crappy way to end a perfect mission!*

"Bear Two has a tally on Lead. What should I do with my bombs, over?"

"Bear Two, Lead here. Recycle your switches and pickle again." It was a risky thing to do, not knowing our exact location over the ground, but my primary concern was for Paul's safety. I could answer for a long round later if he hit a village.

"Roger Lead, I've tried the switches and can't get the bombs to release."

"Bear Two, try punching them off," I advised in desperation. Paul hit the main jettison button and away they went, external tanks and all.

"Bear Two is clean," Paul called sheepishly, as he moved into position on the right side of my aircraft. I was surprised to see him on my wing so quickly but relieved that he had found me. I tried to calm down and breath a little easier.

"Bear Three, do you have Lead?" I asked expectantly.

"Rog, Three has you, but I don't have Four."

What a jolt. We were almost out and Four was unaccounted for. Instinctively, I started a turn back toward the target to look for him. There were no beepers squealing to indicate that anyone had gotten hit and punched out.

"Bear this is Hectic. I have an extra bird, looks like your Number Four man, over."

"Roger, Bear Four is with Hectic." Chris was apparently in good shape, but he sounded a little embarrassed. At last, I could relax and count my chickens. I turned back to the east, hit the deck, and headed for the tankers.

As we coasted out, the weather began to improve dramatically. The radio calls took on a more confident tone as we began to sort things out for a post-strike report to Red Crown. I popped out a Winston and devoured it in three drags.

Mission Successful

Everyone had made it out, and we were on the tankers, getting a final drink of fuel before starting the long flight home. Hectic Lead called Red Crown and reported that we had been successful and were returning without a loss. I could hardly wait to get back to Takhli to assess our film and make an estimate of the number of MiGs we had destroyed.

As it turned out, the weather was not quite through testing us. A late afternoon thunderstorm at Takhli forced us to land at Korat and delayed our triumphant return until after dark. When I finally reached the parking blocks at Takhli, I was exhausted. It had been practically a twenty-four-hour day. The mission had lasted a record four hours and ten minutes. When it was over, we had overcome some enormous obstacles in striking Kep, and we were all proud to be a part of the record-setting mission.

Several days later we made the headlines in the 16 June 1967 edition of the *Stars and Stripes* newspaper.

U.S. Jets Blast 6 MiGs on Ground. SAIGON (UPI)—U.S. warplanes darted past thunderstorms over North Vietnam Tuesday to blast six more MiG jets on the ground, a pair of ammunition dumps and two main rail lines.

A band of F105 Thunderchiefs from Thailand darted past the flak and rolled-in on the sprawling airfield at Kep, 38 miles northeast of Hanoi.

The fighter-bombers sent deadly cluster bomb units [CBUS] blasting into the base and "probably destroyed" at least six MiGs they spotted in revetments.

"As we approached Kep airfield," said Air Force Maj. Kenneth H. Bell, "the sky seemed to be one big mass of thunderstorms. Coming over the field, we found an opening in the clouds and dropped through.

"The flak was really heavy," said Bell. "They were shooting like crazy."

The jets also ripped up the runway, cratering or cutting it in at least four places and blasted tankers, box cars, flat beds and locomotives in the adjacent Kep railroad yard.

The MiGs, all early model 17s declared obsolete in the Russian inventory and sent to North Vietnam, brought to at least 21 the number of communist interceptors destroyed by American warplanes in the past three days.

We had done more damage than we had imagined, and, at last, Kep was on-limits for good. The last line in my diary that night added a touch of irony and insight, *"It's odd, the pleasure a fighter pilot takes in bombing an airfield."*

20

CHAMPAGNE ON THE RAMP

I PROMISED MYSELF THAT I would fly my last two missions down the main street of Hanoi, but it didn't quite work out that way, and in retrospect, it was probably best that it didn't. I might have done something brash and not survived to tell about it.

Even at ninety-nine, we took our missions one at a time. In the deadly business of combat, nothing was certain, and taking the outcome of a mission for granted was often the shortest road to disaster. I decided not to push fate on my penultimate mission.

14 June 67—Wednesday—Wolf #1—A/C# 234—Ron Ferry
Two ship flight, Paul Sheehy #2—The wonderful thing about #99 is that it's really your last but you don't come back a "has been." Good judgment finally prevailed and I decided to take a "single pump" to Route Pack I. My greatest concern was not getting Paul shot down. I was also very worried about bad weather forcing us to recover at Korat again—damn near did.

We came off Blue Anchor for a point target—truck park near Ron Ferry. I warned the other flights that we were rolling in but several F-105s crashed through us to the target. Someone named Wally dove right through our pull-off. The weather was crystal clear so I altered our next roll-in.

We reset the switches and came back around for the rocket pass. Next, we popped over the ridge to strafe a suspected radar site. My gun jammed so I gave Paul the lead. It caught him at a loss. The little tiger stayed in a continuous turn and gave me a work out on the wing but he didn't find a target.

At Bingo fuel, we started back so I could give Paul an instrument check. The weather was ideal for the occasion—it was rotten. Half way home we had to hit a tanker and hold for a thunderstorm sitting over Takhli. Paul did everything exactly right.

With lots of gas we started home. The supervisor of flying [SOF] broke us into single ship for the recovery which wasn't necessary. Once I started down, I began to have some reservations about the weather. There was mud on the runway where an aircraft had swerved off and on through the grass during landing. Vehicles on the runway were a major obstacle when I finally landed.

On the ground, Paul and I started laying plans for tomorrow. I was relieved but excited. At mission #99, you are the #1 pilot in the Wing and the 100th mission air show is your most anxious prospect.

After the debriefing, Paul and I headed for the stag bar to have a drink and talk about my final mission. I don't know which I enjoyed most, the completion of number ninety-nine or the anticipation of flying number 100. I felt optimistic but still cautious. Surely the odds were in my favor but there were several who had gotten this far and hadn't made it.

The flying schedule for the next day was already posted. As I expected, Paul and I were on for an 0525 briefing as Hotdog flight with Jack Hunt as our ground spare. There was a small (100) typed after my name on the schedule, not big but very important. The urge to shout out loud overcame me, and I was filled with a sense of total euphoria. "Shit hot Paul, I don't believe it," I exclaimed. "This time tomorrow it will be all over!"

After a few drinks, I had a compelling urge to buy a round for the bar, but a quiet voice inside me warned me not to count my chickens too early. The right side of my brain knew I needed food and rest but the left side wanted to enjoy the camaraderie at the bar just a little longer. The temptation was too strong. I stayed too long and paid for it the next morning.

Vern Frye always said that I'd be late for my 100th mission, but when I went to bed that night I thought the expectation of the day would be enough to get me up on time. I set the alarm for 0400, tested the ringer, and that was the last sound I heard until I was awakened by a loud knock on the trailer door.

Startled, I came out of bed hoping I wasn't too late to fly the mission. Jack Hunt was at the door. He was halfway laughing when he told me that both Paul Sheehy and I had overslept, and it would be impossible for him to spare for us both. "You'd better get your butt in gear and get down to the briefing," Jack said in a drawl typical of his dry sense of humor.

I dressed quickly and headed for the flight line. All I could think about was a hot cup of coffee and how good 100 percent oxygen was going to smell to my aching brain. What a terrible way to begin the last mission of a combat tour and one of the most significant days of your life. "Next time around," I admonished myself, "I'll do it Vern's way."

Mission Briefing

Thank goodness the mission briefing at wing headquarters was abbreviated. It gave us time to review the flight at the 354th Squadron before takeoff. Paul handed me a copy of the flight plan. The mission had three diverse alternatives. The primary target was a military complex in northern Laos, just across the Vietnamese border from Dien Bien Phu. The secondary target was a highway intersection on the southern edge of Route Pack One near the DMZ. And the third possibility was an armed reconnaissance mission in the mountainous region of Package One along routes that connected with the main coastal road between Dong Hoi and Ron Ferry.

I looked at Paul with a grin. "That's a lot of territory to cover for two guys with splitting headaches."

"Don't panic," he said. "We already got words to recce the routes to the ferry."

"Thanks for telling me smart ass," I said jokingly. Paul and I both grinned and laughed nervously.

We were going back to Ron Ferry on an armed reconnaissance mission. The recce route began at a river junction just across the border from Laos in a sharp valley between two karst mountain ridges. From there, it wound east through high country toward the coastal valley and ended at Ron Ferry about 5 miles south of Dong Hoi on the eastern shoreline. Good old Dong Hoi, the defenses there were usually light, but could be unpredictable.

For once, the weather forecast was ass-backwards as far as I was concerned. It was good in the target area and forecast to be crummy on return to Takhli. On my last mission, I could bomb in any kind of weather, but I needed clear skies at home for the air show that Paul and I had cooked up.

The aircraft that I was assigned was the same one I had flown the day before, but for some reason it had not been loaded with bombs and rockets. Time was really tight, and it looked like I might have to push Jack Hunt out of the spare or launch him and fly my mission another day.

At the very last minute, number 234 was uploaded in time to make the start engine time, and I was Hotdog Leader by the skin of my rinny-tin-tin. I got the queasy feeling that things weren't going my way. "Get thee behind me superstition," I said to myself. "This will be my day come hell or high water."

By the time I got strapped into the aircraft, started the engine, and was ready to taxi, it was past the normal time for check in but I finally pulled out of the chocks at exactly 0706 hours, just as scheduled. I still think Jack Hunt was a little disappointed.

"Takhli, Hotdog One taxiing from hardstand Bravo Seven with the numbers. Hotdog check in!"

"Hotdog Two," Paul answered.

"Spare on frequency," Jack said, with a touch of envy in his voice.

The word spreads fast when you're on your 100th mission, and everyone was pulling for me. In the arming area, the chaplain was beaming. I could tell he was giving me a cheerful blessing while I said a prayer and the ground crew armed the airplane.

The arming chief held up the armament safety pins and gave me an enthusiastic thumbs up. The streamers from the pins fluttered in the breeze as he held them proudly over his head while the rest of the ground crew saluted us. The pins were out and we were ready to take the runway. I signaled Paul to lower the canopy, added power, and swung out in a right turn toward the runway.

"Takhli Tower, Hotdog number one for runway one-eight with two."

"Roger, Hotdog. Cleared into position and hold."

"Roger, Tower. Hotdog leader has pins, canopy, lanyard."

"Two has pins, canopy, lanyard."

Everything was set. We ran up the power and made all of the normal system checks. I looked over my shoulder at Paul on my right wing, and he nodded that he was ready to roll.

Before I pushed the mike button to ask the tower for release, the radio cracked with the call I had been waiting nine months to hear.

"Hotdog flight is cleared for takeoff for number one-hundred, good hunting!"

"Roger, Hotdog rolling, burner NOW!" It was exactly 0723 hours, 15 June 1967. I'll never forget that day.

As the nose of the airplane sliced into the smooth morning air, I knew I was making my last takeoff in the F-105. It was a poignant moment that I wanted to savor, but the radio brought me back to business. "Hotdog Two is airborne, check your lanyard, Lead," Paul called, checking my tendency to forget to disconnect the low altitude lanyard from my parachute D-ring after takeoff. I looked down, stowed the lanyard, and sat back to enjoy the ride to the tanker. We had an 0800 rendezvous with Blue Anchor 73.

Off Blue Anchor

We both refueled without difficulty. As we dropped away from the tanker, it looked especially graceful silhouetted against the blue morning sky. The tankers were indispensable, and we put a lot of faith in the crews who flew them. Our success depended on them, and I had grown to appreciate their unselfish, can-do attitude.

"Thanks for the gas, Blue Anchor. Hotdog off to the east, hope to see you soon. Hotdog go button twelve."

"Hotdog Two on."

"Roger Two, target is zero-five-zero for ninety-nine, green'em up!"

In twelve minutes we were over the western edge of Package One. The mountains were clobbered-in with fog, but I could see a narrow road leading east through a valley so I started a gradual, weaving descent looking for something worth hitting on my last mission. Surely some of Uncle Ho's midnight haulers were under the trees and watching anxiously as we desperately searched for signs of their tracks.

Flying at treetop level, we crisscrossed through valleys and scoured the roads between the mountains and Ron Ferry without finding a target. I was frustrated and angry. "What makes you think the North Vietnamese would leave trucks out on these roads just for your 100th mission," I thought to myself.

I was so anxious to find a good target that I caught myself wishing that I had waited for a mission in Six-Alpha. Once I had dreamed that I made a touch-and-go landing at Phuc Yen and strafed the planes on the ramp as my final salute to the North Vietnamese Air Force. That would have been much more fitting than bombing a desolate ford at Ron Ferry.

"Hotdog, check your four o'clock low," Paul called on the radio.

As we turned back toward the mountains, I spotted tire tracks leading into some trees next to a ridge guarding a narrow highway, a perfect place for a hidden truck park. I glanced over my shoulder at Paul, pointed down at the target and pulled up to roll-in.

"Lead's in, stick with me," I radioed Two.

"Roger, Lead, I'm with you."

I had rushed the roll-in and the dive angle was too steep. It was a rotten pass, but I tried to save it by bunting the nose over to track the target. When I hit the release altitude, I pickled the bombs and pulled out hard down the valley, hoping not to go below the ridge line. The ground was rushing up fast, and I was worried about ground fire.

Paul dropped back and way below me. He was dangerously low and obviously in trouble. "Lead, Hotdog Two has hung bombs. Give me a little."

"What the hell was going on?" I asked myself. "It was Kep all over again. He must have pushed the wrong pickle button."

"Hotdog Two, jettison the load and get back up here," I shouted over the radio. I felt bad about snapping at Paul, but I was tense and concerned about his safety. When I looked back, he had dropped his bombs and was closing nicely. As usual, he was right with me.

With Two back in the fighting wing position, I swung back around to access the damage to the target. It looked as if my bombs had started some secondary explosions, a good sign that we had caught a few trucks napping. I let the nose down to gain airspeed and setup for a rocket pass. As the target passed my wingtip, I rolled-in steep, centered the pipper on some objects on the road that looked like trucks, and rippled thirty-eight rockets in a single pass. Orange fire and smoke from the curling rockets blanked my windscreen as I pulled out straight ahead, grunting from the pressure in my G-suit.

The rockets hit long. Damn! I was tempted to swing around for a strafing pass but something told me to call it a day, so I headed west. "Hotdog, that's it," I called as I motioned for Paul to move up into a line-a-breast position.

On the way to the post-strike tanker, it dawned on me that I had seen North Vietnam for the last time. For a moment, I regretted that I hadn't waited for better weather in Package Six to complete my tour. But, suddenly I was overcome with a deep sense of relief and satisfaction. I was only an hour away from my final pass and salute to the team at Takhli. The feeling was almost overwhelming. Euphoria, pride, and even a touch of melancholy swept through me. I had faced the most formidable challenge of my life successfully. I was alive. I was done!

The tanker was on station and it didn't take long to get the fuel we needed. We each topped-off and dropped away in close formation. "Red Anchor Three-One, Hotdog has full tanks, dropping off port. Thanks, it's my last mission."

"Roger Hotdog, good show and congrats from the crew of Red Anchor Thirty-One, fresh from the States."

"Hotdog, go button four and check in," I called excitedly.

"Lead, Hotdog Two is on."

"Roger, Brigham. Hotdog fifty miles east of Forty-Three, level at two-four-zero, squawking ident, request radar vectors, over."

"Hotdog, Brigham has radar contact, cleared to descend. The weather at Forty-Three is twenty-five-hundred foot overcast, winds light. Landing runway one-eight-zero. Cleared to Point Bravo, call leaving the frequency."

"Roger, copy Brigham," I snapped coolly. I couldn't wait to get back to Takhli.

When as we broke out under the clouds, I changed over to tower frequency and checked in. The air was smooth and moist, and we were doing better than 600 knots indicated airspeed. Graceful white streamers arched off our wing tips as we made the turn onto initial approach. We were 5 miles out.

As I lined up on the runway, I saw the blur of something headed right at us and closing fast. Instinctively, I broke down hard and to the left. For an instant, I was back up north avoiding SAMs, but it was only a formation of four Thai F-86s on a training mission. "What a hell of a note on a hundred-mission pass," I thought out loud. "A midair collision with four guys going the wrong way in the traffic pattern with their heads up and locked."

I turned back to line up on the runway and lowered the nose gently to pick up airspeed. It was the event I had planned over and over again in every detail. I was on top of the world.

"Takhli Tower, Hotdog on initial for a hundred-mission pass," I called on the radio, barely able to contain myself.

We were level at 100 feet above the jungle trees and screaming. The airplanes were solid and Paul was glued on my wing in position. The first pass would be a wake-up call.

"Takhli, Hotdog is one mile out on the trees."

"Roger, Hotdog, cleared for your pass. The pattern is yours, over!"

As we approached the threshold of the runway, I let the nose ease down further, and the airplane leaned forward like a fine race horse. The long, slender pitot boom mounted on the radome split the centerline of the runway like a javelin. Crowds of people had gathered in front of the squadron buildings. The aircraft parking ramp was full but motionless. The ground crews had stopped their work to watch the show.

Midway down the runway, I started a hard, climbing turn to the left. The cloud level was solid at about 2,000 feet, so it would be impossible to do any over-the-top maneuvers. I had to stick with climbing, over-the-shoulder turns, and level-rolling maneuvers. I had planned three passes, a formation victory roll, and a reentry for landing.

I kept the turn tight and started the nose down toward the field. We were in a left, descending arc pulling a solid four Gs, and it felt wonderful. I rolled out of the turn with the nose still below the horizon, accelerating and headed straight across the ramp toward the trailer area and the Officers' Club.

"Tower, Hotdog crossing east to west."

"Roger, Hotdog, tower has you in sight."

We leveled out 50 feet above the ground, aimed straight at the crowd. I hoped I wasn't pressing too hard. In the bat of an eye, we flashed past the ramp and pulled up to the left for a high arching turn that would bring us back down the runway to the north for a low pass from right to left in front of the crowd. Paul was still tucked in tight on my wing, and so far, the show was going according to plan. The formation roll was on the back of my mind as I got set for the second pass.

"Tower, Hotdog half-mile south."

"Roger, Hotdog, cleared for a pass up the runway."

I rolled out of the turn and lined up with the centerline of the runway. I eased the nose down closer to the runway and let the airplane settle. We were right on the deck, low enough to see our shock wave raise dust billows on the runway. I signaled Paul with my thumb to hold it a little high, but he was already up there.

At 600 knots and no more than 20 feet above the ground, things happen fast. Our formation was solid as the crowded ramp raced by through the left side of the canopy. Although blurred, I could see some of the expressions on the faces of the people as they looked out practically level at our formation.

Colonel Scott was one of the faces in the crowd, and I wondered what he might be thinking as he watched us bend the limits on his rules for 100-mission air shows. He had a flare for flamboyance but he also appreciated those who respected his guidance. I hoped he would understand just once.

At the north end of the runway, I pulled up smoothly into a steep climb to make a 180-degree, high, arcing turn over my left shoulder—a tight whifferdill—and come back down the runway for a formation roll and my final salute before landing. The low clouds made it difficult, but Paul hung in there like a trooper, and we came over the top of the turn almost inverted at 400 knots with a solid four Gs. I lined up with the runway in the last part of the dive and leveled off at 500 feet above the ground to provide for some margin of error in the formation roll.

"Tower, Hotdog is in from the north for a victory roll."

"Roger, Hotdog. Be careful!"

Just before midfield, I pulled the nose up about 15 degrees, stabilized, and started a roll to the left away from the wingman. I knew Paul would stay in position. It was up to me to complete the maneuver with enough ground clearance.

Around we went as smooth as silk. As we passed through the inverted position, the ground started coming up a little too fast, so I added just a touch of forward stick pressure and continued the roll. Paul bobbled a bit but adjusted quickly. As we came back to the horizontal, wings level position, we bottomed out of the roll a few feet above the ground, close but with room to spare.

I held back pressure on the stick, continued the roll to the left, and entered a left-climbing turn to reenter the pattern for my final landing. The flybys were good, the formation roll worked, and the only thing that was left to do was make a good landing.

The usual way to complete a 100-mission air show was with a tactical pitch-up from the deck for a normal, overhead landing pattern. Under normal circumstances, a pitch-up break was a pretty way to get a formation of fighters on the ground quickly. As embellishments were added, like higher and higher speeds on the initial approach, the pitch-up pattern became more difficult to adjust to and could be quite dangerous for an inattentive pilot.

"Takhli Tower, this is Hotdog on a low turn to initial, two miles out. Request landing, over."

"Roger, Hotdog. Cleared on initial for one-eight, no other reported traffic, winds are light and variable. Altimeter two-nine-nine-five, call turning base, over."

"Rog, Tower, Hotdog."

I realized that we were lower and faster than we should have been but adrenaline was clouding my judgement.

Over the runway, I started a sharp, high-G pull up to the left, and Paul followed two seconds later. "Hotdog on the break," I said crisply.

The next thing I knew I was on my back on the downwind leg of the pattern, far too hot and tight for a comfortable turn around the base leg to a final approach. Good sense said "take it around and try again" but ego said "salvage it, babes, it's the last one." I hoped Paul had made a better adjustment.

Ego prevailed and I continued the high-G turn down toward the runway, hoping to bleed off enough airspeed to get the airplane around and lower the landing gear in time for a smooth landing. As the airspeed passed through 300 knots, I put the gear handle down, set the leading and trailing edge flaps to the extended position, and pulled back hard on the stick to make the turn to final.

I was too close to the runway but I kept pulling. I felt the airplane shudder, and the left wing started to tuck under, the first warning signs of a stall and spin. I released some back pressure and added power. The airplane responded, but my traffic pattern was crappy. I called "gear down and locked" and continued the turn, recognizing that I would overshoot the final approach for a long and hot landing.

"Hotdog, recheck your landing gear, clear to land."

I looked back inside the cockpit and the indicator lights were all green, which confused me. "Why did he ask me to recheck the gear," I wondered, "when they're all down and locked?" While I was staring at the landing gear lights in the cockpit I was also losing precious altitude.

Finally I snapped back, "Gear is rechecked, Tower. Hotdog is going to be long and hot on the last one."

I dished out of the turn wide of the runway and started to S-turn back to the centerline. Paul called that he was on an extended base leg with three green, and I was relieved that he was able to compensate for my sloppy pattern.

Even with everything out for maximum drag, I came in hotter than a two-peckered goat, and the airplane sailed over the normal touchdown point. Almost 2,000 feet down the runway, the main landing gear finally touched the pavement.

I lowered the nose and pulled the drag chute handle. The end of the runway was coming up fast, and I only had a couple of seconds to decide whether to use the arresting hook. "Not on the last mission," I thought, as I felt the sudden deceleration of the drag chute. "It worked," I shouted, as I was pressed forward against the shoulder straps, thank goodness God looks after fools and fighter pilots.

I turned off the runway and released the drag chute as I pulled into the de-arming area. Paul was right with me. I opened the canopy and looked out at the ground crew. Their faces were beaming.

I put the safety pin back in my ejection seat, saluted the ground crew smartly, and pushed up the power to taxi back to the parking ramp. Several fire trucks were speeding down the parallel taxiway toward us to escort us back to the ramp in the 100-mission processional. It was a tradition that marked the occasion at Takhli and the only time that fire trucks met airplanes other than during an emergency.

Of all the proud moments in my life, the next few were probably the most glorious and fulfilling. I had seen others come back and they all looked just like I felt at that moment. It was like running the last few yards of a race for your life that you *know* you have won.

The fire trucks swung around in front of us and began to spray arcs of white water from their nozzles. As we proceeded, several more vehicles joined the procession. We taxied in close formation behind the leading vehicles and extended our refueling probes in unison as a salute to the crowd gathered along the taxiway.

"Hotdog, peckers up, ready ... now!"

The warm jungle breeze felt good on my face and I sat back to enjoy the most important parade of my life. It was the poignant moment of tradition I had worked so hard for. I was joining the ranks of those who had succeeded in the face of overwhelming odds, and those who had gone down trying.

As we turned into the parking area I spotted the familiar blue sedan of the wing commander. Colonel Scott was standing on the ramp and waiting at my parking spot with a host of others. He was the only one in a tan uniform, and he stood apart from the crowd the way commanders always do. I knew he would have something clever and engaging to say.

As I pulled in, the crew chief crossed his arms over his head, signaling that the nose wheel was on the parking spot. I braked to a stop and shut the engine down. As the engine spooled down, the crew chief came up the ladder to the cockpit. He was smiling from ear to ear. I gave him a thumbs up indicating that the airplane was in commission. He took my helmet, put it in my green, nylon helmet bag and shook my hand enthusiastically.

"Good show, Major. How's the airplane? It's scheduled for the afternoon mission" I reassured him that the airplane was okay and ready for loading. He seemed proud enough to have flown the mission himself, and in many respects, he had. The ground crews did a magnificent job of keeping us in the air and they did it tirelessly.

As I came down the ladder, I noticed the long, red welcome mat that was used to honor such occasions. My name had been added to the list of 100-mission finishers. The white, stenciled paint was so fresh that I was hesitant to stand on it. For a moment, I just stood there silently staring down in awe and disbelief.

I saluted Colonel Scott and he shook my hand warmly. He had a twinkle in his steel blue eyes as he let me know tactfully that I had pressed his limits a little too hard. I got the message and that was the end of it. He looked genuinely proud and happy.

Colonel Broughton saluted and surprised me with a bear hug. He presented my 100-mission flying suit and held it while I stripped down to my underwear. I had on my lucky, red-and-white, checkerboard skivvies, and the crowd got a big kick out of it. Lieutenant Colonel Nelson McDonald, the new commander of the 354th squadron, was looking on with pride and envy, but the skivvies surprised him. Colonel Mac had a dry sense of humor.

100-Mission Flying Suit

I hurried to don the coveted 100-mission flying suit, but my boots kept sticking in the baggy legs. I thought I would never get it on. When I finally managed to slip it over my shoulders and pull up the zipper, the crowd responded with a loud cheer and applause.

The suit was covered with patches—wing, squadron, and SAM Killer—but the one on the left shoulder stood out above the rest. It read "North Vietnam—100 Missions—F-105" sown in bold white letters on a bright red and blue background. My gaze fixed on the patch, and I felt tears begin to well up in my eyes. The crowd hushed as Colonel Mac reached out and touched the coveted patch for good luck. It was a poignant moment.

Paul Sheehy made his way back from his airplane and pushed through the crowd to congratulate me. He had an open bottle of champagne. We toasted each other and shook hands. As we toasted, I put my hand on his shoulder and thanked him while a photographer took our picture. "Trusted wingman gets a pat on the back from a grateful leader" would have been a proper caption.

I had ordered several dozen bottles of champagne for the flight-line celebration, and corks began to pop everywhere. Someone drenched me with a spewing bottle, and it started a chain reaction. The ramp erupted with streaming arcs of precious bubbly. Champagne ran down my face, hiding tears of joy and sadness. I didn't really care that much for champagne, but I took several delicious gulps from a bottle. It could have been Dom Perignon for all I knew, but that didn't matter. The celebration had been christened.

I thought of Vern Frye, who had finished several weeks earlier. As a strict teetotaler, Vern surprised everyone with cases of ice-cold U.S. Pepsi for his flight-line party. Pepsi was better than water, but the object was to honor the ground crews who worked so hard on the airplanes and give them a chance to unwind and get to know the pilots a little better. The airmen appreciated Vern's gesture, but I'm sure they expected something more than ordinary U.S. Pepsi.

The champagne kept flowing and the cameras kept clicking. Finally, the official photographer asked the 354th Squadron to stand together for a group photo with the airplane. Fifteen pilots, mostly captains and majors, gathered behind me as I knelt on the welcome mat holding a bottle of champagne poised over an ice bucket.

I had flown with each of the men in the picture but we were still somehow strangers. Gradually, I had become their senior and watched each one of them replace someone I knew much better. It was the last shot of us together and a good one. It captured the mood and said a lot about camaraderie, commitment and spirit.

Even the 100th mission required a maintenance and intelligence debriefing. When I was finished at wing headquarters, I went to the Thai barber shop next to the Officers' Club. I needed a haircut, a shave, and a relaxing massage from one of the pretty young ladies who were the barbers.

Both my mustache and I had flown our last mission. Only superstition and my respect for tradition had made me put up with the itchy thing in the first place. I sat down in the chair, took a swig of medicinal whiskey and relaxed for the shave I had longed for. For the first time in months, I felt completely relieved and I wanted to savor the moment.

When the barber was through, she timidly offered me a small, dusty mirror. The bulletproof mustache was gone, and I looked happy but exhausted. I paid her and headed for the trailer. I wanted to sleep forever.

Before I lay down, I poured a stiff drink of whiskey and made some notes in my diary. I had some thoughts that needed to be put on paper.

Bittersweet Reprise

In some respects, my last mission was a disappointment. I felt relieved but the relief was accompanied by melancholy and despair. The danger was finally over, but so was the excitement and the feeling of belonging, a paradox and a bittersweet experience.

The closing days of my combat tour were emotionally charged. Fear, anxiety, and confidence were always present but in differing proportions. As I passed the ninety-mission mark, I felt like I was over a hump and into the final countdown. Optimism and confidence grew steadily as I faced fewer and fewer missions. The light at the end of the tunnel became a source of new hope and assurance.

Like any event we look forward to with great anticipation, my final mission had come at last and was over too quickly. I felt empty, and was mentally and physically exhausted. I had learned to take each mission on its own merits, but I wasn't prepared for the letdown that came with finally being finished.

During the last few missions, I began to feel like my security was somehow founded in tradition. "Surely I can't get shot down now," I would reassure myself. "I'm too close to finishing." It was a comforting thought but I knew better.

Certainly, my skill had improved with each mission, but the odds didn't change and risk didn't have a favorite mission. Every F-105 looked the same to the enemy, but superstition and faith played a role in pilot confidence and a confident pilot was a more effective warrior. That's why we wore mustaches, bush hats, lucky underwear, religious medals, had favorite aircraft, and avoided unlucky call signs.

I took my favorite Thai waitress' number button on my last mission because of superstition. One had never been shot down or lost on a mission, and it was a sentimental tradition. I also carried a bright Chinese party hat on my last mission. If I got shot down, I wanted to infuriate the North Vietnamese with my audacity. It was an outrageous gesture, but it was my way of thumbing my nose at the odds and the enemy.

Out of selfish pride, I was disappointed because I had agreed to fly my last mission in the lower route packs instead of waiting for a chance to make a more spectacular finish in Package Six. The raid on Kep would have been more fitting as a final curtain dropper, but it came just two days too early.

Enough second guessing. Deep down, I was genuinely relieved and very thankful. After all, I was the last one from the 67A short class at Nellis to finish. Bob Waggoner, Don Asire, Gene Conley, and Gene Beresik weren't so lucky.

With a sigh of resignation, I closed my diary.

Drinks for the House

Paul woke me up in time for my 100-mission party in the stag bar. Betting I would make it, I had prearranged everything the day before, so all I had to do was get there. I wanted the party to be the best one yet, and it may have been, but I didn't last long enough to enjoy it. Even U.S. Pepsi would have been too much for my exhausted system. After a couple of rounds of whiskey, Paul helped me back to my trailer and that was it until the next morning.

When I woke up, it was early in the morning on 16 June 1967, and I hoped that the party was over. I took a shower and went to the club for some breakfast and a look at my bar bill. It was a gasser.

21
SWEEPING UP

NORMALLY, MOST OF OUR pilots were on their way home within forty-eight hours after finishing. It was a sensible policy that required streamlined personnel action, and it was appreciated by the pilots and the families who had waited so patiently for their safe return. In my case, the circumstances governing my departure were anything but normal.

The *Turkestan* Incident

Earlier in the month, on the second of June, Ted Tolman had strafed a ship anchored in the small port of Cam Pha northeast of Haiphong. Ted and his wingman, Major Lonnie Ferguson, were outbound from a target they had struck on the northeast railroad when the incident occurred.

As Ted approached Cam Pha on an armed reconnaissance of the area, the guns surrounding the port started shooting and provided a target of opportunity that needed silencing. When Ted and his wingman rolled in for a strafing pass, streams of tracers came up from the deck of the anchored ship. Instinctively, Ted centered his pipper on the ship and fired a burst from his 20mm-cannon at the guns on deck. In a matter of seconds, the engagement was over, but the unidentified ship would turn out to be a vessel of Soviet registry named the *Turkestan*.

Due to bad weather, Ted was forced to land at an emergency recovery base short of Takhli. During the intelligence debriefing, Ted answered routine questions about the mission, but he chose not to volunteer any information about the strafing action. Although he wasn't sure about the origin of the ship, he suspected that it might have been from the Soviet Union.

Upon return to Takhli later that night, Ted reported directly to Colonel Broughton, who was the acting wing commander. Ted told Broughton exactly what had happened, and they discussed the potential consequences of the incident. Colonel Broughton decided to overlook the action in hopes that it would go unnoticed or blow over quickly. "Where's the gun-camera film?" Broughton asked Tolman. It had been sent to the base photo lab for processing. To remove any trace of evidence, Broughton had Ted's gun-camera film brought to his trailer and exposed it. It was a deliberate decision made under very agonizing circumstances.

Two weeks later, the wing received word that General Ryan, the hard-nosed commander of PACAF, would arrive at Takhli early the next morning, 17 June 1967. His unexpected visit came just in time to interrupt my departure plans.

General Ryan arrived at Takhli in his personal KC-135 with an armada of staff and his top general officers. Ostensibly, their purpose was to conduct a normal staff visit. Few of us knew or even suspected that they had come to investigate the alleged strafing incident.

Colonel Scott had returned and resumed command of the wing, but Colonel Broughton was tagged to put together a welcoming, overview briefing for General Ryan and his staff. Because of the unannounced purpose of the visit, Colonel Broughton decided to present General Ryan an abbreviated mission briefing, to include his own unvarnished views of how the air war was being conducted. Unwittingly, Colonel Broughton was setting himself up for an angry confrontation, which would be used as a stage to indict and embarrass him.

As the wing stan/eval officer and the most recent 100-mission graduate, I was asked to help prepare the briefing and standby during the presentation to answer any questions deflected my way. Ironically, Ted Tolman would have been asked to assist as well, but he was on R&R in Okinawa, only a phone call away.

When General Ryan arrived he was in an ugly mood. His stern scowl reflected his mood and reinforced his reputation for having a gruff, no-nonsense approach to business. He had been at Takhli a few months earlier and raised hell about our bombing, so we didn't expect a four-star at-a-boy, but no one was prepared for the hostile reception Colonel Broughton received during the briefing.

From the outset, it was clear that General Ryan had an axe to grind, and he started with a vengeance as soon as Colonel Broughton finished the briefing. "Everyone out below the rank of Colonel!" Ryan bellowed rudely. Except for his staff, he cleared the room so he could grill Colonel Scott, Colonel Broughton, and Colonel White, the newly assigned director of operations.

When the group exited the meeting, Colonel Broughton's face was ashen and practically expressionless. After a vicious chewing, General Ryan had personally fired him and threatened to bring court-martial charges against him, along with Ted Tolman and Lonnie Ferguson. The cat was out of the bag. The inquiry had started, and a blanket of anxiety fell over Takhli.

Ironically, I had noticed the *Turkestan* lying in port on my way into Kep on my ninety-eighth mission. I made a mental note to take a better look at it on the way out, but it completely slipped my mind, as we fought our way back to the coast through flak and heavy thunderstorms. Had I remembered the ship, I probably would have reacted much like Ted did and angrily pulled my own trigger on the *Turkestan*, hoping to sink the ship and close the whole damn harbor.

The Soviets were backing the North Vietnamese and their bullets were no less deadly. Lethal tracers had no nationality. As far as we were concerned, ground fire called for silencing, regardless of its origin.

The investigation gathered steam very quickly. The atmosphere in the command section turned chaotic. The air police cordoned the building and patrolled the area for controlled access. Anyone vaguely connected with the mission was brought in for questioning, as the headquarters building became the scene of a first-class inquisition.

Ted Tolman was flown back hurriedly from Okinawa for questioning by General Ryan. When Ted reported, he found himself face-to-face with a man who wanted the facts and had his hand on a telephone to the president. "I want the truth, Tolman," Ryan said gruffly, without returning his salute. For an instant, Ted thought that Ryan might hit him, but he was determined to tell it like it happened.

Once it was determined that I had not flown the mission in question, my desk was commandeered by Lieutenant General John Vogt, General Ryan's number one henchman, and I was summarily directed to leave the headquarters. For some reason, General Vogt kept his dress hat on when he moved through the building. As he approached my desk to dismiss me, he walked like a robot and looked almost comical. The bill of his cap was pulled down, almost touching his nose, so I could barely see his eyes. I didn't question his order, but I wondered if he was vain about his bald head or just plain forgetful.

Colonel Scott and Colonel Broughton were inundated with the investigation. Consequently, the job of running the wing fell on the shoulders of the director of operations. Colonel White was certainly capable, but he was new and needed support.

Colonel White asked me to stick around for a few days to help him run the combat operations of the wing. My body said no but my heart and my sense of duty made me stay. Colonel White was one of the most professional and convincing leaders I had ever met and I just couldn't say no to an officer and friend of his caliber. Besides, Ted Tolman was one of the best combat leaders in the wing and my closest friend and confidant at the time. I was willing to stay just to see how he was treated.

I hoped the delay would not last more than an extra week. But aside from just helping out, I thought I might get a chance to fly again and perhaps put off, ever so slightly, my reporting date to the Air Staff and a desk in the Pentagon.

The investigation continued around the clock for several days. Those of us in the combat operations center tried to concentrate our limited resources on the daily operations of the wing, but we couldn't help but observe what was going on and wonder. Rumors spread through the building about damaging testimony and reported telephone conversations with President Johnson, but by and large, those of us on the outside of the investigation were kept guessing.

I had one chance meeting late at night with Ted Tolman in my trailer. He brought me the Nikon camera I had ordered from Okinawa and left quickly. He looked very tired and drawn, which was normal for Ted, but I could sense he was going through mental agony.

In a matter of days, the investigation team packed up and left as quickly as they had arrived. The inquiry and the litigants moved to Clark Air Base in the Philippines for formal court-martial proceedings. Charged with "conspiracy to withhold vital information from the U.S. Government during wartime," Colonel Broughton, Ted, and Lonnie must have felt deserted, as they prepared to face some grave consequences for a combat action they felt was justified.

Suddenly, it got very lonely at Takhli. Three pilots who had risked their lives for their country had been whisked away and hung out to dry in an uphill fight for their honor and professional future. I felt betrayed. The charges brought against them were an indictment of everyone who had flown a mission north and warranted an open hearing before people who had faced the music.

After a messy trial, Ted and Lonnie were found not guilty and released by the court. Colonel Broughton didn't fare so well. As their standard bearer, he was found guilty of a minor charge of destroying government property and fined $600, his career was over.

I didn't see Colonel Broughton again until the following fall in Washington, when I attended a ceremony at which he was presented the Air Force Cross just prior to his retirement. The irony of the occasion was disturbing.

To my surprise, I rejoined *Colonel* Ted Tolman several years later as a classmate at the Air War College. Against the odds, he had been promoted. His determination and grit had not diminished. Ted was a wiry fighter and a stubborn down-easter who didn't know how to give up. Fortunately, the Air Force leadership had finally understood what it was like to fly fighters over North Vietnam.

Hanging It Up

When I flew my last combat mission I was prepared to hang up my spurs and press on. For me, completion meant a wild party, a flight to Bangkok, one last fling at the hotsie bathes, shopping at James's jewelers, and a flight to San Francisco. The thought of hanging around Takhli for a few extra days never crossed my mind. The necessity to stay required some rethinking and emotional adjustment on my part.

I found myself on the horns of a dilemma. Even though I was ready to quit, I would be tempted to fly more missions and perhaps make good on my promise to paste Hanoi on my last flight. In a way, it was a frightening thought because it opened the door for pride to ask the old question of "How much is enough?" Was I smart enough to recognize my last flight and finally call it quits?

As a compromise, I considered limiting my flying to test hops. The maintenance people always needed help, and I could enjoy just flying the F-105 locally. "After all, I may never get another chance to fly another fighter," I argued with myself over and over again. On the other hand, if I flew test hops, I might as well fly combat because test hops would be like kissing your sister after a night out with a Playboy centerfold, I reasoned as I struggled with the dilemma.

I finally reconciled that I had flown my last combat mission in the F-105, and like it or not, probably my last fighter. If I started flying missions again, it would be terribly difficult to stop again, like kicking a cigarette habit one cigarette at a time. Legally, an extended tour required the approval of the headquarters, and I wasn't about to fight that red tape. If I flew, it would be without the blessing of headquarters and they didn't need any more jolts from Takhli, not right then anyway.

Colonel White only wanted me to help with the routine duties in operations while he carried on as the acting commander. He was faced with doing three jobs and flying missions at the same time. Once I resigned myself to the idea of doing staff work and not flying anymore, I enjoyed supporting the missions. Even though I knew I wasn't going north, I still felt the anxiety and sensed the danger of each mission, particularly during the morning briefings. I had to fight the temptation to fly "just one more" every time I heard the engines start on the ramp.

Working with Colonel White as his assistant was a privilege and pleasure. He was pleasant, cool, and unshakable. The wing was in good hands. I
found myself wishing I could stay. With the addition of his leadership and
confidence, the wing was surely in for a good year.

As soon as things settled down to a normal and manageable combat
load, Colonel White recognized that it was time for me to press on to my
next assignment. I was scheduled to leave Takhli on an afternoon flight to
Bangkok on the twenty-third of June, nine months to the day after I had
flown my first mission.

As I left my office for the last time, I stopped to admire a framed picture
of the F-105. The aircraft was silhouetted against a gorgeous evening sky. I
had looked at the picture often but never considered taking it home. One of
the NCOs watching said, "Go ahead, Major, take it with you. We can get
another, and no one will know the difference." Without hesitation, I took it
off the wall.

That evening, I decided to have a few drinks at the club and go into
Takhli village for a delicious Kobe beef dinner. Before I knew it, I had had
too many martinis and couldn't find anyone interested in going with me.
Against my better judgment, I decided to go alone and make the best of it.

As was customary, I hired a Thai taxi in front of the club and slid into
the back seat for the short 10-mile ride to the village. The driver seemed
unusually surly, but I figured it was a reaction to my robust, perhaps overbearing behavior—the juniper in gin brought out the worst in me.

Halfway to town, the car came to a stop without explanation. It was
pitch dark. The road was deserted and flanked on both sides by klong
water. Nothing was in sight except a set of headlights that blinked on and
off twice just ahead of us. It was a setup! I had walked into a trap half-
bagged with $400 in cash in my pocket, my going home travel money, how
stupid.

Before I could react, both rear doors of the taxi opened, and two small
men jumped in beside me, shouting in angry, high-pitched voices. The driver responded and the car lurched forward, as he started driving toward
town again. As we passed the other car, it swung around and followed us
closely.

My heart was pounding. Adrenalin rushed through my body and my
brain came on-line quickly in spite of the gin. What a going away present!
After flying 100 missions against professional killers, I would get rolled on
some crummy back road and tossed in the klong by a couple of punks high
on opium.

The three men jabbered wildly as the car sped down the narrow road,
weaving from side to side. The two intruders had on red headbands, and

the one on my left held a knife at my side. They appeared to be Thai, and they may have been political dissidents, but their identity wasn't important. They were angry and wanted something. I figured I was dead if we stopped again or reached town under their control.

Impulsively, I threw my arms up and got a hammerlock around the necks of the men beside me. With my fists locked in front of my chest, I squeezed my arms with all the strength I could muster. I was determined to strangle them or break their necks, whichever came first, and I damn near succeeded.

About a mile out of town, I told the driver to continue to the restaurant or I would kill his buddies. He nodded, but I was worried about the guy with the knife in my side. If he wanted to use it, I was a goner. Time stood still. I tightened my stranglehold. With panting gasps, both of my captives went limp. It felt like they had passed out, but I didn't take any chances. I squeezed even harder.

We entered Takhli village and drove slowly past all the night spots. Reluctantly, the driver parked in front of the restaurant. The car was aimed down a shallow incline, with the headlights shining directly on the entrance. Hoping to attract attention, I told the driver to honk his horn and keep honking.

Several waiters came to the door of the restaurant but seemed reluctant to investigate the commotion. The other car had parked behind us. The driver stayed in his car and was probably confused by what was happening. For the moment, it was a standoff. Without help I was in a delicate predicament.

I told the taxi driver to get out of the car, open all of the doors, and go to the car behind us. When he opened the left rear door, instead of leaving, he just stood there. It was time for action. I released my hostages and bolted. As I pushed out through the door, the driver tried to close it. The door caught my right leg, but my momentum swung the door back on its hinges and sent the driver reeling down the embankment.

The other driver had gotten got out of his car and tried to deck me, but I simply ran through him. The punks in the back seat had revived enough to make a feeble attempt to hold me, but there was no stopping. With a lunge, I exploded through the front door of the restaurant, startling both waiters and patrons. I was some kind of upset and excited.

As soon as I was safe inside the restaurant, both cars sped away quickly. Several drinks later I regained enough composure to order a steak and try to enjoy dinner. I was concerned about getting back to the base safely. I had a hunch that my "friends" still had a score to settle and might be waiting.

The restaurant was frequented by base personnel so I hoped someone might come in whom I could join for the trip home. After an hour or so, no one had shown up, but as I suspected, the thugs did return and were parked outside waiting. I couldn't see them clearly, but I was sure who it was, and I hoped at least two of them were black and blue from the necks up to their red bandannas.

The owner of the restaurant sensed my predicament and warned me about trying to run the gauntlet on my own in another taxi. He volunteered to call a friend with a car whom he trusted. I accepted his offer and had a drink while he set the wheels in motion.

When his friend arrived, he parked out back and came in like an unsuspecting patron. Once inside, we worked out a plan that turned into a real 007 thriller. We went out through a window in the men's room and slipped into the getaway car as quietly as possible. I lay down in the back seat to exit the parking lot, but the men in the waiting cars smelled a rat and followed us. The wraps were off and my return to the base became a three-car race for the main gate just ten miles away.

My rescuer turned out to be a Thai Air Force officer. His old Mercedes was barely fast enough to stay in front of our pursuers, but it was wide enough to block their attempts to pass and crowd us off the narrow highway. They tried bumping us once, but neither of their cars was a match for the solid Mercedes. We were betting they didn't have weapons, or if they did, that they wouldn't dare use them.

As we approached the turn into the main gate of the base, the driver started honking the horn to attract the attention of the Thai air policemen. We slid through the turn and our pursuers kept right on going. What a relief, we had won the race, but my dinner was a knot in my stomach.

Exhausted, I went straight to the provost marshall to report the incident, but I should have gone to my trailer. The interview was somewhat embarrassing. After all of the clamor, I was unable to accurately describe the cars or remember their license numbers. I could still remember the tail number of my 100th-mission bird but I couldn't recall important information about my abductors. Where was my trusty grease pencil when I needed it?

The next morning, I was sore all over and had a whale of a hangover. Thankfully, all I had to do was finish some last minute paperwork, say a few goodbyes, and throw my things together in time to catch an airplane.

Lunch cured my headache, and I was tempted to take my first swim in the club pool, but opted instead for a relaxing walk to retrace the steps I had taken soon after I arrived at Takhli. When I returned to my trailer that evening, I made the last entry in my combat journal.

22 June 1967

I have just completed my last day in the combat theater at Takhli. The doctrine study is complete. Looks like Ted, Col Broughton and Fergie have had the Snitzel. I spent the afternoon touring the base on foot. Again, I watched the Thai recruits training and I have reached a pathetic conclusion. The Asians are cruel and vicious people—even the Thais—their pleasant demeanor corrupts and snaps with power. I watched as a combat veteran, as a man who has found his notch in armed warfare. I watched from the shade of the magnificent trees which give the only respite from the heat and humid smell of the jungle.

When I finished the entry, I looked at what I had written and began to reflect. There is a streak of cruelty and viciousness in all of mankind. True, but I was starting to think too seriously, so I did something I hadn't done in a long time. I went to bed early.

C-130 to Bangkok

It was the twenty-third of June 1967. I woke up refreshed, ready to pack up and move out at last. After breakfast, I checked my mailbox and turned in my combination. I had received an official letter from the Pentagon, which looked ominous, so I waited until I returned to the trailer to open it.

The letter was from my future boss in the Air Staff welcoming me to the challenges of research, development, and operational requirements; what a mouthful. Disappointed, I sat down and stared at the letter. My attempts to wiggle out of a Pentagon assignment had been in vain. My pleas to stay in fighters had gone unanswered. I wasn't really surprised but the letter made it official and it looked final.

I dashed off some last minute notes and put my papers, the letter from Washington, and my journal in the side pocket of my B-4 bag. I was ready to go, and the 354th Squadron truck was due any minute.

I tried to say something nice to the maid in Thai, but it was difficult. Bless her heart, she wanted me to take her to America. I never did like calling her Water Buffalo, but that's what she seemed to like, and she smiled when I said goodby. She pointed to the small refrigerator next to the desk, indicating that she wanted anything I might leave behind. I needed a cool drink so I opened the door to inventory the contents: a Beefeater bottle full of water, a Beefeater bottle full of gin, a Johnny Walker bottle half-full of Scotch, and a six-pack of Snappy Tom. By mistake, she had gotten into the gin once before, so I told her to stick to water and leave the rest for the next occupant. Whoever he was, I thought he might enjoy a house-warming gift.

The squadron truck was right on time. We loaded my gear into the back and headed for base operations. Anyone who ever walked through the trailer area at Takhli will remember the sound of the large gravel crunching under foot. I still hear those tires rolling through the gravel as we left "Maj. Bell" and the Bulldog plaque on the door of my trailer.

The C-130 to Bangkok was scheduled to leave base operations shortly after noon in the heat of the day, at about the same time the afternoon strike usually launched. Major Jack Hunt had finished his missions the preceding week and joined me for the flight home. We groused about having to leave Takhli in a C-130. At best, the flight would be hot and bumpy.

After we checked in with our baggage, we were told to standby in the boarding area. As the minutes ticked by, the time for the afternoon F-105 launch got closer and closer. I warned the C-130 pilot that we ought to get off ahead of the fighters or we would be in for a long, hot wait. "During a launch," I told him, "nothing moves until all the 105s are airborne and the spares are back in the blocks." Usually, that took about an hour, and that was a long time to sit on the ramp in the jungle sun inside a screaming, hot C-130 with an overloaded air conditioner.

In spite of my warning, the C-130 crew waited and called for boarding right on schedule, just minutes ahead of the afternoon mission launch. It was a mistake and I knew it. Just as we boarded and sat down on the uncomfortable, side-saddle, nylon benches in the C-130, I heard the distinctive sound of start cartridges firing on the fighter ramp. The tankers were already taxiing.

Jack and I looked at each other. Surely the pilot would have sense enough to let us go back to base ops to wait for a delayed departure. But, to our amazement, we heard the auxiliary power unit chug as the starter engaged the engines. The high-pitched scream of the turboprops resonated through the cargo compartment, and the load master closed the rear boarding door.

We were smothered with heat needlessly. Instantly, my flying suit was soaked with sweat. Clouds of vapor spilled uselessly out of the air vents overhead. The little air we got was cool and moist, but the air conditioner was no match for a closed cargo compartment and twenty sweating passengers. "This is a hell of a way to treat a couple of war heroes," Jack said to me angrily. I agreed, but we waited, and I could have shot the jackass flying the airplane.

After a miserable delay on the taxiway, we finally took the runway and started rolling. The Hercules engines strained forward, and the acceleration pushed me sideways against Jack's shoulder. I pulled forward with my left arm and craned my head around to get a last fleeting glance of Takhli through a small porthole on the side of the fuselage. The base disappeared quickly behind us, and that was it. The 354th Squadron building looked deserted. The bread truck was parked in front, but no one was outside waving, it was business as usual for the Bulldogs.

The flight to Bangkok was as rough and as hot as predicted. Heading due south, it would take less than an hour to make the Don Muang airport just north of the city. I was ready for a cool dip and a yard of beer at pool side. We had reservations at the Siam Intercontinental, my favorite R&R haunt, and one of the best hotels in Southeast Asia.

After landing, we checked in with the military passenger desk and confirmed our reservations on a contract carrier. We had seats on a Continental flight leaving Bangkok on the twenty-fifth, which gave us less than forty-eight hours to cover all the bases. We hailed a taxi and hired him for two days. The fare was a carton of Salems. They only cost us $1.50 but they were worth a fortune to the driver.

The Siam Intercontinental looked great as we wheeled into the big, shaded driveway. It was an ideal hotel because it had all the luxuries of an American hotel in an Asian setting. The pool was beautiful, and the management was accustomed to the ways of American pilots and attuned to our needs. The rooms were elegantly large, very private and air-conditioned.

Several of the international airlines used the Siam for crew rest, so there was usually an opportunity to meet a lovely lady. The bar at the Intercontinental was well known as the watering hole for the rich and beautiful, as well as the daring and hasty. It was a perfect setting for F-105 pilots.

I registered, checked my room, and headed for the pool. The water was refreshing, and there were some familiar faces in the crowd that had gathered beside the pool for early cocktails. I joined a group of Air America pilots and their ladies. They had just arrived for a break from their clandestine flying jobs in northern Laos. It was an interesting group, and the next thirty-six hours looked indeed promising.

After cocktails, I went to the Cat's Eye Lounge in the Hotel President. I wanted to say goodbye to Subhanee. Even though we knew our relationship was temporary, we had built a friendship that deserved a proper ending.

The bar was crowded and Subhanee was busy. Her bright almond eyes flashed but she pretended not see me. She must have sensed that I was leaving, and she wasn't prepared to say goodbye on such short notice. I would have preferred a more intimate setting, but I was never sure where to find her. She didn't have a telephone and she kept her home life very private.

I took a seat at the bar and admired her delicate beauty. Her movements were gracious and supple. Without asking, she served me a drink and paused briefly. Our eyes met long enough to convey a farewell that was both tender and final. I took a sip of the drink and left the rest behind. It was difficult because I knew I would never see Subhanee again.

The waiter in the dining room recognized me and asked if I would have my standard fare: a large Caesar salad with a double order of beef fondue. It was a delightful meal that I always enjoyed. After dinner, I left without so much as a glance in the Cat's Eye bar. I was tempted to go back, but I returned to my hotel for a good night's rest. Subhanee would have to remain a memory.

The next morning, I had breakfast and was off by midday for the last stop on my must-do list. Everyone finishing a tour bought a lot of fine jewelry on their way home. Gold and precious stones, especially sapphires, were excellent buys and James's Jewelry was the place to shop.

The salesmen there were gracious to a fault. They went to great lengths to make you feel comfortable and prime you for a sale. It didn't take me long to settle on a couple of princess rings, a beautiful sapphire brooch, and several strings of beggars beads. I bought my dad an antique set of gold cuff links set with black star sapphires. I knew he wouldn't wear them, but they said what I wanted to say. When I left, the salesman gave me a traditional silver Thai money clip, which I carry to this day.

I had two items left on my things to do before leaving Bangkok checklist: brass candlesticks and a visit to the renowned floating market. Large candlesticks were a must for Americans stationed in Thailand and very popular gifts, but for me they would have been just something else to polish. I crossed them off my list, trying not to feel cheated or guilty.

The floating market was a major tourist attraction that was open all day, but the best time to see it was early in the morning. I had wanted to visit it before, but somehow I never got there. I chuckled to myself when I thought about some of the guys I knew who had bought color slides of the market in the hotel gift shop to make their wives think they'd been there. On my last morning in Bangkok, I intended to go but decided that sleep was more important.

Homeward Bound

Jack Hunt and I checked out of the hotel, and the driver loaded our things in the taxi. On the way to the airport, I had an attack of sentimental melancholy. While I was pleased to be going home, I didn't welcome the end of combat and the camaraderie of flying. The dilemma preyed on my mind the rest of the way to the airport. I couldn't shake it. Everything I saw reminded me of a fond memory. The last nine months of my life seemed to replay before me.

The Don Muang Airport was busy. Darting taxis honked their way in and out of the congested departure area. Over the top of one of the low terminal buildings, I spotted the tail of a Continental Airlines 707. The small American flag on the tail caught my eye and snapped me out of my nostalgic mood. My combat tour was over and I couldn't wait to get going.

The Continental bird I had seen from the street turned out to be our airplane. It was a contract flight, and every seat was filled with a returning U.S. serviceman. There were at least ten stewardesses on board to make the long flight comfortable. Our instructions said we were required to wear uniforms so Jack and I wore our 100-mission flying suits.

I was surprised to find that two of the stewardesses were old friends of mine from Manhattan Beach. They were young, beautiful, and refreshing indeed. It was an incredible reunion, and I enjoyed the extra attention they gave me. "Fasten seat belts and prepare for takeoff," brought a cheer from the passengers, and a rush for their seats by the stewardesses.

After a few hours in the air, we started a descent for landing at Kadena Air Base on the island of Okinawa. I thought of a similar stop I had made going the other way only months before, and the memory of my unexpected stay at Wake Island seemed a thousand years old.

The pilot announced that we would have to debark for the refueling operation but asked the passengers to remain in the terminal in order to minimize our ground time. My cramped legs needed a stretch and I welcomed the break.

As I started down the stairway to the ramp, I spotted Vas Vasiliadis leaning on crutches behind a wire fence. I could hardly believe it was him. He was wearing a bright orange flying suit and smiling from ear to ear. I hadn't seen him since just before he was shot down in early May.

We greeted each other, and he said something in Greek that was probably vulgar but very fitting. Vas had crushed his leg and hip in his high-speed bail-out over Laos. He was pleased with his rapid recovery and happy to be alive. Proudly, he showed me how well he could walk with crutches, and we enjoyed a good laugh. He said he wore the flying suit to remind himself and anyone else that he was determined to make a full recovery and return to flying.

I appreciated his thoughtfulness and thanked him for taking the trouble to meet the aircraft. He didn't tell me how he knew I was on board, but that was Vas. We gave each other a warm hug and I reboarded the flight. I wouldn't see him again for several years but I knew he would fly again, and he did, plenty.

It takes a long time to fly across the Pacific Ocean, and it was difficult to keep track of how many times the sun rose and set on the trip. When we coasted in over northern California, I was dead tired, but the country below looked absolutely beautiful and I couldn't hold back the tears. I think I saw an extra shaft of sunlight over San Francisco and the Golden Gate Bridge but that sounds corny, and I couldn't swear to it.

We landed at Travis Air Force Base at midmorning on 25 June 1967. There were no bands or cheering crowds, but I felt like a million dollars when I stepped off the airplane. I gave the stewardess a big kiss and headed for customs. I had a date with a homecoming party in Los Angeles and was anxious to get there.

Jack and I caught a ground limousine to San Francisco, and we both fell asleep before we had gone a mile. I had changed into my tan summer uniform but I kept my flight jacket on, hoping people might notice the 100-mission patch.

We must have looked like a couple of real dudes when we walked into the main terminal at the San Francisco airport. It was jammed with people going everywhere. They all looked tall and the women were especially beautiful. I was surprised that no one gave us a second glance. I don't know what I had expected but I didn't expect to go unnoticed. I felt like going up on the mezzanine and shouting "Dead Beetle!"

I bought a ticket on the next shuttle flight to Los Angeles and shook hands with Jack a couple of times. We wished each other well as Jack turned and left for another part of the terminal. I was in a rush and didn't stop to think that I would probably never see him again.

The PSA flight left on schedule and I got one of the last seats available. "Welcome on board the PSA shuttle," said a welcoming voice over the intercom system. "Our flying time to the Los Angeles International Airport will be one hour." I settled back and watched the California shore go by.

I was excited and the butterflies were warming up in my stomach. Several old friends from Manhattan Beach promised to meet me with a band and champagne. The closer we got the more I hoped they would forget the band and bring Scotch instead of champagne.

We landed, and as I was walking through the long tube up to the terminal in Los Angeles, the butterflies were up in force and my heart was pounding. I could hear what sounded like a homemade band playing something patriotic, and then I saw a crazy group of a dozen people singing and waving small American flags. They held a sign that read "Welcome Home Ken Bell, the Bar at Panchos is Open." I was very pleased and terribly embarrassed, but none of the other passengers seemed to notice. That's Los Angeles.

We shouted and hugged and kissed and toasted with champagne as if we owned the place. The rest was a blur. The party moved to Panchos Bar, then to the beach, and finally to a home of friends. I hated to be an ungrateful guest of honor, but I couldn't hold my eyes open past eight o'clock that evening. It had been a very long day and my body clock was still in Thailand, twelve hours ahead.

After a couple of days of rest on the beach with my friends, I was ready for the last leg of my journey home to see my parents and close friends in El Paso. I knew they were terribly anxious to see me, and I wasn't sure that I was going to be able to handle the emotions of the occasion. I imagined that I would rather be coming home in an F-105, it would have been more flamboyant and much easier emotionally.

As we descended to land, I felt the thermal bumps coming up off the desert and I knew I was close to home. We passed directly over downtown El Paso. I looked out under a bright blue sky and saw Mount Franklin, the high school and college I had attended, the neighborhood park, and our house, nestled in the foothills of the mountain. Everything was in place and looked familiar.

As I stepped into the terminal, my eyes misted over and and my knees began to tremble. I felt very proud and I wanted to radiate that pride and confidence to my parents. When they saw me, their faces lit up with smiles and they started waving as though they thought I hadn't seen them. There were lots of people between us, and several friends waving signs but I was focused on my dear parents.

My mother looked older and a little frail but her crystal blue eyes were dancing. Tears were streaming down her face. My dad took my hand and said, "Welcome home, boy." We embraced, and it was then that I realized how difficult it had been for both of them. They had waited an eternity for that moment.

I don't remember who was in the welcoming party, but everyone there wanted to talk and ask questions at the same time. We made our way to the luggage claim and finally to the car. The exhaustion I had been fighting for weeks finally overwhelmed me. Dad suggested that we make our traditional homecoming stop at Smitties restaurant for a barbecue sandwich and beer.

As we drove home after lunch, my dad asked how I felt about going to the Pentagon. I knew he was relieved that I was through with combat and out of the cockpit, at least for a while, but I told him very honestly that I was terribly disappointed and felt let down.

Dad loved politics, and I knew he was delighted and very proud of the fact that I was going to Washington. He had only visited there but he figured that a job on the Air Staff could be the beginning of an important career. He encouraged me to take the assignment in my stride and make the most of it. As far as he was concerned, anyone who had a chance to go to Washington ought to come home president, especially a smart boy from the 16th District of Texas with a good combat record. I appreciated his confidence, but I knew he had no understanding of the wide gulf of interest that separated the E-ring on the fifth floor of the Pentagon from Congress and the Oval Office.

As we talked, it was clear that he wanted me to put my fighter days behind me and look for a new, challenging opportunity at the headquarters. He knew I didn't like the idea, and I'm sure he could sense the struggle that was going on inside me. He kept urging me to look at the assignment with a positive attitude.

Halfheartedly, I smiled and assured him that I would give it my best shot, and he looked satisfied. I didn't have the heart to tell him that I would have given anything for a set of orders reassigning me to Nellis, or better yet, to another tour of combat.

When we finally made it home I didn't think I could answer another question. The weather was very hot and my head was splitting, but the house was cool and quiet, and everything was just like I had remembered it so many times. I just wanted to crawl into the bed in my old room and sleep forever. When I did, the sheets felt as soft as ever. I closed my eyes and said a prayer, "God, thank you for bringing me home safely."

Mentally, I was still on double pump in the cockpit over Hanoi, but at last, I could relax. I could close my eyes without worrying about the weather, about the next day, about the target, or about my new wingman. I didn't have to mark off the sorties north, the long count up to 100. The only people shooting at me would be Pentagon executive officers, civilian systems analysts, and harried general officers who were contemptuous of the analytical approach to warfare but powerless to do anything about it.

I'd miss the F-105 and the guys I flew with. I'd especially remember all of my buddies who didn't make it to 100 missions. But I had. I'd made it back and I was in my own bed. The sheets felt fresh and cool.

It finally sank in, I had succeeded and could begin the next chapter in my life. I sighed a deep a sigh of peace and contentment, rolled over, and slept the deep, untroubled sleep of a warrior home from combat.

Next target: Washington!

GLOSSARY

Angels: Altitude in thousands of feet.

AOB: Air order of battle.

APU: Auxiliary power unit used to assist in starting an aircraft.

ARCP: Aerial refueling control point.

Atoll: Soviet built air-to-air, heat-seeking missile.

Bandit: Enemy fighter aircraft.

BDA: Bomb damage assessment.

Beeper: Emergency locator beacon installed in the parachute.

Bogey: Aircraft sighted of unknown origin and intent.

Bomblet: Small bombs carried in clusters inside a larger bomb casing.

Boomer: refueling boom operator.

Bread Truck: Crew van used on the flight line.

Burner: Jet engine afterburner (A/B).

Button: Aircraft radio channel number.

CBU: Cluster bomb unit, bomblet.

CCTS: Combat Crew Training Squadron.

CEP: Circular error probable in weapons delivery.

Channel 31: Tacan station identifier for Udorn RTAFB.

Channel 43: Tacan station identifier for Takhli RTAFB.

Channel 51: Tacan station identifier for Ubon RTAFB.

Channel 79: Tacan station located in central Laos.

Channel 89: Tacan station identifier for Nakhon Phanom RTAFB.

Channel 97: Tacan station located in northeastern Laos.

Channel 125: Tacan station identifier for Korat RTAFB.

Check Six!: Radio call advising a pilot to look directly behind his aircraft.

CINCPACAF: Commander-in-Chief, Pacific Air Forces.

Class-67A: F-105 combat crew training class at Nellis Air Force Base, Nevada.

Clean: All external stores have been jettisoned or removed from the aircraft.

D-ring: Pull-handle used to open a parachute.

DCO: Deputy Commander for Operations.

Dead Beetle!: Term used to start a bar room game in which the participants must fall to the floor and remain motionless. The first one to move buys a round of drinks for the bar.

Doghouse: Free bombing area in eastern Laos just west of the Mu Gia Pass from North to South Vietnam.

Doppler: Navigation system in the F-105 that used the "Doppler effect" on electronic signals transmitted from a beacon on board the aircraft to determine aircraft position over the ground.

Double-pump: Expression of excitement or anxiety derived from a term normally used to state the pumping rate of fuel from a tanker to a receiver.

Downtown: High-threat area around Hanoi in North Vietnam.

Down-wind: Portion of an aircraft traffic pattern that parallels the runway downwind, opposite to the direction of landing.

Drag chute: Parachute that is deployed from the rear of an airplane after landing to aid in deceleration.

Drop tank: External fuel tank that can be jettisoned.

Duckbutt: Twin-engine, amphibious SA-16 rescue aircraft.

ECM: Electronic counter-measures.

Egress: Leaving the target area.

ELINT: Electronic intelligence source.

En route: Flying from one point to another toward a destination.

EWO: Electronic Warfare Officer who operates electronic equipment aboard an aircraft; for example the crew member in the back seat of the F-105F Wild Weasel aircraft.

F-105D: Single-seat, fighter-bomber aircraft manufactured by Republic Aircraft.

F-105F: Two-seat F-105 aircraft used for training and modified with special electronic equipment for use as a Wild Weasel.

FAC: Forward air controller.

Fansong radar: Radar used to detect and track targets for the Soviet built SA-2 surface-to-air missile system.

Flameout: Complete loss of power in a turbojet aircraft engine, usually due to lack of fuel.

FNG: F——ing New Guy, a term of endearment.

Frag order: A fragment of a total operations order that executes a coordinated operational mission.

Fragged: Ordered to attack a certain target as part of an overall mission plan.

GCA: Ground controlled approach. Using radar, ground controllers provide pilots with heading and altitude information to assist in landing during bad weather.

G-load: Force of gravity exerted on a pilot and aircraft during turns and acrobatic maneuvers.

G-suit: Pressure suit worn by pilots to counteract the effects of high G-loads during combat maneuvers. Referred to as "chaps."

GIB: Term of endearment for the pilot in the back seat of an Air Force F-4 fighter.

Go: Aircraft mission; for example fly the morning "go."

Golden BB: An unavoidable bullet that finds its mark by luck or fate.

Gooney Bird: Nickname for the C-47 transport aircraft.

Green'em up!: Command to prepare the aircraft cockpit and armament switches for combat. All switches on and ready to fire.

Hanoi Hilton: Prisoner of war camp in Hanoi.

Hickam AFB: Air Force base located in Honolulu, Hawaii near Pearl Harbor. Headquarters for the Pacific Air Forces.

Hooch: Wooden, jungle barracks.

Hot: Too fast or too long for a landing or during a dive-bomb pass.

Hydroplane: The tendency for aircraft wheels to ride up on water at high speed, resulting in a loss of directional control.

IG: Inspector General.

ILS: Instrument landing system.

Initial: The initial approach to a runway for landing; typically 3 miles from the airport, 1,500 feet above the ground and 400 KCAS in an F-105.

Innercomm: Radio communication system within an aircraft.

Ironhand: Code name for Wild Weasel missions conducted against enemy ground radar missile sites.

JCS: Joint Chiefs of Staff.

JCS targets: Targets in North Vietnam listed by number (for example 76.00) and specifically designated for attack by the JCS in Washington.

Jink: To maneuver an aircraft continuously and abruptly in order to avoid being hit by enemy ground fire.

Kadena Air Base: Major USAF installation on the island of Okinawa. Used as a staging base for KC-135 tankers during the war in Southeast Asia.

Karst: Sandstone mountain cliffs found in the jungles of Southeast Asia.

KCAS: Calibrated airspeed in knots.

KIA: Killed in action.

Klong: Irrigated fields usually rice fields or swamp.

Kobe beef: Tender, pampered beef specially prepared by the Japanese in the port city of Kobe.

Korat RTAFB: Royal Thai Air Force Base located at Korat in south central Thailand. Code name, Channel 125, Korat was the home of the 388th Tactical Fighter Wing equipped with three squadrons of F-105Ds and one squadron of F-105F Wild Weasel aircraft.

Kuala Lumpur: Capital city of the Federation of Malaya.

M-60 Gatling gun: 20mm gun mounted in the F-105 capable of firing up to 6,000 rounds per minute.

McClellan AFB: Major USAF logistics center near Sacramento, California that provided the depot support for the F-105 aircraft system.

McConnell AFB: Air Force Base near Wichita, Kansas where replacement F-105 pilots were trained by the 23d Tactical Fighter Wing "Flying Tigers."

MER: Multiple ejector bomb-rack carried on fighter aircraft.

MIA: Missing in action.

MiG-17: Swept-wing, single-seat Soviet fighter designated "Fresco" by NATO. Powered by a single turbojet engine providing 6,990 pounds of static thrust with afterburning. Initially, the mainstay of the North Vietnamese Air Force, the MiG-17 was armed with three 23mm guns.

MiG-19: Swept-wing, single-seat Soviet fighter comparable to our early "Century Series" jet fighters. Used in very limited numbers by the North Vietnamese Air Force.

MiG-21: Most widely used single-seat Soviet fighter. Designated "Fishbed" by NATO, the aircraft had a delta-shaped wing and was powered by a single turbojet engine providing 13,000 pounds of static thrust with afterburning. Armed with a twin-barrel 23mm gun and Atoll missiles, the MiG-21 succeeded the MiG-17 as the mainstay of the North Vietnamese Air Force.

MIGCAP: Fighters assigned to fly cover for the strike force of F-105s. Usually F-4s from the 8th or 366th Tactical Fighter Wings.

Nakhon Phanom: Most northeastern U.S. base in Thailand. "NKP" was on the Mekong river close to the Laotian border and was the main operating base for rescue operations as well as the center for a number of clandestine operations.

Neg!: Short for negative, meaning no.

Nellis AFB: Air Force base near Las Vegas, Nevada where pilots received F-105 Combat Crew Training. Also home of the USAF "Thunderbird" aerial demonstration team.

No Joy!: Cannot see you or do not have radar contact.

Nuke shape: A simulated nuclear bomb that is complete except for the warhead.

OPREP: Operations report usually summarizing combat mission results.

POL: Petroleum, oil, and liquid fuel storage.

PACAF: Pacific Air Forces.

Package Six: The numbered Route Package in North Vietnam that was centered around the Hanoi-Haiphong area in the north. Referred to as "Downtown."

Pathet Lao: Communist Laotian forces situated mainly in northern Laos and around the Plaine des Jarres.

Penang Island: A small island in the northwest federation of Malaya.

Pentagonese: Slang term for expressions used in the Pentagon.

Pickle: To release bombs or external stores using the "pickle" button located on the grip of the control stick in a fighter aircraft.

Pipper: Aiming point at the center of the gun-sight.

Pitot boom: A streamlined, slender boom that protrudes from the aircraft into the airstream to measure the difference in static and dynamic pressure. The difference, pitot pressure, is calibrated to present the indicated airspeed of an aircraft.

Plaine des Jarres: Central plains in the highlands of Laos that was a Pathet Lao stronghold.

Podjarka: Traditional Thai fruit dessert.

Poopie suit: A waterproof suit worn by pilots during over water flights when the water temperature is below a point deemed necessary for survival.

Pop: The pull-up point used to initiate a dive-bomb pass from low altitude.

POW: Prisoner of war.

QRC: Quick reaction capability; for example, the QRC-160 electronic jamming pod developed to counter the Fansong SAM radar.

RON: Remain over night.

R&R: Rest and relaxation break in combat.

Radar ground map: Radar return from the ground that is presented to the pilot on a radar scope in the cockpit. Used to navigate, locate targets, and deliver weapons from low altitude.

Rapcon: Radar approach control used to aid aircraft approaching an airport for an instrument approach in bad weather conditions.

Recce: Reconnaissance.

Red Crown: Airborne command post that controlled the Rolling Thunder missions over North Vietnam.

Rescap: Fighter cover of a downed pilot or rescue effort.

RHAW: Radar Homing and Warning equipment used by aircraft to detect radar signals from enemy aircraft and ground radar installations.

Ridge: Thud ridge in the Red River valley of North Vietnam.

River Kwai: Famous river in central Thailand.

Rog: "Yes, I understand!" Short for roger.

Rolling Thunder: Code name for air operations flown over North Vietnam in 1965-68.

RTB: Return to base.

S.H.: "Shit hot!" Pilot slang for very good!

Saberliner: Nickname for the North American T-39 aircraft.

Sahwahdee: Thai expression for hello and goodbye.

SAM: Soviet built SA-2 surface-to-air missile.

SAR: Search and rescue.

Scatback: Call sign assigned T-39 courier aircraft flying between bases in Thailand and South Vietnam.

Seiko: Popular Japanese watch. The trade name became the synonym for any wrist watch which was big and had a date and day display.

Singhah beer: Thai beer which uses formaldehyde as a preservative.

Six o'clock: Position directly behind an airplane using a clock face as the reference.

Sky Spot: A bombing technique using the radar return from a beacon equipped aircraft and a ground or air controller to position a flight of fighters over a target for a bomb drop in bad weather.

Slick: Synonymous with a "clean" aircraft. All external stores jettisoned and all aircraft systems retracted; for example, landing gear, flaps, and speed brakes up or in.

SMAMA: Sacramento Air Materiel Area depot.

Snakeye: 500-pound bomb with retarding fins installed.

Snitz: Expression meaning a person has "had it" or has "bought the farm." Short for snitzel.

SOF: Supervisor of flying. A duty assigned to senior flying personnel in a fighter wing.

Speed brake: Hydraulically actuated brakes that extend into the air stream to slow an aircraft in flight.

Squawk: Transmitting a coded signal with an airborne transponder that can be interrogated and displayed on a ground radar screen. "Oak flight is squawking one-four-zero-zero."

STAB AUG: The stability augmentation system in the F-105 that helped stabilize the hydraulic flight control system.

Stan/Eval: Standardization and Evaluation.

Start cart: A pyrotechnic cartridge used to start the F-105 on the ground autonomously.

Steel Tiger: Code name for air operations flown over Laos.

Stick and rudder: Expression meaning the fundamental basics of flying.

TOC: Tactical Operations Center.

Tacan: Navigation system transmits range and bearing information to aircraft.

Takhli RTAFB: Royal Thai Air Force Base located near Takhli village 100 miles north of Bangkok. Code name, Channel 43, Takhli was the home of the 355th Tactical Fighter Wing equipped with three squadrons F-105 aircraft including the F-105F Wild Weasels.

Tallyho: "Have you in sight!"

Tan Son Nhut: Major South Vietnamese (RVNAF) air base located near Saigon. Served as the headquarters for 7th Air Force, the major air command in Vietnam.

TAS: True airspeed of an aircraft.

Tet offensive: Major offensive staged by North Vietnamese and Viet Cong forces in South Vietnam early in 1968.

Thud: Nickname for the F-105 which became its *nom de guerre*. It was used originally in a derogatory sense to describe the sound made by a heavy weight F-105 hitting the ground. Other names included Ultra Hog and Squash Bomber.

Thunderchief: Official nickname for the Republic F-105 fighter-bomber aircraft.

Travis AFB: Air Force base in northern California, northeast of San Francisco. Major terminal for military airlift of personnel serving in the Pacific.

TOT: Time on target.

Trekmate: Partner during a one week trek in survival training at Stead AFB, Nevada.

Ubon RTAFB: Royal Thai Air Force Base located near Ubon in the southeastern corner of Thailand. Code name, Channel 51, Ubon was home for the 8th Tactical Fighter Wing equipped with the F-4 Phantom.

Udorn RTAFB: Royal Thai Air Force Base located in northern Thailand south of Vientiane, Laos. Code name, Channel 31, Udorn was the home of the 32d Tactical Reconnaissance Wing and served as a primary recovery base for battle-damaged aircraft.

UHF/VHF: Ultra-high frequency or very-high frequency radio.

Uploaded: Armament and fuel have been reloaded on an aircraft and it is ready to fly a mission.

VFR: Visual flight rules.

Vientiane: The administrative capital of Laos, in the northwest central part of the country on the Mekong river.

Vis: In-flight visibility.

Wienie: Term of endearment for well-meaning but otherwise useless staff officers.

Whifferdill: Vertical turning maneuver in an aircraft.

Wild Weasel: Nickname for aircraft equipped to detect and strike radar missile sites.

Wingman: A pilot flying an aircraft in formation on the wing of a leader.

Words: Code words for a target, mission execution, and mission results.

INDEX

01 Oct 66, **Captain C.G. Nix**, 421 TFS, Route Pack I, POW • 21 Oct 66, **Captain D.J. Earll**, 469 TFS, Route Pack I, MIA • 27 Oct 66, **Major Dale A. Johnson**, 333 TFS, Route Pack I, KIA • 02 Nov 66, **Major R.E. Kline**, 421 TFS, Route Pack V, MIA • 04 Nov 66, **Major R.E. Brinkman** and **Captain V.A. Scungio**, 13 TFS, Ironhand, JCS 18.90, Route Pack VIA, both KIA • 11 Nov 66, **Major Art Mearns**, 354 TFS, Northeast Railroad, Route Pack VIB, MIA • 02 Dec 66, **Captain M.L. Moorberg**, 34 TFS, JCS 51.10, Phuc Yen POL Storage, Route Pack VIA, KIA • 05 Dec 66, **Major B.N. Begley**, 421 TFS, Route Pack V, MIA • 08 Dec 66, **Lieutenant Colonel Don M. Asire**, 354 TFS, JCS 19, Route Pack VIA, KIA • 13 Dec 66, **Captain S.E. Waters**, 421 TFS, JCS 19.00, Yen Vien Rail Yard, Route Pack VIA, KIA • 10 Jan 67, **Captain J.P. Gauley**, 34 TFS, A/A 62-4265, Laos, KIA • 21 Jan 67, **Lieutenant Colonel Gene O. Conley**, 354 TFS, Northwest of Hanoi, Route Pack VIA, KIA • 29 Jan 67, **Major Larry Biediger** and **First Lieutenant Claude Silva**, 354 TFS, Ironhand, JCS 21.11, Thai Nguyen Rail Yard, Route Pack VIA, both KIA • 18 Feb 67, **Captain D.H. Duart** and **Captain J.R. Jansen**, 388 TFW, Ironhand, Route Pack III, both POW • 04 Mar 67, **Major Ralph Carlock**, 357 TFS, Route Pack III, KIA • 10 Mar 67, **Major Dave Everson** and **Captain Dave Luna**, 354 TFS, Ironhand, JCS 76.00, Thai Nguyen, Route Pack VIA, POW • 11 Mar 67, **Captain Charlie Greene**, 333 TFS, JCS 76.00, Thai Nguyen, Route Pack VIA, POW • 11 Mar 67, **Captain Joe J. Karins**, 357 TFS, JCS 76.00, Thai Nguyen, Route Pack VIA, KIA • 11 Mar 67, **Major Jim E. Hiteshew**, 354 TFS, JCS 76.00, Thai Nguyen, Route Pack VIA, POW • 15 Mar 67, **Lieutenant Colonel Pete Frederick**, 357 TFS, Route Pack III, MIA • 19 Mar 67, **Lieutenant Colonel J.C. Austin**, 34 TFS, Route Pack I, MIA • 02 Apr 67, **Captain J.A. Dramesi**, 13 TFS, Route Pack I, POW • 10 Apr 67, **Major John O'Grady**, 357 TFS Mu Gia Pass,